ONE WE

D1429104

Japanese Urban
Environment

The publication of this book is financially supported by a grant-in-aid for the publication of scientific research results provided by the Japanese Ministry of Education, Science, Sports and Culture.

Dedicated to the Japanese people who have admirably exhibited strength, patience and resilience throughout the traumatic event of the earthquake in the Kobe region in January 1995.

Japanese Urban Environment

EDITORS

GIDEON S. GOLANY

Distinguished Professor of Urban Design
The Pennsylvania State University

KEISUKE HANAKI

Professor of Environmental Engineering
The University of Tokyo

OSAMU KOIDE

Professor of Urban Engineering
The University of Tokyo

PERGAMON

UK	Elsevier Science Ltd, The Boulevard, Langford Lane, Kidlington, Oxford OX5 1GB, UK
USA	Elsevier Science Inc., 655 Avenue of the Americas, New York, NY 10010, USA
JAPAN	Elsevier Science Japan, Higashi Azabu 1-chome Building 4F, 1-9-15, Higashi Azabu, Minato-ku, Tokyo 106, Japan

First edition 1998

Library of Congress Cataloging in Publication Data
Japanese urban environment/editors, Gideon S. Golany, Keisuke Hanaki, Osamu Koide. —1st ed.
p. cm.
Includes bibliographical references and index.
1. Urban ecology—Japan.   2. Cities and towns—Japan.
3. City planning—Japan.   I. Golany, Gideon.
II. Hanaki, Keisuke.   III. Koide, Osamu.
HF243.J3J36   1998
307.76'0952—dc21   97-31720 CIP

British Library Cataloguing in Publication Data
A catalogue record for this book is available from the British Library.

ISBN 0-08-0433596

Typeset by Gray Publishing, Tunbridge Wells, Kent
Printed and bound in Great Britain by Redwood Books Ltd

Contents

List of Figures

Chapter II-E

List of Tables

Contributors' Biographies

Mitsuyuki Asano

Dr. Mitsuyuki Asano is a professor in civil engineering at Waseda University, Japan. He specializes in urban transportation, planning and related environmental issues.

Dr. Asano received his B.Eng. (1966), M.Eng. (1968), and his D.Eng. (1980) in engineering from Waseda University. Recognition was granted to him for his D.Eng. thesis by the City Planning Institute of Japan (1980).

Professor Asano previously held positions with the Building Research Institute and the Public Works Research Institute, both under the Ministry of Construction and the Metropolitan Expressway Corporation. He is a member of various professional associations, including the City Planning Institute of Japan. He has published many articles on transportation, including an article on "Microcomputer based data management systems for urban transportation planning" in 1988.

Gideon S. Golany

Dr. Gideon S. Golany has been a distinguished professor of urban design in the Department of Architecture at the Pennsylvania State University, USA, since 1970. Dr. G. Golany specializes in geospace design, urban design with climate and new-town planning.

Golany received his B.A. (1956), M.A. (1962), and Ph.D. (1966) from the Hebrew University, Jerusalem; his M.Sc. (1966) from the Technion-Israel Institute of Technology; and a Dip.C.P. (1965) from the Institute for Social Studies, The Hague, The Netherlands. He has taught at the Technion-Israel Institute of Technology, Cornell University and the Virginia Polytechnic Institute and State University. He has been a visiting professor at the Hebrew University; Ben Gurion University at the Negev; the University of Western Australia; the Open University in England; Xian Institute of Metallurgy and Construction Engineering, Xian, China; Waseda University in Tokyo; University of Tokyo, Japan; and other universities throughout the world. Golany is an Honorary Professor of the China Academy of Sciences (during this century only fourteen scientists throughout the world have received this title). He is also Honorary Advisory Professor from Tongji University, Honorary Professor from Xian Institute of Metallurgy and Construction Engineering and Honorary Professor of China Academy of Management Science. He is a foreign director of the China Research Society of Ancient Architecture. Golany is a recipient of the U.S. National Academy of Science Award to conduct twelve months research in China, the Faculty Scholar Medal for outstanding achievement in the social and behavioral sciences, the Research/Creative Development Award at Penn State and the Fulbright Research Awards to India, Turkey and Japan. Dr. Golany is listed in: *Who's Who in America, International Who's Who of Intellectuals, Who's Who in The East, Notable Americans, Dictionary of Distinguished Americans, Who's Who in the World, International Book of Honors* and others. Besides numerous monographs, articles and papers, Golany has written or edited more than twenty-five books, including: *Ethics and Urban Design* (1995), *Vernacular House Design and the Jewish Quarter in Baghdad* (1994), *Chinese Earth-Sheltered Dwellings: Indigenous Lessons for Modern Urban Design* (1992), *Design and Thermal Performance: Below-Ground Dwellings in China* (1990), *Urban Underground Space Design in China; Vernacular Practice and Modern Lessons* (1989), *Earth-Sheltered Dwellings in Tunisia; Ancient Lessons for Modern Design* (1988), *Design for Arid Regions* (1983), *Earth-Sheltered Habitat: History, Architecture and Urban Design* (1983), *International Urban Growth Policies: New-Town Contributions* (1978), *New-Town Planning: Principles and Practice* (1976) and others.

Keisuke Hanaki

Dr. Keisuke Hanaki is head of the Division of Urban Environmental Systems at the Research Center for Advanced Science and Technology and the affiliated faculty with the Department of Urban Engineering at the University of Tokyo, Japan. Dr. Hanaki specializes in the effective utilization of energy in urban areas, particularly in the conservation of the urban environment by studying global warming and the effective use of energy, analysis of the thermal environment in urban areas and biological waste-water treatment.

Professor Hanaki received a B.Eng. (1975), a M.Eng. (1977) and a D.Eng. (1980) from the Department of Urban Engineering at the University of Tokyo, Japan. Dr. Hanaki held academic appointments in the Department of Urban Engineering at the University of Tokyo and Tohoku University of Japan; the University of Pittsburgh, U.S.A. and the Asian Institute of Technology, Thailand.

Dr. Hanaki has held memberships with the International Association of Water Quality, the Japan Society on Water Pollution Research, Japan Society of Civil

Engineers, Japan Sewage Works Association and the editorial board of the journal *Bioresource Technology*. He has refereed many international journals and conference proceedings and has reviewed papers, presentations and university bulletins in English. Dr. Hanaki has contributed to many books in Japanese, including chapters in *Global Environmental Engineering Handbook* (1991), *Research Methods of Environmental Microbiology* (1993) and *Separation and Purification Technology Handbook* (1993).

Takashi Hirai

Mr. Takashi Hirai is a Managing Director of Nikken Sekkei, Ltd, Tokyo, Japan and specializes in the present and future development of central metropolitan Tokyo.

Mr. Hirai Received his B.Sc. (1961) and M.S. (1963), both in architecture, from Kyoto University, Japan. Mr. Hirai is registered as a first-class architect. He has served on many projects, the most recent being the Pacific Convention Plaza of Yokohama, the Japanese Patent Office, the Fukuoka Tower, the Fukuoka and Tokyo Garden Palaces, the Kawasaki Underground Shopping Center "Azalea," and the Tokyo Dome "Big Egg," for which he received a prize from the Architectural Institute of Japan (1989). He was a lecturer in the Department of Architecture at Tokyo Metropolitan University and is a member of a number of Japanese institutes and research committees. Mr. Hirai has co-authored Office Renaissance (1986) and wrote *Toward The Realization of the Underground City* (1991). He also has written on the subject of "The direction of near-future underground construction in Tokyo."

Toshiaki Ichinose

Dr. Toshiaki Ichinose is a chief research engineer of the Center for Global Environmental Research, National Institute for Environmental Studies, Japan.

Dr. Ichinose specializes in the urban environment system, particularly in the energy consumption and its impact on the urban climate, the effective utilization of energy in urban areas and the theoretical analysis of the urban evolution.

Dr. Ichinose received his B.S. (1987) from the Department of Geography, M.Eng. (1989) and U.S. D.Eng. (1996) from the Department of Urban Engineering at the University of Tokyo, Japan.

Dr. Ichinose held academic appointments in the Department of Urban Engineering and Research Center for Advanced Science and Technology at the University of Tokyo, Japan.

Dr. Ichinose has held memberships with the Japan Society of Civil Engineers (JSCE), the Association of Japanese Geographers and the Meteorological Society of Japan. He received a prize from JSCE for his research paper on the "Evaluation of the effective use of sewage heat in urban areas using a geographical information system."

Toshimasa Itaya

Mr. Toshimasa Itaya is a project engineer of the engineering division of Shimizu Corporation, Tokyo, Japan. Mr. Itaya has primary responsibility for designing district heating and cooling systems and the co-generation power system of wide area regional planning. He has developed software for the optimum planning of district heating and cooling systems using exhausted heat.

Mr. Itaya received a B.Sc. in architecture (1987) and a M.S. in environmental engineering (1989), both from Waseda University, Japan. He holds memberships with the Architectural Institute of Japan and the Society of Heating, Air Conditioning and Sanitary Engineering of Japan. Mr. Itaya has worked on numerous projects: as designer for the Ginza 5.6-Chome District Heating and Cooling Project; as a consultant for the Akita Gosyone-Tiku Regional Development Project; as the system engineer for the Development of Engineering Tool for District Heating and Cooling and Co-generation System Project and for the Development of a Simulation Program for Unused Energy Utilization Project; and as the system designer for the Development of Air Condition Control with Fuzzy Theory. Mr. Itaya is an authorized first-class architect.

Hikoji Iwai

Mr. Hikoji Iwai is the former managing director for the Teito Rapid Transit Authority of Tokyo, Japan and a lecturer in city and regional planning, Chuo University. Currently, he is vice president of Ohba Consulting Company Ltd. Mr. Iwai's expertise is in the improvement and management of the subway network in the Tokyo Metropolitan area, in the design of comprehensive urban transport plans and in the promotion and improvement of traffic facilities for upgrading railways and new road construction.

Mr. Iwai received a B.Sc. (1958) in civil engineering from Tokyo University and a Diploma in comprehensive planning (1966) from the Institute of Social Studies, The Netherlands. Currently, Mr. Iwai is director of the City Planning Association and the Residential and City Research Institute to promote projects and research. For the past thirty years, he has worked in the Ministry of Construction, playing a leading role in the design of comprehensive urban transport plans for implementation throughout Japan, including the promotion and improvement of traffic facilities for new road construction and the upgrading of railway systems. Mr. Iwai was deputy mayor of Hiroshima and was instrumental in inviting the Asia games to Hiroshima (1994). In preparation for the games, he was involved in planning all the sports facilities as well as large facilities for the city itself, such as a new light rail system. Mr. Iwai has also been involved with the improvement of an Asia highway network with the Division of Transport and Communications of the Economic and Social Committee for Asia and the Pacific Region (ESCAP); the International Technological Cooperation Projects of the Foreign Affairs Ministry; and numerous projects as an advisor, including a comprehensive transport plan for the city of Tehran, Iran, and a transport training center at the Philippines University.

Mr. Iwai has co-authored five publications including a *Manual for Making City Planning in Thailand* (1988), *Underground Structures Handbook* (1987), *Urban Development Policy and Land Readjustment* (City of Nagoya) (1984) and *Development of Regional Cities* (National Land Agency) (1982).

Masaji Kaneshima

Dr. Masaji Kaneshima is the general manager of the Engineering Division of the Shimizu Corporation, Tokyo, Japan. The Shimizu Corporation is considered to be among the five leading construction companies of Japan. Dr. Kaneshima specializes in engineering, in wide area regional planning and in research and development projects for various types of buildings.

Dr. Kaneshima received a B.Eng. (1971) and a D.Eng. (1976), from the Tokyo Institute of Technology, Japan. He is a registered authorized first-class architect. Dr. Kaneshima has been the developing project manager for the artificial thermal environmental laboratory, the mechanical/electrical engineering and design of buildings, the project manager for the Urban Utility Systems and for research on new uses of energy in East Asia.

Dr. Kaneshima holds memberships in the Architectural Institute of Japan, the Solar Energy Institute of Japan and the Society of Heating, Air Conditioning And Sanitary Engineering of Japan. He also serves on the Solar Energy Committee of the New Energy Foundation, the Advanced Co-Generation System Committee of Japan Gas Association, the Urban Utility Committee of the Architectural Institute of Japan and the Heat Pump Technology Development Center.

Kiyoko Kanki

Dr. Kiyoko Kanki is a research associate at the Department of Environmental Systems, Wakayama University, Japan. She currently specializes in urban and rural land-use planning combined with ecological landscape aspects.

Dr. Kanki received a B.Eng. (1989), a M.Eng. (1991), and D.Eng. (1997) at Kyoto University. She held the position of guest researcher at the Institute of Landscape Ecology and Landscape Design, at the Aachen Institute of Technology, Germany (1992–1993). She currently holds memberships of three sub-divisions (Regional Environment, Local City, Urban Planning Education) of the Urban Planning Committee and one sub-division (Regional Planning) of the Global Environment Committee at the Architectural Institute of Japan. She is one of the advisers of rural landscape design at the Japanese Ministry of Agriculture.

Dr. Kanki is the member of the Architectural Institute of Japan, the City Planning Institute of Japan, the Japan Society of Civil Engineers and the Rural Planning Association.

Tadahisa Katayama

Dr. Tadahisa Katayama is a Professor at Kyushu University, Japan and specializes in the field of environmental engineering of building and urban areas.

Dr. Katayama received his B.Eng. (1963) at Yokohama National University and M.Eng. (1965) and D.Eng. (1968) from the University of Tokyo. Professor Katayama held academic appointments at Yokohama National University, Kyushu University, Kyushu Institute of Design and the University of the Ryukyus in Japan. He has served as director of the Society of Heating, Air Conditioning and Sanitary Engineers of Japan; chairman of the Tohwa Institute for Science at Tohwa University; and councilor for the Architectural Institute of Japan and the Japan Association for Wind Engineering. Prizes have been awarded to Dr. Katayama by the Japan Association of Standards (1971); the Architectural Institute of Japan (1991); the Society of Heating, Air Conditioning and Sanitary Engineers of Japan (1991); and the Heat Transfer Society of Japan (1993). He holds memberships with the Architectural Institute of Japan, the Society of Heating, Air Conditioning and Sanitary Engineering of Japan, Meteorological Society of Japan, Japan Association for Wind Engineering, Japanese Society of Biometeorology, the Visualization Society of Japan, Society of Environmental Science of Japan and the Heat Transfer Society of Japan. Dr. Katayama has written a large number of research papers supporting his work and has contributed to five books on the subject of the thermal environment, including *Analysis and Design for Wind Environment in Urban Area* (1993), *Building Environment* (1992) and *Passive Cooling for Houses* (1991).

Ken-Ichi Kimura

Dr. Ken-Ichi Kimura is a professor in the Department of Architecture at Waseda University, Tokyo, Japan. Dr. Kimura specializes in energy conservation in buildings, the architectural utilization of solar energy, solar shading devices, thermal comfort, visual comfort of daylight, indoor air quality, room acoustics and moisture absorption in interiors.

Professor Kimura received his B.Arch. (1957), M.Sc. (1959), and his D.Eng. (1965) at Waseda University, Japan. Dr. Kimura has held academic appointments at Waseda University; the Massachusetts Institute of Technology, Boston, U.S.A.; and the National Research Council, Ottawa, Canada.

Dr. Kimura has served as a member on many national and international committees. He served on the board of directors for the Architectural Institute of Japan; as president of Japan's Solar Energy Society; as president and chairman of the Society of Heating, Air Conditioning and Sanitary Engineers of Japan; as chairman of the Design Competition Committee—Solar Energy Development Association and Research on Natural Energy—Special Energy Project, Japanese Ministry of Education, Science and Culture; and as fellow of the American Society of Heating, Air Conditioning and Refrigeration Engineers.

Professor Kimura has cooperated with and consulted many design projects throughout Japan. He received the research paper award from the Architectural Institute of Japan (1982) and from S.H.A.S.E. (1972, 1973, 1983). He has organized many international conferences and symposia, among them, the International Symposium on the Use of Computers for Environmental Engineering Related to Buildings; the International Symposium on Thermal Application of Solar Energy; and the World Solar Energy Congress. Dr. Kimura has published ten books, including *Theories of Architectural Environment*, Volume 1 (1991) and Volume 2 (1992), *Introduction to Solar Houses*, Omusha (1980) and *Environmental Engineering* (Building Technology Series No. 2) (1976).

Fumihiko Kobayashi

Mr. Fumihiko Kobayashi is a research associate of the Department of Civil Engineering, Kanazawa University, Japan. He currently specializes in the conservational development of historical towns combined with grand landscape conservation aspects.

Mr. Kobayashi received a B.Eng. (1992), and M.Eng. (1994) at Kyoto University. He was a member and co-author of several survey project reports on the conservation of natural and historical assets by the Japan National Trust. He currently holds a membership in the sub-division of the local city in the urban planning committee at the Architectural Institute of Japan.

Mr. Kobayashi is the member of the Architectural Institute of Japan and the City Planning Institute of Japan.

Osamu Koide

Professor Osamu Koide is professor of urban engineering at the School of Engineering, the University of Tokyo, Japan. Professor Koide specializes in national and regional planning, urban disaster prevention planning including fire and crime prevention and information technology in urban planning as well as urban developments.

Professor Koide received D.Eng. (1985), from the University of Tokyo, Japan.

Professor Koide Serves as a member of the National Urban Planning Committee, Ministry of Construction, a member of the Fire Prevention Committee, Tokyo Fire Department, a board member of the Institute of Social Safety Science and as a directing member of the Urban Safety Research Institute.

In addition, Professor Koide is a consultant on a number of regional and urban development projects including the Tsurugashima City on information technology and city development, the Iwaki City, Itoh City, and Kasugai City

Urban Disaster Prevention Plan, as well as the Okayama City Urban Disaster Prevention Plan.

Kisho Kurokawa

Dr. Kurokawa established his firm, Kisho Kurokawa and associates, in 1962. Dr. Kurokawa is one of the world's most prolific architects. He has gained international acclaim and awards for his designs built around the world.

Dr. Kurokawa studied architecture at Kyoto University and graduated from the Graduate School of Architecture, the University of Tokyo.

Dr. Kurokawa's work has been evolving away from modernism, which sought to emulate the functionalism of machinery in its design, toward his own philosophy of symbiosis, which reflects natural, organic systems and seeks to include cultural reflections and differences. In his approach, architecture is freed by advanced technology to express itself in new ways. In other words, form no longer has to follow function. In a world where trends become international overnight, Dr. Kurokawa sees combining this international face with the distinctions that make each culture and region unique, thus producing buildings that reflect a "both/and" rather than an "either/or" approach.

Dr. Kurokawa has written thirty books, including Intercultural Architecture: the Philosophy of Symbiosis, which was a best seller in Japan. Among his many awards and prizes are the gold medal from the Academy of Architecture in France and memberships as an Honorary Fellow in the American Institute of Architects and the Royal Institute of British Architects.

Dr. Kurokawa has designed buildings in North and South America, Europe, China, Japan, Southeast Asia, and Australia. Among his current projects are the Pacific Tower in Paris, Melbourne Central in Australia and an addition to the Van Gogh Museum in Amsterdam.

Yasuo Masai

Dr. Yasuo Masai is professor of geography and head of the Graduate Program in Geography at Rissho University, Tokyo, Japan. Dr. Masai specializes in urban geography and urban land-use mapping.

Professor Masai Received his M.S. (1953) at Tokyo Bunrika University; Ph.D. (1960), Michigan State University, U.S.A.; and D.Sc. (1962), Tokyo Bunrika University, Japan, all in geography. Dr. Masai has held academic positions at many universities, among them Ochanomizu University, University of Tsukuba, Tokyo University, Rikkyo University, Saitama University, Gunma University, Chiba University, Akita University, Iwate University, Mie University, Utsunomiya University, Seijo University, Ryukyu University, and Michigan State University, U.S.A.

Dr. Masai was recipient of a Fulbright scholarship and was designated a distinguished contributor for the promotion of education by the Union of Educational Societies (1989) and a distinguished cartographer by Japan's

Cartographers' Association (1992). He currently serves as president of the Japan Cartographers' Association; past president of Japan Society of Geographic Education; councilor of the Association of Japanese Geographers, the Human Geographical Society, the Tohoku Geographical Society, the Association of Geographical Sciences, and the Environmental Information Center, Map Information Center, and other associations. Dr. Masai previously served as chairman for the National Committee on the Pacific Science Association; the Commission on Urban Cartography, the International Cartographic Association; and the editorial board of the Association of Japanese Geographers; and advisor to the National Atlas Committee, Ministry of Construction and Japan–U.S.A. Cultural Conference and the Ministry of Education. Dr. Masai has authored and co-authored 160 books and has written a large number of articles. His most noted books are *Atlas Tokyo* (1986), *Urban Problems in the Third World* (1986), *Dictionary of Environmental Sciences* (1985), *Living Environments of Japan* (1978), *Urban Growth in Japan and France* (1978), *Learning of International Understanding Education* (1977), *A Comparative Study of Japanese and American Cities* (1977), *Dictionary of Geography* (1973), *Living Map of Tokyo* (1972), *Environment of Cities* (1971), and *Japanese Cities* (1970).

Hiroshi Mimura

Dr. Hiroshi Mimura is a professor emeritus and former professor of the School of Architecture and the School of Global Environmental Engineering at Kyoto University, Japan. He is also a professor of Kansai University of Social Welfare. Professor Mimura currently specializes in urban and community planning.

Professor Mimura received a B.Eng. (1957), a M.Eng. (1959) and a D.Eng. (1968) at Kyoto University and a Diploma of Comprehensive Planning from the Institute of Social Studies, The Hague, The Netherlands. He held the position of Architectural Engineer at the Osaka Prefecture, where he was a team member of the Senri New-Town Design Staff. He currently is one of the councilors of the Architectural Institute of Japan, the Chairman of the Urban Planning Committee, a historical townscape specialist for the Historical Assets Protection Committee at the Japanese Ministry of Culture, a townscape conservation specialist for the Japan National Trust, the councilor of the Center for the Redevelopment of Pollution-Damaged Areas in Japan and the chairman of Kyoto City Housing Policy Committee.

Professor Mimura received honors and prizes from the Architectural Institute of Japan (1985) and the Institute of Urbanology (1983). He has published several books in Japanese, including *The Urban Planning of Small Scale Industries Agglomeration* (1978), *Human Settlement Policies in Urban Areas* (1980), *Introduction for Urban Housing Learning* (1989), *Improvement of the Urban Living Environment* (1991), and *The Urban Planning of Regional Symbiosis* (1997).

Tatsuya Nagai

Mr. Tatsuya Nagai is former deputy general manager, Technology Division of Taisei Corporation, Tokyo, Japan. He specializes in the design and planning of buildings and urban facilities with recent emphasis on research and development management, facility management and long-range planning. Mr. Nagai has interests in the environment and human behavior, social infrastructure engineering, frontier space for human habitation, and productivity and quality of construction.

Mr. Nagai received a B.Sc. in architecture (1960) from Waseda University, Tokyo, Japan, and a M.Sc. in civil engineering (1968) from Polytechnic of Milan, Italy. Mr. Nagai holds memberships in the Operation Research Society of Japan, the Association for Promoting Advanced Science and Technology of Forest Resources Utilization, the Japan Facility Management Association, the Man–Environment Research Association, and the Japan Institute of Hospital Architecture. Mr. Nagai has been involved in many design projects throughout Japan, Korea, and Bangladesh. He has presented papers at numerous international conferences and has ten books published in Japanese, including *Visual Technology of Building, Civil Works and Urban Development* (1993), *Visual Report on High Technology in the Construction Industry* (1990), *Dictionary on Building and Civil Engineering* (1991), *Concrete* (1995), and *Earthquake Antidisaster Engineering* (1995).

Hideo Obitsu

Mr. Hideo Obitsu is manager of the Department of Project Planning, Sales and Marketing Division, Obayashi Corporation, Tokyo, Japan. His expertise is in project planning.

Mr. Obitsu received a B.Eng. (1976) in Urban Engineering, University of Tokyo, Japan, and a M.C.P. Degree (1987) in City Planning, Massachusetts Institute of Technology, Boston, U.S.A. He is a first-class licensed architect and a first-grade licensed construction manager, both in Japan. He holds memberships in the City Planners Society, Japan Building Contractors Society, and Japan Project-Industry Council.

Mr. Obitsu has published articles and co-authored the book, *Data Files of Construction Management and Planning and Expectation for Future Urban Development*.

Toshio Ojima

Dr. Toshio Ojima is a professor in the Department of Architecture at Waseda University, Tokyo, Japan. He specializes in urban environmental planning, district heating and cooling, infrastructure, facility management, and remote sensing. Dr. Ojima is a prominent scholar and one of the leading Japanese experts in the design of the infrastructure.

Professor Ojima received his B.Sc. (1960), M.Eng (1962), and D.Eng. (1966) in engineering from Waseda University, Department of Architecture, School of Science and Engineering, Japan. He has taught at Waseda University and the University of Tokyo; has lectured at Kogakuin University, Tokyo University of Art, Nagoya University, Kyushu University, and the University of Kyoto; has served as Advising Professor at Zhejiang University, China; and was a researcher at the Academy of China. Currently, Professor Ojima is the director of the Advanced Research Center of Science and Engineering at Waseda University, president of the Japan District Heating and Cooling Association, president of the Architectural Institute of Japan, and Chairman of the Japanese Urban Problems Committee. He holds key positions in public and government committees.

Dr. Ojima is a recipient of awards from the Architectural Institute of Japan and the Society of Heating, Air Conditioning and Sanitary Engineers of Japan. He has been involved in major national and international projects, such as Expo '70, Expo '75, and Expo '80, New Tokyo International Airport, Tsukuba Center Area, the Tama Center Area, and the Environmental Planning of the Barcelona Olympic Indoor Stadium. Dr. Ojima is author of ten books, including *Object to Development of Tokyo Bay Area* (1992), *The High-Rise Building and Future City*, (1992), *Imaginative Tokyo—Projects By Toshio Ojima, Process Architecture* No. 99 (1991), *The Reconstruction of Tokyo, Housing in the Future* (1988), *Chikuma-Shobo* (1986), *Tokyo—Design for the 21st Century* (1986).

Toshio Oyama

Mr. Toshio Oyama is a member of the affiliated researching staff of urban environmental systems at the Research Center for Advanced Science and Technology, the University of Tokyo. Mr. Oyama specializes in social system simulation including mass transportation, traffic system and land-use.

Mr. Oyama received M.Eng. (1983) from Keio University, Japan. Mr. Oyama is a consultant of urban traffic simulation and planning, including Sendai City for the Big Earth Quake, Yokohama Station and others.

In addition, Mr. Oyama serves on several regional planning and redevelopment projects, including the Makuhari Area Development, as a member of Shimizu Corporation, a Japanese Construction Company.

Mr. Oyama is a member of the Architectural Institute of Japan, Institute of Human Engineering, Japan, and the Institute of Human Environment.

Mr. Oyama is the co-author of two books, *Revision of Tokyo, Era of Livable City and Multimedia Technology* and *Construction Companies*.

Takeo S. Saitoh

Dr. Takeo Saitoh is professor in the Department of Aeronautics and Space Engineering at Tohoku University in Sendai, Japan. Dr. Saitoh specializes in urban warming, global warming, solar energy, energy storage, and computational mechanics.

Professor Saitoh received his B.Eng. (1965), M.Eng. (1967), and D.Eng. (1971) from the Department of Mechanical Engineering at Tohoku University. He taught at Sagami Institute of Technology, was a visiting scholar at the Solar Energy Applications Laboratory, Colorado State University, U.S.A., and was a member of the Comprehensive Energy Research Council of Ministry of International Trade and Industry, Japanese Government. He is affiliated with numerous professional societies, serving as a member of the board of directors to the Japanese Association of Refrigeration, Japan Solar Energy Society, Heat Transfer Society of Japan, Combustion Society of Japan, and is an honorary member of the Co-Generation Research Society of Japan. Professor Saitoh is presently vice president of the Japan Solar Energy Society. He also has presided as chairman to numerous other councils, bureaus, corporations and societies.

Dr. Saitoh was awarded the Academic Prize Medal from the Japanese Association of Refrigeration (1987), the Komo Prize (1994), the Computational Mechanics Award (1996), and the Contribution Award from Japan Society for Mechanical Engineers. Besides publishing over 200 technical papers, monographs and reviews, Dr. Saitoh has authored or co-authored ten books, including *Global Warming and Urban Warming* (1992), *Computer-Aided Heat Transfer* (1986), and *Advanced Heat Transfer* (1984).

Susumu Sakamoto

Mr. Susumu Sakamoto is managing director of the Takenaka Corporation, Tokyo, Japan. He specializes in urban design.

Mr. Sakamoto received a B.Eng. (1962) and a M.Eng. (1964), both from the Department of Architecture at the University of Tokyo, Japan. Mr. Sakamoto was part-time lecturer in the Department of Agricultural Engineering at the University of Tokyo. He is a first-class architect in Japan.

Mr. Sakamoto has served as councilor to a national committee of the Center for Research and Management of National Property. In addition, he holds membership on research bodies for high-rise building's redevelopment, the Ministry of Construction; Local Resort Development, Ministry of International Trade and Industry (MITI); application of private company's vitality to urban development, MITI; and member of the Leisure Development Center. He is also affiliated with professional associations of the City Planner Association of Japan, Japan Urban Design Institute and Urban Renewal Coordinator Association of Japan. Mr. Sakamato authored the book, *Model Project Proposal for Urban Complex Building, Building Center of Japan* (1992).

Yukio Sano

Mr. Yukio Sano has been the senior managing director and group president of the Architectural and Engineering Design Group of Kajima Corporation. Prior positions held at the Kajima Corporation since his appointment there in 1960 include general manager, chief architect, director, and group senior vice president of the Architectural and Engineering Design Group of Kajima Corporation.

Mr. Sano received a B.S. (1960) from Waseda University and an M.A. (1967) from the University of Pennsylvania, U.S.A. His professional honors include the Building Contractor's Society Award for the Akita Sky Dome (1990), the Togin Kurita Building (1955), and the third senior high school attached to Nihon University (1952). He was also the second prize winner of the Supreme Court Design Competition (1969). He recently received the AIJ Prize (Architectural Institute of Japan Prize).

In addition to these accomplishments, Mr. Sano's creative output includes the Isumo Dome (1992), Hotel Nikko Fukuoka (1989), Dai-idhi Hotel Tokyo Bay (1988), Hotel Bellevue (Dresden, 1985) and the American School In Japan (1983).

Mr. Sano is a trustee of the Architectural Institute of Japan and a Member of the Design Committee of the Tokyo Society of Architects and Building Engineers.

Motoyuki Takabu

Mr. Motoyuki Takabu is division head of the Engineering Division and Senior Executive Director of Shimizu Corporation, Tokyo, Japan. Mr. Takabu specializes in mechanical/electrical engineering, the design of various kinds of architectural buildings, planning and strategic management in engineering in a wide area of regional planning, research and development for environmental control.

Mr. Takabu received a B.Sc. (1960) from Waseda University in Tokyo, Japan. He is registered as a first-class architectural engineer by the Ministry of Construction; a Consulting Engineer by the Science and Technology Agency; and a Building Mechanical and Electrical Engineer by the Association of Building Mechanical and Electrical Engineers. He holds memberships in the Architectural Institute of Japan and the American Society of Heating, Air Conditioning and Sanitary Engineers of Japan. In addition, Mr. Takabu has served on numerous committees, including the Research and Development Committee of the Engineering Advancement Association of Japan; the Super Heat Pump Energy Accumulation System Working Group; a Large-Scale, Energy-Saving Technology Development Promotion Committee of the Moon Light Planning Office, MITI; the Heat Pump Technology Development Center; and the IEA International Heat Pump Committee.

Nobuyuki Takahashi

Dr. Nobuyuki Takahashi is assistant professor with the Advanced Research Center for Science and Technology, Waseda University, Tokyo, Japan. His area of interest is the effect of modernization on the waterways of Japan.

Dr. Takahashi received a B.Eng. (1968), from Asano Institute of Technology and a M.Eng. (1981) and D.Eng., both from Waseda University. He has served as director of Kanagawa Institute of Economics (1974) and has held professorial positions at Asano Institute of Technology, College of Tohoku Science and Technology, and Waseda University. He received the Presidential Prize of Japan's Architectural Association (1996). Dr. Takahashi is currently a member and director of the Architectural Institute of Japan.

Professor Takahashi has published several books, his most recent being *Ecological Planning at Downtown in Tokyo* (1992). His other works include, *The Urban Environmental Capacity in Shanghai City* (1989), *Urban and River* (1989), and *Waterfront Planning in the World* (1987).

Fumio Tsubouchi

Mr. Fumio Tsubouchi is currently the general manager in the Department of Group Planning at the Architectural and Engineering Design Group of the Kajima Corporation.

During his tenure at the Kajima Corporation, Mr. Tsubouchi has served as chief in the Office of Group Strategy and worked in the Administration Department, the Total Quality Control Promotion Office, and the Planning Department.

Mr. Tsubouchi received a B.Eng. (1971) from Tokyo University. His professional accomplishments include programming on various projects for Nihon Sumou Kyokai, the Mitsubishi Corporation, and the Mitusui Resort Development.

He is a member of the Architectural Institute of Japan, the City Planning Institute of Japan, and the Design Committee of Building Contractor's Society.

Tsutomu Uenomachi

Tsutomu Uenomachi is presently the deputy manager of the Infra-Project Planning Department of the Engineering Division of the Kajima Corporation.

He received a B.Design in Architectural Design (1985) and a M.Design in Architectural and Urban History (1987) (Division of Living Environmental Studies) from the Kyushyu Institute of Design.

Mr. Uenomachi was awarded "best prize" in the Surf '90 "Nagisa" Design Idea Competition by the Kanagawa Prefectural Government (1989). His professional accomplishments includes the Atema Highland Resort Project (niigata pref. Japan) and Schematic Design (1990–1993). He is also author of a Survey Report on the Traditional Structures of Arita Uchiyama (1985).

Mr. Uenomachi is a member of the Architectural Institute of Japan and the Design Research Association of Japan.

Yoshiro Watanabe

Dr. Yoshiro Watanabe is Professor of Construction Engineering, Graduate School of Engineering, Hosei University, Japan, and an advising professor at Tonji University, Shanghai, P.R. China. He specializes in city and regional planning.

Professor Watanabe received a B.Sc. (1950) in technology, and D.Eng. (1976), both from Tokyo University. He has been professor at the University of Tsukuba, Japan, and was technical deputy-general for the City Bureau, Ministry of Construction. Dr. Watanabe has received numerous honors, awards and prizes including the Ishikawa Encouragement Prize (1961) and the C.P.I.J. Monograph Prize (1976), both from the City Planning Institute of Japan, the Prize of Merit from the Minister of Construction in Japan (1987), the Prize of Distinguished Services from the Minister of National Land in Japan (1988), and the Assiduous Scholar of Engineering (City Planning and Regional Planning) from the Minister of Science and Technology (1958).

Dr. Watanabe has been affiliated with many national and international committees and professional associations. He has served as director to the Japan Society of City Planning, the Japan Society of National Land Planning, the Eastern Regional Organization for Planning and Housing, and the Japan Society of the Mono-Rail; also, as vice chairman to the Japan Society of the Coastal Zone; and as chairman to the City Planning Institute of Japan and to the all Japan Association of Masters for Land Readjustment.

Professor Watanabe has published twenty-three books, his most recent being *The Story of the New Frontier* (1991), *Urban Traffic* (1989), *Environment Science II, III* (1989), *Socio-Economic Planning* (1987), *Rearing City for Twenty-first Century* (1980), *Atlas of City Planning* (1978), *Land Development* (1977), *A Method of Town Planning* (1977) and *Business Traffic System* (1975).

Preface

The vision for this book was born in 1992, when I was invited to be an Endowed Chair Professor for almost six months at the University of Tokyo. Prior to this appointment, I had spent almost one year as a Fulbright Awardee in various Japanese urban centers conducting research. Throughout the course of my studies in Japan, it became increasingly evident that Japanese urban environments differ considerably from those in the U.S.A. and their differences extend well beyond their physical shapes and geographic locations. Rather, my observation and experiences revealed a dynamic synthesization of traditional Eastern philosophies and other distinctive socio-cultural influences within these urban confines. The integration of such forces in everyday Japanese life provides an interesting model for urban designers in the West because of the relative "success" of many of the larger Japanese cities. Many large U.S. cities are marked by crime and decay, but Japanese urban centers experience relatively low crime and a high degree of cleanliness. They are among the world's leaders in urban innovation, application of creative design techniques, design for socio-cultural consideration, and solutions for accommodating large populations.

The goal of this volume is to give an insight into the uniqueness of the Japanese urban environment with all its contributing factors. We view the urban environment in its comprehensive unity which embraces natural and artificial factors; these factors reciprocally interact and dynamically introduce an infinity of new forms as well as situations. We in the West have made a conscious effort to raise our environmental awareness; we are often trapped into one sight of the environment and consider physical forms, water, air, and soil quality as an expression of the environment. This has led us to almost ignore socio-cultural and human relations, socio-economic and historical factors as well as their influence and dominance on the physical environment. We have always known little of and have been curious to explore, the dynamics, management and social implications of oriental cities. In comparing our urban environment to that of the Japanese, numerous questions are raised. We are also exploring what lessons we in the West can draw from the Japanese case, since we are struggling with acute urban conditions and problematic issues. This book is an attempt to fill the gap in our knowledge of the Japanese urban environment. It is my strong conviction that to understand the Japanese cities, it is necessary to have the input of a team of Japanese individuals who represent the diverse facets of the Japanese urban society and who naturally incorporate their Eastern philosophy into their work.

My previous work focuses primarily on the relation of the various philosophies, associated with certain countries, to urban design in each respective nation. Eastern philosophy of urban design varies from western philosophy. In the West, urban growth tends to be dictated by technological achievement, perseverance, and progress at almost any cost to the environment. However, in Japan, like other Oriental countries, the culture is rooted in ancient philosophies and has historically interpreted the environment through the unity of nature, humans, and heaven; contemporary urban growth has threatened this triumvirate of elements. I have found the ancient Japanese approach most intriguing because of its comprehensiveness, sensitivity, and timelessness in providing valuable lessons for modern day, western urban designers as well as for professionals in related fields. To better understand how this ancient Japanese philosophy is incorporated in the modern city and is beneficial to urban growth, one must go directly to the source of this manifestation—the urban designers, architects, scientists and builders responsible for the successful synthesization of the old and the new of the Japanese city. This type of investigation will not only provide the West with practical ideas for urban design based on the philosophies of the East, but will also be an impetus for using its own history and cultural identity as a resource for future growth. This book magnifies the intrusion of the contemporary Western urban development on the traditional metropolitan Japanese environment.

The selection of the contributors was a lengthy process. During my stay at the University of Tokyo, I was able to personally interview and select the writers from a large number of leading Japanese figures who are all prominent scholars and practitioners in their profession. My intention has been, on one hand, to introduce an interdisciplinary group of theoreticians as well as practitioners who represent a wide range of the Japanese society and on the other hand, to be consistent with the main theme of the book in presenting the multidimensions of the Japanese urban environment. During the preparation process, the contributors and editors have become fascinated with the idea of a comprehensive theme introducing the Japanese urban environment to the English reader in both the developed and the developing countries globally. In addition to the overall orientation which was given and explained to each contributor, each writer was provided with a frame as well as a proposed structure of the paper (preface, introduction, sequential division of the paper's body, conclusion, footnotes, bibliographical listing, and the like).

This book has numerous strengths; they range from the volume's comprehensiveness in dealing with the subject to its focus on the environment. In addition, the rich, diverse backgrounds of the contributing professionals offer a unique firsthand view of the Japanese natives on the subject. The writers are representatives of numerous facets of Japanese society such as academia, the business world, as well as private and public sectors with an emphasis on urban planning and design. Except myself, all contributors representing their views on their urban environment are Japanese. They wrote each chapter especially for this book as a product of thorough and original research. It is my hope that their native familiarity with the subject will render the reading of Japanese Urban Environment contemporary as well as fascinating.

Thematically, this book focuses on the Japanese urban environment which comprises native culture, integration and preservation of self-identity within the technological urban dynamics of change. It is my belief that the strong sense of the Japanese for teamwork and loyalty towards their employer, as well as each other, is the foundation for the positive development of their urban environment. The "Introduction" will provide an indepth analysis of the Japanese urban environment and its components.

Technical difficulties were not outside the realm of this book compilation. Most of the contributing specialists are not in command of the English language and originally wrote their chapter in Japanese. Interpreters who may not necessarily have been acquainted with the subject then translated the chapter into English. Consequently, the editing process became lengthy and it was a challenge to bring each article to its required cohesiveness. Many chapters underwent more than three rounds of editing; each revision was submitted to the contributor for re-evaluation. This explains the absence of references to some extent since not all the contributors are fully acquainted with the Western writing format. Their papers are the original, intellectual product of their research, such as the case of internationally renowned architect Kisho Kurokawa. To provide the reader with reference material for further study, we introduced a comprehensive English bibliography on the Japanese environment in this book.

Comprehensive treatment of the Japanese urbanscape is the core of this volume. Japanese scientists and scholars discuss their environment, its social and cultural features, land and waterfronts, and the many aspects that have led to the enhancement of the Japanese social quality of life. Because of the unique approach of the Japanese, many of their projects have received much attention in the West (for example, the seventy-eight modern shopping centers scattered throughout Japan). The contributors' goal is to present the uniqueness of Japan's urban environment in all its socio-cultural aspects, comprehensively, from the practical, philosophical, and historical perspective to modern times. The outcome is an enlightening book for the western reader.

This book is to the best of my knowledge the first project of its kind in the English language. It highlights the cultural evolution, the social cohesiveness, and the solidarity of the average Japanese person for their institutions as the basis for the quality of urban life. Most Japanese cities are characterized by low crime, safety at night and daytime, a collaborative and team-oriented society, with a deep interest in art and beauty, pride, and last but not least, obedience and sincere respect of the individual for local government as a trusted public enterprise.

The preparation of this book is the product of a collaboration between the University of Tokyo and Pennsylvania State University. I extend my sincere thanks and appreciation to the Research Center for Advanced Science and

Technology of the University of Tokyo and its former Director, Professor Setsuo Ohsuga, for their support and for hosting me during my stay in Japan. I express my gratitude to Dr. Rodney Erickson, Senior vice president for Research and Dean of the Graduate School as well as Professor Neil Porterfield, Dean of the College of Arts and Architecture, and Dr. Edward Williams, Associate Dean for Research, for their practical and moral support. Without their support, this book would have not have come together.

My deep appreciation is extended to my many Japanese friends and colleagues who have firmly supported this project from its inception. Among them is Professor Keisuke Hanaki and Professor Osamu Koide of the University of Tokyo, and Mr. Toshio Oyama, former Cooperative Research Fellow of RCAST. Special appreciation goes to the five leading construction companies (GCS) who made the Urban Environmental System Program at RCAST feasible: Kajima Corporation, Obayashi Corporation, Shimizu Corporation, Taisei Corporation, and Takenaka Corporation. They all deserve appreciation and thanks for their contributions.

Finally, my thanks and appreciation go to each of my editorial assistants; Ms. Ruth Vastola, who extensively worked on the manuscript with me during the first editorial round, as did Ms. Claudia Link. I would also like to thank Ms. Kerstin Roan, who was deeply involved with all the final rounds of editing, for her professional quality work of the entire manuscript with me. Without her, this compilation would not have been finished in time and not have met its ultimate goal. It is the dedication, perseverance, and careful treatment of the details of all three editorial assistants, which made this publication possible.

August 1997   G. S. G.
The Pennsylvania State University

Introduction: Japanese Urban Environment

Gideon S. Golany

FOREWORD

In the Westerner's eyes, Japan is an exotic, mysterious, puzzling and remote society. Yet, it has become close technologically and internationally, as well as more open to us than ever before. What is the uniqueness and the distinction of Japan? Has technology really brought us closer? We feel that the key elements lie in the socio-cultural strengths and their relation to the new, advanced technology. Culturally, socio-economically, identity-wise, geographically and historically, Japan is distinct from its surrounding nations and from the Western world. Until recently, Japan was still able to retain its strong traditions, cultural norms, as well as ethics in a time of change. In the twentieth century, much of Western technology, social and economic values as well as a dominant urban style were introduced into Japan. Japanese society was able to find integrative norms and to establish a synthesized balance between the past and the recently developed urban environment. Unlike the surrounding world, the changes of the Japanese urbanscape have been consciously and continuously steady; at the same time, the Japanese retained the sound quality of their urban environment with comparatively low crime rates. Consequently, the secret of Japanese urban quality has roused the curiosity of the West. The goal of this book is to highlight the uniqueness of the Japanese urban environment, its historical dynamics, the contributing factors which shape it, as well as to explore and analyze its current and future trends.

The following introductory observations are to highlight, explain, and compare, to some extent, the nature of the Japanese and Western urban environment. To understand the past and present Japanese urban environment as well as to comprehend its prospective future, it is essential to outline the roots of the most basic cultural and ethical values which the Japanese have retained over time. With the end of this century, we are heading towards a global, cross-cultural interaction particularly between East and West. For us as Westerners, the Oriental East, and within it Japan, has always been an exotic, mystical, and distinctive world which attracted our attention but which we struggle to understand. This introductory chapter is our contribution to further the understanding of the Japanese culture and its urban environment.

The Japanese urban environment is an extremely valuable case study since it still has a strong culture and tradition, despite the fact that urban Japan has undergone a metamorphosis since World War II. It is here where West and East have truly met and interacted. Throughout the twentieth century, all facets of the Western and recently the Japanese urban environment have continuously and dynamically grown and changed. We define the urban environment in its totality as both an artificial and a natural environment.

The artificial environment, which is reflected visually and abstractly in the *invisible city*, is complex and consists of two dimensions. The first, the physical dimension, is shaped by human activities; the second, the invisible city, is generated by socio-cultural and human interaction. Recently, throughout the world, both have been characterized by the intensive dynamics of change and this tendency will continue in the future. As urban designers, social scientists, and other related professionals, our challenge is to understand and predict the dynamics of the reciprocal relations between these two dimensions. It is the cultural and behavioral parts of the artificial environment that should demand the greatest attention and understanding. Yet, the city should not only be viewed as a formation of one or several factors, but rather as comprehensive reciprocal forces that create the "final product." In essence, such a final product has never been static, but evolves continuously. Even though Japan is an extremely traditional country, the postwar era brought changes to some facets of the Japanese mind and urban environment. The accelerated interaction with the Western life style and technology even altered the overall image of the formerly holy Japanese emperor. Japan has accepted the technology and economic system of the West but refused to adopt the socio-cultural values and has successfully retained its own identity to a large extent. As may be expected, these technological changes occurred in the city, rather than in the village. Yet the latter will not fall behind the city since urban lifestyle and economy are likely to become a dominant force there also.

URBAN JAPAN'S PAST AND PRESENT

Since the multiple complexity of mankind has been the dominant factor woven into the city's evolution, the city has become the most complicated project ever ventured by humans. In Japan, like other technologically advanced countries, the urban setting is a contemporary, living organism. The Japanese have conceived their socio-cultural values and ethics as their first priority and retained them as a continuum of their treasured ancient heritage. This has led and guided the retention of the urban environment in Japan as a whole and its physical form particularly, in the neighborhood structure. The Japanese example shows that we cannot design an effective future city without studying and understanding the urban past as well as its socio-cultural, physical and artificial environments.

The Japanese interpretation of socio-cultural values into physical urban forms has historically carried on with the attitude "design without designers." In the past, people used their observational skills, intellect and instinct to form a community that we view today as creative, harmonious, sensitive to nature, indigenous, and original in its use of local materials. As in the West, it is true that the scale of contemporary urban design and architectural creativity is larger and more complex than in the past, which makes construction more difficult and challenging. The Japanese have not lost their ancestors' sensitivity toward the natural and socio-urban environment to the extent Westerners have. This Japanese attitude was primarily presented in the conservation of the physical setting of the traditional Japanese urban neighborhood. In the West, however, the knowledge that an understanding of an integrative past and present as the foundation of the future, as well as the fusion of socio-economic values with physical forms, was lost. This has resulted in a lack of ethics in urban design and the management of urban growth.

URBAN JAPAN: CURRENT AND FUTURE TRENDS

For the Westerner, the early impressions when visiting a Japanese city tend to superficially define it as exceedingly similar, if not identical, to other Western cities and those of technologically advanced countries. Yet, the careful Western observer, who is sensitive to cultural and behavioral nature, will soon find the distinction between the Japanese and the Western city.

The foremost characteristic of the Japanese city is the invisible city which lies hidden within the Japanese who carry it with them on a daily basis. In the case of Japan and other ancient cultures of the world, the vitality of the invisible city is composed of historical layers which were deposited and evolved to a solidly unified continuum; they are the vibrant force behind the visible city. In short, the invisible part of the Japanese city consists of the culture, individual and collective dignity, social values, norms of behavior, individual attitude toward governments, gender interactions, the integrative community, family and individual norms as well as the complexity of viewing art as representative of culture and nature. This latter attitude is presented not only in the drawings but even in the introduction and display of food at the table. Thus, art is introduced to every facet of life and treated as such in different forms; it establishes an atmosphere of tranquillity and containment in everyday Japanese life. For the average Japanese person, there are rules of conduct, often ceremonially introduced, which establish the norms of his or her daily behavior.

As would be expected, the invisible city is also subject to change within the dynamics of an urban growth evolution, yet, among the Japanese, it has still stayed within its confined basic principles which define its abstract identity. These norms and ethics of the socio-cultural identity determine the physical forms and configurations of the Japanese urban environment, as well as its neighborhoods, as a concrete entity to a great extent. The introduction of the Western urban forms and architecture have certainly influenced the physical part of the

Japanese urban environment, but it has far less influenced the invisible city of Japan and it is this retention which characterizes the Japanese urbanscape today. It is our opinion that the basic characteristics of this Japanese urban environment are solid enough to predict its continuity in the foreseeable future.

Although the origin of urban Japan's metamorphosis can be traced back to pre-World War II, the postwar era is the setting for the major physical alterations of Japan's urban environment. The overall changes are outlined in the following:

- Urban growth and extreme imbalance between the percentage rates of the urban and rural Japanese population.
- Growth of urban size. This growth consumed the bulk of land suitable for agriculture and has led to a significant increase in land prices, especially within the large cities of Tokyo, Osaka, Kobe and Kyoto. This development has a correlated impact on the quality of management, finance, delivery of services, cost of infrastructure, design, construction, and the overall quality of urban life. The Japanese, however, were able to manage their urban growth and control it effectively, operationally, and financially. The centers of their large cities are clean and safe. We in the West have been struggling with the unmanageability of our cities, which have been moving from one major crisis to another.
- The rise of the urban middle class was a result of economic growth, improvement of job training and education, and above all, the openness to the trade with the West. This development has enhanced urban services, increased consumption and waste, improved the standard of living, yet changed the use of urban land.
- The introduction of innovative and sophisticated technological systems into the Japanese economy have enabled Japan to compete with the most technologically advanced countries of the world and to increase its trade internationally. This development forced Japan to step out of its traditional isolationist policy and to become seriously involved with international affairs. It ranks equal, therefore, with the industrialized nations. This recent trend promises further serious changes and improvements in the Japanese urban economy. Technological changes took place not only on the level of the production of machinery but also of highly sophisticated communications and information equipment which, in turn, bring urban Japan closer to the world. Due to this major change in its urban environment, Japan now uses an outside labor force, for the first time in its history, to perform much of its services. This consumption has attracted large numbers of migrants from Korea, China, India, the Middle East, and parts of south-eastern Asia to the labor market of Japan; the wave of immigration, however, is met with reluctance by many Japanese. The dominant majority of these migrants moved to the large cities of Japan, creating socio-economic and ethnic problems which still need to be resolved. This migration has also entailed the need for the enhancement of the Japanese human rights movement. This overall development fosters a condition that carries the potential for ethnic friction and conflict.

It is now noticeable that the Japanese community has become increasingly mobile, more than ever before, in Japan and throughout the world. As a part of this mobility, some Japanese now seek leisure and exposure to the outer world in the form of tourism. Others are motivated by an interest in the financial investment in technologically advanced countries. Obviously, such international mobility will lead to enhanced human interaction among heterogeneous ethnic groups and to create pockets of integrated, ethnically-mixed urban communities of foreign immigrants within Japan. We can also anticipate the increase in uniformity of the physical urbanscape comparable to the international one which will create some loss of indigenous and national urban distinction for Japan. All in all, these are major changes on the level of economics, technology, related matters and, to a limited extent, in architecture and housing design. However, major changes did not take place on the socio-cultural level which makes the Japanese city different from those in the West.

JAPANESE ENVIRONMENTAL ETHICS: EAST AND WEST

Environmental design is the science of shaping our surroundings for the benefit of mankind. As dynamic intruders in this world, humans are also environmental designers, for better or worse. Environmental design has two focuses: the natural and artificial environment.

Natural and Artificial Environment

The natural, physical environment surrounding us is a synthesis shaped by a continuing process of dynamic interactions between many positive and negative forces. The forces are interconnected and consist of the dynamics of climate, hydrological cycles, tectonic forces, soil evolution, solar energy, flora cycles, fauna activities, and a synthesis of site character with all of these components. Each of these forces is strong and dynamic and has the features of five elements: a cyclical pattern, a reciprocal influence, an equilibrium, a newly created form, and a predictable process and product.

The artificial environment intrudes on the natural environment. This intrusion occurs at underground, ground, and above-ground levels. Human activities on these levels are diverse and encompass construction, agricultural processing, social development, and economic pursuits. Such human activities, when not designed properly in coordination with other intruding forces or by exhausting vital resources, often have destructive results for both nature and mankind. To be specific, the artificial environment is continuously shaped by urban and rural construction, technological growth, the dynamics of economic and socio-behavioral systems, cultural development, art and spiritual expression, as well as political systems, which all influence comprehensive productivity. Thus, the characteristic elements of an artificial environmental model differ in equilibrium from those characteristics of the natural environment. The features of the former comprise technology, overall dynamics, and the consumption as well as disposal of goods.

Artificial environmental design ranges from the planning of small-scale housing units to the large-scale layouts of cities and their surroundings. To optimize this design, people must systematically intervene with the process to improve and enhance the environment through physical design. Environmental design strives for an equilibrium to be achieved between the artificial physical creativity, resulting from a deeper understanding and the reciprocal influences of natural forces. In short, environmental designers should consider all forces mentioned above and the "symphony" that orchestrates them. Although these large-scale concepts are universal, philosophically and practically, a different interpretation of the environment between the Orient (Japan) and Western societies exists.[1]

Japanese Environmental Philosophy

The Japanese have historically viewed the environment as distinct and unique because of the unity of the triumvirate of nature, humans and heaven. Their major philosophy has been to view the reciprocal relations of humans and nature, humans and heaven, and heaven and earth, through the art of esthetics.

Humans and nature are bound together and viewed as an integral part of each other. The term *environment* is associated with the natural environment, morality, as well as the ethics of human conduct toward this environment. The ultimate goal is to achieve harmony between the two and create a pleasing ambiance. Japanese society, with a proximity to its natural resources needed for survival, was understandably sensitive about the well-being of its natural environment. Consequently, architecture and urban design have become an indigenous part of the natural environment, evolving with it and not against it. Society adapts itself to the environment and therefore, a mutual coexistence and equilibrium between the two is established. Thus, environmental design is perceived by the Japanese through the unity of society and the balance within the family, neighborhood and community. In short, the Japanese notion of humans and nature is that they are unified as one system and the survival of humans depends on the survival of nature. We in the West have recently revived this notion by establishing green zones and parks within and close to our urban centers. In conclusion, the Japanese perceive the triumvirate elements of heaven, earth, and humanity as a continuous, balanced relationship in which they coexisted in harmony with each other in the past.

Western Environmental Philosophy

Comparing the pattern of the reciprocal relations between heaven, earth, and humans of the Japanese philosophy with the Western pattern, we find conflicting views. Although we in the West would agree on the vitality of these three elements of the Japanese theme and their significance for survival, we differ in practice in the conduct of the relations between the three elements. According to traditional Japanese philosophy, humans should not intervene with nature and heaven (cosmos, gods and rhythm of cycles) but work with them. In the West, our sophisticated technology and intellectual innovations have changed our immediate natural environment rapidly, often with little, if any, sensitivity to nature. In this pattern, we are creating a strong, reciprocal influence between humans and the earth, as well as humans and heaven, while traditional Japanese philosophy is unidirectional (earth and heaven influencing humans).

The ultimate Western view of the environment appears to be similar to that of the Japanese at the outset. However, contemporary Western practice conflicts with that of Japanese philosophy. With the immense scale of contemporary urban dominance in the West, we have routinely detached ourselves from nature. In addition, the West does not view nature as the exclusive source of survival. These two conditions have played a large role in leading to a sense that nature is extraneous to human existence. Moreover, the West is accustomed to imposing its rules on the natural environment. Only recently have we begun to realize the urgent need to work with our environment according to principles, codes, and ethics, however, it should be understood that Japanese contemporary practice has recently begun to alter the indigenous philosophy mentioned above.

ETHICS OF URBAN DESIGN

Ethics are norms and standards formulated to retain order and healthy management of the social and environmental setting. The term *ethics* is commonly used in relation with morality and behavioral conduct of the individual and society,but we will use this term in the context of the urban environment. Our previous research findings indicate that communities and individuals developed their socio-cultural ethics to be used diurnally and to form the rules for survival.[2] Consequently, these moral principles are applied to community and individual decisions when creating the components of physical urban artificial environments such as houses, streets, neighborhoods, and the city itself. The sequential process of socio-cultural ethics which shapes the physical form has evolved throughout history and produced the indigenous physical environment we always praise. In our discussion, we are using *urban* or *environmental design ethics* accordingly. The physical cityscape of urbanity is molded by the culture of the people, their inspiration, and their ethics as well as their behavior in daily life. The Japanese work ethic is unique and differs from the West. The work ethic of the Japanese is characterized by team cooperation, mutual responsibility, submissiveness, loyalty, and a strong dedication to their endeavors. Their system has proven to be innovative, efficient, and productive.

In Japan, for the last half century, there has been intensive interaction and, to some extent, confrontation between the ethics of the traditional indigenous society imbued with highly sophisticated socio-cultural values and those of modern society characterized by advanced technology. The arena of these confrontations of values has been, and will continue to be, the Japanese urban centers rather than the rural areas. Japan has been able to find the synthesis between those two systems of values and, to an extent, successfully fused them without losing its socio-cultural identity.

Another contemporary conflict of human values Japan has experienced is the difference in ethics between rural and urban dwellers. The rural influx to Japanese urban centers has certainly brought changes to the urbanscape. Japanese vernacular rural communities have been characterized by the ethics of simplicity, dignity, pride, conservatism, tradition, clan pedigree, hard work, deeply-rooted social values preceding those of materialistic values and many others. On the other hand, modern urban society of Japan has recently been affected by materialism, political power struggles, and the codes of institutionalized legality rather than humane ethics, leisure with ties to prosperity, and some changes in traditional social values.

Although these clashes of values (the ethics of the traditional and modern on the one hand, urban and rural on the other hand) are of different origins, they are basically similar, yet not identical and have a deep impact on the urban socio-cultural quality, as well as the urban environment as a whole. Both sets of ethics are dynamic and require space as an entity with resulting physical features. Japanese urban ethics have also produced a distinct new urbanity characterized by a different human identity and the resulting city entity with which we are so familiar.

Our previous discussion revolved around a practical analysis of the Japanese urban environment with a limited comparison to the Western world. This volume is the compilation of the urban Japanese experience which has been introduced by a team of diversified backgrounds. It would have been difficult, if not impossible, for a single person to write such a comprehensive book which provides an overview of the numerous forces of today's Japanese urban environment and explores its future trends. Despite its conservatism, Japanese urban society is dynamic and has succeeded in creating an equilibrium between most facets of urban life. These facets include urban government and management, urban economic stability, cleanliness and safety, the daily mobility of more than 5 million residents throughout the city of Tokyo and its surroundings, as well as many other achievements.

Comprehending the Japanese accomplishment in the diversified levels of urban dynamics is, by itself, a lesson which the East and West can draw by virtue of being exposed to the Japanese stage of transition. At the same time, cities of less technologically developed countries are experiencing a transitional urban process similar to the one taking place in urban Japan. Their conflicting values and ethics are similar to those of urban Japan.

CONCLUSION

The compilation of this book is divided into four leading subjects which are to be described in the following. It is the vision of *Japanese Urban Environment* to clarify the social, as well as cultural, impact on the quality of urban life and the ways local leadership enhances it.

A. Social, Cultural, and Physical Determinants of the Japanese Urban Environment

It appears that Japanese cities have been able to master the post-World War II era as a transitional period with social, technological, and relative environmental achievements. These accomplishments will dominate the trends in the Japanese urban environment for the foreseeable future. Traditional urban evolution was often without pre-design, but relied heavily on the cohesiveness of socio-cultural values in advancing the Japanese urban growth process (Koide and Oyama chapter). In contrast, contemporary Japanese urban design has become a revolutionary process which originates on the drafting table. It is our observation that underlying both design processes is a similar concept inspired by Japanese culture (Kurokawa and Hirai chapters). Although much of Japanese urban and environmental design was originally borrowed from ancient Chinese theory and practice, it carried with it the triumvirate of the balance between modern ideals and the inspiration of nature, as well as human and environmental notions. It should be mentioned that in spite of this achievement, the Japanese failed to retain their typically Tokyo urban waterfront by converting the many water canals of their capital to highways (Fakahashi chapter). Urban designers of Tokyo now mourn this loss. The Japanese recently realized that both indigenous, as well as modern design, are a process of trading-off losses and gains, but at the same time, the Japanese need to retain their inspiration, so they can preserve and practice their customs.

B. Environmental Quality

In the average Japanese mind, the quality of the urban environment is to be achieved by multiple factors such as individual, community, and governmental contributions. Such an understanding requires individual contributions for the cleanliness and safety of the streets; a community effort in keeping neighborhoods quiet and free from unnecessary traffic; and sensitivity of the urban local government to the residents' needs in providing the standard infrastructure. These efforts are all equally important in enhancing the quality of the urban environment. The neighborhood structure is an integration of the physical entity with its population's socio-cultural and historical identity and the history of neighborhoods can be traced back to their roots in the villages from which Tokyo grew. In spite of the fact that a reasonable number of Tokyo's residents were rural, or originally migrated from other urban centers, the integration of socio-cultural identity with the propinquity of residential areas provides a sense of pride and belonging.

The distinctive socio-cultural features of Japanese urbanscape lie in the strong traditional culture of its residents. In Japanese metropolitan centers crime, homelessness, and poverty in the social and physical cityscape are rare. The cities have accepted Western technology and architectural styles yet have almost exclusively retained their Japanese socio-cultural features. This integration is noticeable in daily life as well as in a city's overall atmosphere. Japanese metropolises also embrace environmental ethics which raise the urban planners' consciousness of issues which the Japanese have been trying to resolve, like urban warming (Saitoh chapter) and industrial pollution. Urban performance as a whole does have an impact on the thermal performance of the neighborhood and the houses (Kimura and Katayama chapters). Social and environmental awareness is a unique characteristic of Japanese urbanscape. Recently the urban Japanese as a whole, the designers, and urban environmentalists in particular have become extremely concerned with the diminished (almost vanished) traditional waterfront of the city, largely formed by canals and rivers (Takahashi chapter).

C. Cityscape Infrastructure

Another achievement of the Japanese urban environment is the urban governance and infrastructure system. Metropolitan Tokyo has been growing to an immense size, physically (exceeding 2150 km^2) and demographically (more than 12 million people). Within this dual immense development, the Japanese established twenty-three wards (*ku*) governed and managed cooperatively, which efficiently provide the infrastructure (Ojima chapter). Within each ward is a governing hierarchy of city (*shi*), town (*machi*), and village (*mura*); the origins of this system can also be traced through time. However, these governing bodies have decentralized management responsibilities, which enhance community service, enforce community self-recognition, reduce bureaucracy, and increase community and individual identity (Takabu chapter). The urban transportation network makes Japanese daily mobility possible and comfortable, since the place of work is mostly far from the place of residency. Several million of the population commute diurnally within one city or between cities. In observing such a movement in cities, such as Tokyo, Kobe, Kyoto, and Osaka, one cannot help but admire the efficiency of the transportation system as well as of the operation of buses and subways to facilitate this mobility (Iwai and Asano chapters).

D. Urban Planning—Future and Present

The planning of the city of the future at the dawn of the technological revolution encompasses a variety of possibilities. With the recent technological innovations and changes, the design of future urbanscape enters a new dimension (Obitsu, Sano, Sakamoto, Nagai, and Watanabe chapters). Japanese urban planning is one step ahead of the West as it consciously incorporates traditional values with the technological revolution, in a synthesis of the city of the future.

The twentieth century has been characterized by a conflict between the two major blocks of nations, the East and the West. The forthcoming twenty-first century urban environment will be distinguished by accelerated urban growth as well as population mobility, a blend of socio-cultural groups within the urban landscape, and the interaction (or maybe the conflict) of ethnic groups searching and rediscovering their traditional ethnic roots. With the disappearance of the cities' ethnic homogeneity, as it is happening in Japan, an international flavor will prevail in the medium and large cities. Tokyo is one example where the beginning of a steady change in Japanese traditional, ethnic, and homogeneous urban society is taking place. An influx of minorities, such as Koreans, Chinese, Iranians, Thais, Europeans, and Americans have migrated to Tokyo since World War II. A similar phenomenon is currently taking place in European cities, such as London and in many Canadian, as well as Australian, cities.

With the revolutionary and rapid changes in electronic technology, Japan, as it has for the past few decades, will continue to take its share in the communication superhighway, transmission of information, and other related developments. In spite of its traditional tendency for isolation, Japan will continue to move closer to the international community; this will, in turn, affect the quality of its urban environment, whether for the better or worse, it may be too early to determine at this point in time.

NOTES

1. Golany, G. *Ethics and Urban Design.* New York: John Wiley & Sons, 1995, 19–26.
2. Golany, G. *Ethics and Urban Design.* New York: John Wiley & Sons, 1995, 1–9.

Part I

Social, Cultural, and Physical Determinants of the Japanese Urban Environment

Part I: Introduction

Part I discusses three interrelated and important elements which have determined the Japanese urban environment through time; they are the social, cultural, and physical factors of the Japanese city.

The elements of culture and social, and physical forms as well as their interrelation have always been of concern to the Japanese people. This concern existed traditionally among the Japanese indigenous society and continues to a large extent among today's architects and urban designers. Indeed, contemporary Japanese architecture introduces the single structures of the modern city as an imitation of the Western type with some or no indication of the indigenous style. It is the interior parts of the building which have retained their traditional cultural and physical style. Dr. Kisho Kurokawa, a forerunner of modern Japanese thought and architecture, introduces this relation between culture and form in an elaborate philosophical, yet practical way in his discussion. He outlines the fundamentals of Japanese and Western philosophy and their impact upon urban planning as well as architecture (Japan: wood; harmony with nature; symbiosis between part and whole; West: stone and concrete; system of dualities). He conceives the cultural tradition as the multifaceted determinant of the invisible city. Religion, for example, is viewed in its substance as well as its expressive architecture as an important part of the city culture.

Another pivotal subject is art as an expressive element within all facets of Japanese urban culture. Internally, within the house and through the interaction of people, art received much attention to include the ceremonial/ritual performance along with any form of social interaction within the family and with outsiders. Externally, it has played a central role in public gathering spaces such as restaurants. Kurokawa's theory of symbiosis focuses on the concept which takes its name from ecological and biological concepts and puts forward ideas developed from traditional philosophy and culture. The symbiosis of culture and philosophy is a philosophy of "both-and" rather than "either-or" as Charles Jencks put it. Culture, art, and form enter a close relation, which gives the Japanese city its characteristic uniqueness. The future trend of Japanese architecture and urban planning lies in creating an image of life in all facets of society (multivalency in the twenty-first century).

Hirai's chapter deals with the reality of the heart of Tokyo and envisions its future. Tokyo's growth introduced multiple problems particularly to the capital's center; this physical expansion has caused a serious shift of the population from the city to the outskirts and an ever-increasing concentration of business and office buildings in the city center. Due to this development, a chronic shortage of land and skyrocketing land prices have plagued the heart of the city. Hirai closes by suggesting ways to cure the symptoms of the ailing visible and invisible city (new social rules and values, encouragement of cultural activities, etc.).

Another case of urban changes is introduced by Professor Hiroshi Mimura and his colleagues discussing historical and modern Kyoto. When the Japanese capital was moved from Kyoto to Tokyo in the nineteenth century, the former went through a brief period of decline but recovered quickly. Kyoto underwent massive changes with the dawning of the Industrial Revolution and has been expanding ever since. The city consumes its surrounding rural areas by transforming them into dull rurban areas. Mimura has been focusing on neighborhood preservation attempting to incorporate socio-cultural identity and most importantly, the involvement of local residents and the community with the physical preservation process. The author provides suggestions to enrich Kyoto and its surroundings by establishing a rich, harmonious environment with strong, balanced rural elements (e.g. gardens, vegetation, etc.). At the time of its design and development, Kyoto was considered to be the most modern city of Japan; it adopted the design principles and forms of the Chinese urban grid system which proved to be more suitable for today's motor vehicle transportation. At the same time, the design within a single block unit has preserved narrow, quiet streets with a feeling of intimacy and tranquillity. Today, both design elements of the grid and detailed neighborhood structures are contained in Kyoto. Neighborhood preservation retained the positive feeling of a community atmosphere and attractive environment for local residents as well as visitors. Houses in this area serve as a model for today's Kyoto. Therefore, one can still find a reasonable number of the classic, one-story, wooden indigenous houses in Kyoto today which are all well oriented and lighted and come with a cozy patio and small, elegant garden.

Professor Yasuo Masai's work introduces the historical, present, and future Tokyo from a comprehensive point of view. He, too, interrelates the human factor and physical forms of the city. His treatment is comprehensive, yet never loses touch with the details, which enables the reader to grasp the sense of Tokyo's environment. Masai takes the reader on a trip in time through Tokyo, the former Edo. Tokyo's origins date back to feudal times when Edo developed its two characteristic nuclei, which are still a part of the contemporary capital. Combining historical and cultural information on Tokyo, Masai focuses on the city's demographic as well as spatial development and its affects on the urbanscape throughout the centuries. He presents a colorful and illustrative description of Tokyo, a city with 35 million people in its metropolitan region and 15 million motor vehicles; surprisingly, it is still an operable city which exudes an atmosphere of urbanity without much of the stressful impact of the Western metropolitan city. All in all, the Westerner will certainly sense the atmosphere of more a relaxed, diurnally safer and cleaner environment where social cooperation eases any feeling of alienation. The chapter closes with a review of the current problems and their impact on the future.

Finally, both Professor Osamu Koide and Mr. Toshio Oyama discuss the social determinants of the Japanese urban environment. Among the many striking phenomena for the Westerner when visiting the Japanese city are the feelings of safety and security, the kind interaction of the Japanese with each other as well as outsiders, the cleanliness of the environment, and, not less importantly, the distinctive elegant touch of art as it is expressed on the one hand in the treatment in the public green areas and on the other hand, the presentation of food in the restaurant. To the Westerner, the crime rate in Japanese cities is surprisingly low and far lower than in Western cities. In observing eastern Asian cultures, particularly the Japanese, we cannot help but realize that the quality and norms of the individual behavior have much to do with the cultural upbringing of the community and the individual.

To synthesize our discussion, these five chapters have commonly focused on the physical, socio-cultural, historical, and the human aspects of the Japanese urban environment. One cannot help but notice the distinctiveness of the Japanese urban environment and comprehend that its positive atmosphere consists of combined elements which reciprocally interact in creating such an environment. More than any other nation, in Japan it is the culture along with the social dynamics which shape the city environment rather than vice versa. This socio-cultural factor has been the strongest contributing factor to the Japanese urban environment. Although the five contributors in this section have come from different backgrounds and professions, all five chapters discuss the built-up cultural values throughout the historical evolution of the Japanese cities as an essential contribution in creating the Japanese urban environment of today. It is this strength which truly lifts the quality of the Japanese city environment from the physical decay commonly found in some Western cities. Throughout the historical evolution, the population has been fluctuating demographically and structurally while the culture as a whole has been changing at a slower pace. According to our observation in Japan, people keep contributing their share to the positive existing environment of the cities.

G.S.G.

A Metabolism, Symbiosis, and Culture of Japanese Cities

Kisho Kurokawa

AN INVISIBLE TRADITION

Every society has invisible as well as visible traditions. Clearly, a distinct national character and cultural tradition are to be found in religion, philosophy, esthetic sensibilities, lifestyles, customs, psychological backgrounds, sensitivities, and awareness of traditional order. These are all invisible traditions. In contrast, visible traditions comprise architectural styles, works of art, and traditional symbols which are expressed, for example, in roof shapes, decorations, and traditional performing arts. These two traditions, the invisible and the visible, are mutually related. They are an inherent part of the same roots, making it impossible to discuss one without the other. It can be said, nevertheless, that Japanese society places more importance on the invisible traditions than Western society does. To illustrate this, it is necessary to compare the Parthenon with Japan's Ise Shrine.

Let us imagine that an exact replica is constructed of the Parthenon out of the same marble, next to the ruins of the Ise Shrine Temple. People of Western society would regard the Parthenon as a copy and they would not give it the same value as the original work of architecture. Contrary to this, the Ise Shrine, along with the Katsura Detached Palace, were praised by Bruno Taut and Walter Gropius as the sources of modern architecture and its original paradigms.[1,2] The Ise Shrine, in particular, is a classic example of Japanese wooden architecture with a history of 1300 years, but in fact, the Ise Shrine is rebuilt every twenty years.

The shrine is not repaired because it ages and is meant to be destroyed. Part of the original plan called for two sites to be prepared during the initial construction, so the building could be rebuilt on the alternate site every twenty years. There were probably several reasons for this prearrangement. First, wooden structures have a shorter life than stone structures. Second, in ancient times, the practice of recording structures in plans did not yet exist. All the know-how for designing and building a structure was passed down from master to apprentice, from father to son and twenty years was about the span of a generation. This tradition was called *hengu* and it was inaugurated with an important ceremonial offering to the god of the shrine.

The most important reason for the rebuilding of the shrine is that in Japan, although the physical existence or the visible material may have a lifetime of only twenty years, the inheritance of the tradition is preserved and regarded as long as the invisible tradition—the esthetic sensibility behind the object and the sense of order—is passed on spiritually from person to person. Would anyone who sees contemporary Tokyo, Osaka, and Hiroshima imagine that only fifty years ago these cities had been completely reduced to ashes and rubble?

In contrast to Western art and architecture with its esthetics of materialism that seeks the eternal, Japan's esthetics can be called a "mind-only" esthetics.[3] This can be clearly seen in Japan's contemporary cities and architecture which have inherited the special character of this tradition and the way in which it is passed on. When a person first visits Tokyo, they are likely to see it as an international city not much different from Los Angeles, U.S.A. But foreigners who lived for a long time in Tokyo, insist that Tokyo is, in fact, a very Japanese city in character. Tokyo is built with contemporary techniques from contemporary materials and as long as the focus is solely on its exterior, it is difficult to claim that it has inherited Japanese traditions. However, those traditions are alive and well in the lifestyles of Tokyo people, in their high sensitivity to the changes of the seasons and in their sense of order. To express this in another way, the Japanese readily incorporate new cultures, technologies, forms, and symbols from other cultures as long as they have a guarantee that they can preserve the invisible Japanese traditions at the same time.

The author's architectural designs over the last thirty years have consistently incorporated Japanese tradition and philosophy, but these have not necessarily always manifested themselves as traditional forms. Instead, they have remained hidden as the background for the most advanced technologies and contemporary materials. An analogy can be made to the commonly used technique in Japanese cooking called "hidden flavor." It is a method of using a hint of sweetener, salt, or saké in a way that the seasoning cannot be detected, but the end result produces a complex and sophisticated taste. The invisible Japanese tradition is similar in some ways to this "hidden flavor."

Architectural works and the surface of Japanese cities may not seem, at least from their forms and materials, to have much of a link to the Japanese tradition, but the traditional Japanese esthetics behind them can be sensed within their context. This same Japanese tradition can also be detected in industrial design products such as televisions and automobiles, in graphic design, and the fashions created by such designers as Issey Miyake and Rei Kawakubo.

Concerning music, Akira Nishimura, a composer born in 1953, has received numerous prizes for his works, both in Japan and abroad. He attracted inter-national attention when his 1990 compositions *Concerto for Violin Cello and Orchestra* and *Into the Lights of the Eternal Chaos* were performed by the Bruckner Orchestra Linz, with soloist Walter Nohas, under the direction of conductor Kristof Escher. These compositions represent a symbiosis of the compositional technique Nishimura used to call "heterophony" and a Japanese

Pan-Asian sensibility. The compositions have a brilliant merger of a Japanese sense of topos and the logical nature of Western culture.

In Japan, from the start of the Meiji period in the second half of the nineteenth century through Kenzo Tange's work, modernization was believed to be equivalent to westernization.[4] The spiritual traditions that guided Japanese culture up to that time were rejected and materialistic esthetics that viewed structures as inanimate objects were regarded as the organizing principle of modern architecture. Tange idolized Michelangelo and Leonardo da Vinci and he created works based on a "Japanese module" that he established by recalculating Le Corbusier's module forms to a scale appropriate to the Japanese. However, Tange's obsession with the urban hub and symmetrical forms reflected an inferiority complex toward the West.

The first challenge of westernization by Japanese architects took place when this author and Kiyoshi Kikutake, together with the critic Noboru Kawazoe, founded the Metabolist movement in 1960. At first, the architecture and cities of Metabolism may seem to bear a resemblance to the works of Archigram and Yona Friedman, but they were, in fact, the rediscovery of a hidden, invisible tradition.[5,6] The pretexts for Metabolism were the tradition of rebuilding the Ise Shrine every twenty years and the Katsura Detached Palace, which was added to twice in its 150-year history to grow and develop as the New *Shoin* and the Middle *Shoin* were added to the Old *Shoin*.[7] The invisible tradition of Japanese architecture is intimately linked to the Buddhist concept of impermanence (*mujo kan*) (which will be discussed in the following) as well as the provisional concept.

THE PROVISIONAL NATURE

Throughout history, Japanese cities have been under attack almost yearly from natural disasters as earthquakes, typhoons, floods, and volcanic eruptions. Great fires set during the Warring States period and conflagrations, started through carelessness, frequently reduced most of Kyoto and Edo (modern Tokyo) to ashes. The Great Earthquake of 1923 destroyed most of Tokyo and with the exceptions of Kyoto, Nara, and Kanazawa, almost all of Japan's major cities were destroyed in World War II. When a Western city is destroyed, piles of tiles and bricks remain, but Japanese cities were completely obliterated since they were almost entirely constructed of wood. This continuing experience of the loss of cities and buildings has produced doubts about reality, a lack of confidence in the visible and a suspicion of the eternal in the Japanese people.

The fact that Japan is a culture of wood has contributed to the sensitivity of Japanese culture to change, particularly to the vicissitudes of nature and the seasons. Japan is blessed with a very clearly delineated and dramatic seasonal cycle. Japanese culture, as reflected in its poetry, requires the inclusion of a seasonal reference, called a *kigo*. A special feature of Japanese cuisine is the importance of *shun no mono*, the first-harvested or first-caught specialty of the season. People sense the change of seasons in eating such foods and are emotionally moved by the experience.

The attempt to make buildings and cities resemble nature as closely as possible by bringing them into harmony with nature as a part of the larger whole also has been useful in creating a tradition that incorporates natural changes just as they are. This tradition of creating buildings and cities that are as provisional as possible was born from the unique Japanese history. This provisional condition is intimately linked to the core of the Buddhist concept of impermanence. The Buddhist ideas of impermanence, transmigration, and nonself hold that all of the visible world of human beings, the earth, buildings, and cities are nothing but a succession of instants in being.

Buddhist philosophy and the idea of provisionality has been a support of the Metabolist movement since its inception in 1959. The enthusiastic support that the Metabolist group received in the 1960s was partly because Metabolism matched the spirit of the age, an age of miraculous economic growth and change in Japan. Unlike London and Paris, Tokyo was completely obliterated during World War II and a mere fifty years have passed since its reconstruction. A fierce rush into new construction over five decades and its unceasing growth and change have turned Tokyo into a city which the concept of the provisional suits very well.

The provisional status of which the author speaks naturally does not only refer to physical provisionality, such as being short-lived or easy to build, but also to structures built according to the traditional, philosophical concept of provisionality—our main concern. This larger sense of provisionality encompasses architecture as being without a center, an asymmetrical architecture, an architecture that has intentionally forgone consistency. The reason a life science term such as "metabolism" was selected to describe our movement was because we were interested in this kind of provisionality. Life is defined as lacking stability, always growing and moving. Our theme of metabolism, then, is the process of adaptation and change which expresses the constant dynamic changes in our life and in our environment.

FROM METABOLISM TO SYMBIOSIS

Western culture, especially the Western culture based on modernism, cannot be discussed without reference to its special nature based on dualism and binomial opposition. Dualism is the theory which "divides the world, a given realm of phenomena, or a concept into two mutually irreducible elements."[8] As such, dualism is the most fundamental philosophical base of the rationalism of the modern West. Spirit and form, freedom and necessity, good and evil, reaction and reform, art and science, intellect and emotion, humanity and nature, tradition and technology, capitalism and socialism, the individual and the whole—are innumerable binomial oppositions. The significance of dualism and the rational spirit is great, for they have played the role of liberating humankind from the mythological world and leading us to the world of the intellect, based on clear and rational analysis.

On the other hand, our adoption of dualistic thinking and the rational spirit have forced us to reject much that is valuable. For a variety of reasons, philosophical concepts which belong to an unknown realm that has not yet been explicated by science, or are part of an ineffable sacred zone, or are regarded as religious taboos, also have inherent value. Many of these elements of existence are excluded from either side of the binomial opposition. Such elements as ambiguity, ambivalence, multivalence, and myth—extremely essential elements that art has always possessed—have been labeled as irrational and obsolete and are rejected for that reason.

Both the West and Japan need to pay attention to the intermediate zone that exists, in ambiguous form, between the two elements of the binomial opposition and include it as well. To aggressively create intermediate spaces means a rediscovery, a reevaluation of the valuable elements of existence that has been excluded by the West's dualism and binomial opposition. For this reason, topos, regionalism, minor cultures, and noise have become once again themes of contemporary architecture. The new relationship created a symbiosis which does not force the two opposing elements into any sort of compromise. A state in which the two opposing elements coexist but remain as they are, in opposition, is fundamentally different from symbiosis. A symbiosis, however, is the creation of a new relationship, the coexistence of two dissimilar organisms in ecological interdependence, or a mutually beneficial relationship between two elements.[9] It is a dynamic state in which the two opposing elements share, or mutually include, at least some part of each other. This dynamic and symbiotic relationship is formed by the tentative establishment of an ambivalent, multivalent inter-mediate space between the two opposing elements.

The modernism of the West is also a universalism. The strong consumed the weak and eliminated them, so that the culture, the rules, and the standards of judgment of the strong would prevail universally throughout the world. The democratic principle of majority rule can mean that the opinion of 51% of a group prevails over 49%.

The origin of the philosophy of symbiosis, the philosophy of mind-only, is a Buddhist idea that developed in fourth-century India. Buddhist philosophy is almost unknown in India today, but the philosophy of mind-only, brought from India to China, Korea, and Japan, flowered as Japan's Mahayana Buddhism and took firm root there. This particular philosophy rejects dualism and binomial opposition and posits a fundamental stratum of consciousness, the *alaya* consciousness, in which the two are included. Mahayana Buddhism finds the Buddha in many objects. It teaches that Buddha exists in each and every person, plants, animals, and in all of life. The Buddhist doctrine which postulates that Buddha nature resides in all existence, in both elements of a binomial opposition, is the background against which the philosophy of symbiosis and intermediate zones (ambivalence, multivalence) developed in Japanese culture.

Japanese cultural keywords as *ma* (interval) and *Rikyu* (gray) are also inter-mediate zones. *Ma* is the silence between opposing elements. It can be described as a waiting period set between two opposing elements. Zeami, the famous sixteenth-century critic and author of *Kakyo* (a sixteenth-century Noh play script) and *Fushikaden*, described the essence of a performance of the traditional Japanese theater art of Noh as *senu hima*, the moment of silence. Zeami argues that by preserving a gentle feeling in one's heart as one stages a demon or a youthful feeling when portraying old age, the actor will express *hana* (depth), a sophisticated esthetic nature. This is nothing other than the esthetic awareness of two opposing elements in symbiosis.

Since the author first initiated the Metabolist movement in 1959, he has consistently emphasized the principle of life. Concepts such as intermediate zones, open structures, and the information society as a facilitator are in parallel development with the principles of Metabolism since they are all by their natures identical to the principle of life. The philosophy of symbiosis is a philosophy of the life principle that embraces everything from Metabolism on.

The spirit of the age from the turn of the nineteenth century to the twentieth century can be characterized as the age of the machine. Western philosophy of dualism, rationalism, the scientific method, and logos-centrism was part of the intellectual context that supported the age of the machine. It was the cultural essence of the West. Not only Le Corbusier and Eisenstein, but thinkers and artists in all fields proclaimed the arrival of the age of the machine.

Today, the ideas of Metabolism, intermediate zones, and the philosophy of symbiosis are a proclamation of the age of life and are replacing the age of the machine. Thus, the twenty-first century will be called the age of life. The special character of contemporary Japanese architecture and its cities already portray expressions of the age of life.

Within the context of the city, there are many levels on which symbiosis can develop: the symbiosis of past and future; of different generations; of nature and city; of farm, village and urban centers; of the part and the whole; and of different cultures. From the Nara period (eighth-century Buddhist renaissance in Japan), Japanese cities have received influences from China and Korea, and even from India and Persia. Then there was a sudden and strong European influence from the Meiji Restoration in 1868 and after World War II, a U.S. style of rational city planning became the mainstream influence.

In the early 1960s, the author protested against the destruction of the traditional *Shitamachi* (downtown area) that was caused by U.S. redevelopment and proposed a new city planning based on the principles of Oriental medicine.[10] This was a proposal for an Asian method of preserving the historical scale of the downtown area while injecting new functions into it.

The principles of modern city planning, however, are based on the foundation of European rationalism, in which dualism, analytic methods, and division by function are regarded as most important. The idea of zoning is the most functional and rational approach to dividing the city and separating its various functions into residential zones, business zones, industrial zones, and transportation system zones as cleanly as possible.

In contrast to the practice of zoning in modern city planning, the philosophy of symbiosis proposes an integration of more complicated, multiple, and polyvalent functions, or a combination of functions. For example, to modify Modernism's separation of functions, facilities for the elderly could be built in the city centers and in residential areas, the elderly, the handicapped, single people, and families could all live in symbiosis. The separation of racial groups in a city like New York in the U.S.A., for example, could be eliminated.

Another approach to correct the dualism and separation of functions in modern city planning is to revise the excessively clear division made today between public space and private space. Our task is to create a third kind of space, an intermediate zone between public and private, exterior and interior, nature and buildings. In fact, the use of the intermediate zone is one of the traditional elements of Japanese cities and culture.

During the last centuries, Japanese cities, starting with Kyoto, have included communal space that has functioned as an intermediate zone between private and public space to create an extension of living space. The unit of the *machi,* or "town," ceased to be an area demarcated by the roads surrounding the housing. Instead, the houses were built to face each other across the street and formed mini-communities. As the Kyoto merchants flourished, the *roji,* or street space between the homes, developed into a lively area for human interaction. The lattice-work *koshi* (facades) of these town houses provided privacy to those who lived behind them while remaining a structure open to the street at the same time.

The appearance of buildings constructed with openings to the street and urban-type spaces, such as atria, incorporated into buildings, represent a new attempt to create such intermediate zones. A symbiosis of nature and the city can be achieved by including many small-scale parks and pockets of forests throughout the city. This would be in contrast to the giant city parks of industrial societies.

RECEPTIVITY

There is a proverb in Japan, "To lose is to win." In the fifty years since the end of World War II and especially in the last twenty years, Japan has achieved the rank of an economic giant, but its leading role in economics and technology cannot last forever. No matter what happens economically and technologically, Japan will geographically remain a small country. The westernization with its modern society and industrial base that Japan has worked so hard to achieve since the nineteenth century was almost totally lost in the defeat in World War II. Of course, all armaments, military industry as well as most facilities that made industrialization possible were destroyed. As a result, when Japan rebuilt its industries, it was able to quickly install the most advanced industrial equipment of the time, giving it a leading edge industrially. The global superiority of postwar Japanese shipbuilding, automobile manufacturing, and steel industries was a fine proof that "To lose is to win."

Under the forced democratization of Japanese society instituted by U.S. occupation, Japan underwent a dramatic social transformation. The landowner class was abolished, farmlands were redistributed, the *zaibatsu* (a group of wealthy entrepreneurs) were dismantled, the educational system was revamped, the hereditary nobility was abolished, and the armed forces were outlawed. The scope and degree of these changes were even more dramatic than those during the French Revolution. Through its defeat in the war, Japan became a nation freer of class restrictions and more active and vigorous like England or France. The changes were made, as noted above, under the auspices of the U.S. occupational force, but this was not the only impetus for change. Every Japanese person immediately forgot the wartime slogan, "The British and Americans are Devils and Beasts," and passionately sought to adopt U.S. culture. In particular, the American lifestyle as depicted by Hollywood glittered with attraction and seemed as marvelous as a dream.

Looking at this phenomenon from a historical perspective, Japan realizes that the willingness to accept another culture—a foreign culture—and in particular, that of a large country, is also part of the Japanese cultural tradition. In a period of over one thousand years, Japan has developed with an awareness of its neighbors China and Korea, and in the early modern era, of the empires of Portugal, Holland, Germany, and England. In order for "little Japan" to avoid being invaded by these empires, there was nothing Japan could do but continually take positive steps to study them, to absorb elements of these cultures, and preserve its own identity while remaining on friendly terms with them. The importation of foreign cultures continued even during the Edo period, when the country was officially closed to the outside world. The receptivity that Japan needed to survive as a small nation is linked to the spirit of acceptance that Buddhism teaches. It can be seen, then, that the westernization that took place in Japan from the Meiji Restoration on, such as the importation of Western architecture, the Americanization of Japan after World War II, and Japan's absorption of U.S. culture are all linked to the receptivity characteristic of Japan's cultural tradition.

The distinguishing feature of Japan's contemporary architecture and arts is that it does not stop at the mere acceptance of the art of large countries' cultures. There is also an interest in other cultures, including minor countries. Unlike their elders, young Japanese are showing an interest in India, China, and the rest of Asia as well as their own culture. The artist Tadanori Yokoo leans to India for inspiration. The work of the young artist Takayuki Terakado exhibits an attempt to transcend mere westernization. The group of Western-style intellectuals, from architects Kunio Maekawa and Kenzo Tange to Fumihiko Maki and Arata Isozaki, has long been accepted as the trendsetter among Japanese intellectuals. The younger generation of Japanese architects no longer holds to the distorted opinion that discussing Japanese culture and tradition is antimodern. For example, composers Toru Takemitsu and Toshi Ichiyanagi show an interest in traditional Japanese musical instruments. While Kan Izue, Yasufumi Kijima,

Kazuhiro Ishii, Tadasu Ohe, and others are beginning to rediscover the Japanese tradition and to study different cultures the world over in a more flexible fashion and with a lighter touch.

When the author refers to Japanese philosophy as "an order that includes noise," he is influenced by the French philosopher Edgar Morin's theory of noise, as well as Piaget, Jacques Attali, and René Girard. An order that incorporates something different (noise) has the special contemporary meaning of Japan's acceptance of the different. The extraordinary curiosity that the Japanese have for foreign cultures, which will be discussed later, and the enormous quantity of information on foreign cultures offered in Japanese newspapers, on television, and in specialized journals (most of the data remains focused on the U.S.A. and Europe) is a phenomenon not be encountered in any other country. This special feature of the Japanese is also supported by their long tradition of receptivity.

Perhaps modern urban planning has placed too high an emphasis on the whole and on organization. More than one hundred million different life forms exist in the human body (viruses, bacteria, and others). Most of these life forms are necessary for the body to function. The human intestines, for example, cannot function properly without certain species of bacteria. Likewise, a city is also composed of complex and multilayered relations between an organized structure and the multivalent, heterogeneous elements that can be called noise. The city is always changing dynamically as it continually incorporates new elements. The open structure, or receptivity, is a special feature of the Japanese city and one that it shares with other Asian cities.

THE PART AND THE WHOLE: A HOLISTIC STRUCTURE

One of the special features of Japanese architecture, art, and crafts is a pre-occupation with detail; it might also be called the importance of detail. Of course, the same attention to detail can be seen in Western art and architecture at its peak, from the Middle Ages through the Renaissance, Baroque, and Art Nouveau, but Japan's preoccupation with it has been inherited by the makers of contemporary Japanese architecture, art, and manufactured goods as well. This detail cannot be detected, however, in the contemporary architecture of other Asian nations such as China, Korea, or Singapore. Japan's superiority of manufactured goods can be attributed to their efficiency, cost performance, and their service support system, but it must also be traced to the fact that Japanese products exhibit an attention to detail that goes beyond what is required. This also is a special feature shared by German automobile manufacturers, which rank equal with Japanese in excellence.

This emphasis on detail is especially conspicuous in contemporary Japanese architecture. It is partly due to the great variety of materials available in Japan, to its industrial technology and to the expertise of craftsmen, but essentially it is a manifestation of not only a thought process leading from the whole to the part, but also its opposite, from the part to the whole. The craftsman's spirit of seeking to express individuality by variations in detail and the particular Japanese esthetic that places great importance on detail lend to this emphasis. The personality and expression of Japanese city's art and architecture are not very apparent when viewed as a whole, but as the details become evident, an entirely new world is revealed. Up to now, the human race has generally expanded its field of interest to an ever larger world, to the planet, and to the universe. However, if the twenty-first century is to be the age of life, the disciplines of biotechnology, of genetic engineering, and micromachines may also lead this new age toward an interest in detail and to the discovery of the new world of the micro.

The preoccupation with detail is an important key to the author's architecture, as well as a special general feature of contemporary Japanese architecture. It is particularly evident in the architecture of Fumihiko Maki, Kan Izue, You Shoei, and Shin Takamatsu. The importance given to detail suggests a new order that the author has described as the symbiosis of part and whole. In contrast to Western architecture and cities, which are organized in a rigorous pyramid structure from their infrastructure over parts to details, the Japanese feel a stronger autonomy of the parts in their contemporary architecture.

In the author's opinion, when analyzing the great metropolis of Tokyo (*Toshi Dezain*, 1965, Kinokuniya Shoten, and *Toshigaku Nyumon,* 1973, Shodensha), the Japanese capital can be described as a conglomerate of three hundred cities. In fact, the city of Tokyo (formerly called Edo) was built during the feudal period because the lords from other domains were required to keep a residence in the new capital. The city area was parceled out among these various feudal domains and the merchants, temple and shrine priests, as well as craftsmen of each local domain gathered in their lord's section, creating many smaller cities within the larger city.

Tokyo has inherited this tradition and a new Japanese-style hierarchy of a symbiosis of part and whole has been created in the capital. Such a city structure lacks a central core, plazas, boulevards, or landmarks, and may at first glance appear to be a random form. Yet, herein lies the energy of the freedom and multivalence set free by the thinking from the part to the whole and the accumulation of detail. This experimental new order or hierarchy of symbiosis is created by the exploitation of spontaneously arising forces. Consequently, in present-day Tokyo, where the power of private investment is too strong, it is probably correct to say that this order exists between a total absence of order and an order as new and hidden, residing between the two.

Today, there is increased interest in the holistic order proposed by Arthur Koestler (an order in which the part and the whole are valued equally) and in physicist David Bohm's "internalized order" (in which the mechanism for order is internalized in each part). This order in Tokyo and contemporary Japanese architecture are on the verge of creating a new structure different from any in the West.[11]

So far, several special features of Japanese culture and their connections with the present have been discussed. It is not the purpose to assert that Japanese culture is superior to other cultures. Yet, it is impossible to discuss the new currents of contemporary Japanese architecture without reference to traditional Japanese culture and the special features of its contemporary culture which are its context.

Having passed through modernism and industrialization, advanced civilizations are now facing problems in a wide variety of fields. It is unlikely that Western culture, which has played a leading role until now, will suddenly decline, but its guiding principles are losing their power to pull the world along. The author is not predicting a shift from the philosophies of Western culture to those of the Japanese culture, but he is predicting a shift from Eurocentrism to a symbiosis of many different cultures. This period of transition is not, as Kenzo Tange has suggested, a period of chaos. Rather, in all areas a new world is slowly but surely discovered. As long as these changes are looked at through glasses tinted with Eurocentrism, they may appear to be formal chaos. Western materialism interprets the establishment of schools such as modernism, post-modernism, and deconstructionism as visible styles with formal characteristics, but they are a sign of the absence of a philosophy in architecture. It is perfectly acceptable to have, in addition to these "Eurocentric glasses," glasses tinted in many other cultural colors. The Japanese cultural tradition and contemporary Japanese architecture occupy an important place as one of the different cultures.

The preoccupation with detail in Japanese cities is the consequence of the difference in scale of its urban unit. Unlike the U.S. "super block," the Japanese urban unit is quite small. Because of the high price of land, residential lots are especially small, ranging from 100 to 400 m^2. This is what renders the scale of Japanese cities and Asian cities in general to be small and detailed. Walking through the business area of such a city, one would be surprised to see cars parked no more than a few cm away from the shop frontage which is about 3 m away. This extreme urban density is a sign of a new order that is formed when cities are built from the part to the whole.

The author once supervised the establishment of city regulations for preserving scenic views in the city of Nagoya. Instead of regarding the city as a whole, it was treated as a conglomeration of 164 districts, each with its distinct scenic view guidelines. These autonomous districts were part of an experiment which was to demonstrate that the order of the whole consists of individual parts and that it could be maintained by preserving the autonomy of the parts and incorporating all elements.

A DENSE SOCIETY

Of all the nations of the developed world, Japan has the highest population density. In addition, the Japanese archipelago is mountainous and almost all of the flat land is occupied by cities. As far as population density is concerned, Hong Kong, Shanghai, and Mexico City also rank very high, but the ratio of people to living space in Japanese cities such as Tokyo and Osaka is extraordinarily high.

To put this in another way, the average size of a residential unit in the Japanese capital is very small—less than 100 m^2.

Concerning traffic density and congestion, the major cities of the world do not differ greatly, but Tokyo has also by far the densest network of public transportation by train and subway. During rush hours so many people ride these trains that some railway organizations employ a special person called a "stuffer" to literally push passengers inside the train cars. The density of workers in office space is also very high. Since most Japanese offices are simply large, undivided rooms filled with desks, the density is further intensified visually and aurally.

The effect of this physically dense society is an intensifying of the sense of community within companies, regional districts, groups, and the family which creates a groupism or a communalism within a company or a geographical area. The familial nature of each company and the group consciousness of the professions that have created a sort of "village of architects" are extremely strong. There are negative aspects to this, such as envy of those who succeed and rejection of others who have a unique or special talent. Yet, this communalism also produces an extraordinary degree of interest in those outside the group, in strangers, and anything different. This serves as an excellent medium for the cultivation of an extreme sensitivity for awareness of the most minute distinctions.

Perhaps the most remarkable trait of contemporary Japan is the intense availability of information. The extreme curiosity of the Japanese about the outside world, new trends, and new information spans the entire population from specialists to the general public. Every day in Japan, information and news of events from every corner of the world are reported on television, in newspapers and magazines and introduced by a wide variety of professional journals. More information is available about the U.S.A. and Europe than other parts of the world, but truly detailed reports on Africa, Latin America, Asia, Russia, and Eastern Europe reach the general public on a daily basis.

In the profession of architecture, for example, the journal *A + U* publishes detailed expositions every month about architectural styles of many countries of the world. It is published in a bilingual edition and has moved beyond its original function of reporting on Japanese architecture to informing about architecture globally. Its new role as an international journal lets architects around the world know what the trends in other countries are. Strangely enough, the magazine does not publish the work of any Japanese architect, such as Arata Isozaki and the author, even if he or she has completed work overseas.

This enthusiastic introduction of information from abroad, about foreign cultures on the level of mass culture, is a special feature of Japan, not to be found in the U.S.A. or Europe. Through advances in media technology, information is spread to the general public by audio-visual equipment, cameras, video cameras, the lightest portable telephones and pocket computers in the world, word processors, as well as facsimile machines. These highly advanced tools, which process information and communicate, have penetrated Japanese society from the large cities to the farming villages, from the university research centers and giant companies to the neighborhood shops and private homes. Thus, Japan has built for itself a new, incredibly dense information society with an unprecedented amount of accessible data.

Recently Sony developed a data Diskman which is a miniature electronic data file, 12 cm × 15 cm with a complete Japanese–English, English–Japanese dictionary. It also contains a full chart of data on all over-the-counter drugs, a list of good restaurants in Tokyo, personal data on many Japanese key figures, including their addresses and telephone numbers as well as other types of information. Recently, a translation device the size of a fountain pen was invented which can be run over an English word and the Japanese translation immediately appears. With a vocabulary of 30,000 words, this little machine is low-priced at less than 200 dollars. The spread of personal computers and word processors in Japan has not stopped with the young but is embraced by all age groups.

The various information devices also are not used exclusively for business but have found a place in the homes of the general public. Each year these high-tech gadgets are improved by higher performance, lower prices, and smaller size. This sudden development has been made possible by the passion and curiosity of the Japanese for anything new which leads the average Japanese to seek out and purchase the latest items on the market. Recently, high definition television (HDTV) and digital audio tape (DAT) recorders, regarded as crucial in improving the quality of the information society in the future, have already been placed on sale in Japan. If prices lower, these items will, undoubtedly, become popular household items.

With the effect that a dense population and a sophisticated information society can have when combined with economic power, Japan will become an important information center in the future for artists, designers, and architects around the world. Historically speaking, all of the cities that have become world centers, such as London in the Victorian period, Paris under Napoleon, Budapest and Vienna under the Austro-Hungarian Empire, Berlin and Paris again in the 1920s, and New York after World War II, have combined economic power, a densely populated metropolis, and the power to concentrate information. Architects, film directors, artists, musicians, poets, and businessmen have gathered in these centers and demonstrated a marvelous creativity from a symbiosis of different cultures in fierce competition.

Japan and Tokyo are not as open to non-Japanese architects and creative individuals as Paris or New York are. Yet, in the past decade, Japan has opened itself to the rest of the world to an astounding degree. Already more than fifty non-Japanese architects, artists, and designers, including Richard Rogers, Norman Foster, Lenzo Piano, Cesar Pelli, Mario Botta, Michael Graves, Stanley Tigerman, Christian de Portzamparc, and Rem Koolhaus, Rossi, Peter Eisenman, and Hans Hollein have produced works in Japan. Some 30% of Japanese television commercials star non-Japanese and the size of the Japanese market in CDs and tapes is so considerable that foreign artists cannot ignore it.

All of these qualities of a dense society force Japanese architects to adapt and refine their work endlessly. The most minute variations are exaggerated in a densely populated society; this has resulted in a trend among architects to seek differentiation of their work from that of others. Also, Japan's increasing internationalization and growth as a global information hub has given the architecture of Japan's younger generation an extremely cosmopolitan touch. The younger generation is not self-conscious about being Japanese. The new trend to be completely contemporary with the rest of the world has already become a part of everyday Japanese life.

The ideal of modern city planning was Le Corbusier's "shining city" of skyscrapers separated by large empty spaces. The image of the future city was that of a highly populated one; the metropolises of the information age will be densely populated as well. One of the characteristics of Asian cities is their dense population which is also one of the reasons why Asia has achieved a high degree of economic development.

The age of the information society is, at the same time, an age of increased urbanization. Manufacturing took the leading role in an industrial society, but it will lose it in an information society. The industry and economy of the information society will be controlled by the availability of talented workers. This means that cities, where skilled workers tend to gravitate, will again assume a leading role. The communication technology of the information society will undoubtedly continue to develop at a very rapid pace, but the role of direct communication between individuals is likely to continue to grow also.

THE INFORMATION SOCIETY

Among the industrialized nations, Japan is in the process of creating one of the most advanced information societies. As discussed in the previous section, Japan's information society is supported by a dense population, an exchange of intensive information as well as the advance of information technology and the media.

Economically, Japan quickly caught up with the industrialized nations after World War II and is now in the process of transforming itself successfully from a manufacturing into an information society. The leadership of Japanese industry has passed from the heavy manufacturing industries of shipbuilding, steel, petroleum, automobiles, and machinery to information industries. In other words, it has shifted from manufacturing to nonmanufacturing; which already occupies more than 70% of the Japanese gross national product.

The information industry includes banking, broadcasting, publishing, distribution, commerce (wholesale and retail), the leisure industry, education, research, software, design, and the arts. The special feature of the information industry is that, unlike the manufacturing industry which relied mostly on giant companies, medium-sized and small companies will play a larger and more important role. Another difference is that while manufacturing gradually pulled its plants and workers out of the cities, the information industry is located in the cities. It does not produce noise, water, or air pollution, and in addition, it heavily relies on the cities' raw material of human skills.

The information society is seeking to bestow a new role on the metropolis. The basis of Japan's national urban policy has been one of decentralization from giant urban centers to outlying regions. An age of simultaneous decentralization and centralization has begun. This has not, however, meant a denial of the importance of the major metropolitan areas of Tokyo and Osaka. Centralization in this context means not only concentration in Tokyo and Osaka but in the major regional city centers as well. This new urban trend is unfolding parallel to a wave of increasing global urban centralization, including the return of Germany's capital to Berlin and the major reconstruction of Paris. The transformation to a dense information society requires the renovation of the old structure not only of Tokyo but of all of Japan's regional centers, to create new bustling centers.[12] Aggressive renovation and new investment by both the public and private sectors is continuing to provide architects of the younger generation opportunities to build creative structures.

Large-scale proposals have been offered within this social context; an example is the plan for the National Land Policy for the reconstruction of Tokyo by Group 2025 which would create an artificial island in Tokyo Bay. The information society is forcing the fields of architecture, design, and the arts into the public limelight because it is a society that creates added value, a society of the evocation of meaning.

The creation of information as added value, the creation of distinctness, the creation of meaning have all come to be valuable. The reason why Japanese developers have recently come to offer projects not only to established Japanese architects, but also to foreign architects and the younger generation of Japanese architects, is that they have begun to recognize a unique design as an added value in an information society. Experimental works and the cutting edge in Japanese architecture have been realized in this context. Even in the manufacturing industries, design came to have a value equal to performance. In the world of architecture, the design of the facade acquired an independence and possessed a value equal to mechanical rationality and structural technology possibilities.

The technology of the age of the industrial society was a visible technology, as symbolized by the automobile, the railroad, the airplane, the space shuttle, and satellites. The spirit of the twentieth century, supported as it was by the industrial society, was the image of the machine. Thus, the architecture of the twentieth century expressed the spirit of rationality, or formally the machine.

In contrast, the technology of the information age or the technology of the twenty-first century will gradually shift from the macroengineering of space technology to the microengineering of fine detail. The thrust of manufacturing will shift from military purposes to civilian manufacturing and the technology, itself, will shift to invisible technology for media, biotechnology, and communications technology. This transformation in the information society will result in major changes in architectural expression.

The raw expression of technology and high-tech architecture will no longer be suitable for expressing the spirit of the information age. The spirit of the information age of the twenty-first century can be described as a change from the image of the machine to an image of life. An extremely wide field exists of possible methods for expressing this image of life or the spirit of the information age. Such notions as metabolism, growth, information unification, internal order, open relationships, noise, and order that contain heterogeneous elements, multivalency, ambiguity, and the fundamental principle of life and genetic transfer, through which we inherit the past, are concepts that can be applied directly to the architecture of the information society.

The proposals of Peter Cook and other members of Archigram in the 1960s as well as the ideas and works of the Metabolism group reflected this in their architecture of the transitional period from the industrial society to the information society because they pursued the basic principles of life, such as growth and change.[13] At first glance, Richard Rogers's Lloyd's Bank and Norman Foster's Hong Kong–Shanghai Bank may seem to have been developed from the ideas of Archigram and the Metabolism group, but these works do not seek to express or incorporate the technology of the industrial age itself through the technological possibilities of growth, change, and exchange; improved cost performance through cutting edge technology; or a response to mass production. Instead, they inherit the images of an industrial society such as technology and order but move toward an autonomy of the facade.[14] In other words, the image of technology is employed as a sign on the facade. In this respect, these works are, in fact, an experiment in producing a new architecture for an information society.

Japan, a developed nation committed to the most advanced technological developments, has very readily adopted the latest innovations in technology for its contemporary architecture. In this respect, it offers the most favorable atmosphere for the emergence of high-tech architecture. Yet, as the author has stated repeatedly, the most advanced technology—the technology of information—is developing into an invisible technology, forcing the architectural facade toward autonomy, freedom, and the evocation of meaning. With this direction, it is possible for the new architecture that employs the invisible technology to become art. The multivalency of expression and the autonomy of the facade that can be detected in contemporary Japanese architecture and cities have emerged from this set of circumstances.

FREEDOM AND MULTIVALENCY

The changes taking place in the world today are occurring on many levels: from planned economies to free markets, from public works projects to private investment, from nationalism to regional alliances. Japan's growth after the war took place in the context of these developments. Its housing construction and city planning were driven by private investment and the vigor of the Japanese economy has been achieved through the activities of private industry. This has led to the contradictory situation in which Japan's urban infrastructure is always trying to catch up, but it has also changed Tokyo and Japan's other large cities into lively places overflowing with the spirit of freedom. This spirit merged with such aspects of Japan's tradition as its provisional nature as well as the independence of the part in contrast to the whole and has led contemporary Japanese architecture in the direction of an asymmetrical, amorphous, multileveled, and disengaged mode of expression.

In the first section of this essay, the author noted that provisional nature can be found in the Buddhist notion of impermanence. Cherry blossoms are loved in Japan precisely because they are particularly beautiful as they scatter and fall. The Japanese tradition finds the beauty of impermanence in the suicide of a samurai—a belief that, of course, strongly influenced the suicide of the renowned writer Yukio Mishima.

The provisional nature of Metabolism unconsciously tapped into this aspect of traditional Japanese esthetics. In addition to this philosophical and poetic provisional element, uniquely Japanese economic factors have also contributed to rendering contemporary Japanese architecture a physically shortlived, provisional occurrence. Recently, Itsuko Hasegawa's Bizan Hall, which received the Japanese Architects Association Award, was destroyed only five years after it was built. This demonstrates one of the problems contemporary Japanese architecture faces. In Japan, land is extremely expensive and in the large cities, its cost may represent 80% of a construction project's budget which leaves only 10–20% for the actual building construction. As a result, land is everything to the developer and the building is a relatively unimportant, provisional thing.

This spirit of freedom and tendency toward a provisional quality and lightness give Japanese cities in general and their architecture in particular the appearance of disorganization, but they are not chaotic or disorderly. It is certainly not an easy path, but there are hopes for the creation of a new order in which each fragment influences, little by little, its immediate environment, creating a partial order that takes shape as a dynamic balance. We can call such an order a digital order. It is a different sense of order from the scale of classical architecture, from the ideals of Plato and Descartes, the consistency of the hub-and-spokes model or symmetry. The dissembled parts are placed freely, like the stones in a Japanese garden. This free placement of digital signals creates meaning, creates relationships; a digital order is an order of relationships.

Another reason for the birth of multivalency is the principle of symbiosis. The topos and tradition that were banished by the universalism of the age of Modernism, the age of the machine, have been revived and are regarded as important elements in the evocation of meaning. The more important the themes of the symbiosis of tradition and the latest technology, of the part and the whole, of regionalism and universalism, of individuality and the global, of architecture and nature will be, the more varied and multivalent contemporary Japanese architecture is likely to become.

The philosophy of symbiosis is an idea on which the author has continuously elaborated since the start of the Metabolist movement thirty years ago; it is the very conceptual basis of the life principle. The philosophy of symbiosis is extremely useful in the dissolution of dualism and the binomial opposition as well as in the enrichment of rationalism. The increased interest in local environments, ecology, history and topos, as well as the increased importance of the richness of parts, the discovery of divergence and intermediate zones—in fact, all areas of worldwide interest—are effects on the philosophy of symbiosis and the life principle. For contemporary Japanese architecture and cities, the shift from the age of the machine to the age of life and the shift to the age of symbiosis, possess the double meaning of the simultaneity of the world and the rediscovery of the Japanese tradition.[15]

The Japanese social and economic conditions noted above not only create the new directions in Japanese architecture and cities but are also interconnected with all new movements, like those in graphic and industrial design, contemporary music, art, and film. Many works of the graphic designer Ikko Tanaka demonstrate a strong awareness of the signs of traditional Japanese culture; yet, they lack any restrictive ethnicism or regionalism and are highly acclaimed throughout the world.

The works of such representative and universally praised contemporary Japanese composers as Toshiro Kaoru's *Nehan Symphony,* Takemitsu Toru's *November Steps,* and Toshi Ichiyanagi's *Concerto for Koto and Chamber Orchestra, "The Origin,"* incorporate traditional Japanese instruments and music within the framework of Western music. These works are avant-garde compositions which exist in symbiosis with the Japanese traditional. Yet, they have achieved an entirely new type of symbiosis, distinct from folk music or local music. The method of composition is to digitalize the elements of Western music and the distinct Japanese elements, then to freely recombine them to create new, avant-garde music.

A new direction can also be seen in the world of contemporary Japanese cinema. Juzo Itami's *The Funeral* and *A Taxing Woman* take unique Japanese customs and traditions as their themes and examine them objectively, with an outsider's eyes, creating a double code, a symbiosis of tradition with the universal. Yoshimitsu Morita, a film-maker of an even younger generation, has directed a film titled *Something Like ....* It is the story of three people who are not able to specialize in anything and are reluctant to cast aside their amateur status. The resulting film is a splendid expression of a new world of provisional qualities and uncertainty. *Something Like ...* is also a casual, light-hearted reference to the notion of the *simulacre,* put forth by the French philosopher Baudrillard. In this attempt to discover a universality in the unique Japanese lifestyle, there is a connection to the philosophy of symbiosis.

Unlike the analog, traditional style of Akira Kurosawa's Shakespearean approach which faced Japanese history and tradition directly and sought to shape them into films, the new generation of Japanese film directors are depicting non-dramatic stories with a digital, contemporary spirit. Takeshi Kitano's film *A Scene at the Sea* is an example of this trend.

The philosophy of new freedom and the spirit of life permeates the field of sculpture as well. An extremely popular Japanese artist, Katsuhiko Hibino, has as his specialty the ability to create his works from ordinary materials such as cardboard right before the eyes of his audience. One can draw parallels from Hibino to Keith Haring, the American artist who died so young. In his written works, Hibino said, "We call the unit of a person's existence his life, and the unit between sleep and daily sleep eternal sleep or momentary sleep. Is each day a life, or is each life a day? Things, the act of making and the maker create a life in each day, playing hide and seek." In the artist's work we find an immediacy of creating with thinking, provisional qualities, uncertainty, and a conscious amateurism.

In industrial design, including the designs of the automobile manufacturer Nissan, a new trend has recently emerged. Its special feature is the end of the "good design," or the "rational design" that has reigned since the Bauhaus and the appearance of new products that are fun, interesting, tell a story or a typically Japanese line. The Nissan Escargot, Cima, and Beat, which are familiar to the Japanese from TV commercials, are all examples of this new design direction. This new trend in all creative fields is linked in an extremely intimate fashion with the contemporary Japanese city.

NOTES

1. Bruno Taut (1880–1938) was a "German architect/planner associated with the avante-garde Expressionist's Groups in Berlin, immediately after the First World War." Taut left Germany for Japan in 1932. *Who's Who in Architecture,* Richards, J. M. ed. New York: Holt, Rinehart and Winston, 1977; 317.
2. Walter Gropius (1883–1969) was a modern German–U.S. architect and an inter-national leader in modern architecture. He left Germany in 1934. "In 1918 he became head of the Bauhaus in Weimar, one of the best-equipped art schools in the world." *Who's Who in Architecture,* Richards, J. M. ed. New York, NY: Holt, Rinehart & Winston, 1977; 124.
3. "Mind-only" is an anti-dualism concept rooted in Hindu philosophy that was established in the fourth century; it can be called "consciousness only."
4. In the 1960s, Kenzo Tange (1913–) created a modern style of architecture "com-parable in quality with the best international work, yet retaining an unmistakable Japanese character" with a small group of Japanese architects influenced by Le Corbusier. *Who's Who in Architecture,* Richards, J. M. ed. New York: Holt, Rinehart & Winston, 1977; 314–16.
5. "Archigram" is a group of British avant-garde architects who advocated the "Future City" in the 1960s.
6. Yona Friedman is a French architect who also advocated "Future city" in the 1960s.
7. "*Shoin*" is a guest room with a bay window next to *Toko-no-Ma,* an alcove. The

sixteenth-century Japanese upper class housing architecture style is called *Shoin Zukuri.*

8. *Webster's Third New International Dictionary,* Springfield, MA: Merriam–Webster, 1986; 697.

9. *Webster's Third New International Dictionary,* Springfield, MA: Merriam–Webster, 1986; 2316.

10. Oriental medicine, or "Chinese medicine." The Chinese physician does not perform surgery but applies energy to the body and soul, whereby healing power gathers. In this context, the concept applied to city planning means to preserve the downtown area through redevelopment.

11. "New order" is a holistic order based on the autonomy of each part.

12. "Deconstruction" was advocated by a group of French philosophers who criticized the modernism. Here, it is used as the deconstruction of Eurocentricm. Nowadays, many young architects belong to the "deconstruction group."

13. "Archigram in the 1960s" was an avante-garde proposal of the "Future City" criticizing the traditional cities.

14. "Autonomy of the facade" is a concept often used in semiotics; the expression itself creates the semiotic meaning.

15. See the author's *Rediscovering Japanese Space.* New York: John Weatherhill, 1988.

BIBLIOGRAPHY

1. Kurokawa, K. 1992. *From Metabolism to Symbiosis.* New York: St. Martin's Press.

2. Kurokawa, K. 1991. *Intercultural Architecture: the Philosophy of Symbiosis.* London: Academy Editions.

3. Kurokawa, K. 1988. *Rediscovering Japanese Space.* New York: John Weatherhill.

B The Heart of Tokyo: Today's Reality and Tomorrow's Vision

Takashi Hirai

INTRODUCTION

Tokyo, the urban vortex from which all of Japan's politics, economy, and culture emanate, suffers from the asphyxiating effects of an overconcentration of functions. These effects are manifested by the skyrocketing land prices, ubiquitous overcrowding, environmental pollution, huge discrepancy of day/night population, and a seriously questionable quality of life. This list does not end there.

The benefits attributable to the concentration of functions in Tokyo are primarily measured in terms of efficient information dissemination. Although diseased at the heart, Japan's capital city, where everything begins and ends, continues to present opportunities for the progress of internationalization in Japan.

Professional dialogue on the subject of deconcentration and decentralization of Tokyo's functions has been occurring for at least twenty-five years; now, however, the task of reversing the detracting consequences of the excessive concentration of multifunctions, which has evolved over a prolonged period, is urgent and no longer avoidable. Many ideas are now put forward to ameliorate the problems. For example, it has been suggested that multipurpose land use be promulgated nationwide through the improvement of urban subcenters and the creation of dedicated business centers. The intent is to change the national urban structure by planning cities that would contain all necessary social, commercial, and industrial facilities to make those urban centers self-sustaining and financially viable. The projects are, in fact, designated to help urban regional cities and business core cities to become self-supporting, thereby promoting more responsive urban development in the nation as a whole.

Obviously, the respective roles of these regional urban centers and of the supercity, Tokyo, call for clear identification, so their activities can be smoothly integrated in order to ensure success. Unfortunately, there is, as of yet, no definite established vision of the future of Tokyo's heart. However, it is clear that Tokyo's national leading role will be maintained.

Insufficient attention has been given to the problem of Tokyo's infrastructure which has been deteriorating under the burden of the city's dense construction.

The situation is analyzed in this chapter, which concludes with a suggestion for restructuring Tokyo into the ideal functional urban space.

It is our firm belief that future plans for the heart of Tokyo will go far beyond discussions of deconcentration and decentralization, of the city's inhabitability, and of its economies and diseconomies of scale. Inaction is no longer acceptable.

TOKYO'S HEART: TODAY

The Chaotic Cityscape

Central Tokyo has risen in the aftermath of two major catastrophes in the twentieth century: the first was the Great Kanto Earthquake that shook the city in 1923; the second was the destruction of the capital by American bombing in 1945. Tokyo recovered rapidly from the devastation of the earthquake and the war but sacrificed long-range plans for the optimal functional use of the city.

Before the deadly bombing of Tokyo towards the end of World War II, city planning had been based on the European model, while after the war, reconstruction of the capital was influenced by the American cityscape. Japan, then, was willing to adopt foreign architectural ideas as can be seen in many Japanese cities today. This was partly attributable to Japan's location on the eastern fringe of Asia and partly to Japan's historical use of wood for urban structures and buildings. Wooden structures are, however, by their nature, susceptible to earthquakes, wind, and fires, and usually have a short life expectancy. Even with the advent of modern building technology which enables buildings to withstand earthquakes and fires, Japanese citizens still seem to expect a changing cityscape. In addition, today, buildings with low economic efficiency are often destroyed in favor of building new, better designed structures. Thus, "demolish-and-build" is not only a familiar sight in Japanese city centers but has fixed the idea in the minds of city dwellers that the townscape is always changing.

Against this background of change, the new city of Tokyo appears in spectacular contrast, for example, to the stable historical town of Kyoto. For these reasons, modern Tokyo can be described as a mixture of European, U.S., and Japanese functionality. It can be seen as a blending process that seems to explain much about the way the modern capital of Japan has developed.

The Japanese Concept of Construction

Japan's concept of ancient construction is distinct and differs from the concepts of construction of other ancient civilizations. A good example is the variation between the Ise Shrines at Ise and Mie Prefecture of Japan and the pyramids of Egypt. All of these structures have survived either in concept or as a physical entity for 500 years or more. While the latter was constructed of stone and designed to withstand time without maintenance, the former are wooden and have lasted through the centuries only by a process of rebuilding every twenty years. The compound at Ise has two plots side by side specifically for this purpose. The original architects probably considered twenty years as the life of a wooden structure. Thus, the basic idea of an everlasting building differs in Japan and in Egypt. Even though the Ise Jingu complex is a symbol of religious worship, our inheritance is not simply in its structure that is repeatedly torn down and rebuilt every twenty years but in its concept of a technology for design and construction. The concept is both unique and intriguing.

This example, then, highlights a fundamental difference in the building methods between the Far East and the ancient West, or between the "wood culture" and the "stone culture." There is a clear contrast between the massive cathedral structure standing defiantly above a square and the subdued shrine standing quietly in the depths of a forest.

The history of architecture is simultaneously the history of the availability and use of building materials. These materials have evolved from the use of wood and stone to the development of today's modern building technology using reinforced concrete, steel, glass, and tile. This is also true in Japan. As another example, in Paris, where major renovation work was completed in the nineteenth century, demolition and reconstruction also have quite different meanings than those of Japan. However, Japan's rebuilding cycle has remained as it was in the days when wooden structures were the norm. When a city's structures are so frequently torn down and rebuilt, as is the case in Tokyo, the appearance of the city is never constant. There is, therefore, no fixed image that can characterize Tokyo. It is always chaotic, lacks geometrical harmony, and yet offers lively urban activity. That is the state of Tokyo today.

Despite Tokyo's relatively short history, the preservation of structures regarded as cultural assets has become an urgent task. For example, when the present Imperial Hotel was constructed, there was heated discussion as to whether the original building, designed by Frank Lloyd Wright after the Great Kanto Earthquake, should be torn down to give way to new development. This controversial debate became a major issue of public concern at that time. Although the preservationists lost, the issue attracted attention to the "preservational movement" and resulted in the birth of new design techniques now widely used in the rejuvenation of old buildings.

Population Trends in the Heart of Tokyo

The Tokyo Metropolitan Region comprises Tokyo city, Chiba Prefecture, Saitama Prefecture, and Kanagawa Prefecture, covering 3.6% (1.35 million ha) of the nation's land, and contains 25.7% (31.8 million people) of Japan's population.

Tokyo is the unofficial name for the administrative district covering the Tokyo Metropolitan Region. The city itself is divided into two major components. One consists of the twenty-three central wards, which can be described as the city of Tokyo. The remainder of the metropolitan region consists of independent administrative units made up of the surrounding cities, towns, and villages. The heart or core of Tokyo, as defined herein, roughly refers to the remaining twenty-three ward area.

In 1985, Tokyo had a population of 11.85 million, 230,000 more than the previous decade. Since 1985 the rate of increase has slowed down greatly as a result of the population decline in the center of the city. The overall population rate of Tokyo has been dropping since 1987. One of the major causes of the population decrease in the center of Tokyo has been the soaring cost of land, a problem that arose in 1986, causing housing prices and rents to increase drastically which forced residents to move out. A noticable drop in the population of the city center has led to the decline of the local communities, which in turn, creates various other problems like the closing and merging of government schools or the decrease in the number of local merchants and retail outlets. This development in turn deprives the community of services and conveniences and accelerates the exodus of residents.

Changing Land-Use

The most characteristic change in the way land is used in central Tokyo is the considerable increase in floor space—that is, land-use has become highly intensive and efficient. In 1972, the floor area available in the center of Tokyo was about 19,500 ha. This number went up to 32,800 ha by 1990, about 1.7 times its original value. With almost no change in the amount of land in private ownership over this period, the growth in floor area is clear evidence of improved land-use efficiency, particularly for nonresidential floor area.

Such a significant increase in floor area and the implied improvement in efficiency, usually go hand in hand with a change in land-use structure. In terms of the entire region, there has been an increase in the amount of land used for residential purposes, but when in the center of Tokyo, it is office space that has grown considerably. Increasing use of floor space for offices can even be seen in areas designated as residential, retail, industrial, and warehousing zones.

Central Tokyo has clearly been transformed into the core of all economic activity, offering stimulation and entertainment while simultaneously suffering from the severe problems of population decline, the dispersal of its community, traffic congestion, and overcrowded commuter trains. Office space is now abundant and as a result the heart of Tokyo is stripped daily of its vitality. All of these changes are contributing factors to Tokyo's problems.

Historical Role of Tokyo

Tokyo has helped advance the development of Japan, long acting as the center of its politics, economy, and culture. During the Edo period (1603–1868), when Tokyo still bore its traditional name, the city became the seat of the Tokugawa shogunate—the office of the military governor of Japan before the mid-nineteenth-century revolution, whose power exceeded the emperor's. The political development established Tokyo's position as the heart of feudal politics. In the Meiji era (1868–1911), Edo was renamed Tokyo and became the actual capital of Japan under the reign of Emperor Meiji, who was restored to power in the Meiji Restoration of 1868. Tokyo has since played an important role as the center of modern politics, economy, and administration. This centralization of power helped Japan rise as a modern nation during an age of international expansionism.

As capitalist ideas permeated the social structure, the greater concentration of industrial power and population in Tokyo was exactly what was needed to develop an industrial base. Tokyo grew into a gigantic center of commerce and became the great consumer city we see in today's modern metropolis with its concentration of capital and workers.

Although temporarily interrupted by the Great Kanto Earthquake and World War II, Tokyo expanded to become the largest city in Japan. Since the last war, a trio of major cities has developed: Tokyo, Osaka, and Nagoya. Benefiting from having the core functions of the nation's capital, Tokyo has had the most remarkable growth rate as the country has gone through a period of rapid economic growth.

Tokyo now occupies a very important position as one of the pivotal cities of East Asia. It has become a major international city as the economic power of Japan continues to expand and as internationalization and the information revolution continue to progress. Tokyo's importance on the global scene is increasing. In this context, it is hard to see how the excessive concentration and integration of various functions in the heart of Tokyo can ever be altered to achieve a more balanced national urban development.

Tokyo is a place of dynamic political, financial, commercial, industrial, and cultural activity. It has become a supercity that makes great contributions to the economic, social, and cultural development of the entire country in many ways: generating employment opportunities for a network of immigrant laborers; maintaining its position as the leader in academic, educational, and cultural activities; setting new values and ways of thinking; and acting as a clearing house for important information. The history of Japan's development is intertwined with the development of the capital under centralized rule. Within this framework, Japan in its entity has seen successful growth, with Tokyo and other cities each playing their own role.

Tokyo's Worsening Problems and Their Impact

The serious problems Tokyo faces are the result of the unpredictable and unregulated development in a city which experienced the world's fastest growth rate and an unanticipated boom not without a number of side-effects. The unexpectedly rapid increase in the number of cars has contributed to environmental problems. It is clear that urban policies and city planning have failed to achieve satisfactory results. Without a choice of its own, Tokyo has physically evolved into a chaotic, overcrowded conglomerate of people and buildings.

Large cities have attempted to enact regulations that would keep the urban structure compact and prevent sprawl, but all lacked appropriate plans for highly efficient use of urban space. As a result, most city centers have seen accelerated overcrowding without effective measures to control the use of land. In the case of Tokyo's center, the excessive concentration of urban functions continues to intensify with the rush towards internationalization as a "cosmopolis." A surplus of money and the government's low interest rate policy have caused land prices to skyrocket at the core of Tokyo, where the shortage of space is a chronic problem. This condition has pushed office buildings into surrounding residential areas. Eventually, local communities will be transformed by such high-rise concrete invaders. The land price explosion that originated in the center of Tokyo will soon dominate the entire capital region, triggering price hikes in housing. This vicious cycle continues to exacerbate the problems.

Today, the growth of Tokyo seems disposed to advance even further, which is partly due to Japan's need to live up to its economic obligations in the eyes of the world. However, the old problems of over-concentration will not simply evaporate. Land has been divided into tiny parcels which prevents efficient usage; accelerates the delay in implementing urban renewal programs; impedes the ability of "ordinary people" to buy homes; slows down the pace of improvement for public facilities like roads and parks; raises the question of population hollowing; creates problems of water supply, traffic, waste disposal; and raises other environmental pollution concerns.

The greater capital area now has a population of over 30 million, so wide-ranging comprehensive urban policies and city planning have never been more important. This megalopolis has evolved through a kind of borderless expansion in which various urban functions have become interlinked, yet each of the local governments in the greater Tokyo area is still locked into its own administrative territory. There is a lack of coordinated action in all aspects of urban policy making. As a result, Japan remains a long way from realizing a network that organically connects the entire area which could be the setting of a well-balanced sharing of urban functions could occur.

THE CHANGING SOCIAL ENVIRONMENT AND THE ROLE OF TOKYO

The Changing Social Environment

When examining the possibilities for restructuring Tokyo, one realizes that Japan needs a long-range goal which can offer a scenario of future social and environmental changes. Japan should be careful not to be misled by present conditions. Future economic development may be characterized by a greater role of software-based services, cutting-edge technology, and an accelerated influx of people, materials, money, and information into large cities. Consequently, urbanization may have to spread over an even larger area. While the overall potential of land-use around a large city is generally expected to increase, local development within this greater area is likely to have a mosaic pattern due to the decreased efficiency of developing transportation networks in regional core areas.

As for population growth, the total population of Japan is expected to level off around the year 2010; however, the concentration of people in large cities is expected to continue. As a result, the large cities and regional core cities will be overcrowded, while the decrease in population will become a serious problem for rural areas. The demographic prediction also indicates that not all cities will increase in population and develop further. Today, the Tokyo Metropolitan Area is home to about 25% of the nation's population. If this trend continues despite the overcrowding, the development of a national policy on land-use will become top priority and Tokyo will have the greatest need for such a policy. In addition to the previously mentioned issues, Japan will face serious problems in the near future as its society ages. With the productive population migrating to major cities, the social structure of the rural population will rapidly age, possibly toppling local efforts for rejuvenation.

Socially, Japan is likely to witness further internationalization and rapid growth of information use as advanced technology opens up more possibilities. Japanese lifestyles will become more and more diverse. With the trend of shortening the work week, attention will shift to the development of more defined individual personalities. The influx of other nationalities into Japan will also compel the Japanese, a traditionally homogeneous people, to understand and live with the different values of foreign residents. Under these circumstances, we are likely to see movements towards the rediscovery of traditional Japanese values, an understanding of them, and their conservation as a part of the cultural heritage.

The increasing value of information will lead to the rise and fall of corporations and, along with a perpetuity of mergers, Japan will witness the birth of entire new industries. Leisure time will increase and improved transportation networks will encourage a routine of living in the city during the week and in the country on weekends, or vice versa. As people become more mobile, a greater variety of lifestyles will emerge.

Future Role and Functions of Tokyo

If society changes as predicted above, Japan will need to study the future role of Tokyo in the light of such trends. The view that "Japan can thank Tokyo for its success" originated in the concentration of core administrative, business, and informational functions in Tokyo to improve the efficiency of urban machinery; this led to a coordinated accumulation of various hubs in the city.

With its record of efficient urban functionality, Tokyo is likely to grow as a consumer area and to become even an even stronger driving force of the societal engine. Our future need is to learn how to help Tokyo fulfill its existing roles and guide it towards new roles and functions. It will be important to improve and smoothly integrate both physical and abstract aspects of the infrastructure and to combine the new roles and functions in a way that will encourage further development.

In the effort to help Tokyo meet existing demands on its roles and functions, Japan needs to improve various conditions which support it as a center of economic activities and logistics. Therefore, Japan has to encourage the city to initiate the steps which increase the value of products. It is also important to enhance Tokyo's attraction as a city by maintaining the historic quarters with old streets, houses, and their unique atmosphere.

The new focus Japan can anticipate for Tokyo in the future includes the continuation of its function as a center of international finance, international informational networks, and exchange. With these roles qualifying Tokyo for the title of "cosmopolis," the city is expected to play an even greater part in international affairs than it does today. Improved urban land use will thus be essential if Tokyo is to play such a critical role. Tokyo will need a cityscape with trees and plants, a fully developed waterfront, and monumental architecture to qualify as a world-class city of beauty and character.

While maintaining the vitality and strength needed to rise to the challenge of these expectations, Tokyo should also look for greater efficiency and work to create space and time for leisure activities. To realize future renewal projects in the heart of Tokyo and in the greater Tokyo area, Japan must focus on these pivotal issues.

Change in Architectural Style and Urban Facilities

The Tokyo Dome, an air-supported stadium, was completed in 1988 and recorded a total of 12 million visitors in its first year. Professional baseball games and various other events attracted an average of 30 thousand people a day. The success of this stadium lies in its structure. The stadium is completely enclosed and thus provides the opportunity to draw crowds regardless of the weather.

The Tokyo Dome was a trailblazer for a new trend in architecture which makes way for larger and larger structures which frequently offer indoor areas the size of the outdoor plazas seen around the city today. Plazas and squares of this type are generally thought to provide opportunities for new social interaction such as rendezvous. In Japan, the age of artificial indoor public plazas which offer a controlled environment is now dawning.

In addition to their increased size, buildings of the future are likely to be designed within a compound structure. Even today, certain buildings based on new concepts of architecture have been designed with composite features. Occasionally it is possible to see structures with an integrated station building, shopping mall, hotel, and offices, often with a large atrium located in this "mini city." In such cases, there is no single unit of structure; rather, everything is intertwined as part of a large architectural complex. Such large complexes in themselves contribute to the urban function. The development of this concept will lead to cities within cities, an idea born of the need to promote efficient use of space and yet ensure that each component building maintains its own identity.

Big City Appeal

Urban facilities which serve as the basis for academic, educational, and cultural activities also act as incubators of new values. The vitality and appeal of a big city can alter the quality of these activities which can lead to a diversity of cultural experiences. Tokyo offers extremely easy access to culture and art, but now the city needs to grow out of its mold as a receptor of culture and become its generator.

In the city, people are surrounded by a wide range of sensory stimuli—clothing, furniture, interior spaces, architecture, exterior spaces, and the skyline—which combine to form the appeal and aura of the city. Once Tokyo is able to cope with a diverse range of social, cultural, and political experiences, blending the traditional themes of Japan with all current ones, its appeal will grow.

IMPORTANCE OF SOLVING TOKYO'S PROBLEMS

Government Action

The Japanese government has plans to solve Tokyo's problems. On a national level, these plans are to develop a decentralized and urban polycentric country (having several centers of development), encouraging the growth of regional core cities. Plans specifically intended for the Tokyo area advocate the creation of many secondary core cities scattered about suburbs to remove the excessive reliance on the central area. The ultimate goal is to achieve a regional structure based on many subcenters.

These government plans are reasonably effective when it comes to the development of regional core cities which will be designed to take full advantage of the concentration of functions and the efficiency that such concentration offers. The regional core cities will then further the development of surrounding communities in the region.

Another part of the government plan is the creation of business oriented subcenters as self-sustaining economic zones within the capital region to produce a polycentric, decentralized social structure for the balanced development of the entire region. It cannot be expected, however, that such business centers and regional core cities will be immediately independent and form effective self-sustaining economic zones that will help decentralize Tokyo. Since the driving force behind regional core cities has historically been the power of the central Tokyo area, it would be more effective for these core cities to make full use of networking ideas to redefine their links with the capital and to set up their own connections with the outside world. It may then be expected that these cities will be able to function side by side with Tokyo and thrive in the era of advanced information usage, as they implement individual urban plans in a controlled, phased, and strategic manner.

Need for Systematic Improvement Planning in Tokyo

An urban area is not a single unit. As for Tokyo, within its boundaries are numerous structural units including a center, many subcenters, some financially independent city governments, a number of core cities, and many smaller administrative units scattered around the periphery of the metropolitan region. All of these units are organically linked to one another and function in the system according to their tasks; this is also the underlying structure of the entire nation. To illustrate the following, the human body will be used as a metaphor. If the metabolism of a single city malfunctions, the whole city "feels sick," as would happen with the human body. If the metabolism of the capital, or brain in the case of a human, gives up, death will follow.

This holistic view puts together specific urban improvement programs for business core cities and regional core cities and is based upon our understanding of all the connections between the center, subcenters, business core cities, suburban towns, regional core cities, and surrounding administrative areas, combined with each of the roles and functions. Most importantly, the role of Tokyo's center must be redefined since the capital is responsible for supporting the development of all its units. Infrastructural improvements are the first major task in establishing better information and transportation networks which will develop the relations among the components of the spatial system, into cooperative, mutually beneficial relationships.

The important task of restructuring Tokyo requires the discussion about renewal strategies. In particular, the highly efficient, multipurpose use of land must be considered in the light of the predominant international thinking and the increasing value of information. It is crucial to make the most of the concentration of power in the city without downgrading its role. Any reassignment of functions will have to take place systematically and these efforts must result in a quality improvement if the renewal of Tokyo is to become a reality.

Since the dawn of the information age, we have been on an unalterable course towards drastic changes in social and economic structures. The time is long overdue for Tokyo, the hub of Japan's networks, to comprehend this development and develop comprehensive and systematic restructuring plans. A long-range view will enable us to meet the needs of a new era in which systematized urban facilities will serve as the basis for a social capital, including the information and transportation networks.

HOW TO RESTRUCTURE THE HEART OF TOKYO

Basic Viewpoint

Various organizations have considered Tokyo's problems, presented ideal images of its future, and proposed plans for the realization of these ideals. However, even those ideas deemed promising have mostly been abandoned as impractical since their implementation was thought to present too many obstacles of coordination among various government administrations. For the same reason, government administrations have failed to develop programs based on a comprehensive and long-range view. As urban problems become more acute, short-term makeshift plans—usually the imposing of restrictions that promise quick results—are more likely to be proposed and implemented. Yet, they will not provide a lasting solution for the restructuring of Tokyo.

Tokyo's growth has exceeded any expectations and still, administrators are held captive by an outdated image of the city. The programs they prepare are shackled by the conventional norms of city planning. Consequently, irritated by their inability to propose appropriate measures, they have adopted the concept of growth control, an idea that strives to restrict growth itself.

Growth control policies may work for a city whose problems of over-concentration have just surfaced. At this early stage, urban centers can encourage the formation of orderly suburbs and communities, offering stable growth for the entire city. However, restrictions will have only an adverse effect if applied to an area like downtown Tokyo, which has already achieved the world's greatest concentration and accumulation of functions.

This concentration in Tokyo has been the main driving power behind Japan's strength which nurtured the development of regional cities and underpinned the growth of the nation. Control of growth and the dispersion of power has never fueled the rise of regional cities. This fact leads to the conclusion that our policies must be designed to maintain Tokyo's power, that is, to promote restructuring plans which make full use of our expertise in urban design and environmental improvement.

Tokyo's present situation can be viewed as an inevitable social phenomenon relative to the history of other cities and civilizations. Observation of present urban growth around the world suggests that many enormous cities will emerge in the future. It is also logical that Tokyo has reached its present stage due to the progress of social development in Japan and in Tokyo itself. Any move to reverse this global trend, therefore, is likely to have the opposite effect and give rise to greater numbers of regulations. In the end, this could toss the entire nation into a vicious cycle of decay. It would also delay the implementation of radical, but necessary solutions, lead to unnecessary complications, and result in inequalities that could plague society. Shortly, Japan's urban designers and policy makers should devise appropriate guidelines to steer Japan along its natural course of development. While following those guidelines, efforts should be made to solve the problems of excessive urbanization which Tokyo faces and to ensure the vitality of the city. This developmental policy should ensure psychological and physical freedom from the bustle of day-to-day work in the heart of Tokyo.

Transforming Lifestyles at the Heart of Tokyo

New social rules are required if we are to create an environment suitable for the core of a gigantic city. For example, since housing is so dense, it is important to cultivate respect for the privacy of neighbors and to exercise restrictions on some of our behavior.

The availability of urban conveniences should balance the need for certain restrictions. Japanese city dwellers may have to give civic rights to people in urban hotel-type residences. They may also have to consider restricting the access of cars into certain areas and provide acceptable alternatives, such as other means of transportation and mass transit systems that are not objectionable in their own right. Given the limited floor space in homes, it is critical to make highly efficient use of space to create a living environment that does not spatially suffocate residents. With efficient residential design, living in the heart of Tokyo could be comparable to a more relaxed life in the suburbs.

Vitality, as defined in this paper, is based upon the maintenance of urban efficiency and rationality. An orderly social structure in the heart of Tokyo will definitely require firm and fast rules related to work, home, and entertainment. Basic functions, such as those needed to support commerce, will synergize. Encounters with the latest technology and the immigration of people from different cultures will modify existing values, leading to a new form of megalopolitan culture. Eventually, new information and concepts will spread all over Japan and throughout the world.

Historically, wherever a city flourishes, the citizens also see a corresponding rise in culture and the arts. Tokyo, however, has not reached that level yet. Japan would hope to see Tokyo grow more mature not only economically, but also socially and culturally, evolving into a source of new ideas and culture which would be a product of the relaxing environment. We define relaxation in the urban setting to mean comfort based on the basic foundation of safety; a relaxing life in the city is endowed with mind-enriching experiences, in addition to urban efficiency and rationality. Without relaxation, cultural vitality will be threatened. To avoid such a threat, we need amenities such as high-quality living space and pedestrian-oriented areas, open space, rapid transit, and abundant clean energy. A city of vitality and relaxation could be a very attractive place. To appreciate the benefits of such a place, residents must have the social consciousness adaptable to life in the center of an enormous city.

Restructuring the Heart of Tokyo

While there are great hopes for the renewal of Tokyo, the problems hindering such renewal are growing worse. We need innovative ideas to break out of this predicament and enter a new era. Conventional concepts of city planning need to be updated, re-thought, and discarded as necessary. With the establishment of new social values as a prerequisite, the following concrete measures are suggested to set the basic course for the city renewal project.

- To address the flow and exchange of information at the hub of Tokyo, we need to make highly effective use of land at transportation nodes, such as around railroad terminals. To be more specific, complexes of composite structures should be developed to satisfy as many of the various demands as possible: work, home, and entertainment. Such areas of concentrated activity should be limited to prevent the traffic overload from spilling into surrounding areas.

- Urban planners should promote an improved transportation infrastructure to allow the unhindered flow of people and materials and establish sub-systems to support it. For example, spacious parking areas need to be built around outlying railroad stations from which trains connect directly into Tokyo's efficient subway network. In special areas of the city center where land is used highly effectively, the access of cars should be limited and the pedestrian network expanded to increase convenience and comfort. These measures will minimize dependence on the automobile as a means of transportation. Ease of movement would improve significantly if the construction of subways directly under the radial railroad tracks were commercially viable. We need to decrease the demand on roads in the city center by setting up transit systems and transportation networks on both large and small scales, thereby reducing the number of freight vehicles.

- Urban planners should promote by far more efficient use of the limited urban space in the heart of Tokyo while fully considering the environment. In other words, effective use of underground space must be encouraged, for example the construction of underground pedestrian networks or multilayered underground parking areas which would feed into the required new subway stations would ease above-ground congestion. Another example would be the construction of multipurpose underground ducts to help improve the information infrastructure and the construction of deeper subway tunnels stretching out radially from the city center would be one solution for the "commuting" problem.

- The public and private sectors must join forces in the effective implementation of new urban development programs since improvements of the infrastructure generally require cooperation from both sides. For example, any kind of network is useless if it is broken up by public and private land holdings. If the government insists on taking over the management of a facility, consideration of convenience and comfort will certainly come last. To prevent this, the public and private sectors must work together to bring about the renewal of the city in a way that is equally desirable to residents and consumers.

- The conscious evolution into a new city will require the review and reevaluation of numerous present rules and regulations, as well as the introduction of new systems in Tokyo. For example, if there are no regulations to entice new uses of underground space, the deeper subway concept will end up as an "armchair theory." Long-term rules and systems must be reviewed as there is no point in planning new systems if public policy and the law does not support it. In order to bring about the rejuvenation and reconstruction of the city as explained above, we need a comprehensive city plan. The subcenters will need to cooperate in the joint definition of comprehensive city planning to solve our urban problems and to develop an organization which can realize the plans.

CONCLUSION—TOWARDS A NEW CITYSCAPE

Presuming the restructuring of Tokyo's heart is carried out to our satisfaction, what will the new cityscape be like? It will not be a Paris as completed in the nineteenth century nor a New York as developed in the twentieth century. If greater numbers of people are to live, work, and entertain themselves in the core cities, the architectural scale of transportation nodes will have to match the scale of the city. There will then be a chance for greenery to return around the core structural complexes and a cityscape of buildings and trees will develop over large areas.

In addition, buildings that conventionally stood alone will be integrated into large complexes. These large buildings designed by architects and independent entities in outdoor areas will engulf people in indoor space. The character of large-scale building complexes may move from using exterior space to using interior space; one may find a museum or a fine art gallery underground. There would certainly be space for exhibitions, but in reality the museum would have no external facade with which to identify itself. There will be buildings without elevations in the future Tokyo.

The logical prediction is that we will see a change from a two-dimensional cityscape with an array of buildings of similar scale and height to a dual cityscape consisting of large structures and landscaped areas with no artifacts at all.

It will be necessary for city planners and architects to coordinate the various rights of the public and private sectors and to take a new approach to the creation of exterior and interior public spaces. Plazas and parks will be the key exterior spaces, while atriums, malls, and underground promenades within building complexes will become the key indoor public spaces. When we have a network of urban facilities like this, each with public spaces designed to reflect its own characteristics, Tokyo will truly have developed a new cityscape for the twenty-first century.

NOTE

1. The author based this report on "The Heart of Tokyo: How to Restructure It" first prepared by the City Development Committee of the Japan Project-Industry Council (JAPIC) in March 1993. The author is a chief examiner on the committee.

C Urban Conservation and Landscape Management: The Kyoto Case

Hiroshi Mimura, Kiyoko Kanki, and Fumihiko Kobayashi

INTRODUCTION

During the last fifty years, Japanese cities have experienced a rapid trans-formation in growth and technology as have other cities in the world. The case of Kyoto, Japan, with a history of 1200 years shows that there are limitations to applying Japan's former concepts of town planning to meet the demands of its contemporary society. Today, it is necessary to find new concepts to achieve a balance between the development of the cities and conservation of the environment in the innercity districts and suburban zones.

CREATING THE CITIES OF JAPAN

The Ancient Capital City

The ancient cities of Japan were built between the seventh and ninth centuries. By then, the local governing families had been conquered and the reigning emperor ruled the entire country. He established many sites, including a place for religious ceremonies. and also built Miyako, an ancient capital for many aristocrats and bureaucrats in his entourage. Although Miyako was designed after a Chinese city model of Chang An (lasting peace), it was constructed in a very simple form with neither walls nor gates. In contrast to the ancient cities of Asia, Japanese ancient cities did not need tight measures for defense. However, other events such as natural disasters, the ascent of a new emperor, political change, instruction by divination, and the like forced a change in the location of the capital several times. Finally, in 794 AD, Heian-Kyo, located on the basin of modern day Kyoto, became the permanent capital until the nineteenth century (Fig. I-C1).

Heian-Kyo followed the layout of the Chinese city Chang An and was also as large with 4.95 km in length (north–south) and 4.206 km in width (east–west). The emperor's palace was placed in the northern part of the city's center and a main street ran north to south from the palace to the southern edge of the city where the main city gate and a short wall were constructed. This pattern also followed the ancient Chinese urban model. The city of Heinan-Kyo was

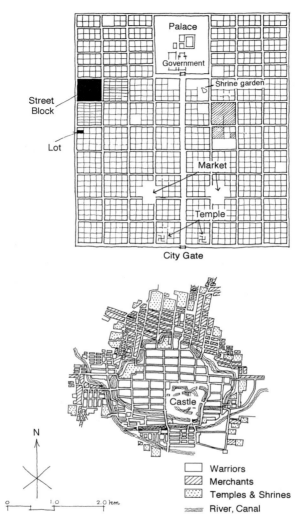

Figure I-C1 Ancient capital city (Heian-Kyo, above) and feudal castle city (Aizu-Wakamatsu, below) (Mimura, 1989, p. 22)

composed of several hundred street blocks of 120 m^2 each which were subdivided into thirty-two lots for the residences of aristocrats; each lot was approximately 450 m^2. Other people living within the city were engaged mainly as laborers for the aristocrats. Their houses were very small and built on narrowly subdivided sites that formed rows along the city's peripheral streets. The central part of each street block was kept open for communal space where a common water well and toilet were located.

Originally, the ancient city functioned as the ceremonial center for national policy and was not developed in an economic sense. Thus, the ancient city had a destiny based on the vicissitudes of the political powers.

Local Feudal Castle Cities

The next emergence of planned cities arrived with the construction of many castle cities during the feudalistic age between the sixteenth and the eighteenth centuries, the era of rivalry among the local lords. After political power became rigidly centralized, older castle towns designed for military defense became useless and were rebuilt as new castle cities. Here, the functions were also more administrative, but in addition the cities became economic headquarters for the regions. The clear pattern of land-use distribution within the city was considered as an almost perfect expression of governing order by the four social classes: warrior, craftsman, merchant, and peasant (who settled in the countryside).

The regional lords were appointed by the *Shogunate*. The *Shogunate* were the officials who governed Japan by their inherited right and who were at the top of the feudal hierarchy from the seventeenth to the nineteenth centuries. In the center of the castle city was a residence for the lord distinguished by a tall castle tower as a symbol of his political power. The residences of the warriors were located in nearby districts. Canals or moats encircled the castle and warriors' residences. Streets for merchants and various craftsmen were positioned outside the castle and the warriors' districts. Even though the population of craftsmen and merchants increased with the economic growth of the city, the share of land allocated to them was kept so small that they were forced to develop a more compact pattern of urban housing and live in higher density.

Several temples and shrines, that were also prepared as headquarters for defense and military activities, were scattered in the city's outskirts. Walls and gates were absent here also. Thus, even though the lord's castle was situated in the midst of the city, it had not been designed to protect its citizens from enemies encroaching from the outside. To protect the castle itself during an attack, the city area was often set afire and burned (Fig. I-C1).

Modern Metropolis

After the Meiji period began in 1868, most Japanese cities grew rapidly with the development of manufactured products, military campaigns, higher education, and commercial activities. The cities gradually expanded outward since there were no walls around the cities for fortification. In this new outer fringe zone, construction of new houses was mixed within existing agricultural lands and villages, and few conflicts arose during development.

To transform the fringe zone into a planned zone, the Land Adjustment Method was introduced. Under this method, parcels of land belonging to local private owners were redistributed after public land for streets and parks was set aside. The rest of the land, which was more than 60% of the present built-up area, was again subdivided into planned lots following the development plan.

In 1923 one the strongest earthquakes that Japan has ever experienced destroyed Tokyo. After this disaster, the city's restoration took on a new form with the layout of a broad, straight street system which had little in common with the traditional city layout. Later, as a result of air raids during World War II, many other Japanese cities were flattened; the postwar restoration was carried out in the same manner as the restoration of Tokyo in 1923. Following these destructive periods, many historic cities lost their traditional heritage and atmosphere during their restoration and in every city a new, similar pattern of modern urban townscape developed. Until the 1970s, most urban redevelopment was conceptually similar to that of reconstruction after natural disasters and wars, and experimental projects for the continuous renovation of the urban heritage were initiated only recently.

STRUCTURE OF THE HISTORICAL CITY OF KYOTO

Process of Urban Formation

Since 794, a city has always remained on the site of the first foundation of Heian-Kyo in the basin where Kyoto is now located. Kyoto had been the capital of Japan for approximately 1000 years until 1868, when the capital was moved to Tokyo.

The central district of Kyoto's built-up area today corresponds very closely to the old city area which was reconstructed after the devastation through the civil war in the fifteenth century. This area is known as *Raku-Chu* or inner Kyoto; the area outside *Raku-Chu*, which is known as *Raku-Gai* or outer Kyoto, was almost exclusively suburban farmland until the nineteenth century. The urban expansion during the modernization of Kyoto in the latter half of the nineteenth century took place in the central part of *Raku-Gai*. In the late twentieth century, urban expansion reached the peripheries of *Raku-Gai* and transformed farming areas into suburban districts called *Kyo-Kou*. The urban structure of Kyoto can be described in terms of urban expansion that took place in three major stages:

- the build-up of the central area;
- the build-up of the peripheral area; and
- the formation of suburbs.

These stages represent urban expansion from the spatial point of view. They also reflect the periods of urbanization from the social point of view but should not be confused with the features of a schema often used to explain ecological transitions that take place as a result of urban functions, i.e. a "concentric circular model." From the spatial point of view, Kyoto is characterized by its innercity area which consists of several core districts that were formed and have persisted at each developmental stage of specific functional urban growth (Table I-C1).

Table I-C1 Correspondence between urbanization and location of industries and other urban functions

Period of urbanization	Ancient city (Heian-Kyo, founded 789)	Medieval development (fifteenth century)	Modern Development (nineteenth century)	Present development (twentieth century)
a. Central built-up area (*Raku-Chu*)	Imperial palace Aristocrat's residence Servant and craftsmen's dormitory	Head temple of Buddhist sect Head schools of hobby arts Production of luxury goods and entertainment Craftsmen's settlement Merchant's settlement	Dissemination to local region Distribution to nationwide market Commercial and urban industrial settlement Administration and business center	Complex area of historical and traditional heritages Traditional areas of arts and crafts Compound inner-city settlement areas Civic and central business district of metropolis
b. Peripheral built-up area (*Raku-Gai*)		Warrior class's villa and temples Farm village	Nationwide sight seeing zones New middle-class suburban development Modern industrial complex Universities and colleges	Worldwide cultural and tourist zones Urban residential area High technology industrial complex Higher education and science center
c. Outskirts (*Kyo-Kou*)	Farm village Distant villa and temples	Farm village	Residential zone for commuters Large-scale industrial and distribution estates	Rurban agricultural and greenery zone Residential new town development Nationwide science and technology research new town

Source: Mimura, H. "Development and Conservation of Traditional Inner City Tyoto with Wood Town Houses." *IFHP/CIB/WMO/IGU International Conference on Urban Climate, Planning and Building,* Nov. 1989.

Compounded Inner-city Structure with Workplace and Residence

The *Honzan* (head temples) of several Buddhist sects were located in old Kyoto which became the nationwide center of religious culture where the *Iemoto* (heads of arts and crafts schools) gathered. However, it was primarily the center of art and artistic activities in the service of the court and religious institutions.

After the capital was moved to Tokyo, Kyoto was overcome by the modernization of urban functions and the expansion of its market to a national scale, but the decline it experienced was only temporary. Until recently, traditional industries continued to operate with modernized renovations within the old built-up area. People working in these industries lived in the proximity which fostered the growth of local centers for consumption and everyday life. A mixed pattern of industrial types is one of the characteristics of Kyoto's urban structure.

Today, Kyoto has a far smaller concentration of regionwide, central management functions compared to Tokyo or Osaka. Kyoto's central business district is not an agglomeration of official buildings only, but it is interspersed with small- and medium-sized traditional manufacturing industries, such as the Nishijin weaving industry, the Yuzen dyeing industry, and the Kiyomizu ceramic industry. People engaged in one industry are concentrated in a certain district where they live and work according to their shared roles in the various production processes from design to manufacturing. In addition, some industries, such as Muromachi textile wholesale, have expanded their district's distribution functions due to favorable production conditions and the distribution of high-class merchandise.

In the latter half of the nineteenth century, the peripheral area immediately outside the old built-up area developed during the modernization process. The intensity of the driving force behind this urban expansion varied among the sectors, but a communalism among them brought about the establishment of a number of public and private universities as well as other institutions of higher learning and research. These educational institutions stimulated not only the innovation of existing industries, but also the local economy as a whole. Apart from the large expenditure of educational and research investments, the money spent daily by the numerous teachers and students also had positive effects on the medium-scale economy.

The needs of modern industries was another key factor in the process of urban expansion. Industrial development was not procured by factors external to Kyoto but by internal factors associated with modern technology and the need for more advanced training of personnel found in the traditional industries. Industries which formerly developed as "advanced industries" have become high technology industries specializing in medical and precision equipment of today.

The new middle-class and modern industrial workers employed in those growing sectors either resided in rental housing or purchased homes in the urban fringes close to the industry. These new developments became the suburbs, which emerged as a result of land readjustment projects and were functionally connected closely to the old districts by a tram-car network.

The concentration of urban functions in a single central core, the suburban residential sprawl, and the transition and decline of intermediate areas, are the general aspects of urban growth based on a concentric circular model. However, such a set of characteristics cannot fully describe Kyoto's diverse urban structure since central Kyoto is formed of multiple core districts of a medium scale, which together constitute the whole inner city.

Typical Town House and Urbanscape

Machiya: Prototype for Urban Residence

Kyoto's ancient city was slowly deteriorating during its term as the capital city from the eighth to the nineteenth century, but during the Middle Ages, it recuperated and became the most prosperous commercial and manufacturing city in Japan. The style of urban housing in Kyoto today is a prototype of the residences developed in this period. The traditional, typical town house is known as *Machiya*, (houses where merchants' or craftsmen's families and their employees lived together and kept their shops and factory spaces). Since merchants and craftsmen were allowed by the government to utilize only a limited amount of urban space at that time, they were forced into high-density settlements. *Machiya* evolved in this manner because the severe limitation on space prevented the introduction of a rational, convenient plan of an effective townscape design which would provide for refined work and living spaces. The main architectural forms of *Machiya* were basically designed around the grid pattern of street blocks in the commercial districts of Kyoto, where each 120 m^2 block had a maximum depth of 60 m. This pattern was inherited from the town planning of the ancient city *Heian-Kyo*.

The rectangular street block created by the urban renewal policy in the sixteenth century had a depth of nearly 30 m and the facade of each site was generally as narrow as 5–8 m. The *Tooriniwa* (an inside corridor) played a very important role in the efficient use of these narrow and deep sites called *Eel Nest* and in reaching a higher quality of living. This corridor ran from the entrance, through the shop and living areas, to the backyard. It served as a convenient corridor for receiving guests or customers as well as for loading goods and domestic works and also controlled the indoor environment. The floor of the *Tooriniwa* consisted of a mixture of clay, slaked lime and bittern, which provided enough humidity to prevent dust from rising and also made a comfortable surface for walking. The *Tooriniwa* was also a means for ventilating smoke, admitting sunlight, and allowing a spaciousness that exaggerated the length of the axis. Toilet and bathroom facilities were located outside toward the backyard. Before modern sewage systems prevailed in the city, excrement and manure were collected by suburban farmers as fertilizer after it fermented. The *Tooriniwa* was also used as a passage to remove the excrement from the back yard area (Figs I-C2 and I-C3).

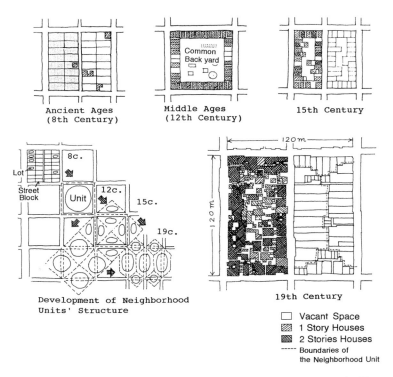

Figure I-C2 Street block and transition of neighborhood units structure in Kyoto (after Nishiyama and Fuji) (Mimura, 1989, p. 22)

The *Zashiki* was a room on the first floor that served as the master's room and formal guest room; its furnishings were changed according to the season. Wooden paneled or wooden framed paper partitions for the winter were substituted with reed screens or bamboo blinds for more ventilation in the summer. *Tatami* (flooring made of rice straw and rush sheet) was also replaced with a reed fabric that held less moisture in the summer. Living in a hot and humid monsoon climate, people made efforts to cool the indoor climate by altering the furnishings and sprinkling water on the garden and frontage for evaporation.

The rooms on the second floor were used for storage and living quarters for employees and the first-floor back rooms facing the court garden served as living rooms for the family. From the large opening of the latter, the family could enjoy the vista of the court garden, their neighboring houses, the sky overhead, and mountains surrounding the Kyoto basin.

In the case of the large houses, the main building in the back was kept for private life and was usually separate from the shop building and *Tsuboniwa* (an inner court garden of about 10 m² broad), which were usually laid out in the front area. The *Senzai* (a backyard garden) was designed to provide comfort. Even

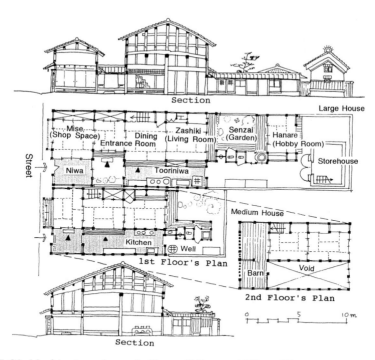

Figure I-C3 *Machiya* town house in Kyoto (Mimura, 1989, p. 25)

though the *Tsuboniwa* and *Senzai* were small-scale open spots in the midst of dense living spaces, both functioned as a vertical duct for ventilation to mitigate indoor sultriness in the summer.

NAGAYA: Tenement Houses

Shopkeepers, employees, and tenants often lived in subdivided tenement houses that were located in the back streets of a city. Initially, the owner of the tenement houses allowed his employees and their families to live in them, but since the middle of the nineteenth century, the owners found it more profitable to rent them. The living conditions were severe. These houses consisted of one or two rooms and their wells and lavatories were communally shared. Thus, residential segregation by social class and income level had not yet developed in the more exclusive areas of town. In spite of the crowded conditions created by the site's shape, the alleys kept the living environment intimate and somewhat private.

Machiya and *Nagaya* housing have been sustained throughout history by the lifestyle of the townsfolk, but recently, the structural organization of shops and houses on streets has been changing due to an outflow of population from the old town to suburban areas. This resulted in the atrophy of traditional industries and the construction of a new wave of tall buildings among the old historic ones (Fig. I-C4).

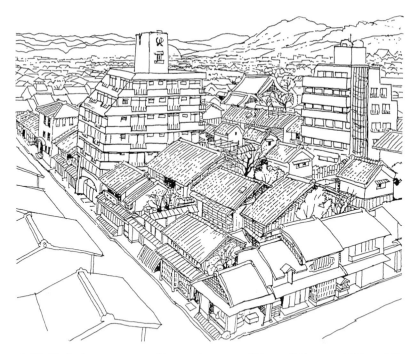

Figure I-C4 Today's townscape of inner-city area of Kyoto (Mimura, 1991, p. 94)

TRANSFORMATION OF URBAN STRUCTURE AND TOWNSCAPE
MANAGEMENT

A New Metropolitan Framework of North–South Axis

Demand for space grows with the expansion of urban activities and the need for
an efficient and comfortable environment to fit modern life. Motorization also
accelerates this process and forces the city to spread to outer districts. Today,
Kyoto is the main core of a metropolitan region inhabited by nearly 3 million
people. Within the dispersed suburban sprawl, the new Keihannna Science and
Technology Research Complex is being developed on a hilly area 15 km south
of old Kyoto. The buffer area between the city and this new town is considered
to be an important site for the next metropolitan structure. This area used to be
a marshland named "Oguraike Pond" and was later reclaimed for farmland;
several other small towns and villages are located around this pond. A new
national highway, a north–south axis of an arterial street and subway, as well as
an outer loop route are planned as a new urban transportation node to connect
these settlements.

In addition to a structured transportation plan, a new development policy for
Kyoto is urgently needed for other reasons. The authors propose the following
be created:

- an ecologically balanced environment with water and lowland nature;
- proper distribution of farm land and urban area including town–village links;
- urban multifunction development; and
- a large parking garage to accommodate the inter-regional mass commuter car traffic while encouraging automobile owners to convert to a new urban-type mobility by rail service.

In the inner-city area, where the heart of the historic city used to be, several problems have arisen, including: (1) serious congestion and air pollution due to the increase of automobile traffic; (2) sprawl of high-rise buildings disrupting the traditional townscape's order; and (3) decrease in the population of the innercity which makes it more difficult to uphold communal activities and culture.

The authors conceive the future landscape structure of larger Kyoto city along a north–south axis. The variation in the topography of the northern Kyoto Basin, the marshy lowland, and the southern hilly area is a crucial factor which should be considered in the planning process of larger Kyoto City. The conservation of the original city of Kyoto would be on the northern basin, while the new city area with the technology districts and intermediate lowland buffer zone would be located on the hills to the south (Fig. I-C5).

Grand Landscape Management of the Basin

As the cityscape of Kyoto is often the subject of traditional Japanese culture, art, and religion, a careful conservation-oriented development policy is required. For this reason, the surrounding mountains have so far been preserved to a large extent. At the foot of mountains, however, where many famous temples and Japanese gardens are located, strict regulations for keeping the scenery beautiful

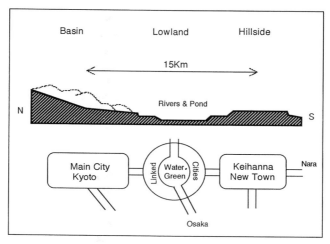

Figure I-C5 A new north–south axis for larger Kyoto city

will be necessary. These regulations are to include, for example, building specifications to control the size, form, material, and colors of buildings, plantation areas, and other structures.

At the bottom of the basin, developers are theoretically barred from erecting buildings of more than 45–60 m in height to protect the environs of historic sites. Despite these strict building controls, even taller high-rise buildings have been constructed through the urban redevelopment project. To stop this development, citizens are called upon to support a "grand landscape policy."

Inner-city Townscape Management at the Communal Level

The inner-city area which is composed of *Machiya* town house units has preserved the character of both the communities' culture and its urban spatial order of low-rise buildings. Problems of the city center today are: (1) the deterioration of the quality of building stock; (2) the replacement of traditional buildings by modern structures; (3) the deterioration of environmental quality because of excess traffic and the dissolution of neighborhood communitites; and (4) the decrease in the population. In addition, the troubled community management has encountered problems with staging annual festivals which have long been upheld by the now disappearing communities. Land-use zoning according to the official planning system has not been capable of solving these problems.

To counter the problems of the townscapes, new efforts to implement a more suitable control system are initiated. One method of control is the *"Machizukuri-Kensho"* (a town building chart), which was established by an organization composed of the town residents. Second, a partnership between the residents and municipality by means of *"Kenchiku-Kyotei"* (additional detailed zoning) and *"Chiku-Keikaku"* (district planning system) is developed. Both efforts involve residents and are regarded as grass-roots projects.

At the same time, the new types of *Machiya* town houses have been recently promoted by both individuals and public housing officials; the design of these buildings originated from the wisdom of traditional town house principles (Fig. I-C6).

TRANSFORMATION OF "RURBAN LANDSCAPE" PLANNING IN THE FRINGE ZONE

The Recent Phase of Urban Environment

Through the 1970s, the main target of Japanese urban environmental policy has been: (1) to prevent the fundamental public nuisances such as air and water pollution; and (2) as a minimum national standard, to prevent overcrowding of residential areas by supplying affordable housing as well as necessary communal facilities. To upgrade the quality of the residential environment, many local governments established a regulation code for the development of subdivisions that would establish the minimum standard of lots, streets, drainages, and so on.

Since the 1980s, new concerns for human culture and the amenities of the urban environment have emerged. In the case of larger-scale development by both public and private sectors, more attractive urbanscape design was introduced and the development of devices concerning ecological aspects such as the preservation of the micro-topographic features, biotopes, and vegetation has begun.

In the urban fringe zone many so-called "mini-developments" have unfolded. These small housing estates have slowly been encroaching onto agricultural lands and villages, transforming rural landscape into a congested *"rurbanscape."* In this zone, environmental standards cannot be attained in the same way as large-scale developments. However, there are ways of integrating the rurban landscape design in the urban fringe zones with these new small developments in the rural landscape.

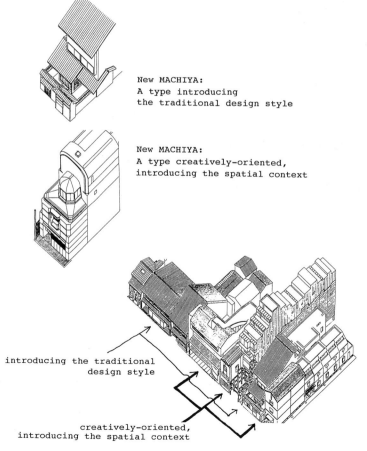

New MACHIYA:
A type introducing
the traditional design style

New MACHIYA:
A type creatively-oriented,
introducing the spatial context

introducing the traditional
design style

creatively-oriented,
introducing the spatial context

Figure I-C6 Examples of new types of *Machiya* town houses and a simulated townscape composed of them (Mimura, 1993, p. 10)

Prototype Structure of Rural Landscape and its Transformation

The typical rural landscape in western Japan is composed mainly of woodland hills, villages, rice fields, and irrigation waterways (Fig. I-C7). The woodlands are usually located on hills behind agricultural villages, which are situated on the flat land or on the gentle slope of the woodland hills, and the rice fields cover the flat lands before of the villages and partly on the gentle slopes. Irrigation reservoirs and rivers run through the rice fields to form a network of waterways that supply all the fields with water.

The main geographical characteristic of this type of rural landscape is the complexity of the microtopography (which can be called "wrinkledness"). This feature is caused by the contour lines that shape the woodland hills creating complicated curves. The villages include houses, small vegetable fields, lanes, a shrine, and a temple, and the rice fields are divided into small plots, which are ordinarily between 30–500 m². This "wrinkledness" hinders efficient cultivation on the one hand, but on the other hand, it contributes to a sound ecological environment.

Among the main components of this landscape are environmentally meaning-ful relationships which are based upon the management by village communities of the stable yearly harvest of rice. For example, irrigation brings nourishment and keeps the rice paddies continuously fertile, as it prevents flooding and soil erosion by retaining the rain in the rice fields and releasing the water gradually. In order to fertilize the fields, people used to make use of materials found around the village such as surface soil from the woodlands and dirt from the bottom of waterways.

However, since the 1960s, the way of farming and living has been transformed into an urbanized routine. As the urban area has expanded into the rural area, residential sites have been constructed in the rural landscape; this increase of new residential sites has turned the rural landscape into a "rurban landscape." Agricultural land adjustment as well as urbanization transforms the diverse environment into a monotonous, poor landscape (Fig. I-C7).

Conceptual Planning for the Rurban Landscape

To render the landscape harmonious and rich, a proper "rurban landscape" is required, where agricultural villages and new mini-residential estate groups can coexist. This could be accomplished through a new development code created to:

- Understand the landscape and environmental context of agricultural villages and their surroundings by establishing an assessment survey method for planners and developers.
- Establish new design codes to conserve the existing agricultural village atmos-phere and prevent new developments from destroying it. The new develop-ment design codes should contribute to upgrade the environment by (1) maintaining the original characteristics of microtopographical features; (2) reproducing and maintaining the biotope of the water reservoir, particularly

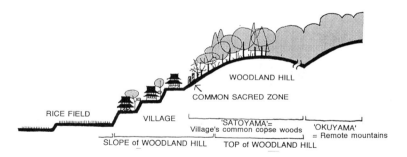

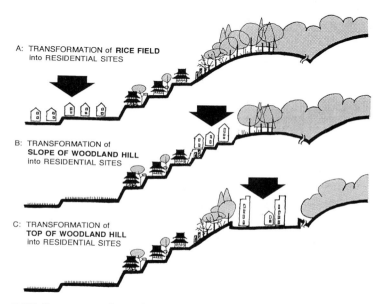

Figure I-C7 Prototype of rural landscape structure and its transformation into rurbanscape (Kobayashi, 1994, p. 2)

its slope, by stone embankment and planting hedges; (3) keeping the optimum size of lots to promote rich vegetation; (4) maintaining the small rice fields and little gardens located between the existing village and new developments; and (5) upholding the traditional, intimate scale and organic-based form.

These concepts, expected to be realized as a "Development Plan" or a "District Plan," aim to achieve a higher quality and harmonious environment.

Analysis of the Rural Landscape as a Context for Design

The authors present a case analysis to examine the structure of the rural landscape and its context as a guide for the code of a new design. As previously mentioned, one of the main characteristics of the Japanese rural landscape is its topographic "wrinkledness," which produces environmental diversity within a small area. Consequently, land-use units are very small, which also contributes to the forming of environmental diversity. On the other hand, the modest scale of the land parcels does not facilitate the planning of the "rurban landscape." Therefore, several steps are necessary to grasp the highly complex structure of the Japanese rural landscape (Fig. I-C8).

Rural Landscape Elements

First, it is necessary step to recognize the "Rural Landscape Elements" that form and comprise the landscape in forming an understanding of the structure of the Japanese rural landscape. These elements are the smallest homogeneous units, similar to the idea of the "biotope." The second step is to identify the spatial perception of the landscape, which may be regarded as units for rural landscape planning. The third and final step in visualizing the structure of the Japanese rural landscape is the perception of the landscape as a network of "Rural Landscape Components."

Assessment of the "Rurban Landscape."

A spatial assessment of the rurban landscape can easily be gained by under-standing the structure of the landscape using these above-mentioned three steps. The transformation of the rural landscape then can be described as the break-down of its underlying network which occurs when the existing "rural landscape components" are destroyed or undergo serious transformation (Fig. I-C9).

CONCLUSION

The Kyoto case study has shown that the city is now at a turning point in its modern town planning system. Currently, the city cannot meet all the needs of

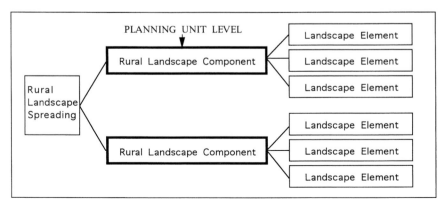

Figure I-C8 Hierarchy of the rural landscape structure (Kobayashi, 1994, p. 6)

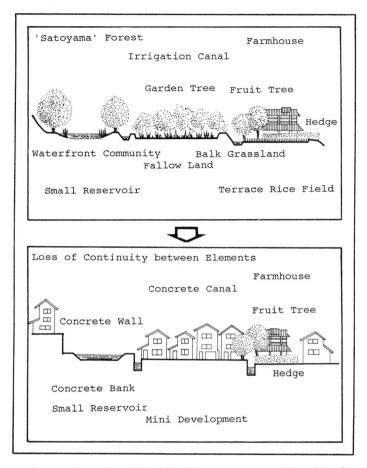

Figure I-C9 The transformation of "rural landscape components" resulting from changes of their existing "rural landscape elements" (Kobayashi, 1994, p. 9)

its citizens. The lessons learned from Kyoto's history should be considered for city planning in the twenty-first century. They may be summarized as follows:

- A city evolves by itself, but planning brings about a valuable heritage from the past to the future. The evaluation of the historical urbanscape should be made not only from the academic point of view, but also as a potentiality for urban cultural and economical maturation. Therefore, the conservation-based development can be understood as a proper concept of town planning today.
- An inventory survey covering a wider scope of the urban heritage is necessary. Modern town planning which depends on simple data of land use, traffic, and

infrastructure has proven insufficient to achieve a creative urban environment. When planning a project, a more intensive survey of the local urban heritage is necessary. The inventory survey should include not only independent elements but also associated assets such as socio-economic features of the community, its characteristic townscape, important biotopes, historically meaningful landscape, etc. Once the urban designer bears in mind these aspects, the essential context of urban structure can be recognized.

- The complexity and diversity of the historic inner city is very appealing. Even in the "scrap and build" method of urban redevelopment, conservation-based remodeling districts should be designated in townscapes of traditional low-rise buildings which will ensure the survival of small- to medium-sized shops, studios, and residences.

- Creative activities with the participation of citizens should be encouraged for the purpose of stimulating debate. Planners and administrators should also recognize the voluntary actions of the residents' groups and offer them support to assist them by introducing professional consultants, presenting the groups' ideas in forums with the municipalities, and so on.

- One of the methods of considering the city's various features as a whole is the landscape analysis which can visually show many elements, such as ecological settlements, historical and cultural assets, and the activities of citizens at the same time. The analysis will be more effective if viewed on three levels: (1) the grand landscape of the city including major topographic features, land-marks, etc.; (2) local temples or shrines and their surroundings; and (3) the microlandscape of town houses, shops, and garden designs.

- In the case of small-scale housing developments in the outlying areas, special codes are needed to induce harmonic development with the traditional environment of agricultural villages. Our case study showed an example of how to enhance both aspects of the biotope and townscape.

BIBLIOGRAPHY

1. Kiyoko, K., Hiroshi, M., and Lim, B. 1990. *The Evaluation of Housing and Environmental Developments in a Local City by the Relation to their Influence upon the View Including "Satoyama."* Papers on City Planning. Tokyo: City Planning Institute of Japan, 25.

2. Kobayashi, F., Hiroshi, M., and Kiyoko, K. 1994. *Rurban Landscape Management Plan and Town Planning, Japanese Case.* The International Symposium on Environment and Land-Use Planning. Seattle, WA: n.p.

3. Mimura, H. 1989. *Development and Conservation of Traditional Inner City of Kyoto with Wooden Town Houses, Kyoto.* Paper presented at the FHP/CIB/WMO/IGU International Conference on Urban Climate, Planning and Building, n.p., November 1989.

4. Mimura, H., *et al.* 1993. *The Practical Methods for Conservation and Succession of Town Houses and Townscape in the Historical City Center* (Nos 9014 and 9110). Tokyo: Housing Research Foundation.

5. Mimura, H., *et al.* 1991. *Ju-Kankyo o Seibi Suru. Improvement of Residential Environment.* Tokyo: Shokokusha Publishing.

D The Human Environments of Tokyo: Past, Present and Future—A Spatial Approach

Yasuo Masai

CONSTRUCTION OF EDO AS A "FEUDAL MILLION CITY"

Over the past five hundred years, Tokyo has grown twice to become the world's largest city: the first time was during its feudal period in the sixteenth century, when its population rose to greater than one million; and the second time has been throughout this century. The construction of the "feudal million city" initially started around 1457, when Ota Dokan, a local warrior-lord built a fortress at Edo. It was abandoned later, leaving practically nothing but ruined fortifications.[1,2]

In 1590, Tokugawa Ieyasu selected this same site for his castle; it remained the center of the renowned Tokugawa era, which lasted for more than 250 years. Its feudalistic society was based on the rule of powerful overlords who held massive landholdings through inheritance and exercised government control over their domains. The castle remained autonomous and upheld control for the benefit of the ruling minority. During this period, Japan's culture changed as a result of two events. Its feudalistic society retreated into self-imposed isolationism from the world which was a fundamental shift from the previous Japanese culture that had been remodeled after ancient Chinese and Korean civilizations. This isolation laid the foundation for the emergence of a unique, traditional Japanese culture—a national "Japanization."

Tokugawa Ieyasu's castle, which kept the name Edo, was erected on one of the many promontory-like dissected uplands of Musashino or Yamanote, looking down upon the brackish swamp of Hibiya Inlet, which was surrounded by marshy lowlands and valleys. The inlet and the marshy lands were filled with soil removed from the moats which were dug to construct a town for retainers, servants and townsfolk.[3] In other words, the alluvial lowlands were selected as the site of the town for the common people, but for the site of the castle, a neighboring diluvial upland was carefully chosen. This form of land-use became the typical way of creating the *jokamachi* or castle towns during the Tokugawa period.

It is unknown whether this form of land-use was intended for building the *jokamachi* at the earliest development stage of Edo. For the Japanese at that time, creating a town on diluvial uplands meant assuming a costly and unfavorable enterprise since uplands were inconvenient sites and short of water. Yet, a large amount of urban land-use areas came to be constructed on diluvial uplands with a height of 15–30 m above sea level. Extensions to the castle and many of the feudal lords' residences were built on these higher areas covered with thick loamy volcanic ashes from Mount Fuji and other volcanoes.[4] However, the Japanese were paddy cultivators and as such, seem to have had an undeniable affinity to the lowlands, at least in the past.[5] Even today, slightly more than half of the built-up areas of Japanese cities are found on alluvial lowlands, indicating the traditional preference for low ands even for urban sites, although diluvial uplands and hilly areas have tended to absorb more urban population in recent years.

Within 100 years, Edo developed from a site with few inhabitants to a city the size of about one million people. The government encouraged population growth and a phenomenal immigration followed. Yet, there were no industrial or technological developments to accommodate a city this size and overpopulation was the result. From that time on, the government tried to discourage the influx of people by limiting freedom of movement under a strict feudalist regime. Individuals on the move and travelers were required to carry passports and with these restrictions, Edo's population did not show any further sharp increase. However, a sizable amount of migration continued to the outlying areas of Edo. In the eyes of Edo's core population, the migrants were considered to be marginal people, both geographically and socially. In other words, the urban peripheries of the administrative city received many people who were ousted or trying to escape from their home villages and towns for various reasons. Squatters were also found scattered mostly at the city's peripheries, on riversides, on swamps, and in the shadows of temples.

The natural increase of Edo's population was not as intense as the population increase elsewhere in Japan. Its growth was thwarted by the poor diet of its residents, cholera, smallpox, typhoid fever, pneumonia, and other problems resulting from poor sanitary conditions. Nevertheless, the marginal newcomers were accelerating Edo's metropolitan population growth to a considerable number towards the beginning of the nineteenth century. It can be estimated that approximately 1.5 million people lived in Greater Edo at the turn of the nineteenth century. Indeed, London and Paris surpassed Edo in metropolitan population during the Industrial Revolution, but during the late eighteenth century Edo reached the worldwide record of urban population worldwide among the developing cities.

FEUDALISTIC URBAN ENVIRONMENTS OF EDO

Urban Land-Use

Greater Edo was constructed along the line of a feudal city plan which exerted a profound influence upon its human environment. Different from all other *jokamachi* (castle towns) of Japan, this city was well characterized by the superdominance of the *samurai* class, a warrior-class people with military and white-collar jobs.[6] In fact, the city provided the living quarters for both *daimyo* (feudal lords) and ordinary *samurai*. Especially common was the use of land for the *daimyo,* including the castle, which altogether occupied 40.5% out of 77 km^2 of all urban land. The feudal lords tended to have a set of residences or mansion estates: (1) the upper, formal residences; (2) the middle, subsidiary residences; and (3) the one or more lower, villa-type residences. Upper residences were used as formal residences as well as the main workplaces for their retainers; middle residences functioned mostly as subsidiaries to the upper ones; and lower residences were used as villas generally located at the urban periphery. All of the lords' mansions had beautiful gardens with trees and ponds and were surrounded by splendid walls or fences. The land was also used for residences of the many retainers and servants, as well as for hostels which sheltered retainers traveling from their provinces. The urban land use of Edo around 1860 is presented in Table I-D1.

Housing and Neighborhoods

Nearly a quarter of the urban land use was for ordinary *samurai* who were working mostly for the shoguns, the military governors of Japan. Many of these *samurai* lived in long wooden terraced houses called *nagaya* with small backyards. Higher-ranking retainers or servants tended to live in detached houses with small yards. The castle, the *daimyo*, and all other *samurai*-class citizens occupied together about two-thirds of the urban lands of 75 km^2 with a density of 15,000 people per square kilometer.

The remaining one-third of the built-up areas were divided into two categories, of which the *machiya* quarters (where townsfolk resided) occupied

Table I-D1 Feudalist urban land-use of Edo around 1860

Land-use	Area (ha)	Percentage
Edo castle	93	1.2
Other Tokugawa possessions	203	2.6
Daimyo upper residences	748	9.7
Daimyo middle residences	321	4.2
Daimyo lower residences	1756	22.8
Ordinary *samurai* houses	1818	23.6
Machiya towns	1626	21.1
Buddhist temples	1027	13.3
Shinto shrines	99	1.3
Confucian temple	5	0.1
Total	7696	100.0

Source: 100 m-grid measurements of 1:20,000. *New Map of Greater Edo* by Y. Masai (1985).

more than one half and religious areas occupied less than the other half. Most of the *machiya* houses were constructed of wood, often in the form of *nagaya*, and without significant yards. Wells and lavatories were shared among up to ten families who constituted a neighborhood. Potable water systems existed in most of the townsfolk quarters. At night, the neighborhoods were closed by lane gates on minor streets, primarily to demobilize unwelcomed visitors (rioters, robbers, unregistered men, etc.). Lane gates were abundant and checkpoints were located at several strategic spots (Fig. I-D1). The population density for the *machiya* was high; on the average, 65,000 people per square kilometer were recorded, as opposed to a much lower density for *samurai* and *daimyo* which averaged around 15,000 people per square kilometer. Greater Edo as a whole housed 20,000 people or more per square kilometer.

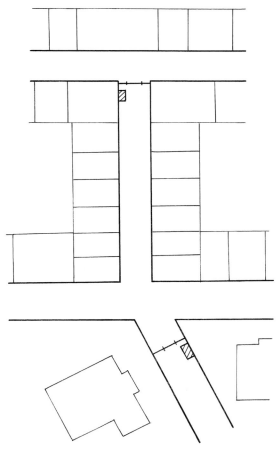

Figure I-D1 Lane gates and watch houses (shaded) in Edo (generalized map)

Buddhist temples, especially larger ones, were commonly located on the peripheries of the city. This may be attributed to practical and strategic reasons: (1) important temples needed to have large precincts and (2) large temples could be used as fortresses during emergencies. Since Northeast was considered to be the direction of bad luck and evil in Buddhism, the largest temple, Kan'ei-ji, was located at the edge of the periphery. Smaller temples were relocated from central Edo city to the outskirts to protect downtown buildings from destruction in case of fire. If a fire developed in the temple, the high roofs did not easily lend to containment of the flames. Well over one thousand small Shinto shrines were built throughout the townsfolk quarters and functioned as neighborhood shrines as well as communal open spaces. Roadside temples and shrines were also numerous, as were family altars for Buddhist and Shinto worship. Practically all families, irrespective of their social status, had family altars.

Urban Form—a Two-Nuclei City

It should be noted that the plan of Edo city had a vague, irregular, and often very complicated pattern. At first glance, one notices the seeming absence of any distinctively recognizable plan. For this reason, the common interpretation of the overall plan of Edo is that it was irregular or unplanned, especially its western half. The author's understanding, however, is quite different; Edo had a distinct plan of "irregularity." It was not shaped by unplanned, natural growth, but was designed to be irregular due to its two nuclei—Edo castle and Nihonbashi Bridge (Fig. I-D2).

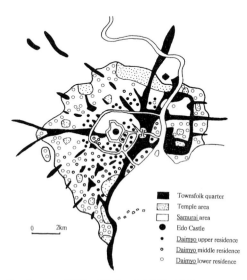

■	Townsfolk quarter
▨	Temple area
☐	Samurai area
●	Edo Castle
•	Daimyo upper residence
◦	Daimyo middle residence
○	Daimyo lower residence

0   2km

Figure I-D2 Generalized map of Edo (Tokyo) 1850–1868

The Edo castle functioned as the political and administrative center for the feudal regime. The castle was surrounded by somewhat irregular but distinct concentric zones of the *daimyo* residences: central upper residences, intermediate middle residences, and peripheral lower residences. Especially apparent was the presence of the three upper residences of the "Three Tokugawa Families" located just outside the western outer moats which served as fortification for the castle. The irregularly patterned western part of Edo consisted of *daimyo* residences, ordinary *samurai* quarters and dotted *machiya* of small sizes—all a result of the feudal planning of this great *jokamachi* (castle town). The convoluted patter of the streets was intended to lead enemies into a maze of irregular, narrow alleys and lanes similar to the labyrinthine towns of the Middle East. Uneven geometric relief in landforms served a similar purpose with an uphill, down-dale road network. Roads with straight stretches of more than 500 m were carefully avoided even on flat lands, where it was physically possible to lay out long straight roads. On uplands, even planned grids had slightly curved roads to lower visibility.

The *machiya* for tradesmen, craftsmen, and laborers had a different pattern. The civil center was the Nihonbashi Bridge, from where road distances to other places were and still are measured. It was located to the east of the castle, at the geographic center of the largest agglomeration of the *machiya* in Edo. For the townsfolk, daily life seems to have been centered around the bridge. The zoning, in general, allowed the townsfolk to live and build their houses right along major streets, including the arterial highways that originated at the bridge in a radial, star-shaped *machiya* pattern (Fig. I-D3). The central *machiya* quarters on the very flat low land consisted of a mosaic of several grids of streets centering around the castle. In this respect, a radial pattern focusing on the castle, not on the bridge, is also recognized, making the plan of Edo much more complicated. It was neither like the gridiron of Kyoto or Nara, nor other *jokamachi* with irregular, grid-iron patterns that create the images of traditional Japanese towns.[7]

The two nuclei, the castle with an irregular concentric form and the Nihonbashi Bridge with an irregular radial pattern, were 2 km apart, which was a sizable distance and too far apart to form a single focus for a radial city. Unlike Moscow, where the Kremlin is located on the Red Square to form a mononuclear, typically concentric-radial form, Edo's binuclear structure, therefore, must have been a product of planning. The irregularly patterned bi-nuclear concentric-radial form of Edo still exists in today's Tokyo, with many more additions of other patterns, sectoral developments, and *laissez-faire* urbanization which developed in later years after the feudal period.

THE MEIJI RESTORATION OF 1868 AND THEREAFTER

During the final stage of the long Tokugawa Feudal Regime, political unrest brought about the sharp decline of Edo's population. A revolutionary movement forced the Tokugawa Government to terminate its long isolationist policy—

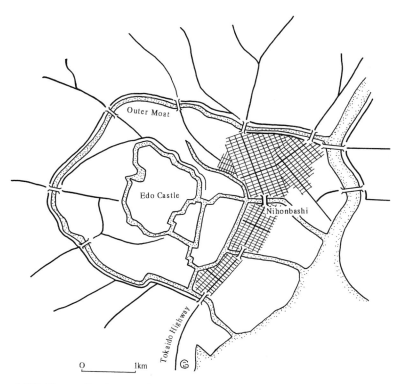

Figure I-D3 Generalized map of central *Machiya* grids centering on the Nihonbashi Bridge and focusing on/facing Edo Castle

a policy which provoked the battles that led to the Meiji Restoration. Some thirty years of unrest associated with the Meiji Restoration accelerated the population decline by the shut-down of the centralized feudalism which had demanded of its people to live in Edo. The population of Edo diminished to a low of 700,000 by 1880 from a peak of well over 1.5 million around 1850. Thus, innovative undertakings were initiated to adjust to a new age.

Introduction of Western Technology

True modernization in Japan did not start until after the Meiji Restoration of 1868 and it was a time of adopting Western practices. Through social reform, industrialization, and modern education, all aspects of Japan's culture, deeply rooted in a long history, were now exposed to powerful Western influences. With much astonishment, the Tokyo citizens must have heard news from Western countries of such innovations as the first hydraulic passenger elevator in a New York hotel (1857), the first transcontinental railroad in "young" America (1869), the first skyscraper (ten stories) in Chicago (1885), and the Eiffel Tower commanding a kaleidoscopic panorama of Paris with the already existing Champs-Elysees. Edo was renamed Tokyo, or East Capital, and its expansion was guaranteed as the new national capital (Fig. I-D4).

Part of the Western industrialization was the coming of the railroad age. To the average Japanese, this was an astonishing event. As commonly known, the

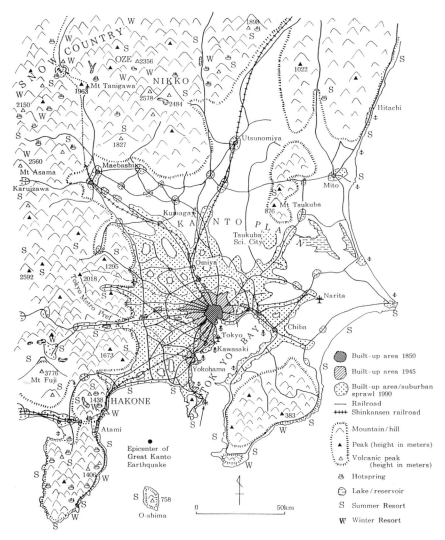

Figure I-D4 Tokyo region 1990—with historical developments. Clockwise urban expansion has taken place in time sequence starting with southern expansion. Now beaches and mountains are within easy access. (Map designed by Y. Masai and drawn by Y. Uchiyama in: *Masai*, 1990, p. 9.)

means of transport was almost exclusively restricted to a pedestrian mode during the Edo period. Under such circumstances, the introduction of steam loco-motives as a symbol of modern technology was extremely impressive to people long accustomed to the slowest means of travel, walking. The railroad not only improved transportation; it also became a factor to be considered in town planning. Japan's first railroad was completed in 1872 between Shinbashi (Tokyo) and Yokohama, the newly opened port-town for Tokyo. The comple-tion of Tokyo Central Station at its present site in 1914 greatly influenced the shaping of the modern downtown area called *Marunouchi*. Even today, many Japanese cannot believe a historical fact occurred in London only five years before the Meiji Restoration—the first underground railway (1863).

Growth of Tokyo

After the Meiji Restoration, as social and political restructuring were stabilized, the population began to grow again at an increasingly higher rate, reaching 2 million by the end of the nineteenth century. Modern factories and buildings were constructed. Major streets had horse-drawn tramways (1882–1903), while a great many *jinrikisha* or rickshaws—a Japanese invention in 1868 intended to catch up with Western civilization—were running on narrow, poorly paved or unpaved streets.[8] Endeavors to develop modern technologies and modern social systems were vigorously pursued to create a modern nation at the eastern extremity of the world, as it was mapped in the late 1880s. Electrification of horse-drawn streetcars, or trams, were introduced to Tokyo in 1903 which elimi-nated the piles of horse dung in the streets. The following year, a steamengine railroad in Tokyo was also electrified. This marked the first "rapid transit system" for the increasing number of commuters. All of these efforts were hampered very severely by the Great Kanto Earthquake of 1923 and the resulting fires. Tokyo, especially the eastern half of the city, became an inferno which claimed one hundred thousand lives.

Just before this catastrophe, Tokyo was developing various kinds of modern establishments under the Imperial Regime. In the early twentieth century, some fifty years after the Meiji Restoration, Tokyo showed very different features of urban structure compared with the feudal city. With less strict urban zoning, a scattering of commercial establishments was developing in areas where *samurai* residences once predominated by law. Much of the former feudal lords' mansion estates were converted into government buildings and military facilities, man-sions for the new elites, larger-size factories, subdivisions for amenities, and others. Educational land use also came to occupy 3.8% of Tokyo, a significant increase (Table I-D2).

EARLY TWENTIETH CENTURY

The idea of a "garden city" was introduced to Japan by Ebenezer Howard just before the 1923 earthquake. The city of Tokyo lagged behind Osaka in accepting this new movement, but the catastrophe persuaded many of Tokyo's downtown citizens to move outward along radiating suburban lines, which had been formerly constructed primarily for carrying farm products, gravel, limestone, and night soil. Garden city-type suburbs such as Den'en-Chofu and Seijo-Gakuen attracted a great many well-to-do people, white-collar workers, and retired people until World War II. Just before the outbreak of the war, Tokyo's population reached a peak of 7 million caused by the build-up along the northwestern coasts of Tokyo Bay with chains of factories that formed the Tokyo–Yokohama (Keihin) industrial zone.

Yet, it was the daily behavior of the inhabitants of Tokyo that made the capital a habitable and hospitable city. For example, the insect population then was quite large, and collectors and hobbyists, as well as children caught cicadas, crickets, and butterflies daily along Tokyo's streets and neighborhoods to add to their collections or as a sport. Some people enganged in other outdoor activities such as hiking, sea bathing, hot spring tours, and fishing, although these were luxuries in which only a few could indulge. The sky could be observed throughout Tokyo and in many areas, without the interference of city lights. One could view the Milky Way, for instance, very clearly in Tokyo at the time. This kind of environment prevailed until the early postwar times.

Impact of World War II Destruction

Between December 1941 and August 1945, the war brought about some unprecedented events for Tokyo. First, the construction of military industries was

Table I-D2 Urban land-use of Tokyo around 1910–1915

Land-use	Area (ha)	Percentage
Company–financial	49	0.4
Commercial–residential	1002	8.4
Residential–commercial	2226	18.7
Warehouse, port, lumber yard	450	3.8
Imperial	420	3.5
Government–public hospital	778	6.5
Military	919	7.7
Manufacturing	523	4.4
Educational	450	3.8
Religious–cemetery	712	6.0
Park green	177	1.5
Mansion	689	5.8
Ordinary residential	3320	27.8
Construction site	211	1.7
Total	11,928	100.0

Source: 100 m-grid measurements of 1:20,000. *Restored Land Use Map Pre-Earthquake Tokyo* by Y. Masai and C. R. Hong, 1992.

very much encouraged by the government and many factories were established in the outskirts of Tokyo. Especially in the western suburbs, where a considerable amount of woodland was found, new factories were constructed, using a large amount of land. (After the war, the factories were converted into schools, housing estates, etc.)

Within the built-up areas, not much change occurred during the first two years of the war, but towards the end of 1944, successive air-raids began to destroy Tokyo. To lessen the damage caused by bombing and resulting fires, many wooden houses were demolished until an extensive network of fireproof zones were formed, especially along railroads and rivers. Several big air-raids towards the end of the war, March–May 1945, together with small daily ones which continued to take place, devastated 70% of the houses and buildings in Tokyo. With very few tall buildings remaining, much of Tokyo could be observed clearly by the naked eye.

The population of Tokyo toward the end of the war diminished to 3 million. Children and elderly people who had been evacuated during the war were returning to the ruined city. Many of these returning citizens were forced to live in deserted shacks built earlier by people who could not find decent places to live. Others lived in small-size wartime shelters dug during the war and built extensions at the ground level to improve their living accommodations. Shanty towns and urban villages mushroomed—many of these hastily thrown up by squatters. The shanty towns were in sharp contrast to the undamaged areas of the city and served as a constant reminder of the war.

An attempt at urban planning was made, but only after individual reconstruction of houses had begun and the population had already started to increase at an uncontrollable rate. Job-seekers, wartime evacuees, war orphans, returnees from overseas, and sundry other shabbily dressed people swarmed into Tokyo in dilapidated trains. Hopelessness prevailed among the majority of people. The dress colors of gray, blue and khaki mirrored the mood of the people. Strikes took place throughout the country, as demonstrators demanded higher wages and political changes. Commuter trains were humble looking, their glass windows often repaired by wooden planks. Overcrowding forced people to stand on the steps of the train cars while the trains were moving. Accidents occurred, some unintended and some intended, and many people were killed. Although the sky was blue, life was gray and miserable. However, some people took advantage of this enormous social and economic growth. Noisy black markets emerged at evacuated spots around the railroad stations. These markets were operated by nonprofessionals amidst an atmosphere of dilapidation. Swarms of hungry people were selling, buying and swapping, making the black markets prosper.

Postwar Reconstruction

The postwar maze gradually eased. After about ten years, Tokyo destroyed nearly all the visible ruins and replaced them with cheap houses. Superficially, the war damage disappeared almost completely and a new, humble townscape prevailed. The economy was developing fast, but the majority of Tokyo's people could not imagine a life of plenty and affluence. Privately owned passenger cars were practically nonexistent even in the late 1950s.

The 1960s, however, were a decade of rapid economic growth. A gigantic renewal plan was issued for Shinjuku to build a new high-rise city out of the shanty town in front of Shinjuku Station's west gate and the Yodobashi Water Purification Plant. The shanty town became a big plaza with modern facilities for motor cars. The purification plant was converted into a new city with a huge complex of tall office buildings, hotels, and recently, the Tokyo Metropolitan Government (City Hall), completed in 1992. The Shinkansen bullet train service was started in 1964, the year of the Tokyo Olympics.

The reversion of Okinawa to Japan in 1972 was seen as symbolizing the end of the postwar period. In Tokyo, streetcar lines were quickly abolished because of the rapid increase of motor vehicles and new subway and suburban lines made their debut. Highway construction continued all over the country. Cars, color televisions, electric refrigerators, electric washing machines, air-conditioners, and many other electric-electronic appliances were no longer considered luxuries, but rather essentials for many families. Factories, companies, universities, and other large establishments were completely or partially relocated to suburban areas, outer fringes, or more distant places. Tokyo's population was planned to decrease to an "optimum" size by encouraging enterprises to relocate to less congested rural areas.

However, Tokyo's population continued to grow and with it increased the level of environmental pollution which reached its worst levels in the 1970s.[9] The destruction of a healthy atmosphere and the historic townscapes proceeded thereafter as elsewhere. The so-called moderate economic growth, somewhere around 5% or less, favored this great city with further metropolitan population growth since many people were misinformed about the extent of the pollution. Nowadays, urbanization encroaches onto the hills, mountain slopes, and into the sea. The result is that in 1994, Tokyo Proper, a 23-ku area (or wards), has 8 million people; the Tokyo Metropolitan Prefecture has 11.9 million people, but the entire Tokyo region has a population of at least 35 million people within its star-shaped urbanized area, extending 100 km or more. This area has developed mostly along the major radial railroads, including the Shinkansen lines.[10]

The overall land-use of the built-up areas of Tokyo proper is astonishingly diverse; the capital features a mosaic of small parcels of land with no single-category land-use area covering 1 km^2 or more, except for the Imperial Palace and the airport. Of course there is a zoning act, but it is so loose and generous that it allows for different land-uses side by side. Simultaneously, a juxtaposition of Japanese and Western architectural forms, with many intermediate forms, has accelerated the image of mixed townscapes. There is a current awareness of the need to purify and unify urban land uses, but this will take a very long time to accomplish. In addition, it is characteristic of Japanese society to intermingle rich and poor neighborhoods. Some voices advocate mixed living of rich and poor Japanese regardless of the economic or social discrepancies. There is, however, an ethnic segregation among Japanese society, although the problem has never been pronounced enough to create ghettos.

DAILY LIFE IN CONTEMPORARY TOKYO

Living in the Shadow of Earthquake Threats

Since Tokyo lies near a major fault line, practically all of Tokyo's citizens contemplate at least occasionally the possibility of a catastrophic earthquake. If a strong earthquake struck before suppertime on a dry December day and with the same magnitude as the 1923 earthquake, the number of deaths would amount to 2 million, according to a government survey. This may or may not come true, but the government of Tokyo and all the citizens must certainly be aware of precaution measures against such catastrophes. The government has already designated many "fireproof" open spaces as refuge bases and some major road arteries as escape routes. The citizens are advised to come to the refuge base located in their neighborhood in an emergency although some of the bases may be too far away to use in conditions of turmoil. Maps showing nearby refuge bases can be found at stations, parks, major intersections and other strategic spots; they also are delivered to homes through *chonaikai* (town associations) or with daily newspapers. However, the great earthquake which just occurred on January 17, 1995 in Kobe, with the strongest magnitude ever recorded in Japan, exerted an unprecedented influence upon Japan's urban society. Perhaps all the preventative measures planned so far will have to be altered. If a shallow earthquake were to hit underneath Tokyo, the damage could be ten times worse than at Kobe.

Daily Leisure

The absence of parks or green open spaces often leaves Tokyo with the description of a city without sufficient amenities. The park area *per capita* for Tokyo is 3.7 m^2, quite a low level even for a densely populated Japanese city. Park areas are slowly increasing, however, with a goal of 6.0 m^2 *per capita* by the year 2000. One of the main reasons why Tokyo and other Japanese cities generally lack vast urban forests or greenery near or within built-up areas is that all Japanese cities are surrounded by extremely expensive, intensively cultivated farmlands without large forests. However, Japanese cities also are close to mountains and hills covered with forests and Tokyo is no exception. The western third of the Tokyo Metropolitan Prefecture (excluding its island portions) is mountainous. These deep mountains still have wild monkeys, bears, deer, and boar sheltered under thick, natural or artificial forest cover. A considerable number of nature-lovers within the Tokyo region travel to the mountains and seashores by train and car.

People can reach the eastern foot of these mountains very easily even from Tokyo Central Station since it is only 30–40 km away. Hot springs are also abundant in the vicinity of the capital. Even ski resorts are numerous and many of them are located within a one-day trip from Tokyo, such as Echigo-Yuzawa, Naeba and Kusatsu resorts. Four national parks are found at the periphery of the Tokyo region, including 3776 m high Mount Fuji situated 100 km west of Tokyo. Even today, the visibility of Mount Fuji eighty days out of the year is a good conversational topic among the citizens of Tokyo, as it was in the old days.

Unlike most other Asian cities, Tokyo tends to have many detached houses with yards and numerous streets lined with trees and bushes which enhances the quality of the urban environment. The author has observed that populations of butterflies, crickets, and cicadas in the Tokyo residential neighborhoods is much denser than in American and European cities, or in Shanghai, Beijing, and Seoul. However, millions of trees and bushes in rural areas have been cut down to make room for space-consuming grassy golf courses, which, most people would agree, are too numerous. Yet, it is true that these grasslands offer a meadow-like landscape that is very rare in Japan and desired by many.

Arteries and Shopping Centers

The daily life of Tokyo's citizens is supported by a dense network of railroads. Tokyo has always made vigorous efforts to construct railroads and the Tokyo region now has a total length of well over 2000 km of a commuter rail system. Several stations in the region are supersized to handle enormous masses of passengers; by far the largest is Shinjuku Station with many converging lines. More than 3 million passengers, shoppers, and commuters use this single station complex daily, followed by Ikebukuro, Tokyo, Shibuya, and Yokohama Stations.[11]

The Nihonbashi area attracted the largest number of shoppers during the Edo period. After the opening of the first railroad terminal at Shinbashi as Tokyo's main station in 1872, the nearby Ginza Street became a modern shopping center which steadily rose in Tokyo's hierarchy of central places. It is the most prestigious center of shopping even today, but the actual retail sales value of Shinjuku Station, 6 km in the west, is slightly higher now. There is a strong tendency among the retail shopping centers or districts to see quicker development in suburban areas and residential satellites. Thus, Fujisawa, Machida, Hachioji, Kichijoji, Omiya, Kashiwa, Funabashi-Tsudanuma, Chiba, and others, each with several large department stores and hundreds of small exclusive shops and restaurants, have been mushrooming (Fig. I-D5). All are in healthy, keen competition with each other. Peripheral centers commonly tend to be car-oriented, but even these particular centers are located at railroad hubs. New Tsukuba Science City, located 60 km northeast of Tokyo, is a shopping center with a considerable number of large department stores, but it is without easy access to railroad stations. A railroad line to connect this center with Tokyo is currently under construction.

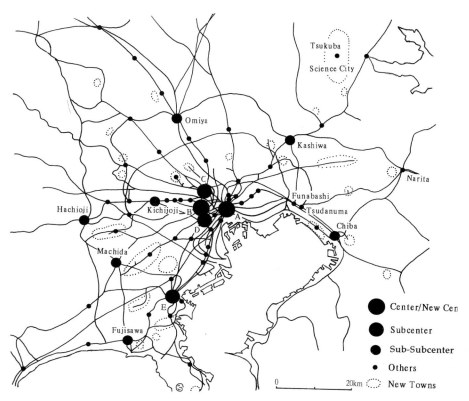

Figure I-D5 Major shopping centers and rail network of the Tokyo region—1994. (A) Ginza-Nihonbashi, (B) Shinjuku, (C) Ikebukuro, (D) Shibuya, (E) Yokohama

With a population of more than 35 million people in the Tokyo region, there are 15 million motor vehicles of various sorts. How to handle such traffic is still an acute problem which calls for an urgent solution. All cars have their own registered parking lots, which causes a significant loss of space that could otherwise be used for mini-gardens or green areas. Lots of demolished houses are often converted into parking areas even in suburbia. Illegal roadside parking, including parking for bicycles, cannot be eliminated which causes traffic congestion and unnecessary accidents.

In Japan's planning restrictions, the minimum width of an urban road is set for 4 m or slightly more, equivalent to a two-car width. If the width is less than that, the law stipulates the roadway is not to have houses built alongside. The abundance of 4 m roads and alleys in Tokyo and throughout Japan is the result of the long years of pedestrian transportation which is thought to have ended in the early twentieth century but, in actuality, is still widely practiced on a daily basis today.[12] Most of the back alleys and paths that were once heavily used as children's playgrounds have been widened to 4 m or more, taking over part of the very expensive, densely built-up areas and demolishing old houses. The construction of wide boulevards is very costly and plans for them are seldom realized. The postwar reconstruction planners envisioned the construction of a network of 50–100 m wide, radial and concentric streets throughout Tokyo, but only a very small portion of this has been built until now. As a consequence, Tokyo "unintentionally" preserves the historically laid out street pattern to a great extent, which makes the city more interesting but creates problems for motorists. The necessity of maintaining the rail systems is paramount here, even though Japan is one of the world's largest producer of automobiles.

FUTURE ISSUES

The Tokyo region currently faces several future-oriented urban planning issues.[13] The most controversial issue may be related to the discussion concerning the relocation of the capital's functions; this problem has been debated for a long time and the debate is still continuing. The super-size of Tokyo, both as a city and metropolitan region, seems to contain all thinkable urban problems: lack of space, long commuting distances, relatively small sized houses, residents' anxiety in case of emergency, etc. These issues may point to the relocation of its functions as a solution since all of these problems have been magnified by the previously mentioned current issues. It is generally understood that the relocation project could be realized only through the dispersal or relocation of the capital's functions within the Tokyo Metropolitan Region, or possibly somewhere in the Tokaido Megalopolis, which is located in the center of the Tokyo, Osaka, and Nagoya triangle. Should the capital be relocated outside the Tokyo megalopolis, a more than one-century old tradition would come to an end. So far, most of the planners and citizens interested in this issue seem to think that the future national capital will be a relatively large sized city at the time of completion. It may not be a Canberra in population size but could be a Washington, DC; the time for a decision of the size of the future Japanese capital has not come yet.

The competition of three gigantic development plans for Tokyo Bay's shores is another urban planning issue not settled yet. Chiba's futuristic new city constructed at Makuhari has been challenged by Yokohama's future plan called "Minato Mirai 21 (Port Future 21)." Japan's tallest building has already been erected within this plan area with the Yokohama Landmark Tower of 70 stories and 296 m height at its center. The most ambitious plan offered by the Tokyo Government is to create a gigantic new city on landfills in Tokyo Bay, in the vicinity of Tokyo's downtown, which will contain various kinds of urban functions focusing on international telecommunication. This artificial city is to be Tokyo Teleport, which would be supported by the Tokyo airports (Narita and Haneda) and the port of Yokohama as the outer port for Tokyo. The combination of teleport, airports, and seaport is considered to function as an exchange of information, people, and goods. A true competitor within Japan could arise in the Osaka region, with its large population and long history, or in Kyushu, which is expected to rise as a grand, sophistiaced economic region in Eastern Asia.

Geographically, Tokyo is expanding even today, following four courses: along the suburban frontier, absorbing farmland, forests, and mountains; along the sky frontier, creating a three-dimensional townscape; on the waterfront, making new large-scale projects possible; and in the geofrontier, advancing into the deep underground space. Within this general framework of development, new measures are urgently needed: (1) reform (including conservation) of historical townscapes, since Tokyo is a historical city; (2) mountain-view (vista) projects, since Tokyo's people have been fascinated with mountain panoramas; and (3) construction of townscapes with green open spaces and footpaths, since people enjoy watching the seasonal changes in the flora, and listening to the insects and birds. These are considered valuable urban amenities which greatly enhance the quality of urban life.

NOTES

1. Yasuo, M. ed. 1986. *Atlas Tokyo* (in Japanese and English). Tokyo: Heibonsha, 42–43.
2. Yasuo, M. 1987. *Jokamachi Tokyo (Castletown Tokyo)*. Tokyo: Hara–shobo, 7.
3. Akira, N. 1966. *Edo and Edo Castle.* Tokyo: Kajima Shuppankai, 43–48.
4. Kaizuka, S. 1980. *Tokyo no Shizen-shi (Natural History of Tokyo)*. Tokyo: Kinokuniya-shoten, 59–60.
5. Yasuo, M. and Tsuneo, S. 1982. Geomorphological locational conditions of the built-up areas in Japan. *Tsukuba Studies in Human Geography.* Tsukuba: University of Tsukuba, vol. VI: 51–64.
6. Yasuo, M. and Yasuo, S. 1979. *Grand Atlas of Edo-Tokyo.* Tokyo: Heibonsha, 174.
7. Yamori, K. 1988. *Jokamachi no Katachi (Forms of Jokamachi)*. Tokyo: Chikuma-Shobo, 13–16.
8. Toshihiko, S. 1980. *Jinrikisha (Rickshaw)*. Tokyo: Kuori Publishing, 48–86.
9. Berque A. ed. 1987. *La Qualite de la Ville: Urbanite Francaise, Urbanity Nippone* (in French and Japanese). Tokyo: Maison Franco-Japonaise, 69.
10. Yamaga, S. 1967. *Tokyo Daitoshiken no Kenkyu (A Study of the Tokyo Metropolitan Region)*. Tokyo: Taimei-do, 42.
11. Cybriwsky, R. 1988. Shibuya Center, Tokyo. *Geographical Review* 78, no. 1: 48–61.
12. Yasuo, M. 1965. Road intersections of Tokyo's 23-ku area. *Geog. Rev. Japan.* 38, no. 11: 79.
13. Cybriwsky, R. 1991. *Tokyo.* Boston, MA: G. K. Hall, 194–234.

BIBLIOGRAPHY

1. Berque, A. ed. 1987. *La Qualité de la Ville* (in French and Japanese). Tokyo: Maison Franco-Japonaise.
2. Brunn, S. D. and Williams, J. F. eds. 1983. *Cities of the World.* New York: Harper & Row.
3. Cybriwsky, R. 1988. Shibuya Center, Tokyo. *Geographical Review* 78, no. 1: 48–61.
4. Cybriwsky, R. 1991. *Tokyo.* Boston, MA: G. K. Hall.

5. Kaizuka, S. 1964. *Natural History of Tokyo*. Tokyo: Kinokuniya-shoten.
6. Masai, Y. 1979. *A Comparative Study of Japanese and American Cities*. Tokyo: Kokon-shoin.
7. Masai, Y. ed. 1986. *Atlas Tokyo*. Tokyo: Heibonsha.
8. Masai, Y. 1987. *Jokamachi Tokyo (Castle-town Tokyo)*. Tokyo: Hara Shobo.
9. Masai, Y. 1985. *New Map of Greater Edo*. Personal printing.
10. Masai, Y. 1965. Road intersections of Tokyo's 23-Ku area (in Japanese and English). *Geog. Rev. Japan*. 3, no. 11: 663–681.
11. Masai, Y. 1990. Tokyo: from a feudal million city to a global supercity. *Geog. Rev. Japan* 63, no. 1: 9.
12. Masai, Y. and Hong, C. 1993. Restored land-use map of pre-earthquake Tokyo. Map.
13. Masai, Y. and Tsuneo, S. 1982. Geomorphological locational conditions of the built-up areas in Japan. *Tsukuba Studies in Human Geography*. Tsukuba: University of Tsukuba, vol. VI.
14. Masai, Y. and Yasuo, S. 1993. *Grand Atlas of Edo-Tokyo*. Tokyo: Heibonsha.
15. Naito, A. 1966. *Edo and Edo Castle*. Tokyo: Kajima Shuppankai.
16. Saito, T. 1980. *Jinrikisha*. Tokyo: Kuori Publishing.
17. Yamaga, S. 1967. *Tokyo Daitoshiken no Kenkyu. (A study of the Tokyo Metropolitan Region)*. Tokyo: Taimeido.
18. Yokoyama, S. 1988. *Shuto (Capitals)*. Tokyo: Taimeido.

E Social Safety and Security through Urban Design

Osamu Koide and Toshio Oyama

INTRODUCTION

Outsiders used to consider Japan to be a peaceful and family-oriented country. It was commonly said that the streets of Japan were safe and its waters open to the public. Now, however, the Japanese people are facing many changes in their society which have lead to urban problems. Japan's population of 124 million people, most of whom reside in large cities, must endure living conditions which are extremely dense. The effect of living in a crowded environment has been exacerbated by the fact that the national Japanese government has proven to be ineffective during extreme urban emergencies, e.g. the Hanshin area earthquake and the Tokyo subway poison gas attack. The cooperation among local governments or between national and local governments has not operated efficiently and failed to keep the streets and homes of Japan sufficiently safe and secure from criminals and natural disasters. Due to these recent setbacks, Japanese people are looking for a new social and governmental system to replace the former system with one that will survive the changing environment of the twenty-first century. In this chapter, the authors describe the current conditions of the Japanese cities, including the local governmental systems, crime, and disaster prevention, which are partly responsible for the state of affairs in urbanized Japan.

CITIES IN JAPAN

Outlook of Japan

Although Japan is a small, island nation, it has a population of 124 million people, about half that of the United States of America. However, the surface area of Japan, at 377,000 km^2, is only 4% the size of the U.S.A.[1] From this data, Japan's population density has been calculated at 329 persons per square kilometer, more than ten times the rate in the U.S.A. The rates are higher, in fact, because Japan is mostly covered with mountains and forests (70% of the land is considered to be mountain and volcanic zone, leaving only 30% of the land suitable for habitation and development). The final rate balloons to more than 1000 persons per square kilometer, or ten people per ha, more than thirty times the population density of the U.S.A.[2]

Japan was once known as one of the safest countries in the world and to some extent it still is. It was common amongst Japanese to think that safety and availability of water are naturally guaranteed; about twenty years ago, residents customarily left their doors unlocked while they were at home. Bolstered by remarkable economic growth, the Japanese thought their country was, in fact, the best country to live.

Times have changed, however. Crime is on the rise now, especially in the cities. The poison gas episode on the Tokyo subway reveals the vulnerability of the Japanese to terrorist attacks. In cities, the number of single households increases rapidly which results in an even higher density ratio than before. The former situation with an atmosphere of familiarity where residents knew their neighbors and community well has disappeared. Instead, people are now suspicious and expect crime rates to rise year by year.

Japanese Cities

Like the Chinese language, each Kanji character has a meaning in Japanese. When expressing the word "city" in Japanese, two Kanji characters are necessary. One of the characters translates into "capital," the other into "market." Historically, the word "capital" referred to the place where large buildings were found, that is, the place where the governors, emperors or rulers of the region lived. The word "market" pertained to the place where people gathered to exchange goods and information. It is believed that the word "capital" developed earlier than the word "market" in Japan, following the change in the role of the city from the center of government to the center of the market.[3]

As with other Asian countries, the agricultural and/or fishing industries used to be located in the villages. To fulfill tax and tenant requirements, the villagers would deliver their locally produced goods to the governors in the cities. As progress in industrial technology increased the rates and amount of production, people started to offer their labor and trade skills in exchange for money rather than agricultural products which enabled them to pay taxes, rent and to buy more diverse goods and foods. This emerging employed population often purchased produce from farmers instead of growing their own and the market as we know it was born. Markets were held at the most accessible gathering area, usually a governmental hub, either near the palace, the castle, or next to the temples and shrines. As such, the cities were characterized by a transition of importance from political to economic centers.

The Definition of a Japanese City

In a Japanese dictionary, the word *city* is defined as an extensive town with a large population and the political, economic, or cultural core of a given region.[4] Currently, however, a city is defined in Japan as an area which meets the four following conditions (with some exceptions in the view of an urban planner):

- An area with a population of more than 50,000 persons. A limit of 50,000 persons is set because a city should be understood as an active place where a certain-sized population would be needed to build mass infrastructure, such as railways, energy supplies, mailing services, etc., and to maintain the city's functions. A population of at least 50,000 would also be neecessary to support the city's industrial activities.
- An area with a population density of more than twenty persons per ha. Although the population of a certain area might be more than 50,000, it would be hard to call it a city if its population density is much smaller than twenty. Internationally, a DID (Densely Inhabited District) is defined as an area with a total population of 5000 persons and a density of more than 40 persons per ha. In the case of Japan, it is thought that half of the DID, or twenty persons per ha, should be the minimum population density of a city.
- An area with a secondary and/or tertiary industry. It is increasingly difficult to define a city from the structure of the employment population distribution. The employment population of the secondary and tertiary industry in an area is usually more than 66% of the total employment population and the population of the primary industry decreases to less than 10%.
- An area with independent management. A city should be managed by one independent government in order to act as a unit area. The single government body should administer the area independently with the help of a mayor and council. In Japanese cities, the councils are partly located underneath the authority of the prefectures and find it difficult to act entirely independently.

Structure of the Cities

According to urban planning laws, 664 cities exist in Japan which are divided into three categories. One of the categories is the megalopolis, including Tokyo, Osaka and Nagoya. A second group consists of twelve cities with almost more than 1 million people each. The area of these cities is divided into wards with some parts of the governmental activities transferred to the ward governments. The third category is made up of the remaining 652 cities. The smallest city in Japan is Utashinai-City with a population of 7836 although it is an exception.

From the viewpoint of comprehensive national land-use planning, the Tokyo, Osaka, and Nagoya metropolitan areas are considered to be the three megalopolis regions (Tables I-E1 and I-E2). Each area includes several cities and the central government determines the comprehensive urban plan for each region.

Table I-E1 Japanese cities

Type	Condition	City name
Mega city	Japan's major cities	Tokyo, Osaka, Nagoya
Designated city	Divided into ward areas	12 large cities including Tokyo
City	Others	Other 652

Table I-E2 Three mega city regions

Regions	Area	Prefectures
Tokyo region	appl. 50 km area of Tokyo	Saitama, Chiba, Tokyo, Kanagawa
Kansai region	Osaka and Kyoto area	Gifu, Aichi, Mie
Nagoya region	Nagoya area	Kyoto, Osaka, Hyogo, Nara

Local Government Systems

Japan is divided into forty-seven local governments which are called prefectures. Each prefecture is led by a minister who is elected into this position; before World War II, ministers of the local governments were appointed by the central government. The prefectures are defined as "wide area local governments" under the Local Government Law of 1956. The management area of the Prefecture is divided into the four following categories: (1) wide area management, including supervision of area development, industrial growth, and social projects; (2) projects which require comprehensive coordination, including education, security, and social welfare; (3) management which requires modifications between cities, towns and the central government; and (4) supplemental works and economic subsidization of city projects, including construction of public facilities. Besides the "wide area" local governments and cities, there are the basic local, city and town governments. They are the political systems which have the most immediate impact on the life of residents.

As the twenty-first century approaches, there have been many discussions on the desirable local governmental system for Japan since the current three-dimensional system has not been regarded as efficient for the citizens of the local areas. Some of the Diet members have proposed to divide Japan into seven to nine districts instead of continuing the rule of a single central government. The mayor of the proposed district would then manage the cities within the demarcated area.

The idea of passing additional power to large cities with a population of more than 200,000 people is also being considered; this proposal would allow for more than 400 cities to manage themselves independently.

The cooperation among the branches of the local government is another controversial subject. It happened in the past that convicted criminals who escaped from prison were not arrested because of the lack of cooperation between police stations. A Japanese joke on this topic illustrates this dilemma: If two policemen appeared at the scene of a man drowning in a river, they would both wait to see to which side of the river he would drift before acting due to the regulations varying between police departments. As to the water supply, it is possible to arrive in one prefecture to find a brimming and available supply of water while there might be none in a neighboring prefecture. The final conclusion seems to be that an overly large central government offers less personalized service to the people, but the overly independent management of an area might impede cooperation between prefectures.

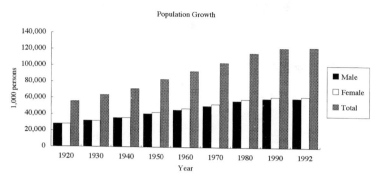

Figure I-E1 Population growth in Japan during most of the twentieth century

POPULATION

Overview

Although Japan's population increases by 0.3% per year, the overall rate of increase is actually shrinking every year (Fig. I-E1). In particular, the natural growth of the population is dropping (Fig. I-E2). As of 1992, the birth rate was 9.8% compared to 18.8% in 1970. The mortality rate has remained steady at around 7%. In order to maintain the current population figure, the birth rate would have to be 2.1 children per family. In 1992, the number was its lowest ever, at 1.5 children.

Despite the decrease in the natural growth of the population, the immigrant population gradually increases. In 1992, 34,000 people immigrated to Japan. Currently, however, as the Japanese economy has stagnated, the number has been decreasing since 1993. Nonetheless, almost 1% of the population in Japan is composed of foreigners.

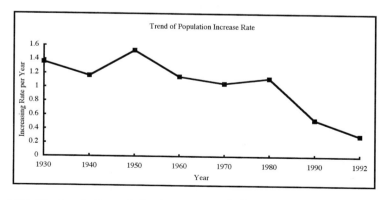

Figure I-E2 The trend of population increase rate in Japan during most of the twentieth century

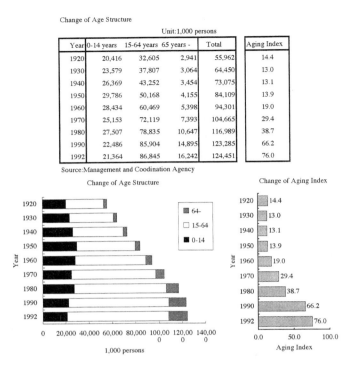

Change of Age Structure

Unit:1,000 persons

Year	0-14 years	15-64 years	65 years -	Total	Aging Index
1920	20,416	32,605	2,941	55,962	14.4
1930	23,579	37,807	3,064	64,450	13.0
1940	26,369	43,252	3,454	73,075	13.1
1950	29,786	50,168	4,155	84,109	13.9
1960	28,434	60,469	5,398	94,301	19.0
1970	25,153	72,119	7,393	104,665	29.4
1980	27,507	78,835	10,647	116,989	38.7
1990	22,486	85,904	14,895	123,285	66.2
1992	21,364	86,845	16,242	124,451	76.0

Source:Management and Coodination Agency

Figure I-E3 Changes in the age structure of the Japanese population (left chart) and change of aging index (right chart) during most of the twentieth century

Age Structure

Japan is facing the rapid aging of its society because of the population breakdown over the last decades (Fig. I-E3). The Aging Index, which is defined as the ratio of the population sixty-five years and older and those people who are fourteen years and younger, was 76.0 in 1992. The number of persons over 100 years also increases every year, reaching a figure of 4152 in 1992. According to the Ministry of Health and Welfare, the total population will begin to decrease in 2015 and the percentage of elderly will rise from 12–25%.

Population Distribution

In 1992, almost 120 million people were living in the Tokyo metropolitan area. The population density was 5400 persons per square kilometer, which makes Tokyo the most densely populated city in Japan. As of 1994, there were 664 cities in Japan accommodating almost 75% of the total population. The region within a 50 km radius of the center of Tokyo is home to 30 million people or 24% of the total population. In the Osaka and Nagoya regions, 16 and 8 million people live,

Table I-E3 The population trend in Japan

Year	Male	Female	Total	Increasing rate
1920	27,981	27,904	55,885	
1930	32,049	31,923	63,972	1.36
1940	35,778	36,032	71,810	1.16
1950	40,943	42,643	83,586	1.53
1960	45,988	47,735	93,723	1.15
1970	51,050	53,011	104,061	1.05
1980	57,250	59,142	116,392	1.13
1990	60,251	62,473	122,724	0.53
1992	60,597	62,879	123,476	0.31

Source: Management and Coordination Agency: 1993.

respectively. Fifty-four million people, or 43% of the population, live within these three megalopolises and they are still growing (Table I-E3).

The total population of Japan is anticipated to reach 130 million in the year 2010 according to the Ministry of Health and Welfare. While the population of the countryside will decrease, that of the three megalopolises, but not their central cores, will increase. In 1992, more than 2 million people commuted to the Tokyo metropolitan area for work or school and spent about one hour each day on the train. More than 3.6 million people commute exclusively into the ward and downtown areas of Tokyo alone. Even though the city center keeps losing permanent residents due to its metamorphosis from a residential to business area, it still remains active.

CURRENT TOPICS OF CITIES

Increase of Single Households

There are more than 40 million households in Japan. This number is still increasing, but the average family size is declining year by year, from 4.14 in 1960 to 2.99 today. Some estimates place the percentage of households with no children at 60%. Single households were about 10 million in 1990, which is almost 25% of all households. The Tokyo metropolitan area comprised 4.3 million households in 1980, with this number still rising. It is estimated that there will be 5 million households by the year 2000. The average number of people in a household is now 2.55 and estimated to be 2.46 by 2000, with single households in Tokyo accounting for 33% of all households.

The shrinking family size has been compounded by the decrease in the number of marriages every year, from 1,029,000 in 1970 to 742,000 in 1991. The number of divorces also increased from 95,000 to 168,000 over the same time span. Conventional urban planning and city management has focused on the notion of the basic, traditional household as a unit of two children and two parents, also including grandparents in many households. The image of the average family is changing, however and becoming more diversified. At least 30% of the Japanese population live alone, only 40% of couples have children, and at least 25% of residences house elderly persons (over 65-years-old). As you approach the center of Tokyo, the trend is more apparent. In Chiyoda-ward, located at the center of Tokyo, the number of children has dwindled so drastically recently that elementary schools are consolidating to accommodate a much smaller student body.

Centralization and Decentralization

While the Tokyo metropolitan area covers only 0.6% of the land in Japan, it also holds 12% of the country's offices and 15% of its professional workers. The office density of the three central wards and Shinjuku ward together is higher than on Manhattan Island in New York City. Such a concentration was caused by the following factors:

- The location of the central government. In Japan, the central government manages all aspects of private companies. When trading or starting new businesses, companies usually seek advice and approval from the government. Since most government offices are situated in the center of Tokyo, it is advantageous to the businesses to be in the close proximity to that area for purposes of communication.
- Concentration resulted in more concentration. The location of many businesses downtown required that the close proximity of services to accommodate both the companies and their employees. From photographic services to restaurants, the bustling office district is a lucrative market for the service industry. The downtown location of these services has led to further clustering of businesses in the city center.
- Total location cost. Within the center of Tokyo, the cost of informational services is very low because companies and offices are so near to one another. Also, compared to the U.S.A., few business trips are required and even though the office floor space is extremely costly, the total expenditure is still lower than in the peripheral areas.

Although there are advantages to having businesses concentrated in one area, the employees of downtown companies must endure long commutes because real estate and consumer prices are much higher in the city center than in the outer wards. The local government also must impose higher income taxes because the businesses activities downtown require more investment for the maintenance of roads, the water supply and sewage treatment.

Since the end of the 1980s, however, the central government has started to develop new business centers around Tokyo. At the same time, the Tokyo metropolitan government also started the development of subcenters within Tokyo, including the Shinjuku area, where Tokyo's government recently moved its City Hall. Due to these efforts, residents anticipated that the situation of Tokyo's center would be eased and that land prices and the rent of office space would decrease. Yet, for fear of a sudden drop in economic growth, the trend toward decentralization has slowed down recently.

Still, the diet and central government discuss the permanent placement of government functions to another area outside of the center city. The focus has shifted, however, from the need to decentralize to the need for security during disasters, such as large-scale earthquakes, e.g. in Kobe.

In conclusion, as Japanese society ages, the typical family unit changes from the conventional family of parents and children, to also include the single or few people household. Additionally, people nowadays face long commutes between their residence and workplace; the short commute of the former days has become a part of the past. It is necessary to think about a social support system to accommodate the recent modifications in the family structure. The target of social support should gradually change from the conventional family only to many kinds of households including single and aged single households. At the same time, the local government needs to redefine new services or further cooperation of services since vast numbers of people spend most of the day time outside their residential region.

CRIME IN JAPAN

Outlook

Japan is known to be a safe country. The crime rate in Japan is about 15% of that of the U.S.A. The difference in murder rates is just as dramatic; in 1992, 23,760 cases were reported in the U.S.A. compared to 1275 in Japan. However, the Japanese cannot feel as secure anymore because the murder rate increases every year in Japan. After World War II, crime rates decreased until 1973, when they started to rise gradually. As the number of criminal cases has increased, the rate of arrests has dropped from 59.9% in 1973 to 36.5% in 1992. While the population has grown rapidly in those years, the crime rate has grown with it (Fig. I-E4). The crime rate has increased for every 100,000 people from 1100

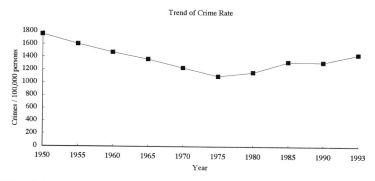

Figure I-E4 Crime rate trends in Japan

in 1975 to 1400 in 1993. Thus, it is no wonder that 87.3% of the Japanese believe crime will further increase in the future.

Police

The foundation of the modern police system in Japan was established in 1874. The Tokyo Police Agency, as it came to be known, was under the auspices of the Prime Minister's office. Currently, there are about 260,000 police officers, which is about one for every 560 citizens. The police system is divided into the following two categories:

- The National Police Agency: This agency, comprising 7600 police officials, is under the guidance of the National Public Safety Commission of the Prime Minister's office. It is the national organization responsible for guiding, supervising, and coordinating the prefectural police. The palace guards are also under the jurisdiction of the National Police Agency.
- The Prefectural Police: The prefecture is one of the units in Japan's police organization. The total number of prefectural police officers is 251,000.

The police officers do not only investigate crimes and arrest criminals, but as part of the "*Koban*," or police box, they are also required to maintain safety and security in a given region. In Japan, there are 6500 *Koban* in various cities. *Kobans* are places to hold lost and found items, educate citizens in traffic safety, offer police consultation and advice, and lastly, the *Koban*'s officers also patrol surrounding neighborhoods. 74% of criminal arrests in 1993 were made by police officers from *Kobans* or police substations in the countryside.

Robberies

Among all crimes, theft or robbery made up 87.6% of the criminal acts in 1992 and this rate has been rising rapidly (Table I-E4). There were 1.2 million cases in 1972, but recently the numbers have exceeded 1.5 million. Almost 50% are thefts of vehicles, that is both cars and bicycles; cases of break-ins comprise only

Table I-E4 Breakdown of crime

	1972	1992	1992–1972	Percentage (1992)
Heinous crimes	8,711	6,338	−2,373	0.36
Violent	53,460	36,630	−16,830	2.10
Theft	1,257,354	1,525,863	268,509	87.57
Fraud	102,125	63,121	−39,004	3.62
Moral, offenses	7,236	6,201	−1,035	0.36
Others	34,342	104,213	69,871	5.98
Total	1,463,228	1,742,366	279,138	100.00

Source: Crime White Paper by National Police Agency.

15% or 225,000 cases. The robbers commonly sought out only expensive goods, although these very cases could well have resulted in murder if the robbery attempts had been interrupted by the unsuspecting homeowners. Thus, measures that will prevent or reduce the number of thefts are direly needed.

In most cases, the thieves enter the houses through unlocked doors or windows. Nineteen percent of all thieves were found to seek out the small windows of the kitchen or toilet. Since these windows are so small in Japanese homes, people often forget to lock them. As a first step to thwarting robberies, it is still important to educate people in Japan about locking windows and doors.

At the same time, 30% of thieves entered a building by simply breaking through glass windows. One solution has been to turn to private security companies for an automated break-in alarm. Once alerted by an emergency signal sent by alarm sensors on all windows and doors, these companies will arrive within ten minutes after receiving the signal. This is only one measure to prevent break-ins and although it is expensive, costing more then 10,000 yen a month, there is no guarantee that the robbery attempt will be aborted.

History of Theft Prevention

After World War II, the approach to theft prevention changed in three aspects. The basic objective was and still is, to arrest the criminals responsible. If all criminals were caught, the threat of imprisonment would be sufficient deterrence. Therefore, in order to increase the rate of arrests, stronger efforts on the side of the police are needed. At the same time, new procedures and strategies would also be necessary to deter people from following their criminal impulses.

The first stage, between 1960 and 1970, was accompanied by a movement to tighten the bonds of the community. Due to the potency of social propriety and family honor, the community has historically been considered more effective at preventing crimes than legal measures. In 1961, the Crime Prevention Union was established in small community units throughout Japan, which marked the beginning of community based deterrence efforts. The movement was very effective at fighting crime in Japan within its first decade of existence. However, with the explosion of the urban population and the accompanying breakdown of the small neighborhood bonds, the Crime Prevention Unions lost their bases of support.

The second stage, between 1970 and 1980, relied on the new innovations to outwit the thieves. Due to advances in technology and remarkable economic growth, more people were able to purchase a wider variety of equipment and devices to protect their homes. In 1980, the police agency announced the development of the "standard key." It was the first official standardization of keys to prevent thefts and break-ins. The use of a common key for the main entrance to a home or apartment building became very popular at this time. However, despite the benefits to the safety and security of homes, people were often inconvenienced by carrying around extra numbers of keys.

The third stage, between 1980 and today, relies on an environmental design. In 1979, the police department conducted research to establish crime prevention standards in urban areas. A report entitled *Crime Prevention Road Model* was published in 1981 by the Aichi Prefecture and evolved from previous research. The concept is based on designing roads wide enough to offer a broad view of the streets and hinges on community support to keep the roads safe. The features of the road design affected both the physical and social aspects of the neighborhood. The police are still gaining from the benefits of the new road measure, but basic criminal awareness and deterrence procedures still need to be developed.

The strategy for security is changing. In the first stage it was focused on the area of management where people used to walk around town at night on patrol. In the second stage, supported by the improvement of the technology and growth of the economy, people started to use several devices for safety, items such as double-key locks, interphones, security systems, and so on. Such devices were small crime prevention methods on a "Point" (equipment) basis. The stages of the history of theft prevention show an evolution from area management, then moving to safety equipment, and finally to the interaction between both the area and equipment. These two factors will influence the implementation of appropriate design measures particularly in housing developments and condominiums.

In short, the design of the physical urban environment and the community is very crucial in the prevention of crime, especially to theft, in modern Japan. Although the concept of crime prevention through urban building and/or design is not common in Japan, a collaboration between such a design system and the conventional Japanese police system would be very effective. Also, as described in the previous chapter, single households on the rise and these people commonly do not have strong ties with the neighborhood. Since little communication and interaction with neighbors is thought of as a merit of city life, it also is a reason for an increase in the chance of crime. In former times, all households joined the *Chonai-kai*, for a block-based community party and crime prevention. People knew each other on the block and recognized a stranger when one was present. In modern Japanese cities, people began to think that the community protection should be handled by the governement and that the block festival was a nuisance. In addition to a need for community crime prevention, the formation of small-scale community life is also necessary as a means of crime prevention. A smaller community would increase the likelihood of community-based crime prevention.

DISASTER PLANNING

Future Outlook

Japan's history is interspersed with attacks of natural disasters. Since the Edo era, many record-setting fires, earthquakes, typhoons, and floods have hit Japan.

The history of natural disaster prevention is closely linked to the history of disasters. Even in modern times, Japan still suffers natural catastrophes, like the Sanriku-Haruka-oki earthquake (May 3, 1933), the Tsunami tidal wave at Okushiri (July 12, 1995), and the Great Hanshin earthquake (1995). For this reason, the management and control of the cities and landscape is one of the most important issues to concern the central government.

Background on the Establishment of Disaster Planning

The first major postwar revision of measures to deal with earthquakes in Japan (and particularly Tokyo) were formulated in the wake of the Niigata Earthquake of 1964. Tokyo had revealed its vulnerability to major earthquakes ever since the Great Kanto earthquake of 1923, but this danger had been ignored in the military buildup that followed almost immediately. The formation of any set of policy measures remained impossible in the aftermath of World War II, as Japan still lacked the appropriate administrative, fiscal, and organizational capacity and resources. Since the mid-1950s, however, rapid economic growth was accompanied by improvements in these areas, as well as the emergence of a number of urban problems. These included a shift in jobs from the countryside to the cities that led to a concentration of the urban population and resulted in pollution and worsening living conditions. It was at this time that a set of policies were established to respond to major earthquakes. The destruction of modern buildings in the 1971 San Fernando Earthquake in California provided useful lessons that provoked the national government of Japan to pursue a national disaster policy. In apprehension of a comparable quake in Japan, the Council for Natural Disaster Planning created an outline of disaster prevention guidelines for large cities.

The worst natural disasters to befall Japan in the early postwar years were caused by typhoons. Following Typhoon Catherine in 1947 and Typhoon Jane in 1950 (both given women's names in U.S. military fashion), storms such as Typhoon Doya-maru in 1954 and Typhoon Karino-gawa in 1958 brought major damage on an almost annual basis. The ravaged postwar landscape and the still inadequate administrative structures could not alleviate the destruction to the property of the residents and the loss of many lives. The Ise-warn Typhoon of 1959 left 4700 people dead. Although reinforcement of the rivers and improvements to the ports were needed to protect Japan against typhoons, insufficient preventive measures were taken or were often taken too late. It was the Ise-war Typhoon that finally prompted the enactment of the Basic Disaster Prevention Law in 1961, which outlined a comprehensive plan of preventative measures and a clear system of responsibilities for dealing with a disaster. Measures to respond to earthquake damage were also formulated based on this law. To ensure that government funding was available after destructive disasters, the Major Disaster Law was passed in 1962, and the National Land Agency was formed in 1974 as the central government's office charged with handling natural calamities.

Japan's policy for diminishing damage from earthquakes has been accompanied by research into quake forecasting. The Earthquake Forecasting Group, established in 1960, drew up an Earthquake Forecasting, Status and Assessment Plan in 1962 that was adopted both as an earthquake prevention policy and a national government program. With the 1968 Tokachi-oki Earthquake, public pressure for earthquake forecasting intensified, leading to the establishment of an Earthquake Forecasting Association in the following year. The role of this most recent research organization was to collect and perform comprehensive analysis of earthquake forecasting data under the National Earthquake Plan.

In the interim thirty years, research into earthquake forecasting has advanced greatly and a variety of measures have been adopted to expand government assistance to victims of disasters. A review of these changes offers the ability to identify problems and issues with the disaster prevention methods now implemented in Japan and Tokyo in particular. These problems are specifically seen when examining the damage assessments that are essential in the preparation of disaster plans.

History of Earthquake Predictions

Any potential damage assessments must be based on predictions regarding the scale and epicenter of a particular earthquake. The following quotation sheds a clear light on the issues concerning earthquake forecasting in Japan: "The National Land Agency held disaster prevention drills based on the expectation of a level 6 intensity reading of an earthquake in the southern Kanto and Tokai regions."[5]

Although the drills are held nationwide on September 1 each year, on the anniversary of the Great Kanto earthquake, it seems strange to see two separate quakes (southern Kanto and Tokai) mentioned together. In the early stages of earthquake forecasting from 1965–1975, it was not possible to make specific predictions about earthquakes and plans were usually based on the expectation of a recurrence of the 1923 Great Kanto earthquake. Subsequently, progress was made in seismology and a Special Measures Law for Major Earthquakes (based on forecasting) was passed in 1978 after the Japanese Association of Seismology identified the possible location of a large earthquake in Suruga Bay in 1976, the epicenter of the Tokai earthquake. This law targeted the study and monitoring of the faults to forecast any future earthquakes and to devise a system of warning announcements. Some 170 towns and cities in six prefectures were designated as Special Strengthened Earthquake Prevention Areas and received training in disaster prevention techniques funded by the national government. The law assumed that damage in the Tokyo area would be slight, but the need for a plan based on the recurrence of an earthquake of the same magnitude as the Great Kanto earthquake prevailed.

In 1988, the Central Disaster Prevention Association published a report by a group of experts organized to investigate policies to minimize the impact of earthquakes. This report suggested three possible scenarios of the damage to expect from an earthquake in the southern Kanto area: (1) the quake would hit at Sagami Trough, similarly to the Great Kanto earthquake; (2) the quake might strike southern Kanto directly, similarly to the Ansei Edo earthquake of 1855; and (3) the quake would occur off the coast of the Boso Peninsula. In 1992, a comprehensive plan to deal with the possibility of an earthquake striking the southern Kanto area directly was published and included special measures.

In the ten years since 1965, Japan's disaster prevention policies have advanced from being nonexistent to identifying the clear danger of the Tokai earthquake. Even though the danger to the Kanto area from this earthquake was regarded as slight, there was no alternative but to continue working with the assumption that the Great Kanto earthquake might recur in the Tokyo area. By the mid-1980s, a number of potentially dangerous earthquakes had been identified and voices have recently risen for the need to warn residents of the danger of imminent earthquakes.

Death Toll Predictions

Damage assessment is at the core of the preparation of disaster prevention plans and policies. Assessment exercises have now been performed three times by the Tokyo Metropolitan government. Table I-E5 clearly shows the differences between the first and subsequent assumptions about injuries. While the first reports suggested a death toll of 560,000 people, subsequent exercises reduced that figure by several tens of thousands each. The reason for this decline is that the majority of earthquake related deaths are thought to be caused by the ensuing fires. Later forecasts have proposed that fatalities would occur over a wider geographical range. The latest estimates included those killed in trains, cars, by falling items, and water damage, but fire continues to be the major cause of deaths in Japan after earthquakes (Table I-E5).

Reports on fires are governed by two factors: the number of individual blazes (including the number of fire sites) and the speed of the fire. Fire fatalities are commonly caused by failed attempts at escape. While the average human's walking pace is 2–4 km/hr, fire can only move at 200–300 m/h, suggesting that those who die are not overtaken by isolated fires but rather are trapped by multiple blazes. For this reason, the most important information in estimating deaths has been to predict how many fires will occur in how many locations.

Table I-E5 Estimation of death by earthquake

	1965	1975	1985
Number of deaths	560,000	36,000	15,000

Source: The Tokyo Fire Department.

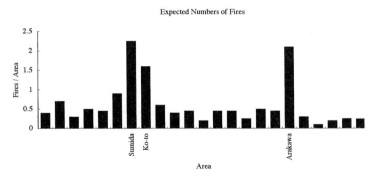

Figure I-E5 Expected number of fires in Japan (Tokyo Fire Department 1992)

The initial forecast of 560,000 victims was expected to be concentrated in the low-lying eastern areas of Koto, Sumida, and Arakawa wards, while the number of individual fires was also expected to be concentrated in the same areas (Fig. I-E5). The second assessment switched to a forecast of multiple casualties in the higher western areas of Setagaya, Suginami, and Shinagawa wards. The decline in expected casualties in the eastern part of the city was the result of the designation of the Shirahige-East area in Sumida ward as a Disaster Prevention Center in the mid-1960s and the adoption of measures stressing the importance of policies in the western part, including fireproofing buildings, clearly marking escape routes to refuge sites, and requiring open spaces between buildings in the mid-1970s.

Does this mean that the eastern part of the city has become safer in the last thirty years while the western areas have become less so? The changes in estimated casualties have resulted not from any changes in the state of the city itself but in the methods used to assess the damage.

Changes in the Method of Disaster Assessment

Assessments of a disaster's scale can be based on the number of fires and the speed at which the blaze spreads. In terms of the number of fires, the assessment method has changed over the years, as described below:

- Stage 1: 1965–1975.[6] Based on documents from the time of the Great Kanto earthquake, a method was employed that relied on the ratio of collapsed buildings in a certain area measured in meters and the fire outbreak ratio. This method is based on statistical regression analysis models. Although the figures are ultimately adjusted depending upon social factors appropriate to each period of time, the employed method basically rests on the features and lessons of the 1923 Kanto earthquake. The depth depends on the period, but the regression model parameters are based on the Great Kanto earthquake.

The result is that today's forecast of damage and fatalities reveal a similar pattern since in 1923, the majority of fires were concentrated in the eastern part of the city.

- Stage 2: From 1975.[7] Full-scale preparations of disaster prevention policies have been developed in the same way as earthquake predictions. Hence research has progressed and new methods have been applied to calculate the assumed number of fires that would result from an earthquake. Research by the Tokyo Fire Department combined an assessment of the fire risk of various structures and equipment with the number of such risks in each region to estimate the danger of fire in each area. It then predicted the total number of fires separately to distribute the risk among each area. Comparative levels of danger were calculated from an analysis of eighty-one types of equipment, with points allocated in relation to these levels and with adjustments made for the structure and use of the building in question. The research found no major differences in the susceptibility of these living environments or levels to fire and no marked differences among regions. The researchers concluded, therefore, that there was no regional variation in the fire outbreak ratio (Fig. I-E6).

As a result, there is no longer any significant difference in the risk level of each region based upon its fire outbreak ratio. This means that there is no difference in the weight accorded to disaster prevention policies. Instead, a different index is needed as the basis for disaster levels which would calculate the speed of the spreading of fire.

Fire Spread

The most frequently used technique for estimating the spread of fire in Japan is known as the Hamada method. It is popular because it takes the wind speed and building density into account. When applied to contemporary urban areas, the structure of the buildings is also factored in the Hamada method which was

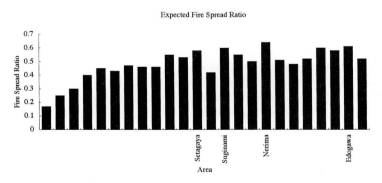

Figure I-E6 Expected fire spread ratio in Japan

developed during World War II as a means of planning urban air defenses. In a research report issued by the Tokyo Fire Department in 1942, the relation between the speed of the wind and the spread of fires was determined to be a principal factor in the deaths of people, as well as the determination of a construction policy in building. A policy to convert the wooden structures into nonflammable buildings is effective to prevent the spread of fires. The Hamada method disclosed that the wind speed has an overwhelmingly greater influence on the speed of fire spread than building density and is expected to maintain the conventional characteristics. The method is very popular among researchers because it allows for adjustments for the building's structure and makes wind speed and building structure the dominant elements in evaluating the speed of fire spread in today's cities. In contrast, wind strength is a natural condition that is independent of regional variation, meaning that, in fact, the evaluation of a region's danger levels in terms of the speed of fire spread is reached according to the structure of the building (the ratio of wooden and non-wooden structures in a city). An analysis of the composition of buildings in Tokyo's ward areas shows that the three central wards (Chiyoda, Chuo, Minato) are the safest, while Setagaya, Suginami, Shinagawa, and others suffer a higher level of danger.

While determining the probability of disasters by fire outbreak density does not produce any differentials, introducing the speed of fire spread as a factor reveals that the areas with the highest concentration of wooden structures are exposed to a higher level of danger. This basis for evaluation has not changed since the mid-1970s, which leads to the conclusion that the Tamanote area on the western side of the city is now thought to be more exposed to danger than before and is the focus of current disaster prevention efforts.

Damage assessments therefore are based on a number of assumptions and multiple evaluation models. However, these models alone do not offer a complete answer and have changed in light of the research over the years. Therefore, we would not have a fully reliable method of forecasting a disaster ensuing an earthquake if one was to hit Tokyo today. As disaster prevention policies are based on extremely logical earthquake assumptions and damage assessments are applied to large Japanese cities (Tokyo, Kanagawa, etc.), they appear to be scientific and accurate at first sight. Yet, the uncertainty of an actual earthquake and the complexity of our society means that these models must be considered only as one possible case study. As time passes, researchers easily forget the above characteristics of the method and people easily reach the wrong understanding of the results which often leads to the setting of unsuitable policies. A line should be drawn between disaster policies and damage assessments in order to reach the most plausible outcome.

Lessons from the Hanshin Earthquake

The Central Disaster Prevention Council published a report in 1992 on the various policies to deal with a direct hit earthquake in the Southern Kanto region.

The earthquake of the Hanshin and Awaji areas in January 1994 struck just as specific policies were being enacted. This disaster offers innumerable lessons to policymakers. The death toll reached over 5500 deaths, expressways were destroyed, wooden structures were obliterated, and mid-to-high rise buildings toppled easily. However, the nature of the damage caused by a direct-strike earthquake and the most appropriate policies to adopt are still being studied, although experts now have a much deeper understanding of the challenges they face.

In particular, while an earthquake of the magnitude of the Great Kanto earthquake will affect a wide region, a direct-strike quake usually impacts on a smaller scale, and the damage to the region is different. As a result, some areas remain unaffected on the perimeter of the disaster zone and can play a major role in providing relief and assistance. The development of a system for assistance between areas was therefore indicated in the 1992 report. The relief structure is multifaceted and diverse; with similar cooperation between government bodies, a system of assistance could evolve between the government and the private sector. One lesson that has been sufficiently drawn from the Hanshin earthquake is that any plan that originates on a drafting board is of no use in actual cases. Further, absolutely no mutual adjustments have been made to disaster prevention plans. Since such plans are drawn up by individual local governments, they are ideally suited to a particular district and do not take the plans created by neighboring areas into account. It should be possible for a prefectural authority to achieve a plan between the cities, towns and villages within its borders, and even though such cooperation does appear to take place, there is not enough consistency in the realization of disaster prevention plans between prefectures. This means that a system of mutual support based on current conditions cannot be expected to be successful. While great efforts are being made to implement more specific disaster prevention plans through practical training, there is a need for a coordinated plan and policies, at least within the Tokyo region.

Traditionally, Japanese were considered a people who took care of the family and lived with an extended family. Currently, the typical, conventional family size is decreasing and the single or nuclear family is becoming more common. There is a need to change existing policies to not only accommodate the conventional family, but also a wide variety of family sizes. Such policy changes are common in urban planning, housing supply, healthcare, and other facets of community life.

NOTES

1. Jetro, 1994. *US and Japan*. Jetro.
2. Asahi, S. 1994. *Japan Almanac 1994*. Asahi Shmbun, October.
3. Guko, Y. *et al.*, 1992. *Urban Planning Words Dictionary*. Shokokusya.
4. Iwanami, 1992. *Kojien Dictionary*. Iwanami.

5. Asahi, S. 1994. *Japan Almanac 1994.* Asahi shimbun.
6. Tokyo Metropolitan Government. 1967. *Study of Fire Damage by a Major Earthquake.* Tokyo.
7. Tokyo Fire Department. 1992. *Report on the Distribution of Fires by Cause and Fire Risk in the Tokyo Area.* Tokyo.

BIBLIOGRAPHY

1. Agency of National Police. 1994. *White Paper of Police.* Tokyo: Ministry of Finance.
2. Kato, A. 1993. *Urban Planning.* n.p.: Kyoritsu Publishing.
3. Ministry of Law. 1993. *White Paper of Crime.* Tokyo: Ministry of Finance.
4. Tokyo Fire Department. 1992. *Report on the Distribution of Fires by Cause and Fire Risk in the Tokyo Area.* n.p.: Tokyo.
5. Yano, I., *et al*. 1993. *Nippon a Chartered Survey of Japan.* n.p.: Kokusei-sya.

Part II

Japanese Urban Environment and Human Comfort

Introduction

A   Present and Future State of Urban Warming in Tokyo Metropolitan Area
Takeo S. Saitoh

B   Contributions of Sea Breeze and Natural Coverings to Urban Thermal Environment: The Case of Fukuoka City
Tadahisa Katayama

C   Thermal Comfort in Japanese Urban Spaces
Ken-Ichi Kimura

D   Changes in Tokyo's Waterfront Environment
Nobuyuki Takahashi

E   Efficient Energy Use in Japanese Cities
Keisuke Hanaki, Toshiaki Ichinose

Part II: Introduction

Part II of this book discusses another dimension of the Japanese city, the environmental issue in its general perspective, and in further elaboration, all five chapters discuss the human comfort. This comfort on the cityscale is perceived from different perspectives by the authors; these are the thermal performance and consequently human comfort (or discomfort) from the macro (Saitoh chapter), macro/micro (Katayama chapter) and micro as related to the indoor comfort (Kimura chapter). The discussion elaborates the macroclimate and landscape as a source for the residents' comfort (cooling) and leisure (Takahashi chapter), and finally, energy efficiency as a source for human wellbeing (Hanaki chapter). Seemingly dealing with concrete issues such as thermal performance within the Japanese urban environment, the chapters are particularly targeting urban dwellers who constitute the center of attention within the urban complex. More accurately, the discussion focuses on two types of environments and the resulting interaction between them.

The urban physical environment consists of two types, one is the natural, which comprises different facets of nature within which the climate is one fraction and the other is the artificial environment, which embraces all physical forms and functions. The design and performance quality of the latter (residence and high-rise buildings, green open space, leisure spaces, industry, transportation, and similar land-uses) are ultimately viewed by the users as most important since they are the beneficiary. The writers' analyses and their explanations should significantly improve the performance quality of these land-uses. The discussion focuses on the interaction between these two given environments, the natural and artificial as well as the micro and macroclimates created within the city as an outcome of their reciprocality. The resulting thermal performance influences, in the long run, the urban dwellers' comfort and is perceived as an important factor in their urban environment. The discussion also embraces two other related subjects; one focuses on the waterfront as a contributing element to human comfort and leisure within the city, the other on energy as a daily necessity within the operation of the city as the dynamic environment of its residents. All in all, the common denominator of the five chapters is the human being. The related issues are undeniably important contributors to the urban environment and, in turn, to the perception and comfort of the urban dwellers.

The focal point of Professor Takeo Saitoh's chapter discusses Japan's urban atmosphere from an environmental perspective. Like other major cities of the world, Japanese cities are now, more than ever before, influenced by their own activities (production of heat, pollution, etc.). In addition, the global system introduces its contribution in determining the overall deteriorating air quality of each and all urban metropolises of the world. Saitoh's second argument is that this international and also regional tendency influences the health and the comfort of the urban dwellers and will continue to do so in the future. Undoubtedly, the entire world, with urban Japan among the leading nations, is heading towards further accelerated physical growth and ever-increasing industrial activities of the metropolitan areas. For Japan, this is an even more pressing issue because of the overall limited availability of land as it is physically located on isolated islands which allow only limited potential expansion. Saitoh's article is similar to Katayama's in that it examines the causes and possible cures for the modern phenomenon of urban warming. Unless the problem of urban warming is taken seriously and we find remedies for it (see Katayam'sa suggestions), it is likely that the phenomenon will claim lives in the near future, if it is not already doing so.

Professor Tadahisa Katayama, as well as Professor Ken-Ichi Kimura, challenge the issue from another aspect of the urban environment, the microclimate and its contribution to human comfort. Other than urban warming and heat production in the city, Katayama reveals the impact of modern building materials on the Japanese urban city's thermal performance. While old building materials created a counterforce to urban warming, modern construction materials reflect the heat and thus increase the overall temperature in the microcosm of the city. In modern times, it has become necessary to find alternative solutions to this problem. Vegetation, ponds, and other water reservoirs as well as the natural sea breeze act as a natural climate control which successfully battles urban warming by creating so-called "cool islands" within metropolitan areas.

Discussing the indoor and outdoor ambient mircoclimate, Professor Kimura's chapter is mainly concerned with human comfort in Japanese metropolises. In the past, the indigenous Japanese house design was and still is focused on this same issue and was designed to suit the local building materials as well as the climate: ventilation, light, sunshine, orientation, and most importantly, privacy, as well as the creation of a cozy and intimate atmosphere. Professor Kimura, in keeping with this tradition, introduces an analysis of the indoor/outdoor microclimate and human comfort.

Part II discusses and analyzes the entire range of the climate in the artificial environment from the macro- to the microscape. Dr. Nobryuki Takahashi introduces his field research findings on the diminishment of traditional canals and other waterfronts which were "flavoring" Tokyo with a traditional country-side touch. While the city of Tokyo rapidly expanded with the Industrial Revolution, its vast historical network of waterways (rivers and canals) disappeared. Waterways were transformed into roads and land for commercial use which had a deep impact upon the city's environment. As a consequence, agricultural land-use decreased and the cityscape was altered greatly. Recent tendencies of reclaiming land have included the project of Tokyo Bay, which will be converted into dry land within the next decade by filling up the bay with city waste. Tokyo is not alone with this development; all major Japanese metropolises have undergone the same, drastic changes with an accelerated urbanization which takes the toll of the rapid destruction of the cities' unique waterways.

Seemingly, the subject of the waterfront does not relate to the previous discussion of Part II, yet it has three implications interrelated with human comfort. First, the water bodies in Tokyo contribute considerably to the cooling of the air in the streets and, therefore, have an impact on the city's thermal performance in the summertime. Second, the lanes of the canals themselves constitute openings within the city and consequently support the ventilation of air that is so needed throughout the humid summer, especially in Tokyo. Third, the canals themselves, because of their scale, penetrate the city deeply with an element of the countryside. Now these canals have been replaced with highways which, in turn, introduce even more pollution to the city.

In his discussion of efficient energy use, Professor Keisuke Hanaki associates this issue to the modern Japanese cities. As the energy consumption increases with the degree of urbanization, the urban planner must examine alternatives to traditional energy resources. Hanaki introduces waste incineration (the by-product methane gas as an important source of energy) as a solution for the severe problems with which Japanese metropolitan areas struggle: The waste accumulation and environmental pollution associated with traditional landfills as well as the conventional production of energy. The sound distribution and recovery of energy (from solid waste, sewage, and river water) is one of the challenges the future poses to the Japanese urban planner whose responsibility it is to combine environmentally sound energy technology with large-scale urban planning. Hanaki sees a correlation between the increase of waste disposal and energy consumption. Therefore, energy production improvement through waste incineration would lead to the improvement of the Japanese urban environment.

To synthesize the discussion of Part II, the human quest for an ever-increasing standard of living in modern times with urban dwellers in the national majority, will demand more and more urban outdoor comfort to be increased along with the thermal macro and microperformance in the cities. Here, the analysis offered by the five writers will be meaningful if it will be translated into effective tools and guidelines for urban designers, architects, policy makers, and other influential leaders, when an urban design master plan is in preparation. On the other hand, the international community needs to cooperate better in presenting its guidelines and be effective in their implementation. At the same time, international and regional legislation should make those tools and guidelines more effective. In any case, the major solutions to the urban thermal performance will continue to be within the hands of the regional and local urban designers and policy makers. Finally, the urban dwellers as the main users of the urban environment, who seek better human comfort, constitute a crucial part of the national and local political power structure and should participate and use their influence effectively.

G.S.G.

A The Present and Future State of Urban Warming in the Tokyo Metropolitan area

Takeo S. Saitoh

INTRODUCTION

Rapid progress in industrialization and urbanization has resulted in the concentration of economic growth and social functions in urban areas. Unplanned and hasty urbanization in modern cities, especially during the three decades following World War II, has caused environmental problems including an increase in energy consumption, an alteration of the local climate (urban warming), and higher amounts of air pollution.

Urban warming is a phenomenon typical of urban areas. Some of its characteristics are a consistent rise in the temperature in an urban atmosphere, an increase in air pollutants like NO_x and SO_x, and a decrease in relative humidity.[1] This phenomenon is known as an urban heat island and has been analyzed using both observational and numerical models.

This paper presents the results of field observations and three-dimensional equations to simulate urban warming in the Tokyo metropolitan area. Included in this study is an investigation of the effects of automobile exhaust and heat emission from buildings on the quality and temperature of air in the Tokyo area. The discussion also presents the results of a three-dimensional simulation of urban warming in Tokyo at present and projected to the year 2031. Lastly, the outcome of a simulation is introduced which studies the effects planting trees and increasing the urban vegetation would have as a means to counteract the effects of the urban heat island.

The three-dimensional governing equations, used as parameters for the urban atmospheric boundary layer, were formulated through the use of a vorticity–velocity vector potential method of measurement. Particular attention was paid to the representation of the buoyancy term in an equation of motion in the vertical direction, thereby describing the crossover and stratification effects of urban warming near the ground surface.

From the viewpoint of numerical stability and suitability of a simulation of an urban heat island, the vorticity–velocity potential method is the most suitable means of calculation. In this study, a numerical prediction was made on the future of the urban atmosphere based on the assumption that the anthropogenic energy release were increased up to five times from its present value. Assessments of the impact of the anthropogenic energy consumption on the urban atmospheric boundary layer are extremely important in the study of global warming. First, survey data was collected on the energy consumption in the Tokyo metropolitan area. Next, three-dimensional simulations were carried out using this data. The simulation results were then compared with the field observation data for the surface temperature. When the energy consumption rate in the model increased five times from its present rate, proportional predictions were made of future rates of urban warming. The data suggests that, if the present consumption rate is maintained, the urban warming rate can be computed for the year 2031 based on this fivefold increase. This present simulation method of calculating the urban warming rate will contribute to the preservation of the urban and global environment.

NUMERICAL MODEL AND THREE-DIMENSIONAL SIMULATION

The numerical model can be classified into two types, a mechanical model and an energy balance model. The former emphasizes flow characteristics and the latter is concerned with the difference between the energy balance of urban and suburban areas. Since Ebenezer Howard reported on the urban heat island phenomenon in London in 1918, there have been a number of observational and numerical studies based on two-dimensional modeling.[2-7] Recently, however, three-dimensional studies have been presented which were made possible by the great advancement of the supercomputer.[8-13]

The three-dimensional governing equations of the urban atmospheric boundary layer were reached using the vorticity–velocity vector potential method. Most of the previous models which have been employed in heat island simulation are based on the hydrostatic equilibrium assumption, an equation of motion in the z direction and simplified by considering the pressure and buoyancy terms. In these models, the equation of motion in the vertical direction is simplified into a balanced equation between the buoyancy term, or the number which is important in buoyancy driven flow, and the pressure term. Consequently, no exact characteristics can be obtained of the crossover or stratification effects which are key aspects of the urban boundary layer. Contrary to this, the present analysis pays particular attention to the equation of motion in the vertical direction. The researchers employed full Navier–Stokes (an equation of motion named after its two founders) and energy equations with a buoyancy term which has been used in the field of heat transfer. This calculation made it possible to describe the crossover and stratification effects near the ground surface for the first time.

AUTOMOBILES AND AMBIENT TEMPERATURE

The author has previously studied field observation data which reported on the degree to which automobiles and energy utilization altered the ambient temperature in Sendai City during the past decade.[14] In this chapter, the author will examine the results of field observations on the ambient temperature in the Tokyo metropolitan area on the day of March 14, 1992.

A clear night was chosen for the observation. To collect data, three automobiles were equipped with measuring devices. Figure II-A1 shows an observation car with an observation probe and Figure II-A2 presents the observation points and the highway locations. The total number of observation points was 359. Figure II-A3 clarifies the results of the early morning field observation (3:00 a.m.–5:30 a.m.) on March 14, 1992. In fact, the ambient temperature fluctuated slightly during this measurement time. We were able to mark the temperature difference by comparing the discrepancy between the initial and final records at the same location. These results showed that the atmospheric temperature in urban areas such as Otemachi, Shinagawa and Shinjuku was as high as 12.5°C while it was only 6.0°C in suburban areas like Koganei and Urawa. The lowest temperature (4.5°C) was found in Hachioji located in the western part of Tokyo. The heat island intensity measured by this observation reached 8.0°C, which is 4.0°C higher than that reported by Kawamura in 1976.[15]

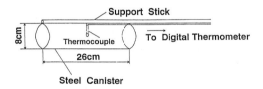

Observation probe

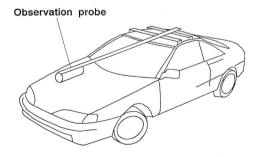

Observation car

Figure II-A1 Observation car with probe

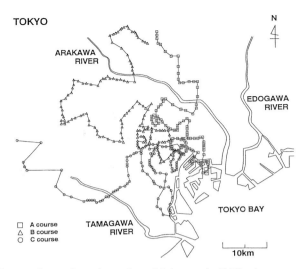

Figure II-A2 Observation points along three highways (solid line)

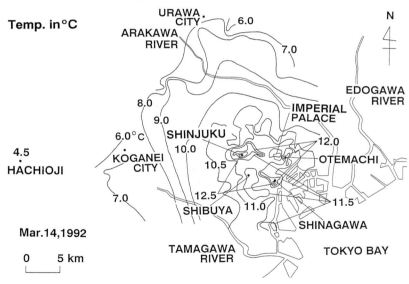

Figure II-A3 Field observation result for ambient temperature in the Tokyo metropolitan area (March 14, 1992)

THREE-DIMENSIONAL SIMULATION OF URBAN WARMING

Heat Island Model

A physical model and coordinate system for an urban atmospheric boundary layer are illustrated in Figure II-A4. The three-dimensional simulation was

FREE ATMOSPHERE

CONSTANT TEMPERATURE REGION

Figure II-A4 Physical model and coordinate system for the urban atmospheric boundary layer

performed for a planetary boundary layer over the surface and soil layer underground. Table II-A1 shows the conditions and numerical values used for the present simulation performed for the Tokyo metropolitan area.

The multilateral element method (MEM) was used as a numerical scheme. In MEM, the triangular or quadrilateral element is used like the finite element method (FEM). The finer mesh divisions were used for regions with high heat emissions (e.g. Otemachi, Shinjuku, Shibuya, and Ikebukuro). Figure II-A5 presents an anthropogenic heat emission map for the Tokyo metro area around 8:00 p.m. during the summer. The data recorded included the consumption of electricity, natural gas, gasoline, petroleum oil, and heating oil. The maximum energy density exceeded 120 W/m^2 in the Otemachi area. The actual energy release included the anthropogenic heat emission as well as the heat storage effect of buildings and structures caused by solar radiation during the daytime.

Table II-A1 Conditions and numerical values used for the present simulation

City for simulation	Tokyo
Computation area	40 km × 40 km in the horizontal Imperial palace is located at the center
Height of planetary boundary layer	3 km
Thickness soil layer	0.5 m
Time	Summer night and Winter midnight
Intensity of general current	none
Anthropogenic heat emission	Measured emission data in Tokyo (1991)

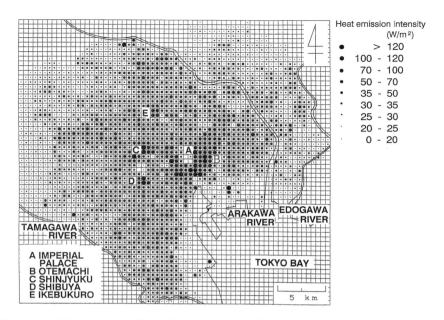

Figure II-A5 Isotherms at the surface (summer, 8:00 p.m.)

Governing Equations

For the analysis, the following assumptions and restrictions were made:

• Boussinesq's approximation is valid. Boussinesq's approximation is the state
  when the density variation is considered only for the buoyancy term.
• Surface roughness is not accounted for.

Three-dimensional vorticity and velocity vector potentials were introduced to
transform the three-dimensional Navier–Stokes and energy equations into a
simple equation system without pressure terms (e.g. $\delta p/\delta z$). This formulation has
been used in the field of fluid mechanics.[16] The governing equations consisted
of three-dimensional vorticity, energy, continuity equations, and equations of the
relationship between vector and velocity potentials. This model is superior in
numerical stability to the velocity–pressure method used in past analyses and can
also easily account for the buoyancy effect. Thus, this formulation was quite
suitable and effective for the simulation of the urban heat island. Employing the
above-mentioned vorticity–velocity vector potential equation, the governing
equations are described below.

$$\frac{\delta\theta}{\delta t} + (v\cdot\nabla)\omega - (\omega\cdot\nabla)v = [(\nabla K)\cdot\nabla + K\nabla^2]\omega\left\{-B_0\frac{\delta\theta}{\delta y},\ B_0\frac{\delta\theta}{\delta x},\ 0\right\} \qquad (1)$$

$$\frac{\delta\theta}{\delta t} + (v \cdot \nabla)\theta = [(\nabla K) \cdot \nabla + K\nabla^2]\theta \tag{2}$$

$$\nabla^2\Gamma = -\omega \tag{3}$$

$$v = \nabla \times \Gamma \tag{4}$$

Here, ω, Γ and v are vorticity vector, vector potential, and velocity vector defined as

$$\omega = (\xi, \eta, \zeta), \qquad \Gamma = (\Gamma_x, \Gamma_y, \Gamma_z), \qquad v = (u, v, \omega) \tag{5}$$

Operators ∇, ∇, and ∇^2 are defined as

$$\nabla = \nabla = \frac{\delta}{\delta x}i + \frac{\delta}{\delta y}j + \frac{\delta}{\delta z}k \tag{6}$$

$$\nabla^2 = \frac{\delta^2}{\delta x^2} + \frac{\delta^2}{\delta y^2} + \frac{\delta^2}{\delta z^2} \tag{7}$$

Relationship between potential temperature θ and temperature T is

$$\theta = \frac{T}{\pi} \tag{8}$$

The previous equation have been made dimensionless in terms of the next variables

$$t^+ = \frac{a}{H^2}t, \ (x^+, y^+, z^+) + \frac{1}{H}(x, y, z) \ (\xi^+, \eta^+, \zeta^+) + \frac{H^2}{a}(\xi, \eta, \zeta),$$

$$(\Gamma_x^+, \Gamma_y^+, \Gamma_z^+) + \frac{1}{a}(\Gamma_x, \Gamma_y, \Gamma^z), \ (u^+, v^+, w^+) + \frac{H}{a}(u, v, w), \ \theta^+ = \frac{\theta_h - \theta}{\theta_h - \theta_c} \tag{9}$$

The boundary conditions for the above equations are written as

$$x = 0, L: \quad \xi = 0, \qquad \eta = \frac{\delta u}{\delta z}, \qquad \zeta = -\frac{\delta u}{\delta y}, \quad \frac{\delta\theta}{\delta x} = 0.$$

$$y = 0, L: \quad \xi = -\frac{\delta v}{\delta z}, \qquad \eta = 0, \qquad \zeta = -\frac{\delta v}{\delta x}, \quad \frac{\delta\theta}{\delta y} = 0.$$

$$z = 0, H: \quad \xi = -\frac{\delta v}{\delta z}, \qquad \eta = \frac{\delta u}{\delta z}, \qquad \zeta = 0. \tag{10}$$

$$\theta = \text{transient } (z = 0) \qquad \theta = \text{constant } (z + H)$$

Energy Balance at the Surface

In this analysis, the next transient energy balance equation at the surface was used

$$\rho_s C_s h_s \frac{\delta T}{\delta t} Q_a + Q_e + HG + S + H \tag{11}$$

Here, Q_a is the radiation from the atmosphere, Q_e is the infrared radiation from the earth's surface, HG is the anthropogenic heat emission (Fig. II-A5), S is the heat conducted to the soil layer and H is the turbulent heat exchange between the earth's surface and atmosphere. Solar radiation is negligible at night and latent heat transport is omitted in these simulations. In most of the past studies, the steady energy balance equation at the earth's surface has been used to determine the temperature distribution at the surface prior to the numerical simulation. This result was used as the boundary condition. However, the most important information is not the special profile but the temperature distribution near the surface. Therefore, to get the exact isotherms, one should employ a dynamic energy balance equation (11). This is an important feature of the present study.

Simulation Results and Discussion

Results of the Simulation for Tokyo on a Summer Night

Figure II-A6 shows the earth's surface temperature at 8:00 p.m. at the end of July. In the rural area, the earth's surface temperature dropped to 24°C due to the sky radiation effect. At the same time, at Otemachi, an urban area, the earth's surface temperature increased to 32°C which was 8°C higher than in the rural area. This temperature difference was apparently caused by the effects of anthropogenic heat emission. Figure II-A7 displays the horizontal velocity vectors at height $z = 120$ m. Even at $z = 120$ m, the heat island intensity amounted to 5°C. Figure II-A8 presents the vertical velocity vectors at $x = 21.9$ km. These results indicate that an urban thermal plume is formed right above the urban area due to a characteristic flow pattern produced by the heat island. Figure II-A9 shows the vertical temperature profile. In the urban area, the height of the mixing layer reached 1 km. Formation of the crossover phenomenon was recognized at about $z = 1$ km, thereby confirming the accuracy of the present calculation.

Results of the Simulation for Tokyo on a Winter Night

According to the computed results for the earth's surface temperature at 3:00 a.m. in December, the earth's surface temperature in the rural area was 3.5°C due to the sky radiation effect. At Otemachi, where there is a significant anthropogenic heat emission effect, the earth's temperature rose to 10°C and the heat island intensity reached 7.3°C. Figure II-A10 reveals a vertical temperature profile. It is clearly shown in the figure that the ground inversion layer is formed in the rural area due to the sky radiation effect.

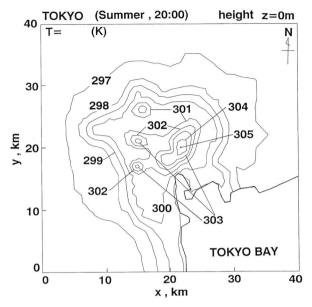

Figure II-A6 Horizontal velocity vectors at vertical height $z = 120$ m (summer, 8:00 p.m.)

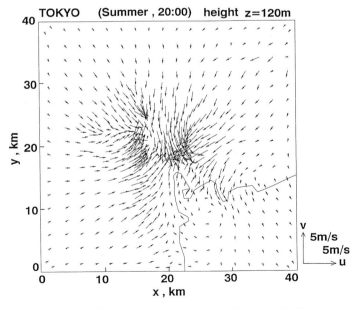

Figure II-A7 Vertical velocity vectors at $x = 21.9$ km (summer, 8:00 p.m.)

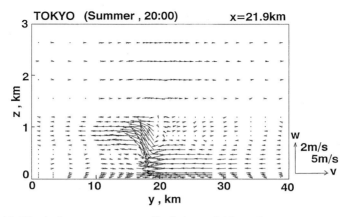

Figure II-A8 Vertical temperature profile (winter, 3:00 a.m.)

Prediction of Urban Warming in Tokyo around the Year 2030

The population rate of the Tokyo metropolitan area has remained constant since the 1980s. However, as the floor area of buildings has consistently been growing, the total energy consumption, including electricity, gas, and petroleum oil, has also been increasing. This trend is caused by technological advancements in office equipment such as the computer, copy machine, and other telecommunication

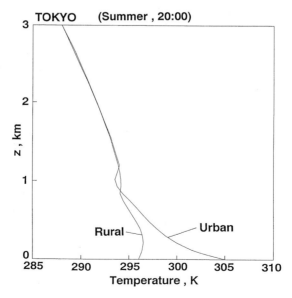

Figure II-A9 Prediction of energy release into urban atmosphere in the Tokyo metropolitan area

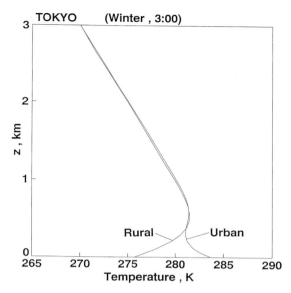

Figure II-A10 A physical model and coordinate system of a tree

devices. It is anticipated that the volumetric density of the high-rise building will increase further in the future which will result in an even greater increase in the energy consumption rate per unit area.

The heat storage effect of the building itself is another important element which generates heat emission into the urban atmosphere. Daytime solar radiation is absorbed and stored in the building, from where the stored heat is slowly released into the urban atmosphere. As a consequence, these two factors will also contribute to future urban warming to a great extent. An overly hot environment needs efficient air-conditioning, which, in turn, consumes a great deal of energy. This circulation forms the so-called "vicious cycle," which results in the steep increase of the energy output into the atmosphere, as shown in Figure II-A11. This energy release consists of the heat storage effect, increment of cooling load, and pure energy consumption.

Initially, the author tried to predict urban warming in Tokyo up to the year 2060, when the carbon dioxide concentration would be doubled. However, as presented in Figure II-A11, heat release measurements for the year 2060 seem to be unrealistic and unreliable at the present time. Instead, the year 2031 was selected, which is the point when the emission rate will be five times its present value. Figure II-A12 presents the simulation result when the anthropogenic energy consumption rate will have increased up to five times (in the year of 2031). In this case, the maximum temperature increments are 11.5°C in Otemachi where in late July, 2031 the temperature at 6:00 p.m. will exceed 43°C. This drastic temperature increase indicates that in the future, the air quality in Tokyo will reach uncomfortable levels.

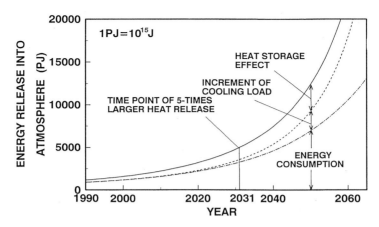

Figure II-A11 Ambient temperature with effect of tree planting in present-day Tokyo

COOLING EFFECT BY TREE PLANTING AND VEGETATION

The principal causes of the formation of a heat island are the presence of extensive surface materials such as concrete and black asphalt, and the anthropogenic heat emissions from residences and factories that are prominent in urban areas. Research has proven that one of the most effective and natural ways of mitigating urban warming generated from these synthetic materials is the planting of trees and other vegetation.

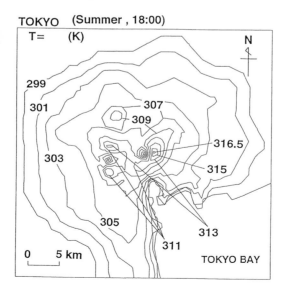

Figure II-A12 Isotherms in Tokyo (year 2030) when the anthropogenic heat emission is increased five times larger than the present value

Trees and vegetation feed on carbon dioxide in the atmosphere, but they also filter particle matter and remove some toxic pollutants from the air by absorbing carbon dioxide into their leaves through photosynthesis. Water from the roots is drawn up through the cambium layer (the thin, moist layer just under the bark) to the leaves, where it evaporates as a gaseous form into the air. This conversion from water to gas absorbs tremendous amounts of heat, thus cooling the hot city air. In addition, trees and vegetation provide shade by covering the barren concrete and asphalt with a canopy of leaves. Planting trees and vegetation, therefore, can significantly counteract the build-up of heat by cooling the air and drawing less energy from overworked powerplants which have already reached their capacity.[17] Further, the presence of trees in a city can obstruct breezes and reduce wind tunnel effects which normally whirl dust in the air.

Considering the benefits derived from vegetation in combating pollution and conserving energy, creating large urban parks is a good first step towards a healthier environment. If a commitment is made to implement this recommendation extensively, the trees and vegetation will curb urban warming in the Tokyo metropolitan area.

Governing Equations

A physical model and coordinate system for the green area illustrated in Figure II-A13 shows the distribution of the vegetation density. The governing equations are described below.

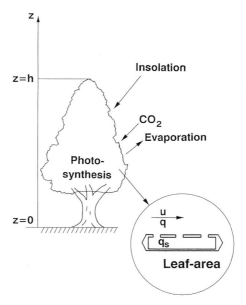

Figure II-A13 A physical model and coordinate system of a tree

The energy balance equation at the roof surface is

$$R(z) + L\uparrow(z) + L\downarrow(z) = 2\varepsilon\sigma T_L^4(z) + H(z) + LE(z) \tag{12}$$

Momentum equation, energy equation, humidity diffusion equation are

$$\frac{\delta u}{\delta t} = \frac{\delta}{\delta z}\left(K_M \frac{\delta u}{\delta z}\right) - c_m s(z) u^2(z) \tag{13}$$

$$\frac{\delta T}{\delta t} = \frac{\delta}{\delta z}\left(K_T \frac{\delta T}{\delta z}\right) k_T u(z) s(z)(T(z) - T_L(z)) \tag{14}$$

$$\frac{\delta q}{\delta t} = \frac{\delta}{\delta z}\left(K_H \frac{\delta q}{\delta z}\right) k_H u(z) s(z)(q(z) - q_s(z)) \tag{15}$$

Diffusion coefficients are given by

$$K_M(z) = l^2(z)\frac{\delta u}{\delta z} = K_T(z) = K_H(z) \tag{16}$$

here

$$l^2(z) = \frac{2k^3}{c_m s(z)} \qquad (z \le h) \tag{17}$$

$$l(z) = kz \tag{18}$$

Simulation Results

According to a survey of the land-use map in the Tokyo metropolitan area in 1987, it would be possible to designate 47% of the whole area to parks and green areas. This is the maximum ratio of green coverage to asphalt and cement. Figure II-A14 shows the simulated result that exists today with the present state of tree planting. Figure II-A15 projects the simulated result of the effect of maximum tree planting by the year 2031. By comparing these results with Figure II-A12, it appears that the planting of trees would decrease the ambient temperature in Otemachi by 4.5°C in the year 2031.

The value of planting trees and other vegetation cannot be underestimated in the effort to reduce the ambient temperature of urban areas. However, the drastic curtailing of energy consumption in cities is of even greater importance in winning this battle against urban warming. Two thirds of the energy presently used could be reduced in the future megalopolis.

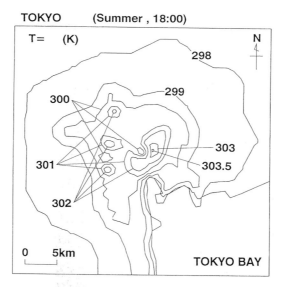

Figure II-A14 Ambient temperature with effect of tree planting in present-day Tokyo

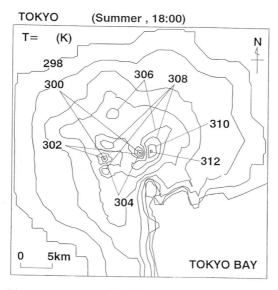

Figure II-A15 Ambient temperature with effect of tree planting in the year 2031 in Tokyo (green coverage ratio: 47%)

CONCLUSION

In this paper, the author presented a three-dimensional model for an urban heat island using the three-dimensional vorticity–velocity vector potential method.

From the present study, the following conclusions may be drawn.

- The field observation made of the earth's surface temperature using automobiles was carried out in Tokyo on a winter night. The scanning observations revealed that the atmospheric temperature was as high as 12.5°C at Otemachi, a heat island in the center of Tokyo, and 4.5°C at Hachioji in the suburbs of Tokyo. The heat island intensity amounted to 8.0°C.
- A three-dimensional simulation was performed for an urban heat island. The model is based on a three-dimensional vorticity–velocity vector potential method. The predictions of this model were verified when the ground inversion layer in the rural area and the crossover effect were clearly recognized.
- The proposed model is effective for the numerical simulation of an urban heat island because its numerical stability is superior and able to be calculated for a long time period. Furthermore, it can easily compute the buoyancy effect.
- A numerical prediction prognosticates that the maximum temperature increment would be 11.5°C by the year 2031 if the anthropogenic energy consumption increased five times from its present value in downtown Tokyo.
- In the near future, the problem of urban warming will become an even more pressing issue than global warming since the growth rate of urban warming is significantly greater.

For this reason, urban warming could be fatal to humans unless it is resolved in the near future.

One of the effective countermeasures to reduce urban heat island phenomena is the borehole/solar seasonal energy storage system for high-rise buildings. This storage system also accumulates solar energy and excess heat from air conditioners. Due to the restrictions on using ground water, the excess heat from air conditioners in the hot summer months is presently emitted into the urban ambient air through the condenser and cooling tower, which results in the heat island formation.

At the same time, the boiler is usually used in winter as a heating system. The boiler emits SO_x, NO_x, and other pollutant gases. It also generates CO_2, which is not desirable as it contributes to global warming, as mentioned before. One feature of this system is its ability to combine the solar energies (solar thermal and photovoltaic) and the excess heat from air conditioners to store these energy reserves in underground borehole units. During the winter season, the accumulated energy will be recovered from the borehole units and used as a heat source for space and water heating. Accordingly, cold energy amassed in winter and stored in the borehole unit would be used as a cold energy source in the summer. Photovoltaic cells located on the south area of the wall would provide electric power for auxiliary equipment including circulating pumps and compressors. By introducing the above borehole system, 70–80% of energy expended in high rise buildings can be saved.

ACKNOWLEDGMENTS

The author extends his sincere thanks to the Computer Center of Tohoku University for use of the Supercomputer SX-2 and TSS. Thanks also go to Mr. Hidetoshi Hoshi, graduate student, who made great efforts to prepare this article.

NOTES

1. Takeo, S. and Hisada, T. 1991. Reduction of air pollution by changing the pollutant emission from the vehicles. *IECEC 1991* 6: 126–131.
2. Howard, E. 1918. *Climate of London Deduced from Meteorological Observations.* London: W. Phillips, vol. 1.
3. Nkerdirm, L. C. 1976. Dynamics of an urban temperature field: a case study. *J. Appl. Meteor.* 15: 818–828.
4. Bornstein, R. D. 1968. Observation of the urban heat island effect in New York city. *J. Appl. Meteor.* 7: 575–582.
5. Oke, T. R. and Fuggle, R. F. 1972. Comparison of urban/rural corner and net radiation at night. *Boundary Layer Meteor.* 2: 290–308.
6. Estoque, M. A. and Bhumralka, C. M. 1970. A method for solving the planetary boundary layer equations. *Boundary Layer Meteor.* 1: 169–194.
7. Bornstein, R. D. 1975. Two-dimensional URBMET urban boundary layer model. *J. Appl. Meteor.* 14: 1459–1477.
8. Saitoh, T. and Endo, K. 1983. Three-dimensional simulation of urban heat island. *Trans. of JSME* 49, no. 445: 2035–2040.
9. Saitoh, T. and Fukuda, K. 1985. Three-dimensional simulation of urban heat island. *Bull. JSME* 28: 101–107.
10. Saitoh, T. and Yamashita, K. 1986. Three-dimensional simulation of urban fire. *The 26th National Combustion Symp. of Japan* 24: 118–120.
11. Saitoh, T. and Yamada, I. 1990. Effect of energy consumption on urban atmosphere. *IECEC* 4: 155–160.
12. Saitoh, T. and Shimada, T. 1991. Three-dimensional mechanism of urban heat island. *National Heat Transfer Symp. of Japan*, 192–193.
13. Saitoh, T. 1992. Supercomputing for urban warming in Tokyo metropolitan area. *U.S.–Japan Supercomputing Conference*, Yokohama, 1–6.
14. Saitoh, T. and Shimada, T. 1990. Relationship between urban warming and energy consumption. *Autumn Annual Meeting of JSME.*
15. Kawamura, T. 1977. Heat island. *Sci. Amer.* 94–101.
16. Aziz, K. and Hellums, J. D. 1976. Numerical solution of the three-dimensional equation of motion for laminar convection. *Phys. Fluids* 10: 314–324.
17. Gray, M. and Young, S. 1992. Growing greener cities. *Living Planet.*

BIBLIOGRAPHY

1. Aziz, K. and Hellums, J. D. 1976. Numerical solution of the three-dimensional equation of motion for laminar convection. *Phys. Fluids* 10: 314–324.
2. Bornstein, R. D. 1975. Two-dimensional URBMET urban boundary layer model. *J. Appl. Meteor.* 14: 1459–1477.
3. Bornstein, R. D. 1968. Observation of the urban heat island effect in New York city. *J. Appl. Meteor.* 7.
4. Estoque, M. A. and Bhumralkar, C. M. 1970. A method for solving the planetary boundary layer equations. *Bound. Layer Meteor.* 1.
5. Howard, E. 1918. *Climate of London Deduced from Meteorological Observations,* vol. 1. London: W. Phillips.
6. Kawamura, T. 1977. Heat island. *Sci. Amer.*
7. Gray, M. and Young, S. 1992. Growing greener cities. *Living Planet.*
8. Nkerdirm, L. C. 1976. Dynamics of an urban temperature field: a case study. *J. Appl. Meteor.* 15.
9. Oke, T. R. and Fuggle, R. F. 1972. Comparison of urban/rural corner and net radiation at night. *Bound. Layer Meteor.* 2.
10. Saitoh, T. 1992. Supercomputing for urban warming in Tokyo metropolitan area. *U.S.–Japan Supercomputing Conference*, Yokohama, 1–6.
11. Saitoh, T. and Endo, K. 1983. Three-dimensional simulation of urban heat island. *Trans. JSME* 49: 445.
12. Saitoh, T. and Fukuda, K. 1985. Three-dimensional simulation of urban heat island. *Bull. JSME* 28.
13. Saitoh, T. and Yamashita, K. 1986. Three-dimensional simulation of urban fire. *The 26th National Combustion Symposium of Japan*, 24.
14. Saitoh, T. and Yamada, I. 1990. Effect of energy consumption on urban atmosphere. *Intersociety Energy Conversion Engineering Conference*, 4.
15. Saitoh, T. and Shimada, T. 1990. Relationship between urban warming and energy consumption. *Autumn Annual Meeting of Japan Society of Mechanical Engineers*.
16. Saitoh, T. and Hisada, T. 1991. Reduction of air pollution by changing the pollutant emission from the vehicles. *Intersoc. Energy Conv. Engin. Conference*, 6.
17. Saitoh, T. and Shimada, T. 1991. Three-dimensional mechanism of urban heat island. *Nat. Heat Transfer Symp. Japan*, 1–6.

B The Contribution of Sea Breeze and Natural Coverings to Urban Thermal Environment: The Case of Fukuoka City

Tadahisa Katayama

INTRODUCTION

Urbanization is characterized by an abundance of artificial building materials such as cement, glass, steel, pavement, and other heat-absorbing and reflecting materials which increase solar absorption as well as heat storage and decrease evaporation for cooling effects. Urban structures take the form of crowded high-rise buildings and paved ground and were developed as a solution to urban growth. They replaced many natural elements like water, open space, and vegetation which cool the air and increase the humidity. Urbanization also occurred without an overall comprehensive urban plan and its structures disrupted existing airflow patterns and their resulting cooling effects. This urban configuration creates "heat islands," a phenomenon of the urban climate used to describe the climatic environment of built-up areas, whereby the density of artificial materials and a sparsity of natural materials create a condition of hotter, less comfortable daytime and nighttime temperatures. Thus, urbanization changes the temperature and airflow patterns of local climates into an "urban climate" characterized by an increased air temperature and a decreased humidity, air circulation, wind speed etc. It would be close to impossible to control the outdoor thermal environment mechanically. Therefore, we have to study cooling effects of natural resources, such as the sea breeze, water, vegetation, etc.

The sea breeze is prevalent in the summer daytime and becomes a natural cooling resource to improve the urban thermal environment. There are few studies to examine its cooling effect quantitatively from a viewpoint of the urban climate; however, many urban areas are not located on the coast. In inland urban areas, water and vegetation are the most readily available natural resources for modifying the climate. Although there are many kinds of studies conducted on the surface temperature and thermal balance of vegetation, the relations between the quantity of vegetation and air temperature have not been sufficiently examined. There is also little information on the thermal effect of water on the surrounding urban environment. This study presents the research results of thermal cooling created by natural resources. First, extensive measurements of air temperature in an urban area were conducted to clarify the effects of wind and land-use pattern on the air temperature distribution. Next, not only air temperature but also surface temperature of pavement, water, and leaves were measured to obtain cooling effects of rivers, lakes, and green areas quantitatively in the summer. Finally, a number of guidelines for the urban designers were drawn to improve the thermal environment in an urban area.

WARMING TRENDS OF THE URBAN CLIMATE

The air temperature in major cities such as Tokyo has become warmer in recent years.[1] This urban warming has also occurred even in smaller, local cities. For example, for the last fifty years, the annual average urban air temperature has been increasing each year in Fukuoka City and in Tokyo, where the area and the population ratio are about one fourth and one ninth, respectively.[2] According to data of 1992, the area of Fukuoka City is about 300 km^2 and its population is circa 1.2 million people. In Tokyo, those same measurements are about 1200 km^2 and 11 million, respectively. The air temperature in Tokyo has been gradually increasing since 1910 and in Fukuoka, since 1920. Since 1950, five years after World War II, this trend has become more perceptible with a significant increase in air temperature while the relative humidity has been decreasing noticably (Fig. II-B1).[3] The warming trends since 1950 are the result of unplanned and rapid urbanization in order to restore the war-stricken area. The remarkable decrease of the relative humidity results from the increase in air temperature and decrease of water vapor caused by the disappearance of much of the area of nonartificial ground surface which includes water and vegetation.

The overall effects of some urbanization elements in Fukuoka City, such as the increase in population, energy consumption, and the area of densely inhabited district (DID), etc. have been less problematic than those in Tokyo, but the percentage increase of each element has been higher in Fukuoka City than in

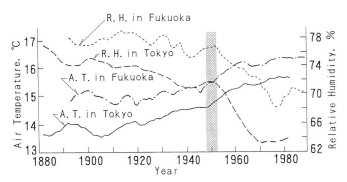

Figure II-B1 Long-term trends of annual averaged air temperature and relative humidity in Fukuoka City and Tokyo metropolitan area

Table II-B1 Changes of urbanization elements in Fukuoka City compared with those in the Tokyo metropolitan area

Elements (unit)	Fukuoka (1960–1985)	Tokyo (1959–1986)
Population of DID ($\times 10^4$ person)	52.9 > 107.7 (+166%)	861.4 > 859.1 (0%)
Area of DID (km^2)	50.2 > 133.6 (+166%)	469.5 > 607.6 (+29%)
Net area of dwellings (km^2)	12.6 > 51.3 (+307%)	99.3 > 301.2 (+203%)
Energy consumption ($\times 10^6$ Gcal)	–	108.8 > 220.6 (+103%)
Electric power supply (GWh)	520.2 > 3468 (+566%)	–

DID: densely inhabited district where the density of population is more than 4000 persons/km^2.

Tokyo.[4] Particularly, in the densely inhabited district in Fukuoka City, the population has doubled, while the population in the innercity core of Tokyo has decreased (Table II-B1). The population growth in Fukuoka City created an immediate need for expanding utilities and services, and the resulting construction took place without any consideration of the climatic effects of this expansion. Growth and concentration of population in an urban area cause increased urbanization and a great amount of energy consumption. Urbanization changes the heat balance at the ground surface and a greater amount of excess heat generated by the energy of the large quantity of cooling and heating units is exhausted into the atmosphere. This directly increases the air temperature.

FUKUOKA CITY LAND-USE CLASSIFICATION

The increase in temperature in an urban area is mainly attributed to the covering of the ground surface with artificial instead of natural materials. Therefore, studying the distribution of land-use for natural elements in the city is the most important source of data for the analysis of the urban thermal environment. Currently, the land-use in many major cities can be quantified in the database of the National Land-Use Digital Information. The land-use is mapped in a grid of cells of 100 m^2 and the ratio of the surface area of artificial structures to natural resources is calculated.

In 1990, the comparisons of ratios of the distribution of land-use in Fukuoka City between 1976 and 1990 were examined in relation to the distribution of air temperature (Fig. II-B2). The original data consisted of nineteen categories of land-use. These were later consolidated into five categories as follows: (1) high-rise buildings; (2) low-use buildings; (3) trunk roads, open spaces, sea shore; (4) trees, cultivated fields; and (5) lake, rivers, and sea (Fig. II-B2). The findings show that of the 800 cells mapped according to land-uses, bare ground, sea shore, the number of low-use buildings has decreased while high-rise buildings have increased.

Since Fukuoka City faces Hakata Bay, it was developed as the largest commercial city on Kyushu Island. Accompanying this growth, an area of high-rise

Categories of land-use
Trees, Cultivated fields
Trunk roads, Open spaces, Sea shore
High-rise buildings
Low-use buildings
Lake, Rivers, Sea

Figure II-B2 Distribution of land-use classified into five categories in Fukuoka City

buildings developed along the coastline from NE to SW along with a private railway which runs inland through the center of the city. Structurally and for the sake of our discussion, the Fukuoka City environment forms three zones: the high-rise buildings in the center, surrounded closely by low-use buildings, and both are enclosed by a zone of vegetation and cultivated fields. The urban development interfered with the cooling effects of vegetation on the buildings.

CORRELATION OF AIR TEMPERATURE AND LAND-USE PATTERN

There have already been many measurements of the air temperature distribution in Tokyo, but similar studies in Fukuoka City have not been conducted until recently.[3] Measurements of the air temperature distribution in Fukuoka City in the summer were taken in the early morning and throughout the day to examine the effects of the wind on the land-use.

Air temperatures were measured by thermistor thermometers with sunshades mounted on eight cars. The measurement points were selected on the roads where the test cars would drive and distributed uniformly over the city. About 120 measurement points were passed by each car within two hours. The total number of measurement points was 958. The difference of air temperatures occurred by a time lag between measurements points, with the base temperature reading taken at 6:00 a.m. and the high point reading taken at 2:00 p.m. The assumption was made that the change of air temperature at each measurement point was similar to that at the Fukuoka Observatory. Numbers on the contour lines (isothermal lines) are the normalized air temperatures calculated by the following equations:

$$(t_i - \langle t \rangle)/^6$$

where $\langle t \rangle = (1/n)\Sigma t_i$, $^6 = \{(1/n)\Sigma(t_i - \langle t \rangle)^2\}^{1/2}$, where t_i = corrected value of air temperature at point i, n = number of measurement points (958) (Fig. II-B3).

The wind vectors at eight points are represented by arrows. In the early morning, wind speeds at these eight points are less than 2 or 3 m/s and the contour lines of normalized air temperature correspond well to the distribution of land-use. That is, the air temperature in the city center, where the prevailing ratio of high-rise buildings is the highest, is contrasted to that in the suburbs with varied vegetation where the air temperature is lowest.[5] On the other hand, in the daytime, wind blows from the sea inland at a speed of about 4–8 m/s and the high air temperature region moves from the center of the built-up area to the leeward side of land (Fig. II-B3).

The investigation area was divided into a 1 km^2 grid and the measured values of air temperature were averaged for each cell. The ratios of the natural covering such as trees, cultivated fields, and surfaces of bodies of water were calculated in each cell of the 1 km^2 grid to examine the relation to the air temperature.[5] The experiment proved that the larger the natural covering, the lower the air temperature. The absolute values of both the correlation and regression coefficients in the calm early morning are larger than those in the daytime when the sea breeze develops (Fig. II-B4). This tendency reverses when the ratios of the artificial covering such as building and pavement are increased.[6]

Cooling Effects of the Sea Breeze

The distribution pattern of air temperature over the city is influenced greatly by the wind as was previously mentioned. Part of the monitoring system of the atmospheric contamination concentration in Fukuoka City includes six observation stations for wind speed and wind direction, and these were used to study the effects of the sea breeze over the city. The observation stations ranged in

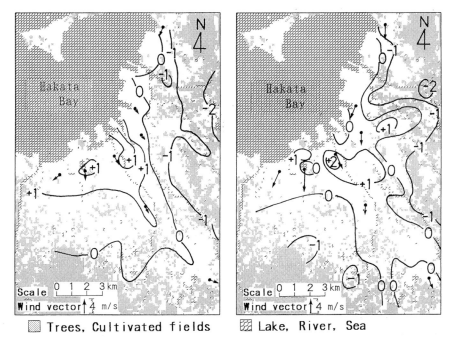

Trees, Cultivated fields ░   Lake, River, Sea ▨

Figure II-B3 Distributions of wind vector and normalized air temperature during summer

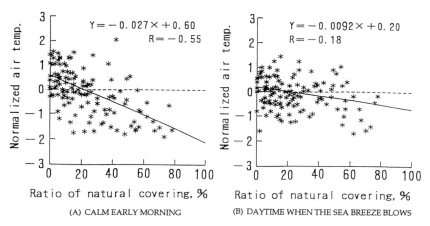

Figure II-B4 Relation between natural covering ratio and averaged air temperature in the cell of 1 km² grid

height from 18 to 43 m above ground. Data on the wind was gathered for two years at six stations and analyzed to obtain the windroses and the frequency distributions of wind speed. The results confirmed that the sea–land breeze develops well across the city and wind speed in the daytime is stronger than that in the night (Fig. II-B5). At each point, wind blows from the sea in the daytime and the prevailing wind direction is approximately perpendicular to the coast line.[7]

Because of its thermal convection, the sea breeze is a natural cooling resource that mitigates the rise of air temperature in summer. Wind direction, wind speed and air temperature were observed simultaneously at three stations located in an almost straight line to the direction of the sea breeze.[8] The distances from the coast line to the three stations were about 1 km, 5 km and 11 km, respectively. Propeller-type anemometers and vanes were used to observe wind speed and wind direction. Air temperatures were measured by thermocouples with

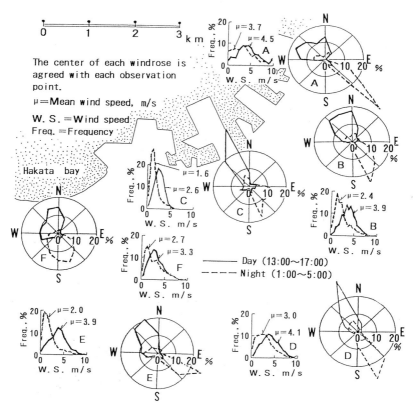

Figure II-B5 Windroses and wind velocity and frequency distributions during the day and night for two years

sunshades at 10 min intervals. The days selected for the analysis were limited to days with a noticeable sea–land breeze, with changes in wind direction and wind speed, and solar radiation. The criteria for the selection were the following: (1) no precipitation during the daytime; (2) an obvious shift in the wind direction from landside to seaside in the daytime; (3) a wind speed that was neither too strong nor too weak; (4) and, a reasonable degree of solar radiation. A sample of the diurnal fluctuations of wind vector and air temperature indicated that the wind shift from the land breeze to the sea breeze was delayed at the landward station. The air temperature fell noticeably when the wind shifted from the land to the sea breeze and remained low while the sea breeze was blowing. The temperature was lowest at the station nearest to the coastline, where the wind shifted from the land to the sea breeze faster and where the air temperature was lower than at the other two landward stations (Fig. II-B6).

The various diagrams in Figure II-B6 (B) indicate the diurnal fluctuations of wind vector and air temperature. The three upper figures show the diurnal fluctuations of wind direction and wind speed at Points P1, P2, and P3, respectively. The wind direction and speed were measured every 10 min simultaneously at the three points. The direction of each arrow marks the wind direction and the length of each arrow the wind speed. The abscissas of the four drawings in (B) show time; daytime is about 6:00 a.m.–6:00 p.m. in summer. The other hours (12:00 midnight–6:00 a.m., 18:00 p.m.–12:00 midnight) denote nighttime. For

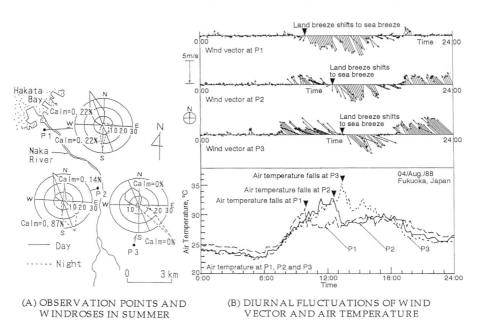

(A) OBSERVATION POINTS AND
WINDROSES IN SUMMER

(B) DIURNAL FLUCTUATIONS OF WIND
VECTOR AND AIR TEMPERATURE

Figure II-B6 Relation between diurnal fluctuation of wind vector and that of air temperature related to the distance from seashore

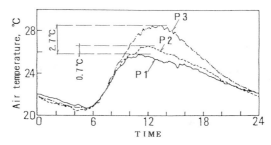

Figure II-B7 Comparison of diurnal fluctuations of averaged air temperature for sea-land breeze days in relation to the distances from the seashore

example, in the uppermost figure, wind shifts from land breeze (very weak) to sea breeze at 9:40 a.m. at P1. The air temperature at P1 (dashed line in the figure in the lowest place) falls at 9:40 a.m. The air temperature at P2 (solid line) and at P3 (dotted line) also falls at the time when the wind shifts.

The results of the diurnal fluctuations of the averaged air temperatures for the sea–land breeze days during four months from June to September (a total of 33 days according to the previously stated criteria) indicate that the air temperature at the seaward station was lower during the daytime. However, there was little difference among the air temperature data at the three stations in the nighttime (Fig. II-B7).

Cooling Effects of a River and a Pond

Most of the seaside cities in Japan have rivers which usually run almost perpendicular to the coastline and empty into the sea. These rivers are an open space through which sea breezes blow freely. Thus, rivers in built-up seaside cities support the cooling effects of the sea breeze and improve their nearby thermal environment.

The Naka River, which is about 100 m wide, flows from SE to NW through the downtown area of Fukuoka City (Fig. II-B6). One of the streets with a width of about 40 m runs nearly parallel to the Naka River for circa 400 m. The street crosses the river at a point about 6 km upstream from its estuary. Measurement points were set at the coast and the cross-point. Between these points, there were four additional pairs of measurement sites, each on the river and on the street (Fig. II-B8).

The measurements were carried out on a clear day in August.[9] In the northern Kyushu District, a typically good day in summer is clear both in the morning and in the evening but is sometimes cloudy during the daytime. When the sea breeze blew, the wind speed increased more over the river area than the street. The wind direction above the river remained fairly constant while the wind direction over the street became irregular and was strongly influenced by various obstacles, such as buildings and road-side trees. When the intensity of the sea breeze increased, the air temperature above the river was clearly lower than above the street in

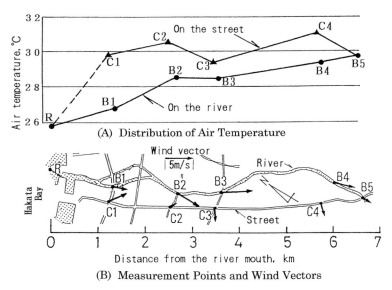

(A) Distribution of Air Temperature

(B) Measurement Points and Wind Vectors

Figure II-B8 Comparison of the distributions of air temperature and wind vector along the river with those along the street at 1:00 p.m. on a clear summer day. C1 through C4 are the measurement points above the street and B1 through B4 are the measurement points above the river. The air temperature at C2 on the street is 30.6°C. This is higher than that at B2 on the river (28.5°C). The pair of two measurements points on the street and on the river (C1 and B1, C3 and B3, C4 and B4) has the same relationship as the air temperature at C2 and B2.

the daytime. The air temperature above the river increased gradually from the estuary upstream. This indicates that the cooler air of the sea breeze blown inland above the river mixes with the nearby hot air and cools the neighboring area of the river. The surface temperature of the river water was lower than that of the asphalt pavement of the street during the daytime. Water surface temperatures fluctuated between 21–27°C, as opposed to the surface temperatures of the pavement in the sunshine, which ranged from 25°C at 7:00 a.m. to 60°C at 1:00 p.m. According to the amount of solar radiation. The difference in surface temperature between the water and pavement reached more than 25°C at about 1:00 p.m. (Fig. II-B9).

The water surface of a pond also remains at a lower temperature similar to that of a river. Fukuoka is one of the rare cities that has a park in its center with a large pond of about 240,000 m^2 which was constructed about sixty years ago. The measurement results of the pond's water surface temperature on a clear summer day were almost constant at 29°C throughout the day, while the surface temperatures of the asphalt pavement and the bare ground ranged from 25–56°C and from 28–47°C, respectively. In the early morning, the surface temperature of the pond water is roughly the same as the asphalt pavement and the bare

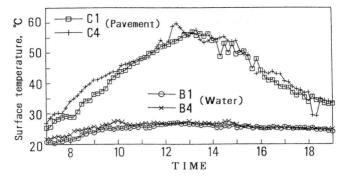

Figure II-B9 Comparison of surface temperatures of the river water with those of the asphalt pavement. C1 and C4 are the measurement points above the street and B1 and B4 are the measurement points above the river, as shown in Fig. II-B8.

ground, and the air temperature distribution on and around the pond is approximately uniform. Therefore, the large pond has almost no thermal effect on the surrounding built-up area. In the afternoon, the surface temperature difference between the pond water and its surroundings becomes larger and the air temperature on the pond becomes 2.5°C lower than that of the distant streets. Isometric lines of −1.5°C, −1.0°C, and −0.5°C can be drawn around the pond in an area of about 700 m × 1000 m (Fig. II-B10). This air temperature distribution demonstrates that a clear "cool island" is created by the pond, and the cooling effect of the pond on the surrounding built-up area is considerable. The thermal effect of the pond gradually decreases in the evening and at night because the surface temperature difference between the pond water and its surroundings also becomes smaller, as in the morning.[10] The air temperature differential between 39 measuring points in an area of about 700 m × 1000 m, including the pond, is low in the early morning and gradually increases, reaching a maximum in the early afternoon and decreasing at night (Fig. II-B11). This temperature differential seems to be highly related to solar radiation, and the standard deviation of the air temperature differential is nearly proportional to solar radiation (Fig. II-B12).

Cooling Effects of Vegetation

By evapotranspiration, vegetation, such as the leaves of trees, turf and grass, keeps its surface temperature lower than that of artificial coverings, such as asphalt pavement, concrete and metal roofing. The crowns of trees also shade the ground surface from solar radiation and keep the ground temperature low. In the shade of the trees, the net radiation is much less on the ground surface of bare soil and therefore, the surface temperature is much lower than it is in the sun (Fig. II-B13). As a result, vegetation in an urban area is expected to mitigate the increase of air temperature during the heat of the summer days.

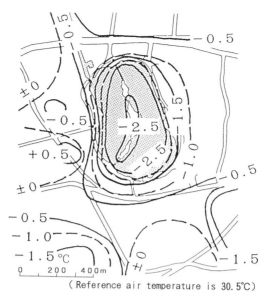

(Reference air temperature is 30. 5°C)

Figure II-B10 Air temperature distribution on and around a pond in a built-up area in the early afternoon on a clear day in summer

In Fukuoka city, there are many open spaces such as parks and precincts of shrines with groves of trees. On clear days in summer, field surveys were conducted to examine the relation between the quantity of vegetation and air temperature.[11] Five open spaces were chosen as the measurement fields with their land areas measuring from 0.18–27 ha. This is equivalent to a small park in a built-up urban area or a large park such as a zoo or a botanical garden. Half of the thirty-two measurement points were located in tree-shaded areas of the parks and the shrines, and the other half were arranged in sunnier areas outside

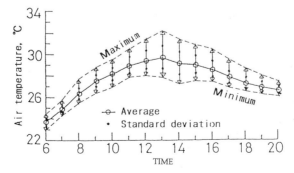

Figure II-B11 Diurnal fluctuation of averaged air temperature with maximum and minimum temperatures and standard deviation

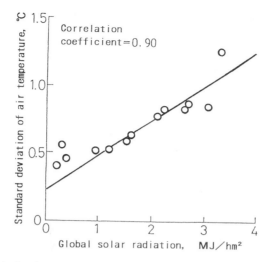

Figure II-B12 Relation between solar radiation and standard deviation of air temperature. The unit MJ/hm^2 is the quantity of heat of solar radiation injected into the area of one square meter of horizontal plane during one hour. 1 MJ/hm^2 equals 2.39×10^2 kcal/hm^2 and 280 W/m^2.

these locations. The green covering ratio was considered as the index of the quantity of vegetation which is the ratio of the circular shaded areas formed by the crowns of the trees with the radius as the measurement point. The shaded areas of the tree crowns were read from expanded air photographs. The air temperatures consistently measured at 1:00 p.m. were correlated with the green covering ratios. The size of the shaded areas varied, with radii of 10, 20, and 50 m. The data proved that the absolute value of a regression coefficient becomes

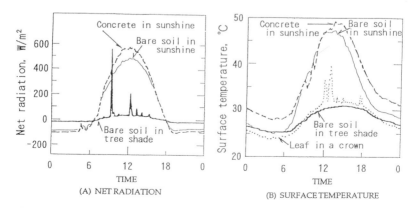

Figure II-B13 Daily variations of net radiation and surface temperature in tree shade and in the sun in summer

larger with the increase of the radius (Fig. II-B14) and the air temperature becomes lower as the green covering ratio increases. In other words, vegetation maintains lower surface and ground surface temperatures and also decreases the air temperature. Most importantly, the crowns of trees also shade the human body from solar heat. As a result, the thermal sensation of a human being is that of becoming cooler and the human comfort is improved in the area with rich vegetation during a hot, humid summer.

CONCLUSION

Even in a smaller city like Fukuoka, the urban warming has rapidly progressed as urbanization has increased. A high temperature zone is observed in the center of the built-up area where the coverage of the ground surface with high-rise buildings is dominant. In a warm climate, the sea breeze and natural covering have a positive cooling effect on these urban zones.

The cooling effect of the sea breeze is notably greater at its time shift from the land breeze to the sea breeze and results in a fluctuation in air temperature. The sea breeze also carries the hot air from the center of the built-up zone to its leeward side. These measurement results indicate that the sea breeze has great potential in controlling the thermal environment in urban areas. When the wind is gentle, the relation between the ratio of natural covering and the averaged air temperature in a 1 km^2 grid is high. Yet, an increase in the ratio of natural

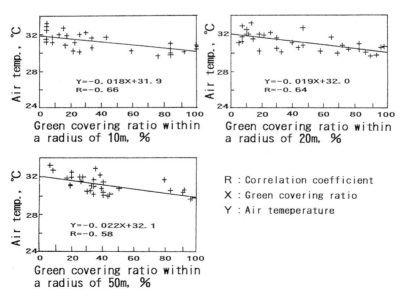

Figure II-B14 Relations between green covering ratio and air temperature at 1:00 p.m. on a clear day in summer

covering from 0% to 100% corresponds to a decrease in air temperature of up to 2.7°C. This suggests that natural covering plays a large role in the mitigation of urban heat.

The water surfaces of a river and pond have lower temperatures compared with surface temperatures of asphalt pavement or a building roof in the heat of the day. The air temperature above a river and pond is also clearly lower than that above a street; the difference between them becomes even greater as solar radiation is increased. Additionally, a river is a useful open space to introduce the sea breeze deep into the urban area. A pond cools the air and this cool zone extends a few hundred meters leeward.

The ground surface temperature in tree-shaded areas is also much lower than ground surface temperature in the sun. The leaves of the trees keep the surface temperature low by evapotranspiration. The cooling effect of vegetation on the air temperature is noticeable in an area with a radius of only 10 m.

In the "heat island" of an urban center, therefore, natural ventilation by the sea breeze plays one of the most important roles in improving the thermal environment, particularly in the hot, humid summers of Japan. Natural coverings such as water and vegetation create clear "cool islands" within hot urban areas. This study confirmed that the larger the ratio of natural covering, the wider and the stronger is the "cool island." The mitigation of urban heat requires the consideration of climatic effects in environmental design for the efficient usage of natural cooling resources. Natural covering should also be recognized as a significant and integral part of urban planning and site selection.

For the efficient usage of the sea breeze and natural covering in improving the urban thermal environment, I have listed below a number of guidelines for environmental design taken from the above-mentioned research results:

- The air temperature in an urban area decreases as the ratio of natural covering increases (Fig. II-B4). Shading a paved road from solar radiation with the large crowns of roadside trees and covering a building roof with vegetation such as turf and bushes are effective ways to keep surface temperatures low during the heat of the day. Therefore, the increase of the covering ratio using these types of vegetation will be effective in mitigating urban heat and will decrease the area and strength of the heat island.
- The sea breeze carries the cooler air from the sea toward inland to built-up areas and controls the rise of air temperature in the summer daytime (Fig. II-B6). Consequently, a street plan that introduces the sea breeze over a city will be useful for the improvement of urban thermal environment. To accomplish this, the building arrangement should be planned to decrease the area of buildings which are perpendicular to the sea breeze flow. Extension and maintenance of a river basin with rows of trees on both its banks will be effective in creating an open space that introduces the sea breeze deep into the urban area. This improvement to a river will allow the possibility of dividing the "heat island" into two smaller parts and will decrease its impact.

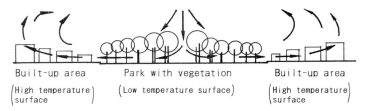

Built-up area   Park with vegetation   Built-up area

(High temperature   (Low temperature surface)   (High temperature
surface)   surface)

Figure II-B15 Thermal convection between a park with vegetation and a built-up area

- Any open space with water and vegetation has lower surface temperatures compared to those of artificial coverings and can create a "cool island" in a hot urban area during the heat of the day (Fig. II-B10).

A "cool island" is accompanied by low circulations which are caused by a thermal connection between the open space and its surrounding built-up area (Fig. II-B15). To increase these flow circulations and to effectively use its cool air, open spaces should not be surrounded by tall or wide barriers such as buildings.

NOTES

1. Landsberg, H. E. 1981. *The Urban Climate.* New York: Academic Press, 84–100.
2. Fukuoka Meteorological Observatory 1990. *Meteorology of Fukuoka During These One Hundred.* Fukuoka: Association of Meteorology in Japan, 43–44.
3. Ojima, T. 1990. Urban pollution. *J. Soc. Heating, Air-condition. San. Engin. Japan* 64: 19.
4. Fujii, S., *et al.* 1988. Influence of climatic factors to meteorological observation items in urban areas. *Summ. Tech. Papers Ann. Meeting, Architec. Instit. Japan* October: 1099–1100.
5. Katayama, T. 1992. Land-use and urban climate in Fukuoka city. *Summaries of 2nd Tohwa University International Symposium on Urban Thermal Environment* September: 1–2.
6. Saito, I., *et al.* 1990/1. Study of the effect of green areas on the thermal environment in an urban area. *Energy and Buildings* 15–16: 493–498.
7. Tsutsumi, J., *et al.* 1984. A study on the sea and land breeze in Fukuoka city. *Proc. 8th Nat. Symp. Wind Engin.* December: 128.
8. Tutsumi, J. 1990/1. Statistical analysis for the characteristics of sea-land breeze and its effect on urban thermal environment. *Energy and Buildings* 15–16: 1003–1008.
9. Katayama, T., *et al.* 1990/1. Cooling effects of a river and sea breeze on the thermal environment in a built-up area. *Energy and Buildings* 15–16: 973–978.
10. Ishii, A., *et al.* 1990/1. A comparison of field surveys on the thermal environment in urban areas surrounding a large pond: when filled and when drained. *Energy and Buildings* 15–16: 965–971.
11. Katayama, T. *et al.* 1991. Field observation on thermal effects of vegetation. *Proc. Int. Conf. Human–Environment Sys.* December: 487–490.

BIBLIOGRAPHY

1. Kawamura, T. 1987. *Atmospheric Environment in an Urban Area.* Tokyo: Asakura.
2. Landsberg, E. H. 1981. *The Urban Climate.* New York: Academic Press.
3. Oak, R. T. 1981. *Boundary Layer Climates.* Tokyo: Asakura.
4. Robinette, O. G. 1983. *Energy Efficient Site Design.* New York: Van Nostrand Reinhold.
5. Saitoh, T. 1992. *Warmings of the Earth and Urban Areas.* Tokyo: Morikita Publishing.

C Thermal Comfort in Japanese Urban Spaces

Ken-Ichi Kimura

INTRODUCTION

Most people living in the modern age experience both indoor and outdoor life. Average office workers spend 90% of their time indoors. Thus, most of the studies on thermal comfort have been focused on ways to maintain a comfortable indoor work environment in order to enhance productivity. However, thermal comfort in outdoor spaces may be regarded as important also, even though the time people spend outdoors is rather short. People usually do not need the outdoors to be as comfortable as the indoors to enjoy urban life. Some people are contended with excessive heat from solar radiation or with a snow-covered courtyard. In these circumstances, people usually adjust to the thermal environment by changing clothes.

It has often been taken for granted that outdoor urban spaces are not heated in winter or air-conditioned in summer. However, problems have arisen in recent times where outdoor spaces are air-conditioned. Atrium spaces, for example, are considered semi-outdoor and are often required to be heated or cooled which results in the squandering of a lot of energy.

In the past, people tried to make the outdoor spaces with an opening to the outside comfortable by providing sun shades, plants, fountains, canopies, pergolas, etc. Nowadays, shadows cast by a building on the street relieve the discomfort from the high intensity of solar radiation in summertime. Underground spaces like concourse and platform areas of subway stations that are crowded with people are not comfortable without air conditioning. In the past, these spaces were too hot in the summer to provide thermal comfort.

There are various kinds of urban spaces with different problems. Solving the problems of thermal comfort according to the conditions specific to the regional climate of modern cities, as well as in ancient urban areas, can yield interesting results.

Traditional Means of Providing Thermal Comfort

The summer weather in most parts of Japan is hot and humid. Various means of rendering the environment as comfortable as possible have been implemented in traditional buildings and outside spaces.[1] Different devices of solar shading are provided outside of buildings. Trees and shrubs are planted in the garden where their natural evaporation process produces cool air. A garden is often pleasantly shaded since densely planted trees permit only a small amount of the sun's rays to penetrate through their foliage. Still, plants allow the breeze to pass through and add to the cooling effect. Rows of trees along a street serve the same function. Old streets are sometimes lined with trees whose high branches and leaves form a kind of arcade. People walking down such tree-lined streets feel much cooler than on sunny, unshaded streets.

Water with *hishaku* (a wooden cup with a rod) is frequently sprinkled on the leaves, stones, and ground surfaces in gardens to cool the air by evaporation (Fig. II-C1). Evaporation from the water surface of a pond in a garden also contributes to a decrease in the air temperature which make ventilative cooling quite effective. Thus, shading and ventilative cooling are the main means of providing comfort during the hot and humid Japanese summer months.

At the same time, people in snowy areas have devised different protective measures from the weather on urban streets. Snow banks sometimes get as high as 3 m in the city areas of the northern Honshu region. Figure II-C2 pictures

Figure II-C1 Japanese garden full of vegetation wetted by *hisaku*

Figure II-C2 *Gangi*, covered sidewalk in snowy district in Japan

Gangi, a distinguished structure which extends from a building along the street to provide entirely covered tunnel-like sidewalks. The snow bank itself acts as a shield for pedestrians against cold winds.

Strong wind often is not only hazardous to building structures, but also gives people an uncomfortable cold feeling. Tall hedges with dense foliage acts as a natural barrier against the prevailing wind. These plants are a frequent wind barrier in windy regions and are an innate part of the local landscape.

Patios and small courtyards provide an excellent thermal balance system as they retain the cool air sunk from the previous night until the early afternoon. This is noticable in the courtyards and patios of southern European cities where the vapor from fountains and vegetation cools the hot air significantly. Traditional Japanese urban houses also contain small patio-like areas called *tsuboniwa*, which are less effective as natural cooling agents than patios, but still allow the air current to pass through (Fig. II-C3). Both *tsuboniwa* and patios are surrounded by buildings, but the former is less structured in shape and more open to the outside to let the air breeze through, while the latter is entirely enclosed.

Basic Criteria of Thermal Comfort in the Environmental Space

The physiological aspects of human thermal comfort do not depend on whether people stay indoors or outdoors. Rather, there are six basic factors that affect thermal comfort: temperature, radiation, humidity, air movement, clothing, and activity level. Depending on the combination of these six factors, the thermal sensation an individual feels can vary greatly. If a person feels neither warm nor cool, the condition is termed "neutral." If the temperature of the environment rises slightly above the neutral condition, one feels slightly warm. As the temperature increases beyond the warm region, one becomes hot. Likewise, an individual feels slightly cool or cold as the temperature drops. The basic assumption for all these situations is the permanence of the five remaining factors.

The radiation exchange between the human body and surrounding surfaces affects the thermal comfort under the same air temperature conditions. For

Figure II-C3 *Tsuboniwa*, a small patio of a house in Kyoto

example, people often feel warmth when part of their body is exposed to an open fire; the sun's radiation has a similar heating effect upon the human body. High humidity in summer causes discomfort while in winter, the thermal comfort is hardly affected by humidity. When the breeze reduces the skin's surface temperature under both humid and dry conditions, the thermal sensation level is lowered. This condition is welcomed in summer and disliked in winter.

It is possible to quantify the thermal sensation level on a vertical scale from +3 as "hot" to (3 as "cold" with 0 for "neutral" (Fig. II-C4). This scale is frequently used for questionnaires concerning thermal sensation under a specific condition. When designing an environmental space, the architect/urban designer must take into consideration the thermal comfort level that will satisfy the average person. The individual preference varies where the predicted mean vote (PMV) has the same scale as the thermal sensation vote (Fig. II-C4). PMV is expressed in the form of a mathematical formula and its value can be calculated by assessing a value to each of the six aforementioned factors described above.[2] For the experiment, the test person slowly walks along the street in light clothing

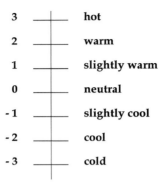

3	hot
2	warm
1	slightly warm
0	neutral
- 1	slightly cool
- 2	cool
- 3	cold

Figure II-C4 Thermal sensation scale

for a clo value of 0.7.[3] The outside condition is a summer day with a dry bulb temperature of 27°C, relative humidity of 60%, mean radiant temperature of 27°C, and air velocity measured at 0.6 m/s. The person's activity level is 1.5 met.[4] The PMV then is a +1.0, which means that an average person in such an environment would feel "slightly warm." If a breeze moves at a velocity of 3 m/s with 1 met activity and the person wears a short sleeve shirt and trousers giving a 0.5 clo, the individual would feel "slightly cool" or "neutral " on the scale of PMV, which would then be –0.5.

There is another way of expressing thermal comfort by the ET* (standard effective temperature). The ET* describes a hypothetical temperature under which a person in the given thermal environment would feel just as though they were under the standard thermal environment at a given dry bulb temperature with a relative humidity of 50%, still air, and mean radiant temperature equaled to air temperature if the person had 1 clo clothing and 1 met activity level.[5]

The ET* can be graphically expressed in the psychometric chart for a given combination of the six factors where the comfort zone is indicated. Computer programs to obtain both PMV and ET* values are available.

CHARACTERISTICS OF THE THERMAL ENVIRONMENT IN URBAN SPACES

The characteristics of a thermal environment in outdoor urban spaces vary greatly from indoor spaces. People commonly accepted being exposed to a somewhat uncomfortable environment while they are in urban spaces, but nowadays, they tend to desire more thermal comfort in any outdoor environment, including urban spaces.

Air Temperature

Urban outdoor spaces are open to the sky and breezes. The air, however, can be stagnant or at times turbulent because artificial control of outside air temperature is quite difficult. As commonly known, the air temperature in modern cities is higher than in surrounding areas which creates the phenomenon of a so-called heat island. This occurrence is believed to be caused by the heat generated by human activities, but the problem has been exacerbated as the evaporation effect from vegetation has been lost by the conversion of the wet ground surface into dry roads and buildings. Warmer conditions are welcomed in the winter, but the situation in summer has become more extreme.

Radiation

Solar radiation often reflects directly onto people; its intensity, however, often fluctuates due to changes in the amount of overcasting. Overheating can be reduced to a considerable extent using the natural shading from trees and artificial shading devices. In winter, however, a soft, pleasant warmth can be felt from solar radiation. Thus, to adjust to the seasonal variation, deciduous trees are often planted in walkways and courtyards.

Precipitation

Protection from rain is likewise difficult to provide. Arcades and covered walkways are common features of downtown shopping areas and markets. Particularly in snowy regions, such covered spaces are also very effective in providing thermal comfort by benefitting from the greenhouse effect which causes the heat of the solar radiation to be trapped. With such a radiation field, covered markets offer much better conditions than open air markets.

Humidity

Humidity control is almost impossible in outdoor spaces since moisture is quickly diffused by the air. In a dry, hot climate, water sprays, fountains and artificial mist procure a cooling effect through humidification. Yet, artificial humidification must be exerted in moderation as excessive moisture accumulation fosters the growth of mold and mildew.

Air Movement

Air movement outdoors is usually greater than indoors. This particularly varies with time and greatly affects the physiological effects of thermal comfort. A convective heat transfer from the skin to the ambient air is accelerated by a higher air velocity along the skin surface. This cooling effect is disliked in winter and welcomed in summer. In the summertime, heat is dissipated by perspiration and the air movement furthers the evaporation of perspiration from the skin surface.

Modern Examples of Thermal Comfort in Urban Spaces

In designing outdoor spaces for the modern urban area, the provision of thermal comfort must be a high priority. The various examples of courtyards, small parks, malls, plazas, roof gardens, sunken gardens, etc. prove that appropriate measures for providing thermal comfort have been taken into account even unconsciously. Shadows are cast by trees and pergolas. The vapor from fountains and ponds cools the over-heated air and also offers esthetic visual distraction.

Canopy with Leaves

The cooling effect of a large canopy of wisteria leaves on people resting in its shade was investigated by Hoyano.[6] The globe temperature measured under the canopy in the shade during the daytime was about 4°C higher than the ambient globe temperature to which a person would be exposed the sun (Fig. II-C5). The shading effect of a canopy with leaves is significant, but the decrease in mean radiant temperature results only if the covered portion of the canopy is several degrees lower than the outside air temperature. The use of vegetation would also help to dissipate heat by evaporation and to enhance the coexistence of vegetation and human lives.

Atrium

Atria experienced a revival all over the world in the 1980s, although their concept dates back to ancient times.[7] The Ford Foundation Building in New York was constructed with an atrium. The Galleria in Milano is famous as the first glass-covered shopping arcade. Many earlier examples of atria in the cold climates of North America and Scandinavia were simple semi-outdoor and semi-indoor spaces where people clad in overcoats could enjoy the outdoors and simultaneously do their window shopping. In this case, thermal temperature within

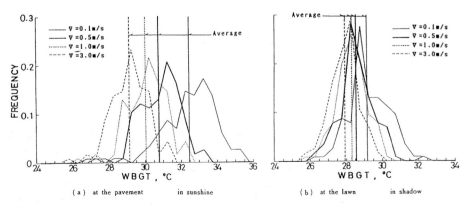

Figure II-C5 Temperature around canopy with leaves

the atria was a mix of the inside and outside temperatures. Unlike streets with melted snow and gusty winds, atria spaces are comfortable and pleasant. Even though they were not heated, the glass-covered space became rather warm due to the greenhouse effect in which the solar radiation became trapped.[8] In many Japanese cities, shopping arcades are common, and their original purpose was to protect the shopper from rain.

Toward the end of the 1980s, however, buildings with an atrium became popular everywhere and large buildings without one became hard to find. Because of the spacious, pleasant atmosphere of the atrium, people became accustomed to more thermal comfort and all-year-round air-conditioning has now become commonplace. Inevitably, most of the atria waste a lot of energy for heating and cooling. Especially when strong solar radiation is transmitted during the summertime and heat accumulates within the structure, cost-consuming air-conditioning is the only means to ease the situation.

The enormous atrium of the World Financial Center in New York City is fully air-conditioned. A person sitting on a chair feels very comfortable among tall palm trees on ground level. However, the warmer air rises and lies stagnant in the upper part of the atrium space. An experiment at the NS Building in Tokyo proved that natural ventilation is not necessary in the air-conditioned atrium. Under the present circumstances, hot air may accumulate within the upper part of the building and heat loss can occur while the cool air stays in the occupied space below (Fig. II-C6).[9] If an atrium was ventilated, however, the warm outside air would permeate the space and, in turn, cause a cooling loss. In warm countries, however, a solar shading device is mandatory for the atrium. Sakamoto clarified this situation by conducting an extensive numerical experiment in a large atrium.[10]

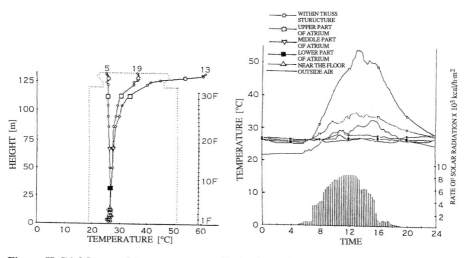

Figure II-C6 Measured temperature profile in the atrium space of the NS Building in Tokyo (Matsunawa, 1987, p. 204)

Urban Canyon

The space between buildings in a city is called an urban canyon. Depending on the proportion of the width of the outdoor space to the height of the buildings, thermal comfort perceived by a person on the ground level of the space can vary greatly. The difference depends on whether the person is located in a sunlit or shadowy area. Sunny streets are comfortable and pleasant in winter, but windy streets provide an uncomfortable environment in winter.

In summer, the problem of thermal comfort in the urban canyon is tied mostly to the hot ground surface overheated by strong solar radiation. Dr. Katayama and his colleagues carried out intensive field measurements in an urban canyon in the city of Fukuoka during the summer.[11] From the measured results of air temperature Qa, wet bulb temperature Qg, a well-known index of WBGT (wet bulb globe temperature) was calculated from the following formulae:

$$\text{WBGT} = 0.7Qw + 0.2Qw + 0.1Qa \qquad \text{(sunny side)}$$
$$\text{WBGT} = 0.7Qw + 0.3Qw \qquad \text{(shadow side)}$$

A rather high correlation between the ET* and WBGT was calculated from the measurements based on the assumption that 0.3 clo and 1.2 met in the wide range of ET* under summer conditions. The experiment also demonstrated that the effect of air movement is considerable, especially in sunlit areas. These results clearly show that the frequency distribution pattern is shifted towards the lower side of ET* in the case of sunlit areas as opposed to the case of shadow areas where only slight effects of air movement can be determined.

Courtyard

A courtyard is an open space surrounded by buildings which can be found in most southern countries. The shadows cast by the surrounding buildings and the ventilation from the vertical airflow provide thermal comfort and protect against overheating in summer. In many cases, open corridors with rows of columns provide thermal relief when the cool air of the night sinks down and stabilizes the temperature until the early afternoon. The cool night air decreases the surface temperature around the courtyard and keeps the mean radiant temperature lower throughout the day. During the day, an upward air movement draws the air through the building.

In a dry climate, the air is humidified and cooled by evaporation of water from fountains or waterways. Sometimes water is sprayed in the air even under humid conditions to cool the ambient environment, as a drop in temperature is more important to thermal comfort than the increase in humidity.

Dr. Katayama and his colleagues attempted another experiment which involved the measurement of the thermal environment in a courtyard space surrounded by five-story buildings. The WBGT of the sunny pavement was dispersed by different wind speed (Fig. II-C7a), but the WBGT of the lawn in the shade was almost unrelated to the wind speed (Fig. II-C7b).

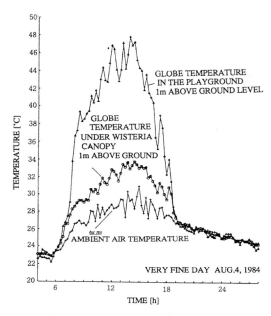

Figure II-C7 Histogram of wet-bulb globe temperature index (WBGT) for wind speeds in a courtyard (courtesy of Prof. Katayama)

Sunken Garden

The sunken garden provides a pleasant, recessed atmosphere for people to relax. It is shielded, by natural walls or a basement building, from the wind that blows across the upper zones and the sunken garden's the surface temperature is more stable than the outside air's. As the sunken garden is an open space furnished with plants, it provides a feeling of being indoors.

In the summer time, the cold air sinks down into the courtyard even in the daytime whenever a vertical temperature differentiation exists. For example, the ground surface temperature decreases when a long wavelength of radiation is emitted on a clear day. The air near the ground is cooled off and sinks down to the sunken garden. This phenomenon is found in the traditional underground houses called *Yao Dong* (cave dwellings) in China and *troglodytes* dwellings (belowground houses) in Matmata, Tunisia. The sunken garden of the Mitsui Building in Tokyo has a large open plaza with trees and a place where people can relax and enjoy refreshments until the late evening, when the air around adjacent buildings becomes cool again (Fig. II-C8).

A river-walk promenade, such as the one in San Antonio, Texas, encompasses a wide space including the air space above the river surface. The river walk, itself, is located about 3 m below the ground level. These walk way spaces are cooler than the space above all year round and even on sunny winter days it is quite pleasant due to the solar heat.

Figure II-C8 Sunken garden of Mitsui Building in Tokyo

EVALUATION OF THERMAL COMFORT IN URBAN SPACES

Although different places have various measures for obtaining thermal comfort in urban spaces, studies on thermal comfort have been confined to interior spaces so far. Theories on thermal comfort must apply to both indoor and outdoor spaces. Specific problems might arise in studying urban spaces, when conducting an investigation based upon questionnaires, as factors other than thermal comfort could intervene with objective results.

As for indoor spaces, the percentage of occupants dissatisfied with the thermal comfort is an index for evaluating the quality of the space. The quality of the space should commonly be assessed when the percentage of satisfaction is less than 20%.[12] In the case of urban spaces, however, acceptability of the thermal comfort would turn out higher than the rate of dissatisfaction because it may be inferred that people enjoying their leisure time outside could tolerate more undesirable conditions than when they are working or living indoors. Thermal comfort studies quantifying the comparisons between outdoor and indoor conditions have yet to be written.

There are some measured results on the thermal environment of urban spaces in Japan which might be useful for future projects as they take the regional climatic conditions into account.

CONCLUSION

Various aspects of thermal comfort in urban spaces have been outlined and discussed in this chapter. The theory of thermal comfort is applicable to both indoor and outdoor spaces. The most significant differences in thermal characteristics between indoor and outdoor spaces are as follows.

First, the environmental factors that regulate thermal comfort outdoors, such as temperature, humidity, radiation, and air movement, fluctuate, are ungovernable and are often inherently violent. Second, those factors are, however, often less severe and more stable than climatic conditions. Third, the human factors are important and vary; for example, clothing, activity level and behavior are different in the outdoor from the indoor environment.

Comfort levels are generally lower in exterior urban spaces than indoors, where the environment is controlled by mechanical systems. It can also be assumed that people are able to tolerate a less comfortable thermal environment in the outdoors where extreme termperatures are not expected to be regulated. However, it is not clear how high their tolerance level is.

Various devices for providing thermal comfort in urban areas and their effects were described. Traditional measures of thermal comfort are interesting, as people in the past had to devise different ways to cope with the severity of the weather. On the contrary, modern designs of atrium buildings, courtyards, sunken gardens, and green walkways are now accepted as ways of providing relief to those who tend to suffer from the intense urban conditions. In some cases, thermal comfort can be satisfied by mechanical means.

Although people might not complain so much about a thermally uncomfortable climate in the outdoors, architects and policy makers should pay attention to the problems of thermal comfort in designing urban spaces. There has been the notion that outdoor spaces must be pleasant, though not necessarily comfortable. Historically, the design of urban spaces had interesting and attractive forms, and they were adorned with fountains, pergolas, and plants to make the thermal environment as comfortable as possible. This principle has not changed in modern cities where people can still enjoy pleasant surroundings. However, in many cases, such as atria heating and air conditioning, conveniences are introduced to make outdoor spaces thermally comfortable. Many of these modern conveniences consume tremendous amounts of energy. As urban spaces are not necessarily enclosed, care must be taken to avoid wasting energy when making the environment thermally comfortable.

There is no definite standard of thermal comfort for outdoor urban spaces at the present as studies on these problems are lacking. Therefore, it is necessary to encourage engineers to examine the thermal quality of urban spaces more precisely and to analyze the consequences of new building methods and designs. This will eventually contribute to an understanding of a sound outdoor environment which architects and policy makers would implement to reach maximum comfort levels for city residents.

As for potential energy shortages and environmental problems, we recommend that different devices be used to create the most acceptable urban areas, bearing in mind local climatic conditions and the preservation of a clean global environment.

NOTES

1. Ken-Ichi, K. 1984. Echotechniques in Japanese traditional architecture—a regional monograph in Japan. *Proc. Int. Conf. Passive Low Energy Ecotech. Appl. Housing* (PLEA 84 Mexico) Oxford: Pergamon Pressa, 1093–1109.
2. Ole Fanger, P. 1970. *Thermal Comfort.* Copenhagen: Danish Technical Press and Florida: Robert E. Krieger Publishing, 1982: 114.
3. "Clo" is a unit of thermal resistance of clothing. One "clo" is 0.18 m^2 K/W to be equivalent to the thermal resistance of business units.
4. "Met" is a unit of metabolic rate of the human body, 1 met is 57 W/m^2 of skin surface area for a standard person sitting on the chair.
5. *ASHRAE Guide Book of Fundamentals.* Atlanta, GA: ASHRAE, 1993: 8–13.
6. Akira, H. and Shokusai, K. C. 1992. Environmental control by vegetation. *Kenchiku Kankyou-gaku 2* Kimura, K. ed. *Theories of Architectural Environment 2.* Tokyo: Maruzen, 151–178.
7. Saxon, R. 1983. *Atrium Buildings: Development and Design.* London: Butterworths.
8. Höglund, I., Ottoson, G. and Öman, R. 1988. Glass-covering of large building volumes—pros and cons. *New Opport. Energy Conserv. Buildings.* Stockholm: Division of Building Technology, Royal Institute of Technology, 153: 109–119.
9. Matsunawa, K. 1987. Atoriumu to sho-enerugii (Atrium and energy conservation). *Kenchiku-Gijutsu (Building Technology)* 430: 201–208.
10. Sakamoto, Y. 1989. Hitoon-Kiryu no modeling to atrium heno oyou (Modeling of non-isothermal flow and its application to atria). *19th Heat Symposium*, Committee on Environmental Engineering. Tokyo: Architectural Institute of Japan, 49–56.
11. Katayama, T., Morikawa, A. and Masuda, S. 1987. Investigation on the formation of thermal environment in an urban canyon. *J. Architect. Planning Environ. Engin. (Transactions of AIJ)* 372: 30–40.
12. *ASHRAE Standards on Thermal Environmental Conditions for Human Occupancy.* Atlanta, GA: ASHRAE, 1992: 2.

D Changes in Tokyo's Waterfront Environment

Nobuyuki Takahashi

INTRODUCTION

Background and Purpose of the Research

One cannot think of rivers, canals, and watercourses in the urban space and the birth of cities separately. In Japan, the industrialization of cities since the Meiji Restoration (1868–1926) has greatly transformed waterways and the urban structure. After 1900, an age of secondary industrial society emerged. People flocked to the cities for jobs and the urban populations increased rapidly. The accompanying modernization and expansion of cities greatly changed the nature of rivers, coasts, and green areas. In order to utilize the land effectively, people modified nature in the process of development.

For example, early Tokyo was a desolate area with many marshes overgrown with reeds. However, during the Edo era (1604–1868), people gathered in specific places which resulted in the strengthening of the urban management system. This created the need for a greater water supply which was satisfied by conducting water from distant places to the populated areas. In the modern era, as the water from rivers became insufficient to meet the local demand, dams were built in places far from Tokyo, and the stored water was brought long distances to satisfy the needs of the capital city and neighboring areas.

Furthermore, water from the nearby rivers and canals, which had thus far been important for living and transportation, was now regarded as an impediment to growth. With the expansion of settlements, an even greater number of people seeking jobs were attracted to the villages. These new enlarged communities experienced a corresponding change in appearance and design. As communities expanded, they formed primary industrial societies relying mainly on agriculture, fishing, and hunting. When production exceeded the demand of the consumers, a division of labor occurred, followed by the emergence of a new social class. The economy then reached a new plateau. This new economic structure was matched by an enhanced social quality of life.

There are three major elements to consider when city development occurs in conjunction with the use of the waterfront environment: water control, water utilization, and water familiarization. The city's basic industrial structure can also be divided into three phases of development: primary, secondary, and tertiary industries (Fig. II-D1).

A primary industrial society is the first stage of city development. A city at this stage is supplied with water by means of riparian works measures. These measures provide for the construction of an irrigation system, embankments, and canals. This is also the age when waterways are the primary means of transportation for products and people.

To promote secondary industries, coolant and water are needed in large quantities. Groundwater has to be drawn, collected, and stored behind enormous water-storage dams. During this phase of industrial development, the demand for a large labor force becomes urgent and the influx of people to the city starts. The construction of pipelines to supply water for the population and sewers to dispose of waste becomes necessary. This evolved distribution system can become

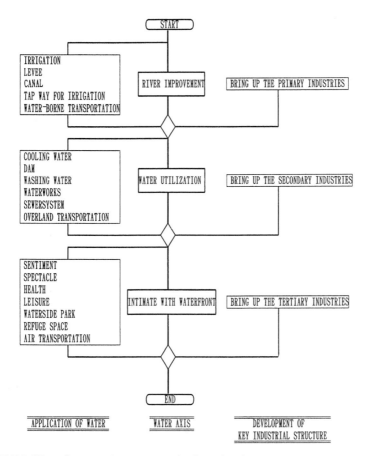

Figure II-D1 Waterfront environment and urban development

complicated. As rapid mass transit systems are required, marine transportation is converted to land transportation. At this stage, the structure of the cities changes greatly, especially in relation to the waterfront environment. In extreme cases, watercourses such as canals are filled to create space for super highways.

However, as the tertiary stage of industry emerges, the logic of filling watercourses to build roads is being reconsidered. With the return to a traditional point of view nowadays, the effects of the waterfront environment have again been linked to the importance of the landscape, health, and leisure which it can provide. At the same time, the remaining vacant areas of a ward should be wisely used as shelters in cases of emergency or natural disaster, as free land is becoming very scarce. This, then, is the dawning of the age where the altered waterfront environment is reclaimed. In various places, plans are currently made to redevelop the waterfront and to restore the function of rivers which had been eliminated. As an alternative means of distribution, air transportation is increasingly used to deliver products that are varied, more expensive, and lighter in weight.

Method of Measuring the Waterfront Line Density Equation

If quantitative measures of watercourses and waterfront lines are taken as elements of the urban environment, these elements can be compared with other city land-use more easily. For example, the concept of waterfront density can be defined as the length of the waterfront line per given area. Its equation is as follows:

$$W_d = \Sigma W_1/S \tag{1}$$

where W_d is the waterfront line density (km/km^2), ΣW_1 is the total length of waterfront line (km) and S is the water basin area (km^2).

CHANGES IN WATERCOURSE NETWORKS IN THE TOKYO METROPOLITAN AREA

The watercourse networks of the Tokyo metropolitan area were constructed during the Edo era; its design was very well planned compared to those of other world cities. The many rivers and canals which flowed into Tokyo Bay were efficiently connected. Urban designers built the canals and watercourse networks bearing in mind the conditions of each location, so the residents could receive the full benefits of the water. However, significant changes in the use of watercourse networks arose as industrial areas expanded and the use of the automobile multiplied. The function and form of the Tokyo metropolitan area was altered and many rivers and canals disappeared.

Today, people are beginning to value waterways and understand the necessity of the waterfront to the Tokyo metropolitan area. Thus, conservation policies are growing in acceptance in the twenty-first century. The Tone River, Tama River, Sagami River, and Ara River flow into the Kanto Plain which surrounds

Tokyo, forming an especially large basin zone. The basin zone of the Tone River is the largest in Japan. However, the Tone River is, in reality, only small when compared with the many large rivers of the world (Fig. II-D2). Yet this river should not be underestimated simply because of its comparatively small size. The way in which the Tone River is related to the human community and its urban systems makes this river first-class in importance and value to Japan.

Figure II-D3 shows the result of further investigation of detail with particular attention paid to rivers and canals in the Kanto area (the Tokyo Metropolitan area). This map shows us that there are many watercourse networks in this area even now.

Changes in the Metropolitan Area

This study's area of investigation consisted of several 10 km concentrical circles with Tokyo at the center. The investigations took place in the years 1914 and 1982 (Fig. II-D4). In the third year of the Taisho Era (1914), Tokyo station was built, giving further impetus to develop that area as the business center of Japan. Thus, central Tokyo was growing into a full-fledged city. The area became more accessible as the steep slopes in the uptown area were leveled down. As a result, the city limits were expanded to include the uptown area, with the population in the central area exceeding 2 million people in 1914.

The population of Tokyo increased at an accelerated pace, reaching 8 million in 1955 and exceeding 10 million in February 1962. Years of prosperity followed for Japan. In October 1964, the long-cherished dream of hosting the Olympic Games in Tokyo came true. In the subsequent years, the Japanese economy continued to expand rapidly, achieving the highest growth of the industrialized nations. Although the double digit growth came to a grinding halt with the Oil Crisis of 1973, the economy has become even stronger since the passing of the oil crisis and has gained a respected position in the world economy. Yet, as a consequence of Tokyo's rapid development into a greater metropolis, the volume of traffic running from the suburbs into Tokyo has been mounting rapidly. Improvements of the railway transportation to accommodate this increasing volume of commuters have become a central issue in the development of the Tokyo Metropolitan area.

The distribution pattern of population and employment in the Tokyo Metropolitan area for this study was determined by using commuting zones classified according to the length of time it takes to travel to Tokyo station, i.e. 10, 20, 40, 60, 80, 100, and 120 minutes. The transition of population and employment in specific time zones is described below.

- The 20- and 40-minute zone began to decrease in population between 1960 and 1970. However, over the same period, the 60- and 80-minute zones exhibited a rapid increase in population, with the outskirts showing a more dense concentration of population.
- Employment continued to increase in the 10-, 20-, and 40-minute zones where population decreased. In the 60- and 80-minute zones where the population

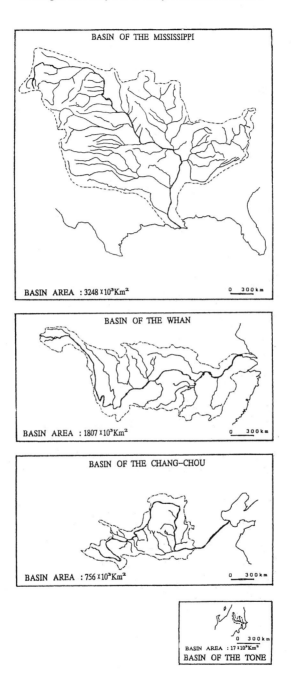

Figure II-D2 Comparison of the basins of the Mississippi, Whan, Chang Chou, and Tone Rivers

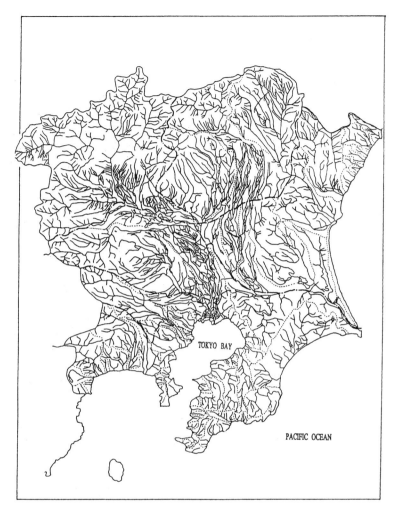

Figure II-D3 Rivers and canals in Kanto (Tokyo metropolitan area)

was increasing sharply, employment also increased considerably. In other words, while employment increased in the central district of Tokyo, it also rose in the outskirts according to the growth in population. The distribution pattern of employment turned out to be quite complex.

Due to the increase in commuter traffic, major railways are becoming more congested every year, especially in the central districts of Tokyo. Since the turn of the century, the capital has attempted to modernize its transportation systems and to take effective measures to handle the increasing commuter traffic. These endeavors are of critical importance to the Tokyo Metropolitan transportation

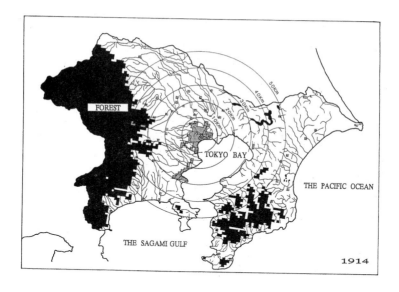

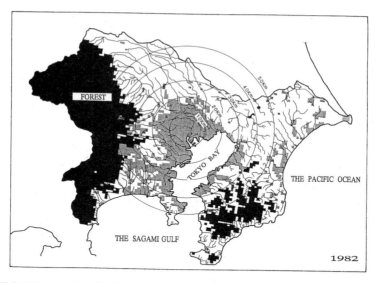

Figure II-D4 Expansion of urbanization and decrease in river area in southern Kanto

plan. In 1939, Tokyo's first subway, the Ginza Line, was opened. In 1951, construction began on the second subway, the Marunouchi Line. In addition to providing maintenance for the JR (formerly the Japan National Railways) and private railways, new subway construction plans have been reviewed several times since the Tokyo improvement committee decided in 1919 to install seven lines covering over 83 km.

Over the past twenty years, the transportation capacity has increased by a rate of 2.50 times per line and the number of passengers has increased 2.07 times. Moreover, in terms of the congestion ratio ((passengers carried/transportation capacity) × 100), loading rates in 1990 were 263% of 1960, 228% of 1970 and 217% of 1980, showing a gradual downtrend every decade. These percentages express the extensive growth of the Tokyo Metropolitan area and the increase in volume of commuting traffic over the decades from 1919 to 1980, when the concentration of population and employment accelerated most intensively. The 50 km radial zone from Tokyo station, which forms the Tokyo metropolitan area, has continued to face the most intensive and rapid concentration of population and employment over the past twenty years, more than any other Japanese city. The population of Tokyo has increased sharply from approximately 15.35–25.47 million, a gain of about 10 million people.

Rivers and canals have been deeply affected by these changes. Figure II-D5 displays the changes in the length of the waterfront lines in the metropolitan area

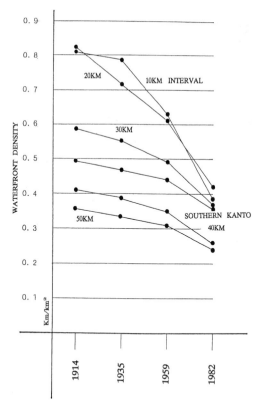

Figure II-D5 Change of watercourse network density at 10 km intervals in the Tokyo metropolitan area

and the southern part of Kanto area (Tokyo, Kanagawa, Saitama, and Chiba prefecture) over the past sixty-eight years. According to this figure, the total length of the waterfront has decreased by 45% in the 10 km area, by 41% in the 20 km area, 30% in the 30 km area, and 15% in the 40 km area. In the 50 km area, which is the farthest distance from Tokyo, the waterfront has decreased by 28%. These reductions to the waterfront were caused by the expansion of urban area and the concentration of population within the city districts.

Change in Tokyo's Twenty-three Wards

For the examination of the condition of Tokyo's twenty-three wards (the Tokyo metropolitan area), the Japanese *mesh* unit of measurement (1 *mesh* = 500×500 m) was introduced for an easy comparison of the total length of waterfront per area. The objective was to investigate the change in length of the waterfront over seventy-one years and in six intervals: 1909, 1918, 1932, 1952, 1970, and 1980. There is a total of 128 rivers in Tokyo—four main rivers, 94 branch rivers and 30 smaller rivers. The total basin area of these rivers is 1752 km^2 and their total length is 884.65 km. The Tokyo metropolitan area covers 618 km^2 and its waterfront line density is 1.43 km/km^2 i.e. 884.65 km/618 km^2.

Edogawa ward boasts the largest acreage of waterfront (Fig. II-D6). In 1980, however, this ward lost 66.7% of its waterfront line density; Adachi ward lost 67.8%, and Katsushika ward 59.2%. In 1909, immense quantities of *mesh* watercourses existed in the eastern part of the twenty-three wards (Fig. II-D7). There were also numerous watercourses in the eight wards of Adachi, Katsushika, Edogawa, Arakawa, Sumida, Daito, Koto, and Chuo. However, around 1970, land reclamation was finished and construction projects were planned to straighten the course of the rivers (Fig. II-D8).

After the Meiji era, cities expanded and secondary industries emerged. It was mainly during this period that the industrial structure changed. Particularly the heavy chemical industrial areas led the modern industrialization in Japan. A flood prevention system was established and the traffic network was modernized. These changes took precedence over other considerations and as a result, the number of watercourses was gradually reduced. In 1909 Tokyo, the waterfront area decreased from 109.80 km^2 to 107.25 km^2 by 1919 and 96.97 km^2 by 1932. By 1980, the area diminished even further to 33.86 km^2, a substantial decrease. In seventy-one years, Tokyo Bay's waterfront line decreased by a total of 75.14 km^2 or 68.4%.

Changes in Chuo Ward

Ieyasu Tokugawa, the first *shogun* of the Edo era, began the construction of Edo city in 1590. During this era, Chuo ward was the place of residence for townspeople. After this period and with the modernization of Japan, Chuo ward developed into the center of Tokyo and Japan. However, several natural disasters

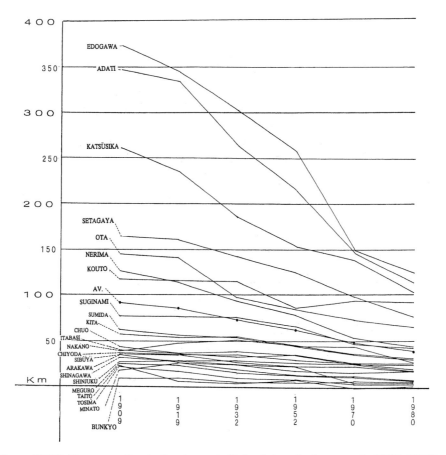

Figure II-D6 Decrease of waterfront area in Tokyo's twenty-three wards (1909–1980)

influenced its development. The Kanto earthquake disaster of 1923 necessitated the introduction of earthquake disaster revival planning. In addition, despite the further expansion of roads after World War II and the maintenance of metropolitan highways, this area has not changed in appearance since its creation. This section focuses on Chuo ward, for it is central to Tokyo and has taken the lead in modernization. The discussion will center on the relationship between this area and its rivers and canals.

The modernization of Japan began during the Meiji era. The Taisho era saw the completion of a network of land transportation in almost all areas of Japan. Railroads, streetcars, and roads were built. During this period, Chuo ward continued to develop within the basic framework established during the Edo era. However, by the time of the Kanto earthquake disaster, 100% of Nihonbashi ward and 88.7% of Kyobashi ward were damaged. This opportunity to rebuild

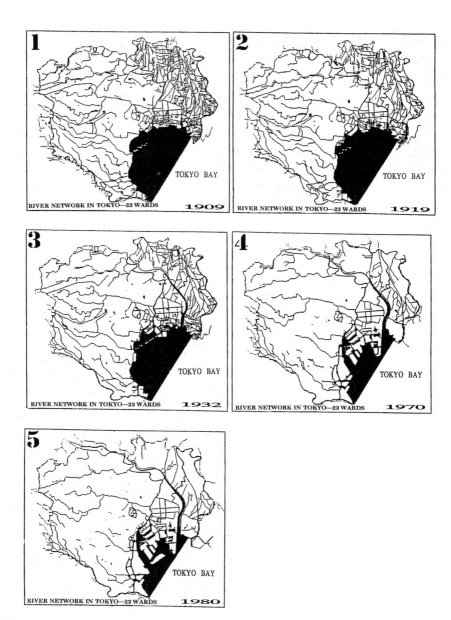

Figure II-D7 Map of the change in watercourse networks in Tokyo's twenty-three wards and decrease of Tokyo Bay area by reclamation

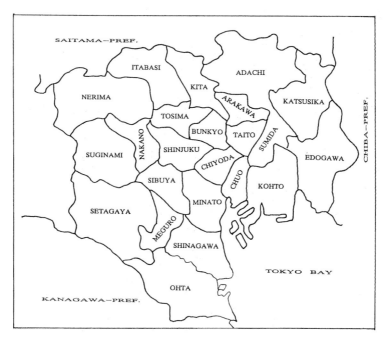

Figure II-D8 The twenty-three wards of Tokyo. The Shitamachi area is located at the right hand side on this map. This area was often hit in the past by typhoons and floods. The left side is called the Tamanote area (uptown).

these wards was accompanied by a revival in city planning. Yet with the air raids of World War II, two thirds of the Nihonbashi and Kyobashi wards were again destroyed. By the opening the Tokyo Olympic Games in 1964, however, it was apparent that the city had maintained its basic urban structure.

The three elements that constitute the transportation system in Chuo ward are watercourses, railroads, and subways. The extensive transportation network of metropolitan highways was a result of high economic growth. In Chuo ward, the Shinkansen (new super high-speed railway) and subways were implemented, and the first one was the expressway of Route 1. At the same time canals and medium- to small-sized rivers were filled and streetcars were eliminated. In Chuo ward the possibility of expanding roads happened at the expense of waterways since the price of land was extremely costly. Over the past one-hundred years, from 1883 to 1982, the waterfront line density in Chuo ward changed drastically (Fig. II-D9). The ward lost 44.29 km of its waterfront which originally encompassed 78.5% of the area. Thus, vestiges of the appearance of Edo gradually disappeared. During this period, business activities were centralized, the night population decreased, and the water area in Tokyo Bay was filled to be used as additional land.

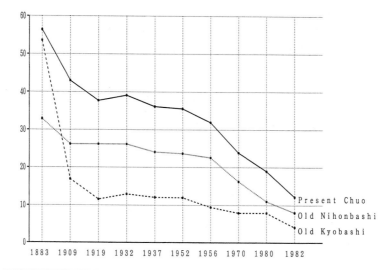

Change of Rivers and Canals in Chuo Ward in Kilometers										
Ward	1883	1909	1919	1932	1937	1952	1956	1970	1980	1982
Present Chuo Ward	56.44	42.96	37.66	39.02	36.11	35.53	31.92	23.81	18.95	12.15
Old Nihonbashi	32.86	26.10	26.10	26.10	24.01	23.56	22.49	16.24	11.01	8.02
Old Kyobashi	53.58	16.86	11.56	12.92	12.10	11.97	9.44	7.94	7.94	4.13

Figure II-D9 Change of the rivers and canals in Chuo ward

To summarize the development of Chuo ward, a hydrographic network map of the ward in 1883 is presented in Figure II-D10. There were 89 bridges, which indicates that watercourses were prevalent and well intertwined. The hydrographic network map of 1980 shows that almost all of the medium- and small-sized hydrographic networks were lost. Although there were once 89 bridges, now only 26 remain. The reason for this development is that certain bridges have become superfluous with the reclaiming of the rivers. The existing ratio of hydraulic networks is calculated at 30%. Overall, 28 watercourses were lost (Fig. II-D11). A total road network map of the present Chuo ward shows its extremely dense situation today (Fig. II-D12). With this review of the development of the transportation network, it is easy to understand the trend toward enriching the road network to compensate for the decrease in watercourse networks.

Restoration of Abolished Rivers

The population of Edo reached one million in the eighteenth century and was the largest city in the world at that time. There are few seaport cities worldwide which have experienced the degree of change that occurred in Tokyo Bay. As mentioned above, as the city developed, people changed the nature of

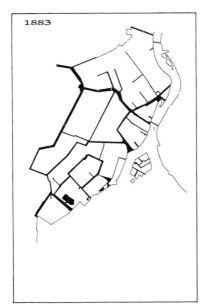
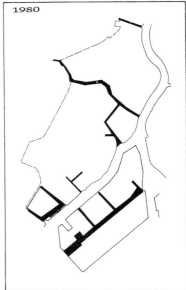

Figure II-D10 River and canal map of Chuo ward in 1883 and 1980

waterways which they perceived as a threat to their existence. There were some watercourses and rivers from the early Meiji period (around 1900) whose names have already been forgotten. This chapter presents a special investigation of rivers throughout the modernization which occurred during the Meiji Restoration and altered the city's structure.

The Taisho era and the Showa era of Tokyo were the ages of the secondary industrial revolution, during which the urban population increased rapidly. As a result, rivers were drained in heedless efforts to utilize land effectively. This invasion was made possible due to the rivers' continuity and the fact that rivers were public land (and thus free). Rivers were filled and buried forever. The original uses of rivers were terminated in order to build roads, railroads, residential areas, and industrial areas, as well as to support the evolving urban structure. Thus, the original use of watercourses, such as rivers and canals, for ship transportation which played a dominant commercial role in early cities, was abolished. During the railway transportation period, the delivery of goods by river declined and with the onset of the automobile age, the relationship between cities and rivers changed completely.

The period from 1909 to 1985 was a time of turbulent change in Tokyo's twenty-three wards. The bridges built during the Edo era were arched so that ships could pass under them easily. In addition, many of them were parallel structures across the river so that coaches, rickshas, and people could cross the bridges easily. There were signs of a turning point during this period, especially

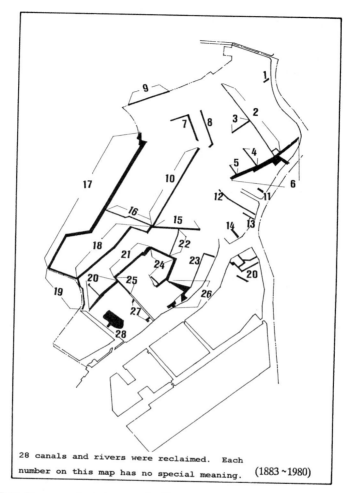

Figure II-D11 Decrease in waterways in Chuo ward between 1883 and 1990

as the country entered an age of high economic growth. Highway construction on outer moats spurred the construction of super highways. Presently, metropolitan highway structures above watercourses do exist—an odd combination.

Six Wards which Changed Greatly

Edogawa ward lost 1293.9 m of its river length in one *mesh* which was the largest decrease of all rivers (Fig. II-D13). The next largest decrease occurred in Adachi ward of 1187.1 m/*mesh*, followed by a decrease of 912.8 m/*mesh* in Chuo ward, 886.4 m/*mesh* in Katsushika ward, 872 m/*mesh* in Koto ward, and 696.3 m/*mesh*

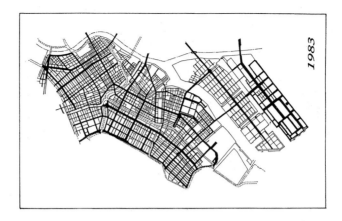

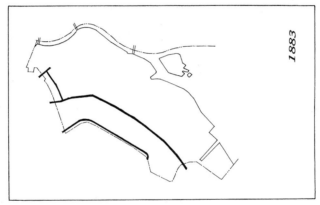

Figure II-D12 Road maps of Chuo ward in 1883 and 1983

in Sumida ward. These six wards lost the most river length among the twenty-three wards. A change of 675.3 m increase or decrease per *mesh* was the average of all twenty-three wards. This section offers an analysis of the six wards mentioned above which have changed comparatively rapidly.

New Uses of the Waterfront in the Six Main Wards

The width of rivers can be divided into three categories: under 3 m, 3–15 m, and over 15 m. Table II-D1 presents the land-use change of reclaimed watercourses in the forty-three years between 1937 and 1980. Edogawa ward has had the most filled-in watercourses, averaging 1.317 million m^2, which amounts to 40.92% of the total six wards. Adachi ward was second to Edogawa with 665,000 m^2 of filled in watercouses, which constitutes 20.65% of the total six wards. Next was Katsushika ward, with 382,000 m^2 or 11.86% filled in, followed by Chuo, Sumida,

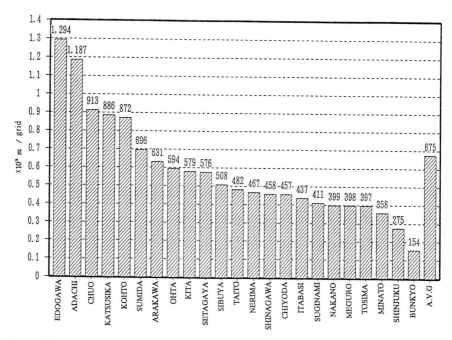

Figure II-D13 Decrease in the waterfront line density of rivers and canals in Tokyo's wards

and Koto ward. In Chuo ward, the greatest area of river, 60%, was converted into roads. 16.5% of the rivers in Koto ward were changed into roads. As for the other wards, about 30% of the total area of each ward was reclaimed for roads.

The rate of land-use conversion from rivers to residential areas was the highest in Katsushika ward, followed by Adachi and Edogawa wards, respectively. The conversion of rivers to industrial land-use areas was highest in Koto ward, amounting to 14.2%. As for the land-use change from rivers to commercial areas, Chuo ward also had the highest ratio. A few land-use changes were made from rivers to agricultural areas in Edo ward, but there were few of these transformations in other wards. On the other hand, many rivers were converted into various other land-use areas. Especially in Edogawa and Sumida wards, land-use change to other usage was about 50% which refers to the construction of parks and green space, parking lots, open spaces, and parks for sports.

Rivers were destroyed according to their width (Table II-D1 and Fig. II-D14). In the three wards of Edogawa, Adachi, and Katsushika, about 70–80% of all remaining rivers were under 3 m wide. The tendency was to fill in the wider rivers for roads. However, less than 50% of rivers remained which were under 3 m in Sumida, Koto, and Chuo wards, which demonstrates that the wider the river, the greater was the conversion from water body to land-use.

Table II-D1 Conversion of watercourses to other uses in six wards of Tokyo (1937–1980)

Ward	Continuation m	Area m²	Conversion of use from watercourse to					
			Road	Housing	Factory	Business	Farm	Others
Katsusika	190,875	382,142	121,075	134,640	18,514	17,123	6557	84,233
	15.8%	100.0%	31.7	35.3	4.9	4.9	1.7	21.5
Edogawa	562,778	1,316,638	399,479	251,311	74,655	40,946	40,718	409,519
	46.5%	100.0%	30.3	26.7	5.7	3.1	3.1	31.1
Adati	313,605	664,541	221,133	216,008	25,531	33,988	4531	153,734
	26.0%	100.0%	33.8	33.0	3.9	5.2	0.7	23.4
Sumida	82,752	288,800	84,931	46,371	5009	11,314	0	141,175
	6.8%	100.0%	29.4	16.1	1.7	3.9	0.0	48.9
Koutou	35,493	244,750	40,371	37,100	34,666	8969	0	123,644
	2.9%	100.0%	16.5	15.2	14.2	3.7	0.0	50.4
Chuo	24,777	322,023	202,693	4608	0	52,370	0	62,352
	2.0%	100.0%	62.9	1.4	0.0	16.3	0.0	19.4
	1,210,280	3,218,894	1069,682	690,038	158,375	164,710	51,806	974,657
Sum Total	100.0%	100.0%	33.3	24.6	5.0	5.1	1.6	30.4

Only Katsushika ward experienced a trend different from the other wards. In this ward, more area was converted into roads than was changed into residential areas. In Chuo ward, there were already few rivers and canals which were under 3 m in 1937. The following are the uses selected for converted watercourses, such as rivers and canals, during the years from 1937 to 1980 in the six wards:

- for water networks with widths over 15 m: the primary use was for roads; the second, for residential areas and the third for commercial areas.
- for water networks with widths of 3–15 m: the primary use was for roads, the second, for residential areas and the third, for industrial areas.
- for water networks with widths under 3 m: the primary use was for residential areas, the second, for roads and the third use was for commercial areas.

Waterfront Line Density and Land-Use in Cities

The city is an ecological system composed of people living within its boundaries and its environment. There is a natural feedback among people, their culture, and their natural environment. Through man's technology, slopes have been altered to serve residential purposes while the damp ground, the river, and

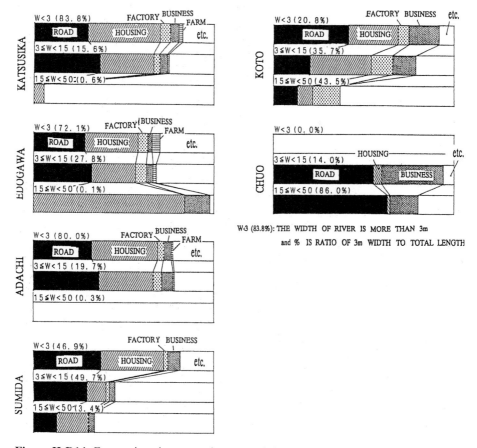

Figure II-D14 Comparison in conversion uses of six main wards in Tokyo (1937–1980)

seashore have been filled. Thus, the original importance of the landform has disappeared. As a result of the inappropriate development of natural landforms, nature has responded to alterations in the form of vengeful disasters. It is not possible to understand the natural characteristics of a region and its proper use unless we think about the natural system and its people.

To make favorable use of the potential returns that land offers, it is important to classify and analyze the form and style of land-use. Urbanization occurs in very complicated steps. If industrial areas, commercial areas, housing sites, residential areas, and fields are used as the index of the expansion of built-up areas, the change in land-use and environment becomes obvious. There is a correlation between these indexes and the waterfront line density (Table II-D2 and Fig. II-D15).

Table II-D2 Correlation coefficient table between waterfront line density and urbanization

	Main six wards	Tokyo 23 Wards
Housing area	0.884	0.573
Farm field	0.877	0.785
Drain pipe length	0.815	0.736
Housing & building	0.803	0.822
Secondary industry population	0.803	0.508
Water pipe length	0.782	0.762
Road length	0.715	0.806
Population density	0.552	0.566
Industrial area	0.385	0.487
Business area	0.221	0.163
Tertiary industry population	0.113	0.285

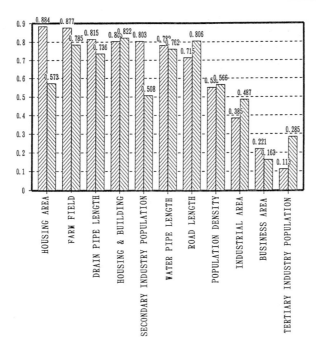

Figure II-D15 Coefficient correlation table between waterfront line density and urban spaces

Decrease of Waterfront Line Density and the Factorial Area Ratio

After the Meiji era, the industry in Tokyo changed greatly with the development of modern production. A cement plant, glassworks, shipyard, and beer brewery were established in and around Shinagawa. In the early 1900s, the two areas of modern industry in Tokyo were the manufacturing of machines and chemical products. According to industry statistics in 1920, the increase of factories in the number in Tokyo was 11.1% and the increase of employees was 11.2%. Industrial areas have often been chosen according to their proximity to coastal areas.

Proximity to the coast was an important condition for selecting factory sites, especially for the heavy chemical industry. Thus, the chemical industry developed mainly along the Sumida River and the canal zone to the east of the river. An industrial area formed on the reclaimed land of Tokyo Bay which stretches over both the Kanagawa and Chiba prefectures. The rise of industrial inland areas and coastal industrial zones has brought about an increase in cargo transportation overland. Consequently, the age of the water transportation evolved into the age of land transportation.

Decrease of Waterfront Line Density and Commercial Area Ratio

The increase of commercial land-use area ratio was predominantly high in Chiyoda, Chuo, and Taito wards. Sixty to seventy percent of these wards already held commercial uses by 1952. As for Chiyoda ward, the commercial area ratio had continued to increase from 1960 to 1980 and finally reached over 80% by 1980. In Taito ward, the ratio was also over 80% by 1970. On the other hand, in the remaining twenty wards, the change in the ratio of commercial area had remained almost the same, that is, under 20% but was increasing annually. The only exception was Minato ward which showed a slightly different change from the others.

Decrease of Waterfront Line Density, Housing, and Residential Area Ratio

In this chapter, housing sites refer not only to living accommodations, but also to areas where office buildings, shops, and factories are located alongside the housing units. In Edogawa, Itabashi, Nerima, and Setagaya wards, the area of housing and residential sites increased rapidly from 1952–1980. With the exception of Shinagawa, Chiyoda, and Shinjuku wards, where the residential area ratio has been decreasing, the housing site ratio of the remaining wards is more than 90%. This considerable change can be observed particularly in Edigawa, Katsushika, Adachi, and Chuo wards.

On the other hand, in Shinjuku, Bunkyo, Shinagawa, and Chiyoda wards, the area of housing and residential sites has decreased every year. In three wards, Edogawa, Katsushika, and Adachi, an increase in the housing site ratio has lowered the waterfront line density. At the same time, in Nerima, Itabashi, Setagaya, and Ohta wards, where the housing site ratio has also been increasing, the waterfront line density has not been declining as to be expected.

Decrease of Waterfront Line Density and the Agricultural Area Ratio

With the expansion of the Tokyo metropolitan area, the traditional agricultural base in cities and suburban areas has collapsed. At the beginning of this research project, an investigation was made in the area where the amount of water for agricultural use was expected to decrease as a result of the reduction in agricultural lands.

$$\frac{\text{decreasing of agricultural lands}}{\text{paddy}} \leftrightarrow \frac{\text{decreasing of watercourses}}{\text{use for paddy}}$$

The project reveals the rapid decrease of the agricultural area ratio in Edogawa, Nerima, Setagaya, Ohta, and Suginami wards. Although the agricultural area ratio was almost 80% in Edogawa and Nerima wards, it decreased to 15% by 1980. At the same time, agricultural land and the waterfront line density in Edogawa, Adachi, Katsushika, Ohta, and Setagaya wards decreased to an extreme extent.

PAST, PRESENT, AND FUTURE OF TOKYO BAY

Tokyo Bay is one of the three largest bays in Japan. The entrance to the Bay is extremely narrow with a width of about 6 km. Its depth is shallow with about 15 m and its area covers only about 120,000 ha. The Bay holds about 18 billion m^3 of water.

The reclamation of Tokyo Bay started during the Edo period. Relying on reclaimed land, the industrial area has expanded greatly since 1955 and is now about 26.456 million ha. Figure II-D16 shows the degree of the reclamation: About 4000 ha of Tokyo, 6000 ha of Kanagawa prefecture and 20,000 ha in Chiba prefecture are composed of reclaimed land. Before World War II, the reclamation was 3.5 ha. Even between 1921 and 1935, only 1000 ha were filled. Today, the reclamation of land in Tokyo absorbs about 4300 ha, in addition to the previous hectares reclaimed.

Change of Reclamation in Each Bay

Yokohama Bay was constructed by filling the Natsushima area in the 1910s and was used as a naval airport before World War II. After that, reclamation was extended to 62 ha by 1967, 68 ha in 1969 along Maboli seashore, and to 12 ha in 1974 for Yokohama Bay. This reclamation began in earnest when 80 ha from the town of Daikoku and 610 ha from the town of Negishi were reclaimed during the fifty-eight years Yokohama Bay Plan was revised. In addition, during sixty-eight years of the revised plan, 34 ha of Hongen wharf and 669 ha of Kanazawa were accepted for reclamation reached completion in 1980.

Today the Minato Mirai 21st Century Plan (MM21) is underway with 76 ha of the 186 ha planned to be renewed. To form Kawasaki Bay, 114 ha were created in Chidori town by 1955, 527 ha in Ukishima and Ougimachi by 1963, and 217 ha in Higashiougishima by 1972. Now the reclaimed land in Ukishima town and Higashiougishima is under way. Harume wharf and Toyosu wharf were maintained in the Tokyo Port Area Plan in 1955. However, with the port area plans

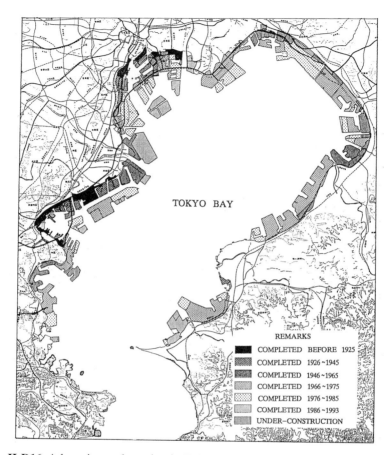

Figure II-D16 Advancing reclamation in Tokyo Bay

of 1961 and 1966, Shinkiba, Yumenoshima, and Ohi were planned to be filled to create 2244 ha. Five-hundred-and-two ha were "produced" for Chuo breakwater and 403 ha for Haneda were created by disposing of waste.

Before World War II, Chiba port area was filled to gain 198 ha and in 1950, an additional 99 ha of filled land were added to create the site of an ironworks. After that, 36 ha were created at this port for the site of a thermal power plant. In Kitasodegaura 399 ha of landfill and 440 ha of landfill from the Nagaura area were used for the site of a factory. Besides those reclamations, 608 ha were gained in the port area for a factory and a public site by 1968. In addition, in the modern port area plan of Chiba Chuo, 2233 ha located mainly in Funabashi were planned to be gained and completed by 1975. Around Kemi River 1546 ha were created as the site for the Kaihin New Town and Makuharimesse. Eight-hundred-and fifty-seven ha in the Urayasu area were used as the site for Disney

Land in 1980. Besides these areas, 1054 ha of additional reclamation is under way or under consideration. In Kisarazu Bay, 661 ha were gained by 1967 for the site of an ironworks and 460 ha in 1975 for the site of a port.

Tokyo Bay as a Refuse Disposal Plant

All waste from the metropolitan area of Tokyo was relinquished inland until 1945. However, since about 1957, the garbage disposal site has been located on the reclaimed land of Tokyo Bay as it became impossible to dispose of all garbage inland. After 1976, almost all of the waste was "eliminated" by filling in Tokyo Bay (Fig. II-D17).

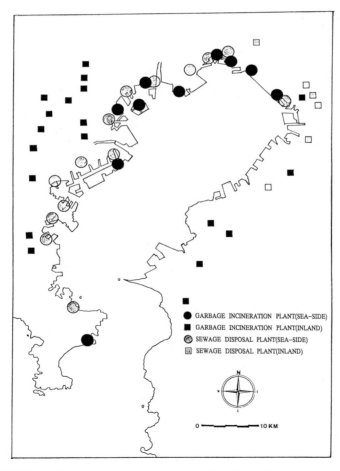

GARBAGE INCINERATION PLANT(SEA–SIDE)
GARBAGE INCINERATION PLANT(INLAND)
SEWAGE DISPOSAL PLANT(SEA–SIDE)
SEWAGE DISPOSAL PLANT(INLAND)

0 —————— 10 KM

Figure II-D17 Locations of sewage disposal and garbage incineration plants near Tokyo Bay

The Ministry of Transportation and the Ministry of Health and Welfare estimate that disposed waste from the metropolitan area will fill 1 billion m^3 of Tokyo Bay within ten years. To deal with this situation, the Fenix Plan was designed to reclaim 600 ha of land in order to meet the demand of about 110,000 million ha of reclaimed land. This project plans to use Minamihonmoku in Yokohama and Ukishima in Kawasaki of Kanagawa prefecture, the area of Chuo breakwater in Tokyo, the area of Kasai and Ichikawa city in the Chiba prefecture as reclaimed lands.

The Environmental Agency estimates that by the year 2000, the accumulated waste from the metropolitan area of Tokyo will be at least 90 million m^3 while the Tokyo and five prefecture summit estimates 70 million m^3 of garbage. Therefore, even if the Fenix Plan is carried out, the area will be consumed in about three years. Moreover, it is estimated that the area which will be used to discard the remaining earth after construction will amount to between 180 million m^3 and 230 million m^3, and that the area of industrial waste will be from 100–220 million m^3. Thus, 2250 ha of the Bay will have to be converted into land in order to bury all the waste from these projects.

Present Coastal Waterfront Line

Tokyo Bay consists of six port areas and two out-of-port areas (Fig. II-D18). These waterfront lines are divided into six parts: a place which citizens can access freely, districts around the port areas, industrial areas, distribution storehouses, an airport, and military bases. Of course, people cannot access these places freely except where they are permitted to do so. The results of research according to this classification are presented (Table II-D3 and Fig. II-D19). 40% of Tokyo Bay waterfront is an industrial area and 36% of its coastal facilities are port areas and distribution storehouses. The American military base and the Self-Defense Force in Tokyo Bay extend over about 31 km, or 4.5% of the area. Consequently, citizens can only freely access 24% of the sites.

The largest port area in Tokyo Bay is Chiba port, followed in size by the ports of Tokyo and Yokohama. If the area beyond the designation of the Fenix Plan is filled, the surface of the sea will decrease further and an even greater change in Tokyo Bay can be expected in the future.

CONCLUSION

After World War II, research was conducted on twenty principle cities which underwent modernization and industrialization and were consequently altered drastically. The conclusions from this investigation were that nine cities, Toyama, Tokyo, Tsu, Osaka, Hikone, Hiroshima, Tokushima, Fukuoka, and Saga have decreased their water surface by more than 10%. As to the waterfront line density, the same rate of decline occurred in Akita, Kanazawa, Tokyo, Shizuoka, Osaka, Hikone, Hiroshima, Kouchi, and Shiga.

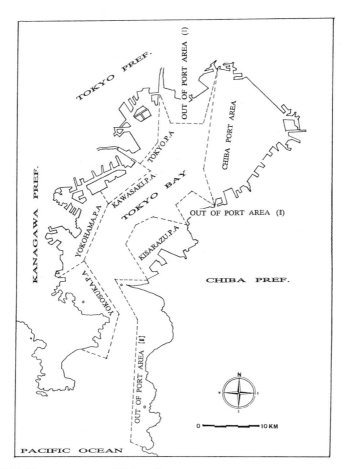

Figure II-D18 Port area map of Tokyo Bay

A change in the structure of the industrial population in developed and developing countries worldwide is presented in Figure II-D20. The primary, secondary, and tertiary industrial sectors in each country undergo different developments. Some cities in the Third World still are at the starting point of the secondary industrial city. The waterfront environment in those cities is inclined to follow the land-use pattern that occurred with waterways in the cities of developed countries. The graph, in fact, implies that developing countries do follow the same trends as developed countries. In the cities where the foundation for the secondary industrial city was prepared, the waterfront environment was destroyed and it has since become extremely difficult to recover the lost water space. The valuable waterfront environment has been eliminated by trying to accelerate the city's development. On the other hand, in cities which experienced a slower pace of industrialization, a beautiful waterfront environment has remained.

Table II-D3 1994 Coastal waterfront line of Tokyo Bay

Port Area	Accessible (m)	Port (m)	Factory (m)	Warehouse (m)	Airport (m)	Force Base (m)	Swimming Beach (m)	Total (m)
Yokosuka	24,357	2581	17,941			33,988		78,867
Yokohama	7604	45,210	95,874			896		149,584
Kawasaki		5601	46,882	9550				62,033
Tokyo	57,341	23,987	56,312	58,813	17,819		5002	219,274
Chiba	35,963	66,441	137,514					239,918
Kisarazu		9781	10,691			1240		21,712
Excepting (1)	22,207	20,129	1941					44,277
Excepting (2)	8631							8631
Excepting (3)	54,918	9170				4241	30,398	98,727
Total	211,021	182,900	367,155	68,363	17,819	40,365	35,400	923,023

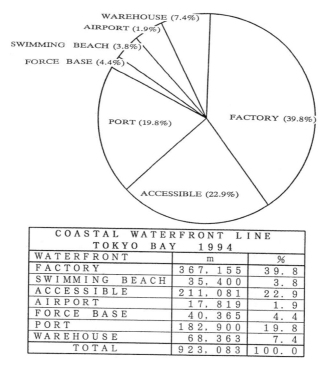

COASTAL WATERFRONT LINE TOKYO BAY 1994		
WATERFRONT	m	%
FACTORY	367, 155	39. 8
SWIMMING BEACH	35, 400	3. 8
ACCESSIBLE	211, 081	22. 9
AIRPORT	17, 819	1. 9
FORCE BASE	40, 365	4. 4
PORT	182, 900	19. 8
WAREHOUSE	68, 363	7. 4
TOTAL	923, 083	100. 0

Figure II-D19 Breakdown of the use of coastal waterfront area of Tokyo Bay

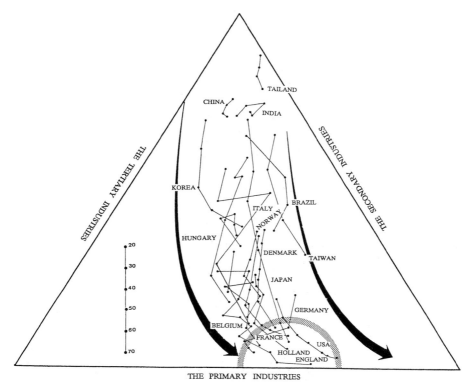

THE PRIMARY INDUSTRIES

Figure II-D20 Distribution of industrial employment in several developed nations

This shows that future tertiary industrial societies should profit from the lessons of others and preserve their waterfront line density. The waterfront environment in the primary industrial period gradually deteriorates during the industrialization because of the tendency to decrease the water area for the sake of the development of modern cities (Fig. II-D21). Yet during the transformation to the tertiary industrial city, people are demanding that the waterfront environment be restored and some cities are endeavoring to seek an improved waterfront environment. Figure II-D22 shows this tendency of historical change in other countries with the change of population over a 100-year time span covering each phase of the primary, secondary, and tertiary industrial development.

- Germany, France, and Italy: The primary industry was replaced first by the secondary industry, then by the tertiary industry (France: 1868; West Germany: 1892; Italy: 1962).
- U.S.A. and Japan: The primary industry was replaced first by the tertiary industry and then by the secondary industry (America: 1898, 1918).

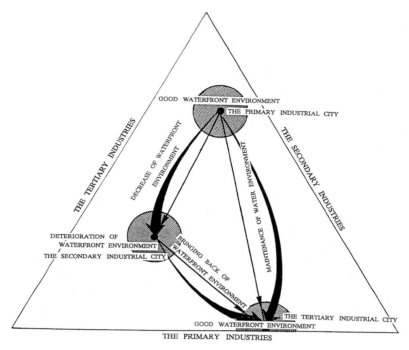

Figure II-D21 Typical pattern of change of waterfront environments and nearby industries

- England: The primary industry was overrun by the secondary and the tertiary industries over 100 years ago (England: 1700).

The period when the primary industry phased into the second or third stage of industry took thirty-eight years in France, thirty-nine years in western Germany, and seven years in America. Italy attained the third stage in only two years and Japan achieved it in three years, which is a remarkably short time. This rapid transition meant that some elements of the city structure were forced to change drastically to accommodate the short-term achievement of the secondary or the tertiary industrial period. Cities in countries like France or England which changed their basic industrial structure over a long period developed differently from cities in countries like Japan and Italy where change occurred rapidly and over a short amount of time. Therefore, the influence of the change in both types of cities was different. In addition, the modernization of the main urban trade during the secondary industrial development was established at the cost of depleting the cities' waterfront environments.

Modern industrial cities have experienced three industrial revolutions during their development. First, the change from production by human labor to

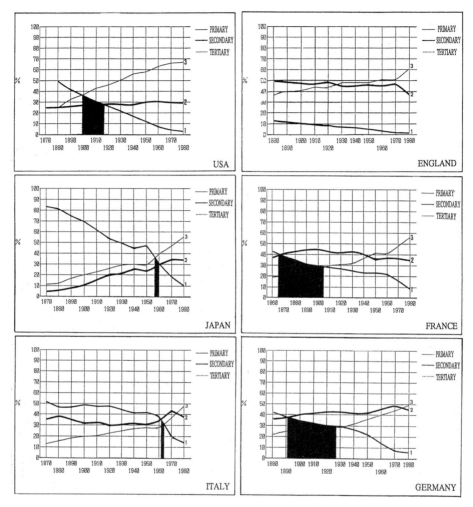

Figure II-D22 Change in distribution of industry over the long term

production by machines created a change in the demand structure. The second revolution began when mass production was systematized into private production due to the transfer of military technology developed during World War II. With these two revolutionary industrial changes, many aspects of social life were also altered. As a result, the spatial structure of factories and homes changed drastically.

Finally, due to the new exploitation of materials and advanced electronics technology, the third industrial revolution has created cities of multiple technologies and information. Sometimes change is characterized only by the images of mammoth skyscrapers that have become identified with future cities. However, to solve the problems which arise during the evolution to the tertiary industrial city, the secret may be to consider returning to a more natural environment. None of the cities in their various phases of industrial development can do without planning the coexistence with their waterfront environment. Waterfront redevelopment projects all over the world are, in essence, plans to recycle facilities around the bay. Ultimately, the remnants of the secondary industrial period need to be recycled in the context of restoring the natural waterfront environment.

On the other hand, the city of the tertiary industrial type (the "information society") needs an information base that can accommodate a safer, richer, and more natural environment. As cities enter the third industrial period, now is the time to recover the waterfront environment which was thoughtlessly eroded during the secondary industrial period.

There are many cities that have passed through the secondary industrial phase and are at the onset of the third industrial era. Some developed countries have even almost completed the third phase. In the future, as countries face further development, the field of city planning must accept the difficult challenge of redeveloping waterfront areas to revive beaches and of recovering lost rivers to restore flowing water. Only through a new awareness of the fragility of nature can the waterways lost during the industrialization be rescued. Tomorrow's city planners must devise a method of developing cities that considers all aspects of the waterfront environment to avoid repeating the errors of the past.

BIBLIOGRAPHY

1. Biswas, A. K. 1970. *History of Hydrology.* Rotterdam: Northern Dutch Publishing.
2. Jyunko, N. 1983. *Sewage Systems.* Tokyo: Asahi Shinbunsha.
3. Kiyoji, T. 1980. *Development of Water Resources.* Tokyo: Sankaido.
4. Koichi, A. 1983. *Thinking About River.* Okyo: Kokinshoin.
5. National Astronomical Observatory 1994. *Chronological Scientific Tables.* Tokyo: Maruzen.
6. Nishio, K. 1983. *Water, Livelihood, Environment.* Tokyo: Recycle Bunkasha.
7. Shinbun, A. 1994. *Japan Almanac.* Tokyo: n.p.
8. Tadashi, A. 1980. *Japanese Water.* Tokyo: Sankaido.
9. Tadashi, A. 1987. *Hydrological Environment in Urban Areas.* Tokyo: Kyoritsu Shutspan.
10. Taichiro, C. 1977. *Regional Development and Water Resources.* Tokyo: Riko Hyoron Shutspan.
11. Teruyuki, S. 1991. *Principles of Water Problems.* Tokyo: Hokuto Publishing.

E Efficient Energy Use in Japanese Cities

Keisuke Hanaki and Toshiaki Ichinose

INTRODUCTION

The energy consumption in urban areas has significantly increased with the dramatic rate of industrialization in society since the Industrial Revolution. The activities of a developed nation such as Japan greatly depend on substantial amounts of energy. Although the cost of energy in Japan is much higher than in the U.S.A., high prices have not critically limited the growth of Japan's economy because other expenses, such as labor, contribute to the total production cost more than does the cost of energy. Therefore, economic incentives to save energy tend to decrease since there are other expenses costlier than energy. However, the increasing awareness of the global warming issue is changing circumstances and attitudes. Saving energy is an absolute necessity in a developed country where the per capita energy consumption is higher than in developing countries. Japan is committed in its actions to prevent global warming by stabilizing the per capita emissions of carbon dioxide so that by the year 2000, emission rates will remain at their 1990 level. The reduction, or at least stabilization of energy consumption and diminished use of carbon intensive fuel, are definitely necessary to achieve this target. The current energy consumption in urban areas, which has grown with the increase in the nation's various capabilities and functions, should be preserved to keep global warming worldwide at its status quo.

However, saving energy is not the only goal of the future city, nor is returning the society to its previous state of development prior to the Industrial Revolution. It is necessary to maintain high standards of living for people by offering sufficient medical, educational, and cultural services, among other considerations and to improve the overall quality of life. It is not easy to save energy and to maintain high standards of living at the same time. It is necessary to develop technologies to minimize energy consumption, to recover energy in urban areas and to apply these technologies. In addition, plans for the infrastructure should also consider methods for saving energy. An analysis of the energy consumption in Japanese cities and possible methods to preserve energy are discussed in this chapter.

CHARACTERISTICS OF ENERGY CONSUMPTION IN JAPANESE CITIES[1]

Energy is consumed in a city for many purposes which range from household to commercial or industrial uses. A city's consumption occurs primarily in four sectors: household; commercial, office and service; industrial; and transportation.

The share of energy consumption (end use basis) in each sector varies from the industrial city to the commercial city. Energy consumption in seven large Japanese cities was analyzed in 1992.

The basic data of the seven prefecture capital cities is summarized in Table II-E1. The consumption of each type of fuel was estimated for each of the four sectors, i.e. household, commercial, office and service, transportation as well as industrial, to see how each sector contributes to the energy consumption rate of the seven cities (Fig. II-E1). Various statistics, both for the user aspect such as a household expenditure survey and the supplier aspect such as electricity supply statistics, were used to estimate the overall energy consumption. The share of the industry sector was almost 50% in Osaka while Sapporo's and Fukuoka's industrial sector used less than 10%. Fukuoka showed a low value since the adjacent city of Kitakyushu has a high concentration of industry. The commercial, office, and service sector, which is typical in cities, was as high as 50% in Fukuoka followed by Tokyo's twenty-three wards. The average value of the annual growth rate in energy consumption in each sector of these prefecture capital cities was compared with the growth of population and GDP (Gross Domestic Product) (Fig. II-E2). Only the energy consumption in the industrial sector grew at a slower rate than the population. Other sectors experienced a much greater increase in energy consumption which was not matched by an increase in population in these cities. The highest increase in energy use was

Table II-E1 Analysis of basic data for seven major Japanese cities

City name	Population[a] (thousands)	Projected urban planning area[b] (km^2)	Annual average temperature (°C)[c]	Heating degree-month[d]
Sapporo	1610	240	8.0	111.4
Tokyo (23 wards)	8100	568	15.3	45.1
Yokohama	3150	326	15.1	49.0
Nagoya	2100	301	14.9	51.4
Osaka	2540	205	16.2	45.3
Kobe	1430	198	15.6	50.3
Fukuoka	1170	149	16.0	40.9

[a]1989.
[b]1989.
[c]Average for 30 years (1951–1980).
[d]Heating degree-month = sum of (18 – monthly temperature in °C) for months in which the average temperature is below 18°C.

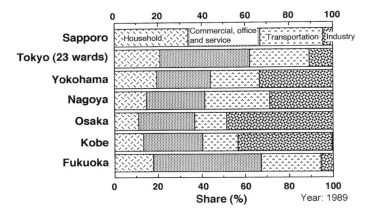

Figure II-E1 Share of energy consumption in each sector of seven large cities in Japan (Hiramatsu *et al.*, 1992)

observed in the commercial, office and service sector which typically represents various functions in the urban area. A significant rise in this sector increased the total energy consumption rate in all these cities. However, the growth in total energy consumption was lower than the growth of the GDP.

Household Energy Consumption

Household energy consumption generally depends on the lifestyle of the owners, floor space of the house, and the climate of the area. However, since the income

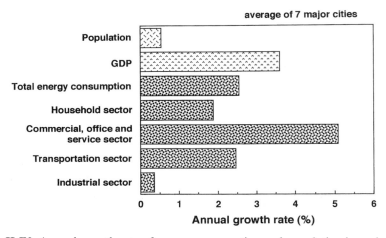

Figure II-E2 Annual growth rate of energy consumption and population in each sector in the period between 1980 and 1988. (The increased growth rate in seven cities, namely Sapporo, Tokyo's twenty-three wards, Yokohama, Nagoya, Osaka, Kobe, and Fukuoka were averaged)

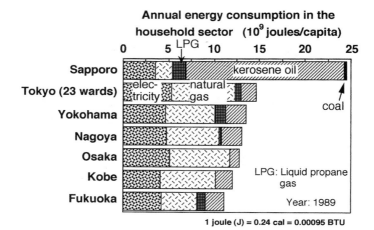

Figure II-E3 Annual per capita energy consumption rate for household use in Japanese cities (Hiramatsu *et al.*, 1992)

level and lifestyle of people vary little in Japan, floor space and climate become the major factors in determining the per capita household energy consumption.

Considering the per capita household energy consumption for the seven cities, a high heating demand for kerosene oil significantly raised household energy use particularly in Sapporo (Fig. II-E3). Fairly small differences in household energy consumption were observed among the other six cities because of their similar climate conditions. Therefore, the per capita household energy consumption varies independently of the type of city as long as the climate conditions are similar.

The measure of energy consumption in different climates is often discussed by using the index of degree-hour, degree-day, or degree-month that represents the extent of cold or heat and its duration. Calculations of the heating degree-month (HDM) shown in Table II-E1 were based on the monthly average temperature by adding the fractions of temperature (°C) lower than 18°C between January and December.

An investigation was conducted on several Chinese and Japanese cities to find the effect of temperature based on available energy consumption data.[2] A correlation between HDM and the consumption of various types of fuels was examined. The kerosene consumption in Japan and coal consumption in China showed the best correlation with HDM. The correlations also indicated the degree of dependency of the annual household consumption on kerosene, which is almost exclusively used for heating in the forty-seven prefecture capitals of Japan and coal consumption in Chinese prefectures for heating using the degree-month index (standard 18°C) (Fig. II-E4). Heating demands in Japan are remarkably sensitive to HDM in the zone where the HDM is higher than a 70 degree-month, whereas heating needs in China are less sensitive to temperature. Such low

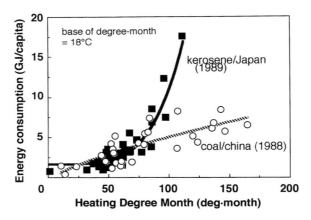

Figure II-E4 Increase of kerosene consumption in Japan and coal consumption in China with the increase of heating degree-month (Ichinose *et al.*, 1993)

sensitivity rates in China might be related to the Chinese system of central planning and enforced energy allocation. The regression curves are expressed as follows:

- Per capita annual kerosene consumption $(10^6 \text{ J}) = 15.1 \times 10^{-6} \text{ HDM} 4.4 - 1638$ (Japan).
- Per capita annual coal consumption $(10^6 \text{ J}) = 224 \text{ HDM}^{0.7} - 583$ (China).

Household energy consumption in Japanese cities was compared to U.S.data based on the cold regions in the North-East and the warm regions in the South (Fig. II-E5).[3] Japanese cities used far less energy for household purposes than U.S. cities even in the warm regions of the southern U.S.A. Kerosene is used in a greater volume in the cold north-east region than in the warm regions (South) in the U.S.A., whereas the use of electricity is greater in the warm regions. Although U.S. cities still consume an excessive amount of energy, this amount decreased between 1978 and 1982, especially in the north-east region and this trend seems to continue. On the other hand, the household energy consumption in Japan shows a clear tendency to increase due to the change in lifestyle which places greater demands on energy.

Commercial, Office, and Service Sector Energy Consumption

The commercial, office, and service sector tends to consume larger amounts of energy each year, although the breakdown of energy consumption in this sector has not been calculated by using the available statistics from Japanese cities. The annual increase in energy consumption in this sector is almost ten times greater than the growth rate of the population in large Japanese cities. The results imply that the per capita increase in energy consumed by this sector greatly contributes to the overall growth of energy consumption rates in Japanese cities.

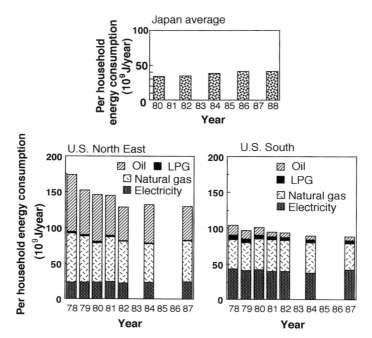

Figure II-E5 Comparison of household energy consumption rates in Japan and the U.S.A (Energy Information Administration, 1991)

Transportation Energy Consumption

The energy consumption in the transportation sector depends mostly on the activities of a city, its spatial distribution, and the extent of its mass transit system. The rate of energy consumption has been determined by dividing the amount of energy burned in transportation by the total number of people who commute in Japan's seven largest cities (Fig. II-E6). High usage of the railway service lowered the energy consumption in Tokyo and Osaka, even though their average commuting distances are longer than in the other cities. The high consumption rates in Sapporo and Nagoya are probably due to a heavy reliance on automobiles.

Energy Consumption and Economic Activities

Although the amount of energy used depends on the type of activities which are prevalent in an urban area, the GDP economic index may be a sound parameter to define the overall activities of a city. When examining the correlation between GDP (expressed in 1985 Yen) and annual rate of energy consumption every year from 1980–1988 for each of the seven cities, Tokyo had the highest GDP and energy consumption levels, as would be expected (Fig. II-E7). Not only was the

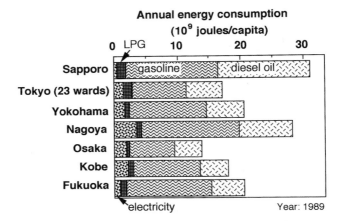

Figure II-E6 Transportation energy consumption per commuter in large Japanese cities (Hiramatsu *et al.*, 1992)

growth in the GDP consistent, but so was the increase in energy consumption for each city. All the data fit into a fairly neat pattern. Thus, the growth in energy consumption was found to correlate directly with the growth in GDP. The regression line is:

$$\text{Energy consumption (J)} = 21{,}000 \text{ GDP (Yen, 1985)}$$

The coefficient in this equation varies depending on social and economic factors.

ENERGY CONSUMPTION IN URBAN VERSUS NONURBAN AREAS

Energy consumption per person and GDP in the seven cities is compared with national average values (Fig. II-E8). The per capita energy consumption in these

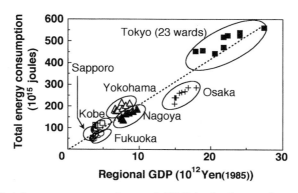

Figure II-E7 Total energy consumption and GDP in the largest Japanese cities. The symbols within the circles denote the years (Hiramatsu *et al.*, 1992)

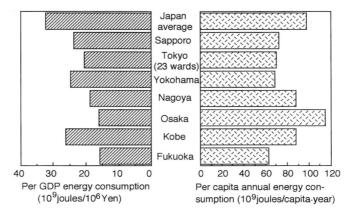

Figure II-E8 Energy consumption per GDP and per capita in seven Japanese cities (Hiramatsu *et al.*, 1992)

cities was smaller than or nearly equal to the national average value except for Osaka which has had high industrial activity. These comparisons indicate that urban areas generally consumed no more energy per person than nonurban areas because cities are mainly commercial or service oriented centers. The energy consumption per GDP was significantly lower in all seven cities than the national average. In other words, urban areas use energy more efficiently to generate economic activity.

However, these facts do not necessarily mean that nationwide urbanization can reduce the total national energy consumption rate. Many urban activities are, in fact, supported by the industrial production located in nonurban areas which significantly contribute to high energy consumption. That is, urban areas are responsible for the relatively high energy consumption rates found in the nonurbanized areas which actually support the cities.

Lower per capita energy consumption in highly urbanized areas seems to be observed frequently in developed countries. This tendency is entirely different in developing countries. Two examples, China and Thailand, are compared with the case of Japan (Fig. II-E9).[4] The per capita energy consumption in Beijing, Bangkok, or the Bangkok region, showed almost comparable results to Tokyo (twenty-three wards). However, these values were much higher than the average value for their nation. Both Beijing and Bangkok consumed three times more energy per capita than the average rate of all of China and Thailand, respectively. This is attributed to the fact that many industries are located in and around the cities and that the lifestyle of urban residents is much more energy-intensive than in nonurban areas. Therefore, urbanization does cause a significant increase in the energy consumption per capita. The increase in both population and per capita energy consumption greatly contributes to the drastic energy increase in the cities of developing countries.

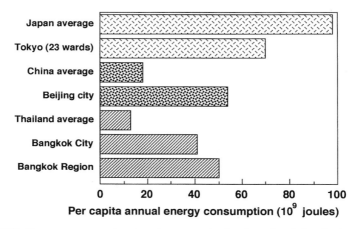

Per capita annual energy consumption (10⁹ joules)

Figure II-E9 Energy consumption in urban areas in developed and developing countries (1. Hiramatsu *et al.*, 1992; 2. Ichinose *et al.*, 1993; 3. Thailand Development and Research Institute, 1990)

EFFICIENT ENERGY USE IN URBAN AREAS

Materials, energy and heat are altered in urban areas and discharged into the environment in a different form (Fig. II-E10). Energy is consumed to pursue various urban activities, but it yields only heat and carbon dioxide, although general urban activity produces diverse types of output. Products, food and raw materials imported to a city eventually become solid waste and wastewater which leave their impact on the surrounding environment. To make the city more environmentally sound, it is necessary to minimize the wasteful use of energy through recycling energy or heat recovery. This advanced technology will convert the heat to energy which can be used again. Possible methods to achieve these aims through proper urban planning and careful infrastructure management are presented in the following sections.

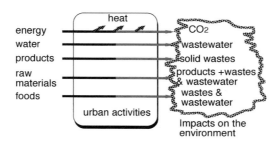

Figure II-E10 Material transformations in urban areas and their impact on the environment

Minimizing Energy Consumption

Minimizing energy consumption in the transportation sector is the most efficient means of conserving energy. The construction of a mass transportation system is a direct way to achieve this goal. Other methods of reducing energy consumption are by improving the freight transportation network and introducing a mixed land-use policy. The commute distance is shorter in mixed land-use areas than in separated, conventionally zoned areas; the former then would lower energy expenditures for individual commuters as well as the entire public transportation network. However, high environmental quality should be maintained when using the mixed land-use zoning system in residential areas. Although the introduction of more sophisticated urban planning which includes the construction of information networks connecting satellite offices, is expected to reduce energy consumption, it is still debated whether such a system would ultimately do so.

Energy Recovery from Solid Waste and Wastewater

In addition to the effort to minimize energy consumption, various ways of recovering energy from solid waste and wastewater treatment should be introduced. Table II-E2 summarizes typical methods used to recover energy from solid waste and wastewater.

Solid-waste management poses one of the most pressing challenges in the planning and management of modern cities since cities produce an ever increasing amount of solid waste. The problem is critical in large Japanese cities which do not have sufficient space for solid waste landfills. Incineration is widely used in these cities to reduce the final volume of waste to be disposed and to avoid sanitary problems. Incineration provides waste heat which can be converted to generate electricity and/or heat.

The amount of energy obtained through incineration can be calculated through the calorific value of solid waste. An average amount of solid waste generated by household, commercial, office and service sectors is roughly 1 kg (wet weight basis) per day per person in Japan. Using the average calorific value of solid waste in Japan of about 10×10^6 J/kg (wet weight basis), the calorific value of the annual solid waste generation is calculated to be 3.7×10^9 J/year per person. This value is much smaller than the per capita energy demand (for example, 70×10^9 J/year is required for Tokyo's twenty-three wards); however, recovering the solid waste of a large population to supply energy to a limited area is a very feasible idea.

Another way to recycle energy is through the methane fermentation process whereby bacteria produces methane in the absence of oxygen. Treatment of solid waste in a designed reactor is possible, but it is more efficient to recover methane gas from solid waste landfill sites. Microbiological methane production takes place over many years in these landfills. Part of the calorific value of solid waste is converted to that of methane gas in the landfill site. Roughly estimated, if half

Table II-E2 Possible methods of energy recovery from solid waste and wastewater

Resources	Method of energy recovery	Potential energy recovery per capita[a] (10^9/person · year)	Advantages	Disadvantages
Solid waste	Electricity and/or heat recovery at incineration plant	3.7	High quality of heat energy obtained	Location of incineration plant is often far from CBD (Central Business District)
	Methane recovery from landfill	0.9	"Greenhouse gas" (methane) emission also reduced	Low recovery percentage
Sewage	Heat recovery from sewage	1.9	Large flexibility in site of heat recovery	Low quality of heat, heating purpose only
	Methane recovery from sewage sludge	0.2	Established process, good fuel obtained	Low energy recovery

[a]See text for assumptions in these estimates.

of the original calorific value is converted to methane gas and half of the gas is recovered from the landfill site, the recovered methane would account for 0.9×10^9 J/year per person. This measure is much smaller than the energy obtained by reusing heat produced during the incineration process. However, recovery and utilization of methane gas from the landfill site is very important from a different point of view. Its recovery can reduce the emission of methane gas into the atmosphere. One of the drawbacks of methane is that it is a "greenhouse gas" and causes global warming. Since methane from the solid waste landfill is considered an important source of energy, its recovery is necessary.[5]

Sewage has the potential to be another important energy source. Energy can be recovered from sewage which has a higher temperature than the atmosphere. Assuming that for every 5°C temperature difference recovered from sewage, the sewage discharge per person is 250 l/d, the recovered energy is 1.91×10^9 J/year per person. The disadvantage is that the quality of the recovered heat is poor and using it with a heat pump for space heating is almost the only way to effectively utilize this energy. On the other hand, the flexible location choice for a heat recovery plant is a great advantage of this energy source. Such a plant can be constructed not only close to the sewage treatment plant, but also at the site with the highest energy demands.

The recovery of energy from sewage through methane production is yet another example of alternative energy.[6] Direct methane conversion from sewage, however, is not feasible in a developed country like Japan due to the poor effluent from the sewage treatment plant. Instead, methane production from sewage sludge can take place in the process known as anaerobic digestion. Assuming each person discharges sewage which contains 100g of chemical oxygen demand (COD) per day and only half of this organic matter is converted to methane in the anaerobic digestion of sewage sludge, 0.2×10^9 J/year could be recovered using this method. This value is smaller than the energy recovered by other sources, but this technology has been in practice for more than fifty years.

System of Energy Recovery in Urban Areas

Energy recovery technology of solid waste, sewage, or river water has long been established in some countries and has already been used in many urban areas. Yet, a more important and practical issue is the reasonable and optimal application of these techniques to urban areas which have an uneven distribution of residential, commercial, or business land-use. A district heating and cooling system is necessary when the recovered heat is utilized with a heat pump. A high density heat demand is preferable in district heating systems considering heat loss and construction costs of the distribution pipes. Thus, central business districts or high-rise apartment houses seem to be suitable sites to install a district heating system. On the other hand, an energy source such as a solid waste incineration plant or sewage treatment plant is normally located in a suburb or fringe zone of the urban area. This discrepancy between the location of supply and the location of the heaviest demand should be considered in planning the procedure of recovering energy.

Another current approach to supply energy is through the use of a solid waste incineration plant (Fig. II-E11). Many of the incineration plants in Japan currently recycle energy; a typical example of heat utilization is the supply of heat to a swimming pool adjacent to a plant (Fig. II-E11a). Energy from solid waste is, of course, utilized in this case, but it does not effectively contribute to the decrease in the fossil fuel consumption in urban areas. A simple way to connect the energy source with its demand area is to transport heat to the central business district (CBD) from the site of a district heating and cooling plant (Fig. II-E11b). However, heat loss and the high construction cost of a transportation pipe are problems that need to be solved before implementing this method. A third method, which would require a drastic change in urban planning, is to relocate the solid waste incineration plant near to the CBD (Fig. II-E11c). The plant could

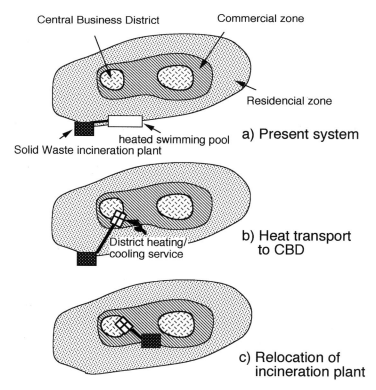

Figure II-E11 Energy recovery and supply systems converting solid waste to various land-uses

be constructed under the ground of a building or park and would function as an energy supply plant. One possible complication with this plan is that it would first be necessary to gain the acceptance of the residents and subsequently the consent of the management to transport the solid waste in and out of the plant.

Sewage heat as a source of alternative energy offers several options to counter the aforementioned problems (Fig. II-E12). The current system is to recover the heat from a sewage treatment plant or from existing pumping stations (Fig. II-E12a). Again, the location of these facilities is not in proximity to the area of high energy demand. One possible option is to construct district heating and cooling plant(s) along the main sewer pipes which usually run through the CBD (Fig. II-E12b). Another option is to combine energy recovery with the reuse of treated sewage. The treated sewage would be pumped from the sewage treatment plant to the district heating and cooling plant at the CBD (Fig. 1II-E12c). The water would then be pumped into a stream which would create a pleasant water environment.

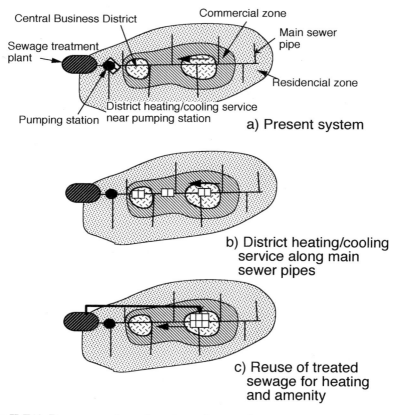

Figure II-E12 Recovery and supply system of energy from sewage

CONCLUSION

Modifying or altering the existing urbanscape to create an environmentally sound city is essential for the future. The restraint of energy consumption and the reduction of greenhouse gas emission will be a most critical factor in future urban planning. The reduction of greenhouse gas emissions should be achieved with all combined efforts by using various techniques. The development of equipment running on low energy and promotion of a lifestyle which expends less energy is also essential. Urban planning can and should play an important role in the reduction of energy consumption. Designing an urban system that functions on a minimal amount of energy, yet maintains the full scope of urban opportunities, is one of the greatest challenges facing Japan in the twenty-first century.

NOTES

1. Hiramatsu, N., Hanaki, K. and Matsuo, T. 1992. Comparison of energy consumption among seven major cities in Japan. *Environ. Syst. Res.* 20: 252–261.
2. Ichinose, T., Hanaki, K. and Matsuo, T. 1993. International comparison of energy consumption in urban area. *Proc. Environ. Engin. Res.* 30: 371–381.
3. Energy Information Administration (U.S.A.) 1991. *Annual Energy Review 1990.*
4. Thailand Development and Research Institute 1990. *Industrializing Thailand and Its Impact on the Environment.*
5. IPCC (Intergovernmental Panel on Climate Change) 1990. *Climate Change—The IPCC Scientific Assessment.* Cambridge: Cambridge University Press.
6. Hanaki, K. 1990. Application of methane fermentation process to treatment of agricultural and industrial wastes with energy recovery. *Proceedings Regional Seminar on Management and Utilization of Agricultural and Industrial Wastes.* Kuala Lumpur. March: 274–81.

BIBLIOGRAPHY

1. Energy Information Administration (U.S.A.) 1991. *Annual Energy Review 1990.*
2. Hiramatsu, N., Hanaki, K. and Matsuo, T. 1992. Comparison of energy consumption among seven major cities in Japan. *Environ. Syst. Res.* 20: 252–261.
3. Ichinose, T., Hanaki, K. and Matsuo, T. 1993. International comparison of energy consumption in urban area. *Proc. Environ. Engin. Res.* 30: 371–381.
4. Thailand Development and Research Institute 1990. *Industrializing Thailand and Its Impact on the Environment.*

Part III

Infrastructure of the Japanese Cityscape

Part III: Introduction

It is the intention of Part III to focus on the infrastructure and its related technological, social, and environmental factors. It is most important to see the dynamics of its perspective since Japan, particularly Tokyo, has paid much attention to the subject since the post-World War II era. The acuteness of the problems associated with the infrastructure result primarily, but not exclusively, from the physical and demographic urban growth. The four chapters tackle this problem from its diverse aspects including the discussion about the future promise.

The magnitude of urban expansion, especially of large metropolitan areas such as Tokyo, has significantly increased the length of all infrastructure networks as the city expanded vertically and horizontally. These extensions include diverse kinds of infrastructure networks, such as the water network, sewage, electricity, cable TV, waste disposal, subways, ground transportation, and others. Moreover, every addition in the vertical city has frequently burdened the existing networks beyond their originally intended capacity. The expansion, as always, has to be translated into the costs of the design, construction, maintenance, and renewal of the existing infrastructure. Most frequently urban infrastructure implemented the changes in pieces occasionally combining old and new which renders the infrastructural system inefficient and increases the cost. In the case of Japan, there is an ideal implementation in which the prospective development of Tokyo Bay for future urban expansion has obviously led to the development of an overall, systematic plan for its infrastructure (Ojima chapter).

The common denominator of the four chapters is the operation of infrastructure which includes an innovative system for the improvement of infrastructural design and its implementation, technology, and the future, which are all interrelated with the urban environment as a whole. We commonly see infrastructure from the technological aspect; recently, with the introduction of transportation and other services belowground, we have become increasingly concerned with other, nontechnological aspects as well. However, we are still using the aboveground space for other kinds of infrastructure (such as transportation) and service networks. In either supraterranean or subterranean case, we are concerned with the social and economic, as well as environmental, aspect.

Both theoreticians and practitioners contributed to Part III. The Japanese are well known for their technological achievements in engineering in general and in belowground engineering in particular. The subject of infrastructure is treated from different angles to include its "hardware" (technical/concrete aspect) (Ojima chapter) and "software" (the social, economic, and environmental aspects) (Takabu, Iwai, and Asano chapters). Professor Toshio Ojima sees an interrelation between the technology and design of the Japanese infrastructure which have a deep impact upon the social quality of life. Due to this delicate relationship, he calls for the constant enhancement of the infrastructure. The future should bring about the development of sophisticated, "intelligent" infrastructure in order to tackle the rising problem with the related technology. Ojima envisions recycling as a potential way of saving the environment rather than merely saving economically. He provides a complex approach to Japan's infrastructure focusing on its history, current problems (waste), future trends (utilization of excess energy, third industrial era and its special needs), planning, and design (Tokyo Bay and subsurface "lifeline"). Land shortage and the changing needs of the Japanese population will be at the center of concern in the future. Conscious urban planning is presented as one of the hopes for the future since it has the potential to maximize the use of land (sub- and supra-surface) within the parameters of environmental ethics.

Mr. Motoyuki Takabu's chapter explores the relation between the enhancement of the infrastructure on a regional scale and the quality of its users' lives. He suggests to decentralize the large network of infrastructure in order to accommodate the large city through a symbiosis with small networks. Infrastructure must not be regarded as a system which serves and transports people but as a means to improve the quality of urban life (using waste heat, creating more green zones, comfortable transportation systems, etc.). Computers and modern technology can be a valuable tool for the assessment process of where and how to plan improvements of the infrastructural system.

Mr. Hikoji Iwai's chapter on the Tokyo subway network is an enlightening example of the city's successful management of its subway which accommodates almost 6 million commuters every day (Iwai). In spite of the fact that the bulk of the network is not equipped with the latest technology, the management and culture of the Japanese people make it work efficiently. In this chapter, the discussion of the "hardware" and the "software" is also essential in understanding the mechanism of the entire system. The Tokyo subway contributes to the improvement of the city's environment in numerous ways. It transports a large number of people on a daily basis and eases aboveground congestion, particularly during the evening and morning rush hours. One of the by-products of the subway stations' construction has been the establishment of modern, below-ground shopping centers which are considered to be among the most sophisticated and efficient of their kind in the world. This by-product directly, or indirectly, is a consequence of the skyrocketing of aboveground land prices. Consequently, the impact of the subway reached beyond the traditional goal of transporting people from one part of the city to another. In short, the Tokyo subway system may claim four original achievements; these are the transportation of people, easing aboveground congestion, the development of below-ground shopping centers, and providing alternative land-use at lower cost.

Finally, as for any other metropolitan concentration, supraspace transportation has always been vital for the livelihood of the city. The aboveground network consists of roads, waterways, and railways. More than any other city in the world, Tokyo enjoys a wide and effective railway network within the metropolitan area as well as extensive connections beyond the city center. In his chapter Professor

Mitsuyuki Asano focuses on this kind of transportation, its impact on the environment, and the cityscape. He examines the relation between the environment and urban transportation systems as well as demographic changes and the transportation system. In the future, the Japanese will have to solve mainly two problems: first, the pollution of public as well as private transportation systems will become a burning issue and second, Japanese society will enter the "age of the aged," with a large population of elderly citizens with special needs. Urban planners are challenged to create a high-quality space of life and transportation.

The common concern of all four chapters is the environment in its complexity, both static and dynamic. The discussion includes the technological impact, relation of the infrastructure with the Japanese culture, and finally the connection of the existing infrastructure with its historical evolution to the present and future. As Mr. Iwai states, the subways are strained 200% beyond their capacity and still operate efficiently. Since the supra- and subterranean transportation are the most dynamic facets of the urban Japanese infrastructure, it is fair to say that it is the quality of the human contribution, thus the culture of the people, which make the infrastructural system work.

G.S.G.

A Tokyo's Infrastructure, Present and Future

Toshio Ojima

INTRODUCTION

The development of Japanese urban infrastructural networks lag behind compared to other advanced countries throughout the world. This was partly due to the fact that Japan was forced to rebuild its cities hastily after World War II. Much of the post-World War II infrastructural network remains today, but it is not sufficient to support the economic, social, and daily activities of the people who live and work in a large capital city like Tokyo. Several projects are considered to create a new infrastructural network underground, which would solve Tokyo's present situation and provide a more convenient and efficient infrastructural design.

This underground infrastructure would be based on modern technology, would require thorough city planning to meet future as well as present needs, and should be promoted aggressively. In fact, a comprehensive basic plan for the urban environment should precede any construction and is more important than the environmental assessment measures used to evaluate the environment after the city is built. Various proposals for the design of Tokyo's new infrastructural network are presented in this chapter.

WHAT IS INFRASTRUCTURE?

In general, the infrastructure of a city comprises belowground facilities and their support facilities. The "suprastructure" comprises the facilities located above ground and their supporting belowground infrastructure. For example, physically, the pipeline and subway are a part of the underground infrastructure, while the buildings on the ground level are its suprastructure. The aboveground system with its supporting belowground facilities form the infrastructure. On the other hand, homes and offices are also defined as the superstructure. The infrastructure in this case would be the facilities that support the district's culture and daily life, such as schools, parks, and museums.

Specifically, then, what does the infrastructure encompass? For this chapter, its definition will include the several main service systems such as the water supply, sewage, transportation, energy systems, and the telecommunication system. The system which contributes to the functioning of daily house or office life, especially in the case of emergency situations, will be referred to as the "life rope" or "lifeline." The "lifeline" is the invisible part of the infrastructure located belowground.

JAPANESE INFRASTRUCTURE

Tokyo's infrastructure is not as modern as that of other advanced countries in the world. Its transportation system along with its urban supply and dispersal facilities such as electricity, gas, water supply, sewage disposal, telecommunication, garbage collection, district heating, and cooling, etc., are estimated to lag thirty years or more behind the development of the infrastructure of various cities in Europe and the U.S.A. In addition to its swift postwar construction, some of this delay can be attributed to the lack of uniform internationalization of urban homes, parks, museums, hotels, conference halls, hospitals, and schools (Table III-A1, Fig. III-A1). To understand Japan's lag in infrastructural development, the reader must first bear in mind the circumstances from which Japan's infrastructure emerged. Second, the reader must analyze the economic base which supports Japan's infrastructure.

After the Tokyo's restoration during the Meiji era, the importance of the lower or underground infrastructure was underestimated and therefore not included in the city planning. This may be due to the urgent need to build an upper suprastructure which would catch up with the building boom in other countries at the time. This trend was a reflection of Japan's policy of the "rich country and strong soldier" that urged to be extensively productive and outwardly powerful. An extensive suprastructure was constructed in an effort to pursue this policy. However, the infrastructure, or the "thing in the under," was consistently regarded unimportant and was thus excluded from the process of the overall

Table III-A1 Comparison of some urban infrastructure in six different countries

Section	Equip. Index	Japan	England	West Germany	France	Italy	U.S.A.
Sewer lines	Total area equipped with sewer lines (%)	(1989) 40	(1982) 95	(1983) 91	(1983) 64	(1980) 55	(1986) 73
Park	Area/person (m²/person)	(1987) Tokyo 2.5	(1976) London 30.4	(1984) Bonn 37.4	(1984) Paris 12.2	(1973) Rome 11.4	(1976) Washington, DC 45.7
Road	Road area in city (%)	Tokyo 13.6	London 16.6	–	Paris 20.0	–	New York 23.2

Source: White Paper of Construction. Ministry of Construction, 1992; p. 87.

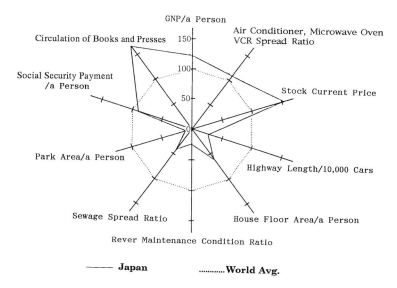

Figure III-A1 Japanese social stock (Ministry of Construction, 1991, p. 80)

planning and construction of the actual city. This attitude still prevails today. Thus, infrastructure is not financed generously even though it is for public use. Yet, some proposals asked for the financing of the infrastructural construction through a common tax base.

After the war, the capital was constructed around its factories in a painstaking effort. At the time, Tokyo was a barrack-type city and did not have a functionally balanced structure. Therefore, facilities to support these aboveground structures are extremely poor. Since Tokyo has grown to become a densely populated city, certain ethics should be upheld in city planning to maintain its balance.

As an analogy, a massive tree endures both the intense sunshine in drought and the heavy wind of a typhoon in the rainy season because its strong underground stalk and firm roots expand deeply into the soil to reach the nourishment of the underground water system. Its root network is well established and balanced with its massive leaf and trunk structure above ground. This analogy can apply to the ideal configuration of a city. A well-balanced city is not one whose only construction considerations are extensive parks or roads. Only recently have the Japanese come to realize this. An American once expressed this best when he said: "The house of Japan is a rat hole."

Transition of the Infrastructure

Japan's infrastructure has changed over time. Before the Edo period, the castle town was often burned as a precaution against seizure during battle. Therefore, facilities for its citizens were not part of the plan for the castle town. The castle, located at the center of town, served to protect the people. During the Edo period, however, the city grew to more than 1 million people in size. Water transportation and traffic systems were well organized and relied on canal and road construction for flood control. The city was a single, harmonious entity composed of a spiritual base of the Japanese Shinto shrine and temples, and the structural base of its bridges. These were laid out against the background of Mount Fuji and the ocean. These views are pictured in the "one hundred beautiful scenes in Edo city" (Fig. III-A2).

The infrastructure then consisted essentially of a canal network used to transport agricultural products to the castle. Its waterways flowed in all directions and were used for the transportation of traffic and goods, carrying of solid waste, the water supply, and drainage. An irrigation system surrounded the rice fields and a wall was constructed to protect the castle. The land was reclaimed to prevent flooding and Edo became known as a city with an ideal low water level. This was the extent of Tokyo city's infrastructure in this period.

Following the Edo period in the Meiji era, the castle lost its responsibility of rebuilding the city. Under Japan's policy of the "rich country and strong soldier," the emphasis shifted to building new industries and strengthening existing ones. This industrial era of Japan was established after its industrial revolution and dates from the beginning of the Meiji era until recent history. During this time,

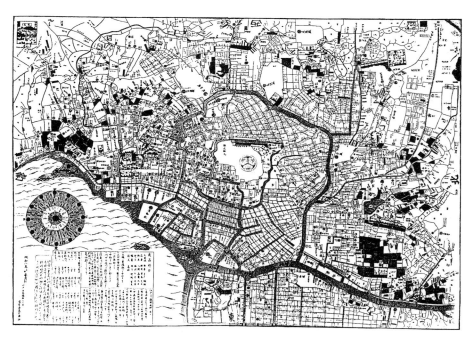

Figure III-A2 Map of Tokyo (Edo) in the eighteenth century (Meiwa Edozu, 1982, p. 52, ©Jinbunsya Co. Ltd.)

the factories and their industrial complexes were considered the most important aspect of city planning. It was commonly thought that people could lead their lives only if they had a place to work. The industry dominated the entire city. Factories were supported with thermal power plants, port facilities, railroads, highways, and a network of transportation systems. These services were the largest part of the infrastructure at that time, with the port facilities, thermal power plants, and industrial waters being the three most important elements forming the industrial complex. At the same time, because of industry's demand for labor, the residential complexes located close to the industrial area also had to be supported by the infrastructure (Fig. III-A3). This was the same infrastructure that supported Japan during its industrial revolution after the war and continues to be used today.

In order to accommodate the domestic-oriented industrial demands for an immense infrastructure, Japan had to reclaim Tokyo Bay as a new land source. The financial support for the reclamation project came from the postal savings and pensions of the postwar generation, who has already spent its savings to pay for investments in the future city which has strengthened the Japanese industry. Factories have relocated close to the vital industry. People competitively bid to promote industry, construct thermoelectric power plants, lay industrial water lines, build facilities to support and increase the efficiency of factory work, and have further reclaimed the land.

In an effort to secure work for the population, the local government attracted industrial development by building the Keihin and Keihou industrial complexes in Tokyo Bay. Keihin encompasses the Tokyo and Yokohama area along Tokyo Bay. Keihou includes the Tokyo and Chiba Prefecture area along the Bay. Those areas were reclaimed for building factories and storage facilities. In fact, the Third and the Fourth Comprehensive National Development Plan were promoted by copying the Keihin and Keihou industrial complexes.

This way, Japan's people, including the local governments, have given financial aid to industry. It can be said that the second industrial base occurred with the coupling of the infrastructure to the factories in local areas. This factory-oriented city plan of Tokyo then spread to local areas primarily to decentralize the work place away from the Tokyo area which was completed by the 1980s. In fact, this second industrial phase occurred throughout all of Japan. A national trunk road and expressway network was built throughout the country to connect the local cities with their industries. A negative consequence of this national transportation network, however, has been severe pollution caused by large diesel trucks, dump trucks, and power plants.

Ideal Situation for the Infrastructure

A high percentage of manufactured Japanese products are exported to many countries. Products such as the motorcycle, camera, transistor, and television have swept over the world carrying the label "Made in Japan." Other nations such as Taiwan, South Korea, and China are also now emerging in their second industrial phase with an even stronger output than Japan had, while Japan, in turn, has exceeded Europe and the U.S.A. in production. If Southeast Asia and China, which have the advantage of a vast population and thus a cheap labor pool, continue to produce at their current rate, Japan will clearly be deprived of its industrial lead in a similar way as Japan took the lead from the U.S.A. and Europe.

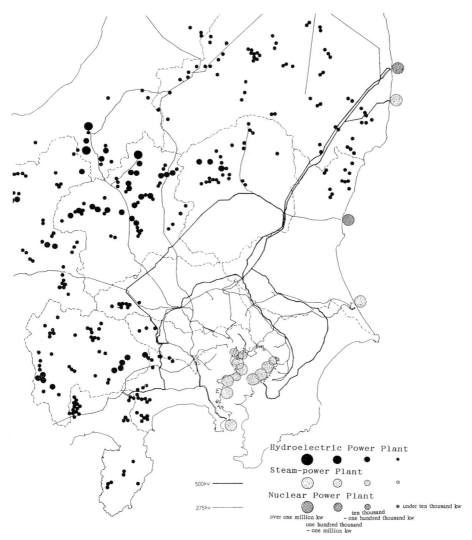

Figure III-A3 Plants and power lines in Tokyo metropolitan area (Meiwa Edozu, 1982, p. 94)

This second industry is causing pollution in the Southeast Asian nations as it has been in Japan, which raised the issue of industrial pollution control. In Japan, the goals of the Fourth Comprehensive National Development Plan are to create pleasant living conditions, comfortable work places, and the basic maintenance of the urban environment. In this plan, the information transmitter, which functioned through the information network, was an important component of the infrastructure. The infrastructure of the third industry in Tokyo, the convention center, science museums, and art museums, formed a one-pole concentration city with a central business nucleus and factories surrounding it. Thus, it is necessary:

- To locate the financial, commercial, and informational bases of the third industry in Tokyo as the foundation of the second industry. This concept of a city where the center of the third industry would support the second industry could also be applied in rural areas.
- To distribute the industrial base to a local area outside of Tokyo. The efforts in Tokyo have been considered successful.

These are the goals of the Fourth Comprehensive National Development Plan.

With the emergence of the third industrial era, which is the transition from the industrial production age to the information production age, Japan has chosen to make its basic infrastructure the future social capital of its people. This third era is marked by a shift from factory production and distribution of products to an intellectual exchange of ideas between human beings.

However, the infrastructure for the third industry is not yet clearly defined. Teleport systems have been considered first because they can be used as an information base to support the fourth industry. Teleports can also be constructed with little investment compared with the cost of investment of thermoelectric power plants or harbor facilities which were used as the basic infrastructure of the second industry.

It is not clear how much of an economic effect this industrial development will have or whether the target for the third industry will actually be reached. All local governments are competing with each other to build museums or teleports without understanding whether this development is actually beneficial to the infrastructure of the third industry. As a result, the following ideas have been accepted as strong arguments of the government:

- To prevent a one-pole concentration in Tokyo, Japan should not make as many public investments in Tokyo.
- The base of the third industry should be extended to the provinces.
- If Japan were to create a deficient environment in Tokyo by decreasing public investment, people would not be able to live there comfortably and would voluntarily move to the rural areas.
- Thus, Japan should endeavor to build an infrastructure that would create a comfortable environment in the local areas.

This effort for a decentralization of Tokyo would be the first in Japan's history.

An unbalanced situation exists between the number of representatives from the local areas and the Diet members of the National Assembly of Tokyo. The Diet members are fewer in number and hold less power than the local areas. Moreover, with the message of the Fourth Comprehensive National Development becoming vague, the National Diet has been considering transferring the capitol of Japan to another city and removing the core function of the Diet from Tokyo. One of the pivotal aspects of the infrastructure of Tokyo was the Diet centralization itself. With this consideration, it seems that Tokyo is losing sight of its direction. So far, it has not been determined when and where the capitol will be transferred or what plan will be used afterwards.

One thing is clear. The future of Tokyo's metropolitan area lies in the construction of an immense office complex with teleports to focus business activity at the seaside of Tokyo Bay. The bay area redevelopment project originally started with the MM21 project in Yokohama, followed by the No. 13 area project, the Makuhari area project, etc. One project after another took shape with the intention of creating a new urban area to replace the old Tokyo metropolitan area.

It is true that Tokyo is likely to practice the "scrap and build policy" if the infrastructure of the third industrial type is not more than an extension of the second industrial infrastructure. This would occur if the industrial complex, which is the current base of the second industry that exists in the Tokyo Bay area today, was renewed. However, it is still thought that business center facilities would become the infrastructure of the city itself. Rather than orienting the planning of an infrastructure to serve the manufacturer, basic facilities are needed that will also target consumers. This type of comprehensive planning for facilities would be necessary for the infrastructural network of the twenty-first century.

Problem of the Infrastructure

The area of central Tokyo used to cover a 60 km range. Recently, a 100 km range was designated as the central area of the city. Today, the range extends to 200 km if the Shinkansen commuting area is included. All of the infrastructure such as the electric power network, communication network, water supply, drainage, and gas pipelines tend to follow the sprawl of the city without a preconceived plan. Some of these services are built underground and some extend over the largest plain in Japan, the Kantou Plain. However, in the long term it is difficult to maintain a complicated mesh of infrastructure, even though it was efficient initially.

The postwar infrastructure in the central part of the city is in dire need of renovation. New housing complexes developed in the suburbs lie in a continuous sprawl. The massive infrastructure of the third industry to be constructed on the reclaimed land in Tokyo Bay is larger in scale than the infrastructure of the second industry built on its opposite side.

However, trying to accommodate the demand of the third industry in an unplanned way would require a liberal investment and a safety management system to maintain the facilities. Moreover, back-up facilities for the infra-structure would become difficult to support because the same infrastructure that secures the center of the city is also needed in the suburbs and at the water front area. This situation would be similar to Japan's condition that existed under its "rich country and strong soldier" policy. At that time, Japan expanded to Greater East Asia by sending its military to the front and acquiring territory, just as the Roman Empire had once done. Ultimately, however, the Roman Empire destroyed itself because of its inability to maintain its vast territory.

Many resources are consumed to maintain, support, and control the network of an infrastructure that extends horizontally. For instance, it requires approxi-mately 10 billion yen a year to maintain a water supply system with kilometers of extended pipe pumped by electric power from Tokyo's metropolitan areas. This creates a great strain on the government's budget. Additional capital is needed to handle the drainage of rain-water in the metropolitan area that runs into the area network sewerage system where it is pumped to a processing plant and then, in turn, into Tokyo Bay. A similar costly operation was used for dismantling the Japanese National Railways throughout the country from Hokkaido in the northeast to Kyushu in the southwest, excluding Okinawa. This operation incurred a tremendous deficit.

Moreover, in an emergency it would not be possible to back up a metropolitan infrastructure made of a congested multiroute network. Unfortunately, the likelihood that the infrastructural network would function continuously is very small. Once one part of the network shuts down, other parts become over-burdened and also slow down or stop. It is extremely difficult to locate the source of malfunction and if the malfunctioning section cannot be repaired, the whole system would stop functioning. The entire city of Tokyo would collapse in an emergency like this. How can Japan continue to depend on this large area network in such situations? The present expanded network cannot provide the answer.

In the U.S.A., a similar multinetwork was created by the Greyhound buses and the Amtrak train which connected every area in the country, but the lines broke down because of their large scale. This network was superimposed on the existing network of roads, railways, energy, and pipelines throughout the U.S.A. The roads were well situated to connect cities, but the country was forced to spend a lot of capital to maintain the bus and railroad lines. That infrastructure is now clustered and operates on a regional basis; only highway infrastructure is still organized on a large scale.

Presently, during the Clinton administration, the last large area network was a system of optical fiber cables for multimedia use, called "the intelligent highway." This large-scale infrastructure exists independently in each city and is broadcast in a very limited capacity to meet the demands of the region. In the U.S.A., the idea prevails that this kind of infrastructure is friendlier to the earth's environment. However, Japan would do better to change this policy and have an infrastructural unit for the area of Tokyo alone, instead of enforcing a huge-scale network system over many areas. Only a minimum system necessary for the area should be interconnected.

In other regions, the infrastructure took various shapes suited to the region. However, it would be more feasible to construct the infrastructure independently, based on the characteristic situation of each region. The high density network area and low density network area should be separated according to the distinct features of each. Only where there is an excess or deficiency of service should the infrastructure be supported mutually. Thus, a strategy for decentralizing the future infrastructure has become necessary.

OPENING PLAN FOR TOKYO BAY

Tokyo supports one fourth of Japan's population. What infrastructure should Japan build now to realize a future that would be more pleasant, safe, healthy and efficient for the city's population?

First, Tokyo needs to install a specially designed infrastructure in the waterfront area. An independent infrastructure in the reclaimed water front area should be built in addition to the usual network of water, electric power, gas, and information systems. The bay area infrastructure has to be unique and independent since this area's soil is too soft to support a large infrastructure in the normal way. If an earthquake were to occur, a liquefaction phenomenon might follow, causing water from the lower layers to be drawn to the surface which might then become too soft to support the construction base. The risk is too great for underground pipe networks such as joints to be damaged severely and the city's supply function would become limited or terminated. Therefore, it is necessary to install a "Lifeline" on the deep stable layer (Fig. III-A4).

Introduction of a Life Anchor

A deep underground network of utility corridors in the Tokyo Bay area has been proposed for the Life Anchor Project. The project specifically calls for an independent basic facility for electric power, water, and information systems. Several anchors would be installed on a stable foundation deep underground to prevent damage, even during an earthquake.

The Tokyo Bay area would be further supported in the case of a disaster by setting up backup facilities (such as an oil tank, a water tank, heat storing tank, private dynamo, boiler, refrigerator, and computers) on the deep and stable subterranean ground under the Bay's shore. The facilities' bases would be connected by deep underground tunnels for transportation. Oil-related articles would be shipped through the pipeline from the entrance of the bay to the plants inside the bay. Other freights would be distributed by containers the same way. Both would require the oil transportation and physical distribution network to be located in these tunnels (Fig. III-A5). These facilities should be able to maintain the city's function in the bay area for at least one week after a disaster.

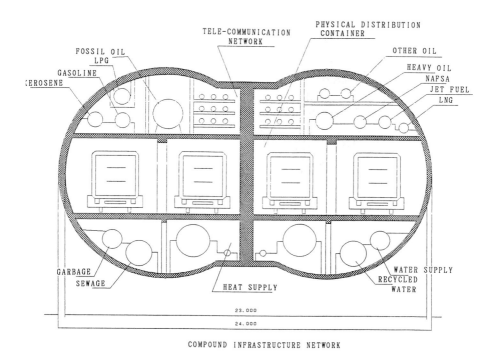

COMPOUND INFRASTRUCTURE NETWORK

Figure III-A4 The deep underground infrastructure as "lifeline" (Ojima, T. 1991, p. 80)

The Oil Transportation Network

About 40% of ships that sail into Tokyo Bay carry oil. It is important to eliminate these ships with their hazardous cargoes from the area and create an area with parks, beaches, and yacht harbors. This can be accomplished by building an outport outside Tokyo Bay; the outport would become the entrance to a new oil transportation network. It would have to be deep enough for a large-scale tanker to moor and connect with the underground network inside the bay. A base for distributing oil should be constructed near plants which heavily rely on oil such as chemical factories, gas factories, thermoelectric power plants, and oil refineries.

The Physical Distribution Network

Changes have been proposed in the distribution network to reduce the number of freight accidents and free some of the bay area for parks and recreation. It is planned to use 10 tn containers in place of freighters.

The bases of the distribution network should be located on the site of an existing or planned large-scale harbor facility area. In the proposed network, 96.9% of the oil and 39.5% of the freight that is now transported by ships would

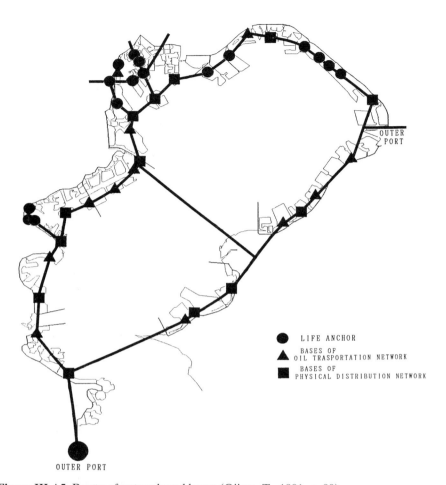

Figure III-A5 Route of network and bases (Ojima, T., 1991, p. 80)

be carried by this network. This would reduce the number of the ships to 18%—
an 82% reduction—or from 280,000 ships to 50,400 ships. In turn, it would also
decrease the number of accidents which currently pose a serious problem.

For the second-industrial-type facilities, 120,000 ha of the Tokyo Bay area can
be zoned for public leisure by relocating the harbors to the seaside industrial
complexes. The Tokyo Bay shore would become a beach park and a site for
highly developed industry and commercial facilities. Hotel and residential buildings, surrounded by trees and landscaping, would replace the existing factories
and industrial complexes. The reconstruction of city facilities that has come to
a standstill would be promoted to create a beautiful bay shore scenery comparable to southern France or Rio de Janeiro.

THE DEEP UNDERGROUND SPACE NETWORK PROJECT

Tokyo direly needs a study on the effective use of water supply and energy consumption, as well as their impact on the environment. Such a study should also consider the establishment of a water recycling facility and a wider range of heat supply. A deep underground tunnel network called the "Cooperate Utility Space Network" has been proposed to alleviate this problem. This underground system would be composed of a vertical tunnel to connect the surface of the earth with a deep underground base and a horizontal tunnel to join each of the underground bases. The recycling facilities for energy as well as water and the pipeline facilities would also be located deep underground (Fig. III-A6). Garbage, unused river and rain-water, unused energy and excess heat, trunk-line networks for the distribution of information, pipelines for oil and gas, and trunk-lines for electric power could be placed in this deep underground space network (Fig. III-A7).

This new urban infrastructure would be most effective and meaningful when introduced to the central part of the city where congestion is heaviest. However, this project is in its proposal stages and not fully completed. Also, no one has spoken strongly in support of its advantages. For example, permission to use the space under roads has not yet been granted by law. Therefore, the construction of a wide infrastructural network under roads has not been realized. However, there are many more problems to be solved before being able to access this space.

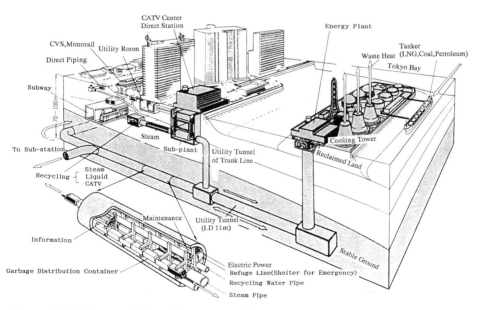

Figure III-A6 Image of urban infrastructure (Ojima, T., 1982)

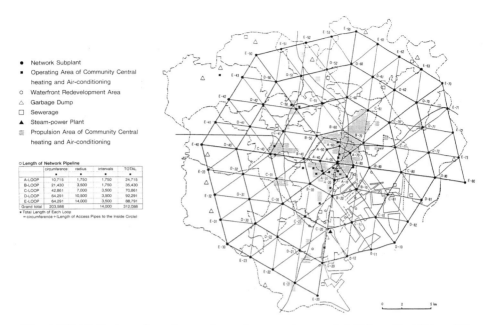

- ● Network Subplant
- ■ Operating Area of Community Central heating and Air-conditioning
- ○ Waterfront Redevelopment Area
- △ Garbage Dump
- □ Sewerage
- ▲ Steam-power Plant
- ▨ Propulsion Area of Community Central heating and Air-conditioning

○ Length of Network Pipeline

	circumference	radius	intervals	TOTAL
	■	■	■	■
A-LOOP	10,715	1,750	1,750	24,715
B-LOOP	21,430	3,500	1,750	35,430
C-LOOP	42,861	7,000	3,500	70,861
D-LOOP	64,291	10,500	3,500	92,291
E-LOOP	64,291	14,000	3,500	88,791
Grand total	203,588		14,000	312,088

● Total Length of Each Loop
  = circumference + (Length of Access Pipes to the Inside Circle)

Figure III-A7 Basic project of extensive underground network 1 (Ojima, T., 1991, p. 99)

Some of the obvious problems are financing this project, providing ventilation, minimizing or avoiding the high risk of disaster, and securing ample space for it. Some companies which run their own networks have already pioneered into the deep underground space. In order to extend its infrastructural network in the future, all of Japan must venture into the underground and effectively use this space.

The transportation systems are also in desperate need of renewal and restructuring, and with the increasing congestion, the deep underground will be the only place suitable for developing this infrastructure. To ease the traffic surge during the rush hour, an underground railway system around the central city would be economically feasible and highly practical. Currently, this transportation system is at the level of actual planning, even though there still are some obstacles to overcome. An underground transportation system for unattended commodity distribution is feasible and would help to reduce traffic jams. These underground facilities need responsible management to avoid traffic situations similar to the supraspace. It should be noted that the later construction is started, the more difficult it becomes to accomplish a well-planned underground system.

To promote the planned use of deep underground space, the main lines of a supply managing facility which are best suited for underground tunnels are to be put together inside a joint tunnel. Meanwhile, there is a growing need for the rearrangement of existing facilities which use space inefficiently due to the lack of a coherent plan. For example, the underground pedestrian network, underground roads, electric and telephone wires have neither been preplanned nor efficiently built.

Upon the completion of the deep underground infrastructural network, sharing routes would increase and more sub-lines could be placed in the joint tunnel. Over a period of time, it would be possible to improve the intricate use of the shallow space under the roads by adding new facilities. This would give Tokyo not only some relief in its traffic congestion, but also reduce the repair costs for roads.

It is important to make advances in improving the existing urban sprawl by keeping volume in the urban center higher ("up-zoning") and lower in the middle regions ("down-zoning"). Specifically, Tokyo's land slopes gently down to the bay and is intersected by many rivers. The points where the rivers divide the land will be particularly useful for redeveloping each district. Underground infrastructures could be planned here to free more land for aboveground use. Water and green areas could be strategically placed to divide the urban area in order to prevent fire disasters or heat islands (Fig. III-A8). By limiting the supply area, some areas could be highly redeveloped while other areas would be kept at a low density. The areas in lower density would serve as a backup when extra space is needed (Figs. III-A9, III-A10). In the near future, the use of the deep underground for infrastructure is inevitable as demands increase.

INTELLIGENT INFRASTRUCTURE

The cable television (CATV) network is one of the important infrastructure networks for a modern city as part of the new age of information distribution. This information network is a system of optical fiber cables which connects the

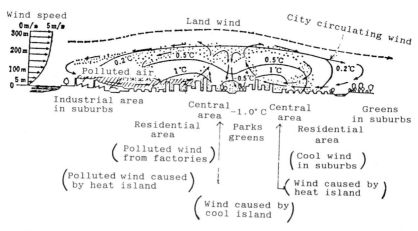

Figure III-A8 Sketch of speculation of the heat island effect on a large scale (Toshio Ojima Lab, unpublished)

Figure III-A9 "Up-zoning" and "down-zoning" (Ojima, T., 1991, p. 91)

entire Tokyo Metropolitan Area and eventually, all of Japan. The availability of the CATV network is still unbelievably low. It covers only about 15% of Japan, while the network in the U.S.A. serves about 70% of the nation.

One of its problems is the way the CATV was originally introduced in Japan. The cable trunk-line of the CATV was suspended in the air with the telephone lines. These overhead lines created an eyesore even though the television image was greatly improved. The CATV will only be successful if Japan is to extend its network without disturbing the appearance of the city environment. The current subterranean cable facilities along with supraterranean electric wires, telephone wires, and CATV cables should be reorganized in the shallow underground during the construction of the deep underground network.

Eventually, satellite broadcasting may render the CATV obsolete. However, the CATV is a valuable information trunk-line which can carry a large amount of information within a very thin optical fiber cable. If all existing kinds of information networks were to be intertwined in the future, this super-information network could carry a tremendous amount of diverse information. The maintenance of the CATV network base in Tokyo is a crucial aspect for Japan if it were to remain part of the world network of visual information. Since the CATV contributes toward improving the quality of life and education, Japan should be willing to finance its construction through its postal savings revenue.

GARBAGE PROBLEM IN TOKYO

The garbage problem in Tokyo still remains unresolved at present. Its transportation and refuge collection methods detract from the appeal of Tokyo in an embarrassing way. It is also difficult to find suitable sites for its disposal. The

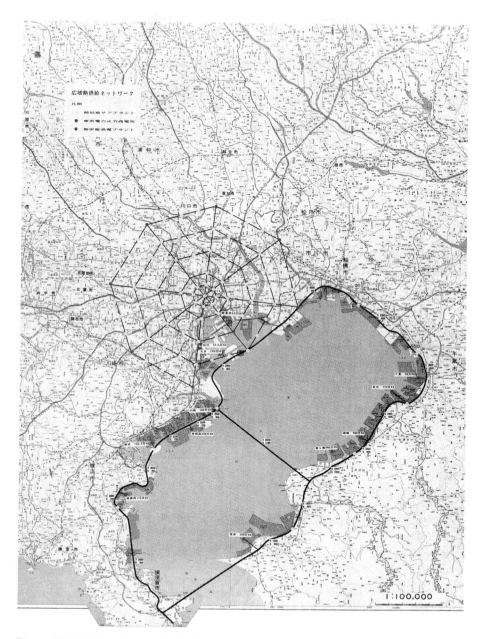

Figure III-A10 Total network of oil transportation of Tokyo Bay (Ojima, T., 1991, p. 91)

amount of garbage produced in Tokyo's twenty-three wards has grown 2.18 times in 1966–1986 and is still increasing. Today, Tokyo's twenty-three wards produce 6 million tons of garbage every year which means that Japan is struggling to dispose of more than 16,000 tons of garbage daily. Many factors account for this increase in waste material, but one of the main reasons is the change in economic productivity to mass production and mass consumption.

The ideal way to solve the garbage disposal problems would be to decrease the amount of waste generated. Yet, it is impossible to return to the lifestyle of ancient times when people's lives were adapted to a natural cycle. With modern industrial production, waste has been increased from many sources and will continue in this fashion as long as Japan maintains its current lifestyle. If Japan recognizes how garbage is produced, it will understand why it is more important to look for a way to recycle garbage rather than attempt to reach the unattainable goal of terminating its production.

In order to proceed with the effective use of waste, it is necessary to be aware of its amount, its contents according to the areas where it is produced, the state of collection methods, and then to introduce an effective disposal system. Recycling is a very important issue, especially in areas where extensive amounts of waste are generated. The issues of garbage disposal and reuse can be divided into three categories.

The first category deals with the problem caused by the increase of waste and how to find a site for a new disposal facility. Reclaiming former disposal areas may be a solution. The second category is the problem of the increased traffic caused by garbage collection vehicles and the illegal littering of the street which creates hygiene problems. The final category concerns the research and development of new refuse collection systems, such as pipe distribution systems, urban incinerator facilities, and recycling systems.

The dispute among Tokyo's wards called the "garbage war" began in 1972 when the Suginami Ward tried to dispose of its garbage in the Koutou Ward. This dispute was finally settled by a common agreement that each ward would be responsible for building incineration plants within its own ward. However, due to the prohibitive cost, eleven wards still have not constructed their own garbage incineration plants. It is very costly to build these plants on land which costs 15 million to 30 million yen per m^2, which adds up to approximately 50 billion yen for a waste disposal plant that would only serve one ward. Thus, the construction expense for all eleven plants would be about 600 billion yen. Instead of building plants for each ward, it seems more economical to introduce a large area network, as previously described, at a construction cost of about 1 trillion yen.

Garbage can be recycled and used effectively as fuel if it is properly collected and adequately disposed. Kitchen waste can be converted into compost and used as fertilizer. Garbage which can be incinerated could generate heat of more than 1900 kcal/kg and then be used as fuel. Recently, the excess heat from a waste disposal factory provided a district heating and cooling facility and its associated facilities, with heat.

The complexity of garbage transportation, collection, separation, processing, and disposal is a challenge for a future city's basic maintenance. Just like a living organism, disposed waste should eventually be returned to the ground. In the future the consumed waste will ultimately remain in the country from which it came. The plan of reducing garbage must take into account the waste distribution, inflow, outflow, disposal, and reduction at such global levels.

In the proposed No. 13 Development Plan of Tokyo Bay, a large city base was constructed for a pipeline. This large initial investment imposed a heavy economic burden on the user according to "the principle of the beneficiaries bear." In Tokyo, a large city base has already been constructed and high rental fees for residences or office spaces are required to finance this project.

USE OF UNUTILIZED ENERGY

After the oil crisis of 1973, the consumption of industrial energy in Japan was reduced by using energy-saving technology imported from the West. The rate of the total energy consumption in Japan is now less than that of Europe and America. However, the amount of energy consumed by the public in homes, offices, or shops keeps increasing, especially in the region surrounding Tokyo. The energy consumption for public use in Japan will probably increase as the quality of life is upgraded by modern conveniences that consume energy. This rate will vary by region and season, and will require tremendous energy supplies. Therefore, it is necessary to develop innovative advanced technology to save energy in the future.

Moreover, Japan has to depend on importing oil and fossil fuels from overseas. Japan depends on overseas imports for 99.7% of its petroleum, 87% of its coal, and 95% of its natural gas. However, the foreign sources of these products have become more limited during the last several decades. Alternative means to supply Japan with a steady, dependable supply of energy are become increasingly more important for the future.

There are many inefficient aspects of Japan's present energy supply system. For example, gas and electricity need to be uniformly supplied and high-quality electric energy must be converted into thermal energy. If Japan keeps relying on gas and kerosene or electricity for thermal energy, there will be a tremendous waste since the indoor temperature of public facilities is about 80°F at most. Therefore, it is necessary to exercise a more delicate, more premeditated use of the energy supply by eliminating energy waste. If we adequately understand the temperature level and convert unutilized energy into a usable energy form, we can plan for a more efficient energy supply that would match the heat consumption.

It is also necessary to consider the impact of energy consumption on the environment. The inland side of Tokyo is covered with concrete and asphalt; this causes a heat storage effect which contributes to the heat island phenomenon. As a result, this area requires more energy for cooling. Also, a variety of air pollutants such as CO_2 and NO_x are generated through the combustion of fossil fuel which causes global warming and acid rain.

Decreasing the individual energy demand, developing alternative sources of energy, and improving the efficiency of the energy supply system, are considered strategies for decreasing the overall energy demand. However, there is a limit to decreasing the amount of energy consumption. The improvement in the efficiency of the energy use or in developing alternative sources of energy are most pressing issues, but they take time to develop. The so-called unutilized energy in the surrounding environment is considered a source of energy that has not previously been tapped. It is crucial to control the heat from the incineration of waste, the heating of the processing water, the heat of thermal power generation and drainage, and the excess heat from buildings, subways, and factories because they increase the temperature level of cities. This, in turn, creates a higher energy demand for cooling and increases the consumption of energy by the public even more. The improvement of efficient energy use will be of merit economically and environmentally (Fig. III-A11). Moreover, employing the unused energy produced from the temperature difference of a large-scale rejected heat source (e.g. waste disposal plants and thermoelectric power plants), requires expensive equipment to collect the heat and produce energy. Therefore, energy should be used more effectively in each region than is currently the case at the level of building units.

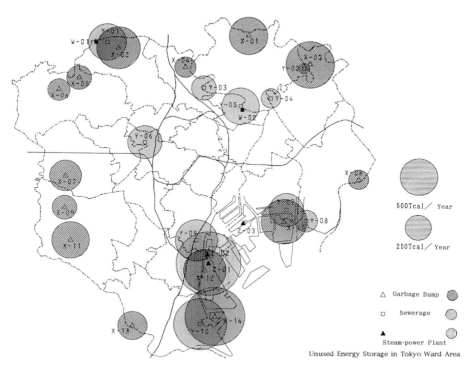

Figure III-A11 Unused energy storage in the Tokyo Ward area (Toshio Ojima Lab, unpublished)

The District Heating and Cooling (DHC) system with its use of untapped energy offers high energy savings, wider availability and could serve as a new infrastructure for the city. The DHC system proposes the installation of a plant in a certain region and the control the concentration of air-conditioning. An aggressive approach is necessary to render the DHC network an effective energy source in the future, not only to curb pollution at the regional level, but to protect the environment at a global level.

The DHC in Tokyo has aggressively been promoted as a solution to the severe air pollution which is still its main purpose as promoted by the Tokyo metropolitan government today. Actually, the area of the DHC system is being expanded in districts where the amount of SO_2 measured in the air is under the minimum according to pollution control standards. It was introduced in twenty-seven places by the end of 1990 and has been considerably expanded within the twenty-three wards of Tokyo. However, the number of the DHC systems using alternative energy sources is low. Two of these systems use excess heat from the garbage disposal plant in large-scale apartment complexes; one uses the energy created by the difference in temperature between the air and the river water and several area systems collect the excess heat from air-conditioning units of transformer substations.

There are several additional sources of high-temperature excess heat, for example waste disposal and sewage treatment plants in all the twenty-three wards as well as the electric power plants along Tokyo Bay. Sewage treatment plants that are expected to be a source of effective low temperature rejected heat also lie in the twenty-three wards.

The DHC network should establish mutual support between each DHC unit to act as a backup unit in an emergency. Since the DHC facilities are able to relieve other units, the facility's equipment is considered highly energy-efficient; it also renovates and updates the equipment without interrupting the energy supply. It may also work more efficiently by interconnecting two or more DHC plants. There is also the possibility of increasing the output of the equipment within each plant.

Creating a network of DHC systems is effective not only for current DHC facilities, but also for facilities where the supply has just started. The city planning behind this network of infrastructure is important. Foremost, as part of the energy infrastructure maintenance of the third industrial phase, it is critical to expand the network of the DHC while preserving the earth's environment through efficient management of the untapped energy sources in Tokyo.

CONCLUSION

The various proposals for Tokyo's infrastructure discussed in this chapter focus on city planning at a technological level. This technologically based planning should be pursued aggressively. A comprehensive preliminary plan for the design of infrastructure in urban areas is more important than environmental assessment measures taken after the infrastructure has been implemented. The ideal condition for the future Tokyo region will become evident after studying a basic, longterm plan for the infrastructure before the suprastructure is constructed. This conceptual way of thinking is crucial, especially in the case of Tokyo.

BIBLIOGRAPHY

1. Edozu Meisho 1982. Tokyo underground project. In: *Kenchiku Bunka*. Tokyo: n.p.
2. Fourth Comprehensive National Development Plan (in Japanese) 1987. Tokyo: Tikyuusya.
3. Masai, Y. 1986. Edo/Tokyo through maps. *Atlas Tokyo*. Tokyo: Heibonsya.
4. Ministry of Construction 1991. White paper of construction. Tokyo: n.p.
5. Ojima, T. 1991. Imageable Tokyo. *Process Architecture* November: 99.
6. Ojima, T., *et al*. 1982. New architectural outline 9. Tokyo: Shoukokusya.
7. Tokyo Metropolitan Government 1988. Development plan of sub-civic center in seaside. Tokyo Prefecture.

B Infrastructural Planning to Upgrade the Social Quality of Life in Regional Districts

Motoyuki Takabu, Masaji Kaneshima, Toshimasa Itaya

INTRODUCTION

Japan's social infrastructure has evolved throughout time and has recently been improved by building centralized public works facilities to serve surrounding areas. However, newly emerging problems have intensified demands on the existing infrastructure. In addition, there is a growing need to provide information as well as human comfort to accommodate an aging population and a maturing society. The cities also struggle with intensified congestion within urban areas due to demographic changes. Solutions to these problems cannot be met by the further expansion of the present infrastructural systems. Instead a new diversified infrastructure is required that is technologically advanced and information-oriented. Thus, new urban designs will be needed to implement and accommodate these new service systems.

This chapter introduces a new concept of a small-scale, decentralized social infrastructure as a solution to the aforementioned problems. It would take the shape of small "district developments" to operate within and complement a "district development program" in conjunction with larger-scale urban infrastructures. To become a realistic solution to Japan's infrastructural problems, these "district developments" can only be successful if they meet with the acceptance and united efforts of the government and the people. They must be specifically designed to provide, in their totality, high quality services satisfying the various needs of the residents.

To further successful construction of the infrastructure, Shimizu Corporation has designed computer models for these small-scale community support systems which focus on optimum facility plans for respective infrastructure programs. The computer model plans are used as tools to aid in the design of actual engineering projects by Shimizu Corporation. A number of examples of these plans are introduced in this chapter.

In addition, the technological capabilities of conventional architectural and civil engineering departments as well as related engineering departments need to be strengthened. Research and development in related fields should focus on and contribute to the construction of a new social infrastructure to meet the future needs of Japan's maturing and changing society. Shimizu Corporation is dedicated to these goals of improving technical capabilities by continuing research and development in related fields and proceeds with the engineering design of projects through computer aided design (CAD) to support system plans. The resulting work will contribute to the construction of a new social infrastructure for the future.

BACKGROUND

Japan's social infrastructure is believed to have contributed greatly to the present economic prosperity and improvement of people's lives. However, various problems have undeniably occurred due to the excessive congestion in the metropolitan area. A review of the nationwide situation shows that some of the supporting infrastructure related to the living environment is less advanced than in the U.S.A. and Europe, which reflects differences in the historical backgrounds of the cultures. Furthermore, from a longterm point of view, it has become necessary to take into account the new problems related to an aging population and a maturing society and to offer solutions that will preserve the environment when preparing future infrastructures.

According to a basic program for public investment which was granted in 1990, a total of 430 million yen of public investment will be made throughout the 1990s. Thus, Japan is responsible to expend the social overhead capital in a quantitatively and qualitatively acceptable manner for building social infrastructure in the twenty-first century.

THE NEED FOR NEW SOCIAL INFRASTRUCTURE SYSTEMS

The present condition of social infrastructure design in Japan needs to be evaluated. Systems contained in the social infrastructure (herein after referred to simply as "infrastructure") which support a city or region range from transportation to disposal and from supply to the environment. The transportational system consists mainly of roads, ports, harbors, airports and railways; the disposal and supply system consists of waterworks, sewerage, electric power plants, gas plants and waste incineration plants; and the environmental system consists of green areas, parks, and beaches which contribute to the improvement of the living environment (Table III-B1).

Considering the gigantic volume of industrial activities and demands of its many inhabitants, the infrastructure in Japan's metropolitan area is considered to function at a very high level of service and is believed to be unrivaled in its stable supply of water, gas and electric power services. However, problems still exist due to the excessive congestion in the metropolitan area. These include traffic jams, water shortages, and the need for a stringent electric power supply to meet consumer demands, particularly in summer.

Although the traffic system, including the railways, functions at an advanced level in terms of technological achievements, the infrastructural systems related

Table III-B1 Examples of infrastructural systems for different services

Infrastructural System	Services
Traffic/Transportational	Roads, airports, railways, ports and harbors, station buildings.
Land/Environmental	Developed land, parks, green areass, beaches.
Disposal/Supply	Waterworks, sewerage, electricity, gas, district heat supply, waste incineration facilities.
Information/Communicational	Telephones, cable television.
Buildings/Cultural	Hospitals, schools, libraries.

to the living environment are less efficient than in the U.S.A. and Europe. This is due to the fact that Japan's infrastructure has had a shorter history of development than those in other advanced industrialized countries. The geographical, environmental and other conditions typical of Japan, such as the large ratio of steep, mountainous areas, create further obstacles for expansion of the infrastructure (Table III-B2). Sewage systems in local cities and other localities remain at a lower level of efficiency. Thus, Japan's problems with its infrastructural networks are twofold. On the one hand, the infrastructure's capacities are overburdened in the metropolitan area where the population demands for various functions are extremely concentrated. On the other hand, the infrastructure is less strained in local cities where population density is low and the demands are less.

As compiled by the Economic Planning Agency, Figure III-B1 presents a longterm projection to the year 2030 for demands of various sectors of the entire infrastructure. Assuming that financial investment is held constant and that inflation is factored into this investment figure for the coming twenty years, the

Table III-B2 Comparison of the efficiency of infrastructural systems in different countries

System	Service Indicator	Unit	Japan	U.K.	(former) West Germany	France	Italy	U.S.A.
Sewage	Rate of Diffusion	%	(1992) 45	(1982) 95	(1983) 91	(1983) 64	(1980) 55	(1986) 73
Urban Park	Area per Person	m²/ person	(1989) Tokyo 2.6	(1976) London 30.4	(1984) Bonn 37.4	(1984) Paris 12.2	(1973) Rome 11.4	(1976) Washington 45.7
Road	Ratio of Urban Road Area	%	Tokyo 13.6	London 16.6	–	Paris 20.0	–	New York 23.2

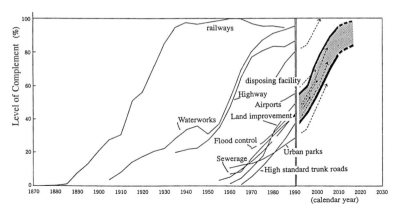

Figure III-B1 Long-term demands on sector-wide levels of future infrastructure (The General Planning Bureau, 1991, p. 58)

capacity level in each sector will improve steadily. Increased emphasis on improving existing infrastructural systems such as sewage disposal, waste incineration plants, and parks, which are already in need of improvement, will greatly enhance the quality of the living environment. New infrastructural systems, such as airports, will also be prepared to meet Japan's needs as an international trading center.

However, new demands will be placed on the future infrastructure which cannot be met by the mere expansion of a current facility's capacity. First and foremost, harmony with the natural environment is of prime necessity. With the growing awareness of the extensive preservation of the natural environment, not only at the regional levels but also at global levels, more sophisticated use of resources and the disposal of toxic substances are required. In order to satisfy these requirements while still meeting social demands, it is necessary to renovate the existing infrastructure and build new systems using more advanced technologies.

Second, the necessity for diversification and sophistication of services rendered by the infrastructure requires an information-oriented system based on international networks. Not only are its functions necessary for the mere survival of urban and residential centers, as well as for ensuring a comfortable environment within work centers and residential living quarters, but they are also essential in offering new information. The creation of various types of environments will become indispensable as a response to the needs of an aging population.

Third, the issue of the necessity of responding to the maintenance and renewal of existing infrastructures is pressing nowadays. Concurrently with the construction of new infrastructure, the renewal of the existing infrastructure will have to be accomplished in a manner that can also meet the new needs of a maturing society. Along with massive renewal of existing infrastructure that crossed its zenith, it has become necessary to modify and equip it with functions to meet the needs of modern times. From now on, it will become even more urgent to develop technologies that accurately judge the timing of renewal for the existing equipment and efficiently carry out the renewal in an efficient manner. Figure III-B2 shows the environmental, service, maintenance, and renewal needs associated with the development and continuation of services provided by the infrastructure.

INFRASTRUCTURE RESPONDING TO DISTRICT DEVELOPMENT

In Japan, a variety of district development projects are planned which require the preparation of a district infrastructure within an overall network that forms an integral part of each district development project. In the metropolitan area, for example, regional development projects that vary in size from several hectares to several hundred hectares are currently planned. The redevelopment of existing urban areas is also projected by using former factory sites in the port and harbor zones of reclaimed land. In local cities, too, district development

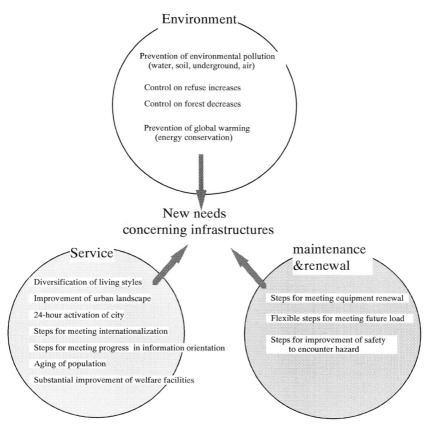

Figure III-B2 Needs which affect infrastructure

projects such as the construction of resorts and residences are planned. Examples of such projects are displayed in Figure III-B3. In conjunction with the redevelopment of existing urban areas, the development of any city adjoining an airport is expected. Thus, improvements will be required to increase the functions and services rendered by the existing infrastructure to serve not only the present urban area, but the newly proposed developments as well. This differs from the conventional large-scale infrastructure which has been designed on a citywide scale. Previously, it was widely assumed that the future infrastructure would be based on the concept of the small-scale, decentralized module which would correspond to a district development project and be planned within a limited scope. However, in order to coordinate many small-scale infrastructural systems according to the size of the district development and then further coordinate the district developments within a large-scale urban infrastructure, the problems mentioned earlier must be resolved first (Fig. III-B4). The features of the small-scale decentralized infrastructural networks which make this plan feasible are outlined below.

- Small-scale networks are able to respond with flexibility to fluctuations in demands on district infrastructures as a whole.
- Since their size is small, they can be easily modified to accommodate future progress in technological development.
- Since they are intended for district development areas, boundaries can be defined and bearers of financial support for the preparation of the networks and their beneficiaries can be clearly identified. Thus, the infrastructural networks can be developed with greater financial control.

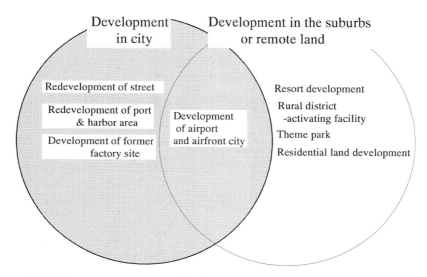

Figure III-B3 Concrete examples of district development

By utilizing these features, it is necessary to prepare an infrastructure specifically intended for areas defined as a distinct district. These can then be specifically designed not only to meet merely short-term capacity requirements, but also to satisfy demands for high quality services which would respond to various needs of their particular district. For this purpose, Shimizu Corporation proposes an infrastructure which will use new technologies and types of operation as shown in Table III-B3. The infrastructure for a district development can include a traffic and transportation system; land and environment system; disposal and supply system; information and communications system; preservation of the environment system; and energy supply system. These systems can then be incorporated into actual district development projects, while technological development is underway for other infrastructural systems.

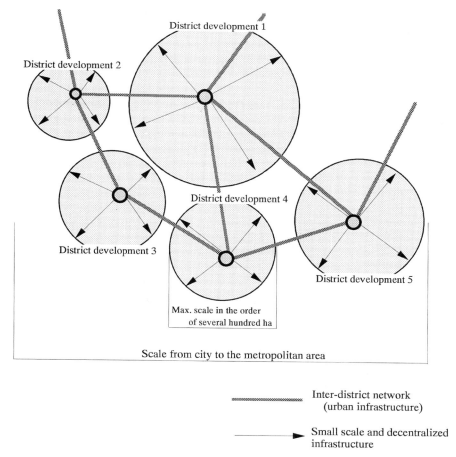

Figure III-B4 shown.

Figure III-B4 A perspective model of small-scale, decentralized infrastructure, and district developments

Table III-B3 New infrastructural systems corresponding to district development

Infrastructural system	District development
Traffic/transportation	Infra-district physical distribution systems, district parking lots, short-distance traffic systems
Land/environment	Artificial beaches, high-level water purification areas, urban space for people to stay close to water, artificial marine facilities, artificial ground, biotope
Disposal/supply	Unused energy utilization systems, on-site power generation, rain-water utilization systems, refuse collecting/disposal systems, natural energy utilization systems
Information/communications	District information systems (area management), district hazard prevention systems
Preservation of environment	Prevention of soil contamination, green areas, preservation of lakes and marshes
Contributive business	Businesses activating rural districts, businesses contributing to district conducted by thermal power/nuclear power plants

Before proceeding with a concrete project, it is necessary to take into account the conditions and existing services for each district development project, to propose new infrastructure as hardware, and lastly, to propose prospective rural area businesses and environmental preservation activities as software.

NEW SMALL-SCALE DECENTRALIZED INFRASTRUCTURE

It is necessary to introduce examples of new small-scale decentralized infrastructure (Fig. III-B5). One of those examples is an urban port or harbor area. In viewing the project's cross-section and perspective drawing, this proposal shows the special importance of building in harmony with the environment (Fig. III-B6). Required plant facilities are installed underground as much as possible to increase the green land area above ground. The neighboring river and beach provide an attractive space where people can relax and enjoy the waterfront. The entire project would improve the living environment.

Infrastructural Facilities to Improve Traffic and Transportation

To accommodate heavy automobile traffic, the construction of a vast parking lot for use by a region is proposed, along with a traffic system for moving people short distances within the district. This would minimize the volume of automobile traffic within the district and diminish traffic congestion and the air pollution from automobile exhaust fumes and traffic jams, thereby contributing to improvements in the environment. Also, the volume of automobile traffic for cargo transportation within the district would be reduced by using a mechanical centralized transportation system equipped with a central collection and delivery center for cargo.

1. Tree planting
2. Purification of canal
3. Multi-purpose public trench
4. Wide area parking lot
5. Underground- garbage incinerator

6. Thermal storage system
7. Area management center
8. Using unused-energy system
9. District heating & cooling plant
10. On-site power generation,

Figure III-B5 City district which implemented the new type of small-scale, decentralized infrastructure

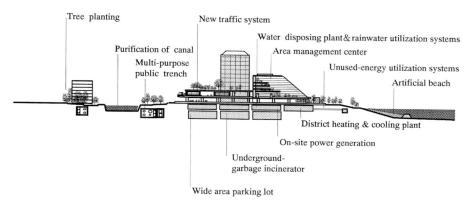

Figure III-B6 A layout image of an urban harbor area with small-scale and decentralized infrastructure

Infrastructural Facilities: Land Development and Environmental Preservation

It is intended not merely to develop the necessary land, but also to create a water purification area as a space for people to be close to water and green land. When developing a district facing the sea, it is proposed to install artificial banks which slope gently toward the water. A planning method must also be adopted for preventing the natural state of the sea from being altered by reclamation (pollution, changed sea current, etc.). Within the district, the artificial ground would be used so that the system's plants, parking lots, and other facilities would be installed below the newly reclaimed ground while areas above it would be amply secured as green land, parks, and pedestrian space.

Infrastructural Facilities to Improve Disposal and Supply

By installing a refuse disposal plant and an on-site power generating facility within the district, waste heat from these facilities could be utilized for district heating and cooling, thereby gaining an efficient energy supply. As a heat source, water used for the district's heating and cooling and unused energy sources, such as river water and treated sewage whose temperature is relatively low, would be used to realize a heat pump efficiency of 50%. Eventually, a cutback of approximately 30–50% on energy consumption would be achieved, compared to the energy consumption not using these facilities. As a result, the CO_2 emission into the air would be cut in half which would make the district development friendly to the global environment. Figure III-B7 shows a diagram of the general flow of the energy supply system. Figure III-B8 presents a system which collects different types of refuse within the district separately and recycles the different types.

As for the utilization of water, a waste-water recycling facility could be installed so that recycled water together with rain-water could be stored for miscellaneous uses such as toilet water, watering vegetation in hot, dry weather, and cooling water for district heating and cooling use. With these recycling uses, the load of city water/sewerage services would be reduced by approximately 25–40%.

Infrastructural Facilities to Improve Information Communications

When planning future infrastructure, a variety of jobs pertaining to all aspects of its network must be considered in their totality. This range encompasses the proposal of a plan to determine its basic design, its business plan, the scale of the facility, and the facility design. In particular, it is mandatory to work out an optimum plan even at the initial stage of planning which considers the predicted future demands and loads of the facility. For this prediction to be realistic, it is necessary to base demand and load estimates on concrete facts by confirming beforehand the facility's required capacity, by assessing the extent to which the facility's construction will affect the neighboring environment and by predicting the future business potential for the facility.

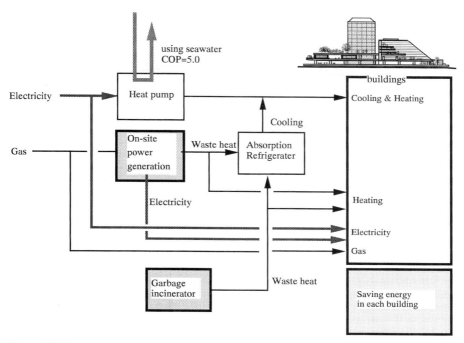

Figure III-B7 Energy supply infrastructure in harmony with the environment

CAD as a Tool for Supporting New Infrastructural Plans

To satisfy requirements, it is crucial to evaluate, using a computer model, each project's multiple and varied requirements in terms of its eventual successful growth into a larger-scale infrastructure. By making advance computer assessments, the project can be quickly evaluated under the various conditions that it will operate before it is built. Through computer simulation, input variables can be modified and outcomes reevaluated to aid in selecting an optimal design plan before the project is built and under the various conditions that the facility will operate.

Shimizu Corporation has developed computer modeling systems to plan new infrastructure, as mentioned earlier. Table III-B4 shows examples of such plan supporting systems which are used in designing actual projects. At the early stages of planning, conditions and parameters related to the facility design can easily be changed through computer modeling. For example, Figure III-B9 displays a method for examining an energy infrastructure. Input variables from a database, such as a district use plan, a street plan, an energy supply facilities layout plan, a district piping installation plan, and an equipment system can give output estimates for the energy consumption of a supply facility, the quantity of pollutants, and the supplying facility's running cost and construction cost. The

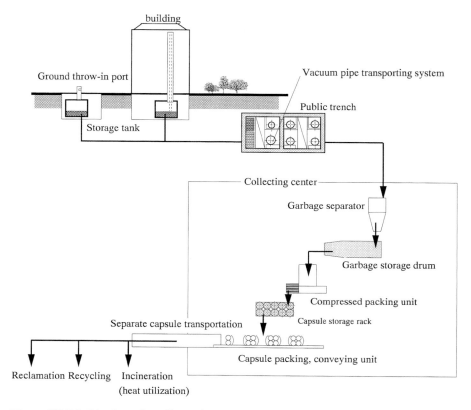

Figure III-B8 District refuse disposal system

Table III-B4 Computer simulation as a tool to support system plans for a new infrastructure

Subject	Infrastructure system plan
Urban planning	• Urban infrastructure plan supporting system
	• Landscape simulation
Disposal/supply	
Energy utilization	• Energy infrastructure plan supporting system
	• General water utilization plan supporting system
Traffic/transportation	• District parking lot plan supporting system
	• Road network plan supporting system
Information	• Area management plan supporting system

computer-simulated model evaluates a wide range of indices from the scale of the facility to the facility's output capacity and the business potential. These systems can then be utilized by designers to select an optimum plan of design

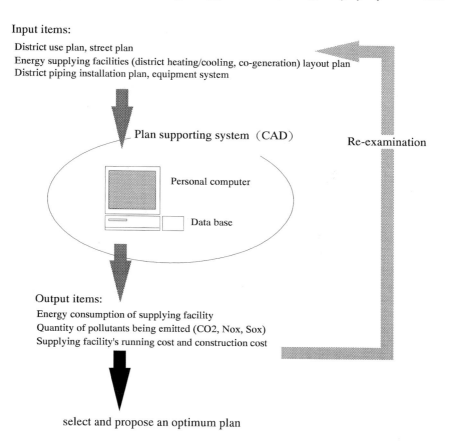

Input items:

District use plan, street plan
Energy supplying facilities (district heating/cooling, co-generation) layout plan
District piping installation plan, equipment system

Plan supporting system （CAD）

Re-examination

Personal computer

Data base

Output items:

Energy consumption of supplying facility
Quantity of pollutants being emitted (CO_2, Nox, Sox)
Supplying facility's running cost and construction cost

select and propose an optimum plan

Figure III-B9 CAD as a tool for supporting system plans with input/output variables of an energy infrastructure model

for the infrastructure. Four of the seven supporting plans for systems presented in Table III-B4 are described in detail in the following.

Urban Infrastructure Plan

By inserting quantitative measures into a computer model at an early stage of the district development, variables, such as topographical features, shape, scale, use, street plan, roads, the required scale of the infrastructure, its construction cost, and its various service systems can be configured to produce a total benefit/cost model. This model can be quickly calculated by the database which contains actual cost figures and results. Thus, an overall business plan, including the infrastructure as a whole, can be smoothly worked out and integrated into the larger urban plan (Fig. III-B10).

At an early stage of planning, changes in the proposed use of facilities, road plans, etc. are frequently made, which often makes it exceedingly difficult to

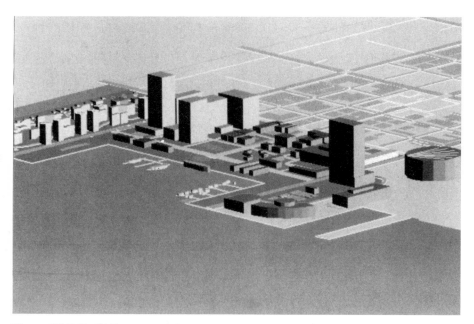

Figure III-B10 CAD as a tool for supporting system plans with input/output variables for an urban infrastructure model

examine infrastructures while also swiftly responding to changes in planning conditions in conventional cases. However, the use of this supporting plan system or computer model makes it possible to respond quickly to such changes.

Energy Infrastructure Plan

A computer model may be used at the stage where a district's business plan and its predicted energy usage needs to be determined in order to propose an efficient energy infrastructure system. By feeding the computer planning conditions to be evaluated, such as the facilities' scale, equipment system, and plant configuration and conduit laying plan for an energy supply system, the quantity of energy consumed and pollutants generated can be mathematically calculated. The supply system then can be evaluated in terms of its capacity and environmental impact; the cost of construction can also be calculated. These inputs also allow predictions of the business potential of a plant and the completed model enables the proposal of a design plan that will provide an optimum energy supply system for the district.

General Water Utilization Plan

To positively utilize rain-water and recycled waste-water within a district, an optimum recycling system can be worked out by applying this plan supporting system through computer modeling. The quantity of water demanded and supplied in the district can be calculated when feeding the computer the data of district conditions such as the use of miscellaneous water supply, the intermediate treated water source and the rain-water collecting site. These calculations can aid in selecting an installation area of a water disposal system at the recycling facility and estimate the cost of its construction and operation to evaluate the business potential of the system.

District Parking Lot Plan

Based on the district's land utilization plan, the computer simulation of variables can calculate the necessary size for the parking lot while performing a dynamic simulation of the automobile flow within the parking lot and on the neighboring roads (Fig. III-B11). By analyzing the queuing time of automobiles going in and out of the parking lot, the impact of building a parking lot upon the neighboring roads and so on, and the model aids in the design of optimum land utilization when it assists in planning the configuration of the parking lot.

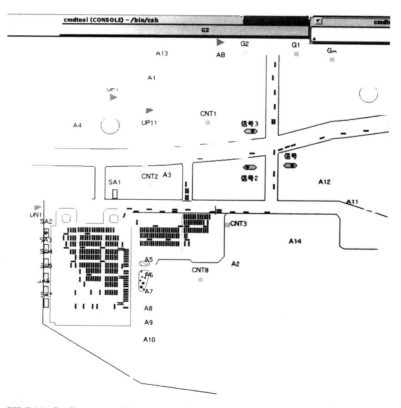

Figure III-B11 CAD as a tool for supporting system plans with input/output variables for an intra-district parking lot plan

Figure III-B12 The image of a city realized through new infrastructure

CONCLUSION

An image of a city where the various small-scale district infrastructural networks are incorporated into a larger district, as proposed by Shimizu Corporation, are presented in Figure III-B12. As introduced in this paper, the drawing expresses a city plan in which small-scale infrastructure intended for district development harmonizes well with larger-scale infrastructure which covers a wider geographical area. Together, this small-scale infrastructure creates a favorable district environment. If Japan fails to prepare the infrastructure as it approaches the twenty-first century, the present generation will lose an opportunity to profit from the natural environment, both regionally and globally, and from the sophisticated services rendered by the infrastructure. Japan will also miss a chance to solve various problems, such as the environmental pollution, aging of population, and outdated building equipment. Thus, the authors feels responsible for enhancing the social quality of life through meeting the needs of the present and future generations.

Shimizu Corporation intends to continue to improve CAD as a tool for supporting system plans to design infrastructural models as introduced here and utilize them in various district development projects.

To make these large-scale and complex projects successful, Shimizu Corporation brings a broad perspective, which transcends conventional ideas and technology, to bear upon the entire process from the conceptualization to start-up. By strengthening not merely the conventional architectural and civil engineering departments, but also the related engineering departments, Shimizu Corporation is also resolved to reinforce the total technological capability for proceeding with projects. By continuing research and development in various fields, the ensuing results will help establish a higher quality of life.

ACKNOWLEDGEMENTS

The authors are very grateful to Mr. Ryuhei Enman, District Development Department, Business Division; Mr. Toshio Oyama, Technological Development Division, Shimizu Corporation; and the many others who have kindly extended their cooperation in preparing this paper.

BIBLIOGRAPHY

1. The Energy Measurement and Analysis Center 1993. *Energy Economy Statistical Handbook.* Tokyo: Japan Energy Economy Research Institute.
2. The General Planning Bureau, Economic Planning Agency 1991. *Social Overhead Capital for Tomorrow Which Must be Created Now.* Tokyo: General Planning Bureau.
3. The Japan Architecture Center 1990. *Proposal of New Urban Habitation.* Tokyo: Japan Architectural Center.
4. The Ministry of Construction 1991. *Visions of Cities in 2013.* Tokyo: Ministry of Construction.
5. The Ministry of Construction. 1993. *White Paper on Construction.* Tokyo: Ministry of Construction.
6. The Urban Infra Technology Promotion Conference 1993. Papers Read at the *Fourth Meeting for Announcement of Technological Research Results.* Tokyo: Urban Infra Technology Promotion Conference.
7. Tokyo Metropolitan Government 1990. *The Environment as Seen from Figures: Collection of Environmental Preservation Data.* Tokyo: Tokyo Metropolitan Government.
8. UC Planning Company 1993. *Nationwide Public and Urban Projects.* Tokyo: UC Planning.

C Subway Network Development in Japanese Cities

Hikoji Iwai

INTRODUCTION

The subway system could be one of the most efficient ways to solve the urban transport problems of Japanese metropolitan areas. The introduction of subways to Japanese cities started later than in Western cities. However, in the past thirty years, a great effort has been made to develop new subway lines in Japan. For the residents of metropolitan areas, time and money spent on transportation and the physical exhaustion from congestion and overcrowding on subways are serious problems that need to be solved. At present, there are many lines operating or under construction. It is necessary, however, to integrate the design of the subways and especially their stations, into a comprehensive plan of subsurface utilization.

In this chapter, the current status of subways is described first. In addition, various problems of the subway system will be raised and suggestions to make the underground transportation network the most effective means of urban transportation will be discussed.

RAPID TRANSIT NETWORKS IN METROPOLITAN AREAS

Historical Evolution and Current Status

The modernization of Japanese society began around 1860. In the transportation sector, stagecoaches and horse trams were introduced first, but they did not last long. In 1895, the first streetcars went into use in Kyoto. After that, they were introduced to other large cities nationwide and streetcars became the major means of urban transportation. However, Japanese urban transportation facilities were still behind the times considering that the basic structure of subway networks in Western countries had been built by that time.

In 1923, a strong earthquake hit the area of Tokyo and Yokohama. Since most of the buildings were made of wood, these cities were almost completely destroyed by the earthquake and its subsequent fires. After the disaster, people began to move into the suburban areas along the new railway lines while commercial services remained in the city center. This event is the origin of the existing land-use pattern with a separation of residential and commercial areas.

Both national and private railroad networks, built for freight and local transportation, started to play a significant role for commuters. Yet, many of these railroads extended only as far as the Japanese National Railway's Yamanote Line in the city, which was a circular line with a radius of about 5 km. Instead, streetcars and buses were necessary to connect these outer limits with the city center. Furthermore, the initial planning for the rapid railroad, which was introduced after the great earthquake, was designed mainly for subways in the city of Tokyo and did not cover more than a radius of 10 km from the city center. The plan did not include the growing suburban area.

The development of subways in central Tokyo started in 1925 as the project of a private company. In 1927, a segment of the Ginza Line began operating between Ueno and Asakusa. By 1939, the Ginza Line, which covers 14.3 km and starts in Shibuya, was the only fully completed line. In the meantime, the subway in Osaka was launched in 1933.

During World War II, the Tokyo area was once again devastated by fire. After the recurrent destruction within a short period of time, people were forced to evaluate the safety of their city and many people opted to move to the suburbs. Again, the separation of land-use between the residential and commercial areas was accelerated. The center of Tokyo accommodated mostly commercial and business functions, while the residential areas were moved to the outskirts of the capital. As a result, the traffic inside the city swelled with the increased number of commuters to and from the suburbs while the traffic inside the circular Yamanote Line became dependent on streetcars (Fig. III-C1).

Around 1960, as the economy boomed, Japan experienced a proliferation of motorized vehicles. The number of automobiles in and around Tokyo rose rapidly. This increase brought along traffic jams and reduced the efficiency of streetcars. Since 1955 in the larger cities and in smaller cities since 1960, the use of streetcars has come to a halt. In Tokyo, streetcars were abandoned and replaced by buses or other vehicles around 1965. At that time, it was expected that the disuse of streetcars would ease traffic congestion. However, this transition did not improve the flow of traffic since the buses and cars which replaced the streetcars proved to be inferior in efficiency and transportation capacity (Fig. III-C2). Finally, officials agreed that it was necessary to construct elevated railroads or subways which would be separated from congested and overcrowded streets.

In modern times, a master-plan for an urban rapid transit network, including subways, is a crucial part of comprehensive city planning. Projects have been undertaken according to the urgency of building these lines. This plan was revised in 1946, 1957, and 1985 to adjust to the conditions which existed at each period of time. At the end of World War II, there was only one fully operational subway, the Ginza Line in Tokyo. During the postwar period, with its devastated economic state, the construction of new lines was launched with the support of

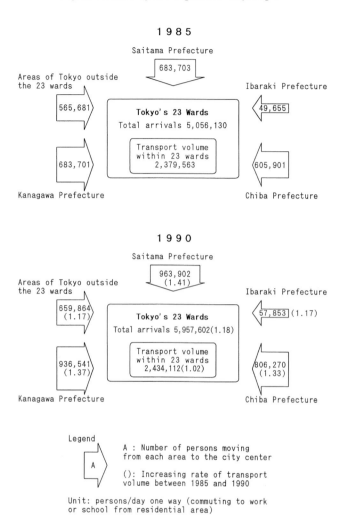

Figure III-C1 Number of persons commuting to work or school from Tokyo's twenty-three wards and neighboring prefectures to central Tokyo (TRTA Subway Brochure)

	RAILWAY	BUS	PRIVATE CAR	WALK·BICYCLE	OTHERS
1968	30.0	6.3	16.1	47.5	0.1
1978	33.6	3.5	17.8	45.1	0.0
1988	39.6	2.8	16.4	41.2	0.0

Figure III-C2 Share of transportation means in Tokyo's twenty-three ward area

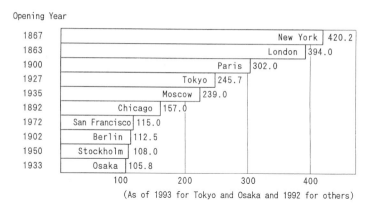

Figure III-C3 Operating length of subways in the world in km (*TRTA Subway Brochure*)

the national and local governments. For the Tokyo Olympics of 1964, several new lines were opened and the subway network improved drastically. Even today, the construction of new lines is still underway. Japan has almost caught up with cities such as London and Paris and several other world cities in terms of extending subway lines the full length of the city (Fig. III-C3). Nevertheless, considering the volume of traffic, still more lines are needed.

In Osaka, the Midousuji Line (full length 4.1 km) was opened in 1935; it crossed the city from North to South. Yet the main mode of transportation then was still the streetcar and bus. Since 1945, the subway system was gradually developed and by 1970, the year of the World's Fair, rapid progress was made in constructing more lines. Other major local cities recognized the need for subways as the main transportation system and lines were added gradually. Yet, the subways in these cities still remain too few with only the exception of Nagoya, where an extensive network of subways has been developed (Fig. III-C4).

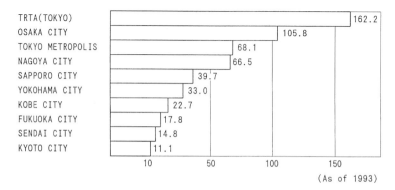

Figure III-C4 Operating length of subways in Japan in km (TRTA Subway Brochure)

Subways in Metropolitan Tokyo

As mentioned before, at the beginning of the 1960s, there were a number of national railroads and private lines which were connected to the terminal stations of the circular Yamanote Line. The only subway line in full operation at that time was the Ginza Line. Between 1960 and 1990, however, the construction of subways was actively promoted and the construction was carried out by the Teito Rapid Transit Authority (TRTA), which also operates the Ginza Line. The Transportation Bureau of Tokyo Metropolitan Government is the agency responsible for the management of streetcars and most of the buses. TRTA is an organization jointly run by the city of Tokyo and the national government. Tokyo is the only city where the central government participates in the management of subways. In other cities like Osaka, construction and management of subways are controlled by the local government alone.

Since the whole metropolitan mass transportation system operated with different networks were owned by different companies, there was a need to establish a collaborative system which would operate the entire network in an efficient manner. This arrangement was called a "reciprocal direct operation." Most of the subway lines in Tokyo are now managed through reciprocal direct operation which connects subway lines with railways operated by other companies. This way, the transportation of commuters from the suburbs into the central business districts and vice versa, now takes place without major inconveniences for the passengers. This operation contributes significantly to the efficient performance of railways. With the reciprocal direct operation, the length of railroads and subways was extended from only 73.8 km in 1960 to 522 km in 1990 (Table III-C1). To adopt this operation, the following conditions must be met.

- Both railways must have common technical structures such as a track gauge, electric suppliers, and control systems. Where the systems are not compatible, trains with suitable equipment have to be installed.
- Both networks must have a balanced demand for transportation.
- The railway crews must be able to drive the other company's trains since the crews alternate driving trains only in their respective company's area.

Table III-C1 Total growth length of railroads in Tokyo in reciprocal operation with subway lines.

Year	Length (km)
1960	73.8
1970	239.0
1980	400.6
1990	522.0

Source: Transport Economy Research Institute, 1992.

This reciprocal direct operation has many advantages, but some complications may occur.

- All of the private railways adopt overhead power supply systems. To connect with them, subways have to use this power supply also. In comparison with a third rail power collector system, the overhead power system would require large tunnels and this, in turn, would increase the construction costs (Fig. III-C5).
- The service plan and schedule must be agreed upon by both companies.

A number of other problems must be currently addressed, such as congestion during rush hours, lack of ring lines, and the need to improve facilities.

Congestion During Rush Hours

The situation at the moment is best characterized by the Japanese term *tsuukin jigoku* (commuting hell). The congestion of trains in big cities during the rush hours is an acute problem which is especially intensified during a few hours in the morning and evening. In central Tokyo, 25% of the passengers use trains between 8:00–9:00 a.m. At the peak of the rush hour, most trains are overloaded more than 200% capacity. In order to ease the congestion, the transportation capacity must be improved.

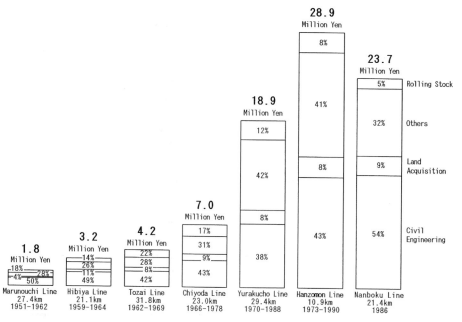

Figure III-C5 Construction costs per m length of the subway lines in yen (TRTA Subway Brochure)

The following three ways are proposed as solutions:

- To increase the number of trains during peak hours.
- To increase the number of cars per train.
- To construct additional lines.

In the Tokyo area, most railways run trains every two minutes during rush hour. By advancing the signal system, the interval between trains can be shortened further, but this will not make a significant difference. As to increasing the number of cars, many trains already have ten cars, which is a considerable length. The enlargement of garages and underground stations is also required, but this is an unrealistic idea considering the unsurmountable difficulties involved. This leaves the third solution of building new subway lines as the most feasible.

On the other hand, it is very important to decrease the demand for subways and to disperse the traffic at the busiest hours of the day. With this view in mind, there has been an effort to relocate the major commercial and business centers to satellite cities such as Yokohama, Omiya and Chiba. Japan has not been successful in moving business functions to local areas outside of metropolitan Tokyo, but within the Tokyo area, cities such as Yokohama are growing as a substitute for the central business district. Thus, the current practice of concentrating all business functions in the central district of Tokyo is expected to be eased in the near future.

Lack of Ring Lines

Subways in Tokyo were built radially from the center of the city, from the business area, towards the suburbs. However, there are not enough ring lines to connect with these radial lines. Streetcars are used to cover the relatively short distances inside the Yamanote Line with a thin network system, but to this point, there is no means of alternative transportation to replace them.

Necessity of Improving Facilities

The population and economic activities in the Tokyo area have expanded more than expected. The commercial area has spread from the Chiyoda, Minato, and Chuo Wards to the Shinjuku, Ikebukuro, and Shibuya areas. As a result, the commuters have outnumbered the demand estimated at the beginning of the construction of the subway network. Not only do trains not have the capacity to allow a smooth flow of people, but the stations are also inadequate. Furthermore, as the technical standards of safety and disaster prevention become stricter, facilities with better quality have become necessary. Air-conditioning and escalators in the stations need to be added and to meet these requirements, stations in and around the central city area are being renovated while business goes on as usual.

CREATION OF NEW SUBWAY LINES

In the Tokyo urban area, the intensity of rush hour congestion, which is one of the major complaints of residents of this metropolis, is beyond the level of passengers' tolerance. However, all the possible attempts to ease congestion seem to have been exhausted; the only remaining effective solution is to add new lines. The railway companies and organizations involved are now working on the construction of new subways or are adding double-track lines to existing ones. Those participating in this venture are not only TRTA and the Tokyo Metropolitan Bureau in charge of subway construction, but also private companies which run lines in the suburbs, local governments, and semi-public companies in the business world. The Ministry of Transportation set up the Transport Policy Council to develop a comprehensive master plan of transport for the entire metropolitan urban area. As for Tokyo City, a plan was made in 1985 to be completed in 2000. Railway entrepreneurs need permission from the Ministry of Transportation to undertake enterprises which will abide by the master plan of the Ministry. This way, the coordination of projects will be maintained.

TRTA and the Tokyo Metropolitan Bureau construct subways mainly in the central business district and its vicinity. At present, several lines are under construction in this area. The attempt has been made to adopt as many reciprocal direct operations as possible. For example, the TRTA Nanboku Line (21 km) has been under construction since 1984 and Meguro station, a part of the Yamanote circular line at the south end, is expected to be fully operational in the near future. At this point, Nanboku is expected to be connected to Tokyo Mekama Line, a private line leading towards the suburbs, under reciprocal direct operation. Eleven out of nineteen stations on the Nanboku Line are planned to be intersected with other railway stations. This will contribute to a more extensive and efficient railway network. By using modern technology, this line will offer the highest security and most convenient service to passengers. TRTA plans to build new subways with as high security and comfort as experienced on the Nanboku Line.

Another important subway line is also under construction in the Tokyo urban area. This line is a long ring line managed by a semipublic company originally founded by the Tokyo Metropolitan Bureau. The line aims to combine many radial lines to improve the efficiency and convenience of the entire subway network and to offer subway service to areas not currently covered by any lines. On the other hand, the construction costs have to be minimized for this line, since ring lines tend to have relatively fewer passengers than radial lines, even during rush hours. As a result, ring lines tend to adopt linear motor driven cars. This is the second time this type of car has been used for a subway in Japan. The linear motor driven car has a flat motor which calls for the tunnels half the size of usual subway tunnels. This line will be the second ring railway line in the central business district of Tokyo. Upon its completion, the network system in this area should be nearly satisfactory. However, this does not necessarily solve the problems of the radial lines during rush hours.

DEVELOPMENT OF NEW TYPES OF RAPID TRANSIT SYSTEMS

In the Tokyo metropolitan area, TRTA and the Tokyo Metropolitan Bureau have outlined the plans for new subway lines while private railway companies are undertaking various measures to increase the transport capacity. However, due to the enormous cost of these undertakings, the feasibility of the lines is limited technically as well as financially.

Buses in big cities are not a reliable transportation means since the streets are chronically congested. As the feeder service and supplemental service of subways, a medium-scaled and relatively economic transportation method is necessary. In major local cities outside Tokyo, a number of subway lines serve as the main mode of transportation, but it does not seem feasible to build more subway lines in those cities. As an alternative, medium-scaled monorails and new transport systems, such as the Automated Guideway Transit (AGT), are being introduced in many of these urban areas.

The Tokyo Monorail Haneda Line was opened in 1964 to cover the 13.1 km between Hamamatsucho station on the Yamanote Line in central Tokyo and the Tokyo International Airport (Haneda). It was the first commercial straddle-type city transit monorail in the world. In addition to its role as an access route to Haneda Airport, it has also contributed to the development of the area along the line.

Now, monorails are being used in other cities like Osaka, Kitakyushu and Chiba for intra-city transportation. AGT is also being adopted as a supplemental transportation in Osaka, Kobe, Yokohama, and Omiya. These urban transit systems have the following advantages.

- Since the cars are relatively light compared to those ordinarily used, the substructure of the driving tracks can also be simple and light, making it possible to build tracks above the existing roads.
- The system allows the operation of cars on slopes and small radial curves.
- Since the track beams can be prefabricated in factories, the field-work at the construction sites can be carried out quickly and easily.
- Since both construction and operating costs are low, these systems have great economic and technical efficiency.

However, as this system requires the construction of bridges over the existing roads, it has several disadvantages: (a) it obstructs the city view; (b) it causes noise on the street; and (c) it casts shadows over the street. It is important to evaluate the advantages and disadvantages of the monorail comprehensively before realizing it.

RAPID TRANSIT SYSTEM AND THE URBAN ENVIRONMENT

Effects on the Urban Environment

As one of the global environmental issues, the problems of air pollution like NO_x still need to be solved. Most motorized vehicles consume oil, which results in the emission of pollutants, such as CO_2 and NO_x, into the air. If traffic becomes heavier, it will bring serious environmental consequences as well as the increased consumption of limited energy resources. Therefore, it is necessary to meet the increasing demand for transportation and simultaneously decrease the emission of pollutants and consumption of energy.

In the urban areas, energy consumption in the transportation sector (automobiles, railways, ships and airplanes) consists of 25% of all of the energy use. Among the transportation methods, automobiles consume most of the transportation sector's energy, 85%. To decrease the energy consumption in the transportation sector, it is crucial to find ways to reduce the gasoline and light oil consumption by automobiles and to find alternatives for these resources.

Nationwide, 30% of the entire transportation is covered by the railway, but its energy consumption is only 8%. Buses contribute to 6% of all the transportation and their energy consumption is only 3%. Automobiles make up 43% of the transportation and 65% of energy consumption. In other words, to carry one person 1 km, automobiles use five times more energy than railways and three times more than buses. Furthermore, during the rush hours in the Tokyo urban area, automobiles consume twenty-three times as much energy as subways do and sixteen times that of buses. Consequently, railways are an excellent means of mass transportation in terms of pollution and energy consumption. Thus, the shift from automobiles to railways should be considered as an important solution to the Japanese traffic situation. However, with the current state of fierce congestion during rush hours, there is very little extra space to absorb the passengers from automobiles into public transportation. To make the conversion possible, the construction of new lines would have to be accelerated while the frequency of operation and the number of cars on each train during rush hours would have to be increased. Yet, the problem of finding space to accomplish this expansion still remains.

Automobiles are used as the primary means for carrying out commercial and business activities in the city. In the Tokyo metropolitan area, 60% of all business travel is by automobile and only about 20% is by railway. Since trains are not filled to their capacity during the daytime, business trips within the city could easily be transferred from the automobile to subway. To achieve this transition, the subway network would have to be reinforced and access to stations would have to be improved.

Other than the problems of energy consumption and air pollution, many environmental aspects are considered when railways are constructed or operated. For example, train cars create noise and vibration. A train traveling on or above the surface might bother the surrounding neighborhoods, but underground, these inconveniences can seldom be felt. Unfortunately, though, if the subway tunnel is relatively close to the surface, it might produce some noise and vibrations in the buildings directly above the tunnel and could disturb the residents' sleep. Still, these problems would be less acute than those of a train on the surface. In the case of an elevated structure, the superstructure blocks sunshine, intercepts electric waves, and spoils the landscape. There is no such problem in the case of subways built underground.

Considering the environmental problems and the difficulty of getting a railway right-of-way above the ground, new railways are being built underground exclusively within a 15 km radius from the center of Tokyo. If the location is in a residential area 15–25 km from the center of the city, building above and below ground will be feasible. For example, a private company is currently trying to construct an additional elevated railway along an existing railway and has received strong resistance from the residents who live along the line. This brings planners to a controversial issue: Is it better to build subways below ground or as surface trains in a suburban residential area? Subways are more suitable as they generate less pollution for the environment and use the more plentiful public space underground. On the other hand, surface railways are superior to subways because of their easier and lower construction and operation costs and the higher comfort for passengers.

Suburban railways built during the period prior to the expansion of the built-up area of Tokyo were laid on the surface. Therefore, they intercept many roads. These railway crossings, however, increase the risk of severe traffic accidents. If train service was expanded to run at two-minute intervals on double tracks, the road crossings would almost continuously be closed. For this reason, it is quite reasonable to consider constructing new railways with elevated or underground structures, but the decision should be made on an individual basis due to the specific conditions of each case.

In the future, the consideration of environmental problems and utilization of land should be given high priority. Consequently, subways seem to be the solution in many instances. In the case of monorails or AGT, which are expected to be useful transportation systems for medium-sized traffic volume, low construction costs endorse its construction. Monorails have been used in Yokohama, Osaka, Kobe, and other cities as a supplemental service to the arterial railway lines. In Tokyo, the construction of two new lines has begun. These types of new transportation methods seem to offer good prospects for practical use if the citizens can accept their environmental drawbacks.

ENVIRONMENTAL CONSIDERATION OF SUBWAY FACILITIES

When utilizing underground space the environment and protection against disasters are critical issues. From a legal standpoint, there are many protective laws like the Railway Enterprise Law, which regulates important technical standards of the railway equipment and operations, the Fire Regulation Law and the Building Code, which regulates technical standards of buildings (railway stations are considered buildings). The protection from fire is the most pressing concern and there are detailed regulations to be met. The basic concept of the fire protection regulations are as follows:

- To remove flammable materials from cars and fireproof the facilities in the stations.

- To install fire alarms, fire extinguishers and fire hydrants to extinguish fire in the early stages.
- To provide smoke extraction apparatuses and emergency lighting in the stations.

Japanese subways, not only new but also old lines, need to be fashioned with these countermeasures against disasters. In addition, since subways in the future are expected to be deeper underground and the distances between stations are to be longer, reinforcing these countermeasures will become even more important. Examples of countermeasures include the use of oil-free cables and the implementation of an open space between the subway and surface level.

The open space in the subway would accommodate the unspecified number of people to and from the subway as well as the large number of staff who could work comfortably, both physically and mentally, for long periods of time. The main factors which contribute toward the physical comfort are ventilation, a noise-free environment, and proper lighting. As for the psychological comfort, ameliorating conditions to prevent claustrophobia, to ease anxiety of losing one's sense of direction, and to allay fears for one's safety become paramount.

As for the psychological problems, the sense of being underground rarely frightens passengers. Stations are brightly lit and constantly filled with people. Fortunately, public peace and order are also well maintained even at night which lessens fears of one's physical safety. Equipment to eliminate physical uneasiness was installed to an almost satisfactory level in the latest subways, as well as in those built in 1980, which originally did not have such equipment. Construction to install air-conditioning in subway cars and stations is still under way. We need further investigation, including insights from the human engineering perspective to make the stations even more comfortable physically as well as mentally.

Subways and Subsurface Space

As the cities grew and times changed, land-use of the urban area shifted from a horizontal to a vertical layout and from a simple to a complex function. In Japan, private landowners control the surface as well as the subsurface. In commercial areas, the subsurface space of private land is used for supplementary purposes such as the underground floors of buildings, parking spaces, and storage facilities. Buildings which have use of commercial underground space increasingly open this area to outsiders. On the other hand, the public space in the urban area, particularly its subsurface space, is used for various public facilities in addition to its original use. Roads are an example of structures with multiple purposes. Besides their original function of offering a means of transportation, roads carry many facilities underground, such the various pipes and cables which reach each household. These include water works, sewers, telephone lines, and big-scaled structures such as subways, underground roads, underground rivers, and parking spaces. The large-scaled structures cannot be moved once they are built. Considering the difficulty of freeing new surface land and the environmental problems that exist in built-up areas, the need for using subsurface space will increase in the future.

The present status of the subsurface space utilization is the result of a lack of medium or long-term planning. New facilities are built when they are needed, but only after modifications are made to already existing facilities. Subways are constructed beneath wide roads, but the roads in Tokyo are not well developed compared with those in other big cities of the world. The subsurface space beneath wide roads is becoming filled with various public facilities. New subways need to be built under narrow roads, or sometimes they have to be constructed under private lands. The old facilities were built close to the surface, but new facilities must be laid deeper in the ground. The oldest subway, the Ginza Line, was built within 10 m of the surface on the average, but new lines are built at about 30 m from the surface. As stations move deeper, access to other lines and the surface becomes poorer. To solve this problem, connecting concourses, pedestrian walkways, and open space for the public in the buildings are used to offer the necessary convenience for subway travel. In the future, not only vertical movement like escalators and elevators, but also more horizontal facilities, such as moving sidewalks, need to be implemented.

FUTURE PROSPECTS FOR SUBWAY FACILITIES

Planning Aspects

As mentioned earlier, increasing the transportation capacity is necessary to ease the congestion during rush hours in urban centers like Tokyo and Osaka. The subway network should also be expanded, so it can offer the most convenient transportation possible for daily use. The need for subsurface uses of public lands will increase for various reasons. Among those needs, subways should be given high priority since they are basic and important facilities to support the city's activities.

The location of subway lines and especially the stations must be examined from various angles and be determined as a part of overall city planning, for they will have a great impact on the future development of urban centers. To encourage more people to use the subway as a convenient mode of transportation, it is essential to offer easier access to the stations from various parts of the city and to facilitate the transit to another subway line inside the stations. For example, it would be useful to connect the concourse levels of the subway stations, underground pedestrian ways, and the public underground passages of the neighboring buildings smoothly. These subsurface spaces should be comprised of a planned network of subsurface pedestrian walkways. In order to provide easier transit for passengers, more elevators and escalators should be installed. As mentioned previously, the substructures of subways are enormous and are almost impossible to be moved once they are built. The existence of these structures will affect the future utilization of subsurface space by other public facilities. These facilities should have their own proper locations of subsurface space according to their functions and characteristics. It is not wise to arrange subsurface space on a "first come, first serve" basis. Authorities concerned with road administration started to work out a basic plan for the possible usage of subsurface road space by various public facilities. However, the location of each future facility should be decided according to this plan.

Engineering Aspects

The ground of Tokyo consists of soft alluvium soil. The eastern part of central Tokyo is particularly soft and there is no solid ground in which to build facilities, unless they are to be located deeper than 50 m. For the structure to be safe and firm in a high-density city setting, high level construction techniques are necessary. For the subway stations, the cut and cover method can be used where the ground is dug out from the underneath road surface, using shield driving methods to dig underground tunnels to the next station. However, if the station is to be very deep, the shield method is used to dig only a minimal amount of earth from the surface. Since the shield method has the advantage of not affecting activities on the surface, it is expected to be improved technically, so it can be used not only for digging circular shaped tunnels, but for other tunnel forms as well.

The main material used for underground structures is reinforced concrete. In the case of Tokyo, underground water tends to erode the underground concrete. However, the concrete which makes up the main part of the tunnels has to be permanent. Therefore, appropriate maintenance and repair measures are necessary. To do this, the following technical developments are important:

- The technique to measure the extent of the concrete's deterioration with accuracy.
- Effective repair techniques in all cases.
- The establishment of investment planning for repair from the point of view of the economic evaluation method.

These problems will soon become apparent in Japanese subways and planners have, of yet, insufficient experience to deal with them effectively.

Management Aspects

Railway projects in the Tokyo metropolitan area are managed by the Japanese Railway Higashi-Nippon (JR), formerly Japanese National Railways, TRTA, the Tokyo Metropolitan Bureau, and private companies. Among them, the subways inside the Yamanote Line are run and managed by TRTA and the Tokyo Metropolitan Bureau. The construction of new lines is also managed by these two parties.

In the Osaka area, as in Tokyo, JR Nishi-Nippon, the Osaka Transportation Bureau, and private companies operate the subways; they do not have semipublic organizations like TRTA. Therefore, most of the subways inside the city are managed by the Osaka Transportation Bureau. Although the subways are municipal enterprises, they adopt self-supporting accounting systems by regarding themselves as an independent enterprise for accounting purposes.

The national government offers low interest loans to those projects, but subsidies are not enough. On the other hand, the subway fare is regarded as a public utility charge and cannot be raised without the government's permission. Due to this, many railway entrepreneurs suffer from budget deficits; one of the largest expenses in their budgets is the repayment of construction loans. They still have to invest money to construct new lines to ease the congestion of rush hours. It does not seem appropriate to cover this kind of investment for upgrading the capacity solely with fares from passengers. Capital investments should be regarded as public infrastructure investments to support the city's activities.

Accordingly, the costs of tunnels and stations might be handled in the same way as the construction of roads, ports, and other facilities. The introduction of new subway lines and stations makes a strong impact on surrounding communities. By improving the transportation convenience with new lines, the subsequent development can bring an area a tremendous profit. Private companies in suburban areas invest in the land along their railway lines and secure a development profit which in turn helps pay off the deficit of the railway projects. However, TRTA and other public companies, which manage the network within the city, are not allowed to develop land along their lines. In this case, the profits from development go into the pockets of the landowners in those areas. It is very difficult to take away the development profit directly from built-up areas, but it would be worth considering charging the community indirectly through land taxation or other taxes. Like in the Tokyo metropolitan area where several railway entrepreneurs run railways, fares can vary according to companies' financial conditions. In Tokyo, lines by TRTA and those by the Tokyo Metropolitan Bureau consist of one subway network, but there is a small difference in the fares. Regarding transit between different companies, the fares are calculated separately although there is a partial discount system. This results in relatively high fares even for short distances. From the passengers' point of view, fares should be set at the same rate no matter which company owns the line. It is necessary to set up a united fare system that would use one business organization to run the entire subway network.

CONCLUSION

In large Japanese cities, urban railways, including the subways, have played and will continue to play the main role in public transportation. The following three factors must be accomplished to maintain this role effectively.

- To offer satisfactory services to passengers.
- To uphold good standards of facility management and operation of cars.
- To preserve a healthy financial situation.

Judging from the urban transportation situation in Japan, the most serious concern is that the congestion of cars heading for the city center during rush hours is burdensome to the passengers. To increase the transportation capacity, capital investment must continue to flow. However, this large investment can hurt the company's financial situation which is one of the crucial conditions mentioned above.

Fortunately, in recent times, the national government and local self-governing bodies have begun to help subway constructions financially by providing subsidies and interest-free loans. While continuing these efforts, it is also important to develop new business districts with plans to switch the flow of passengers in the opposite direction—from the center to the outskirts of the city where congestion is not yet as severe.

Thus, excessive concentration of transportation to the city center will be eased. To achieve this goal, the sound coordination of transportation planning and urban development projects are indispensable.

BIBLIOGRAPHY

1. Civil Engineer's Association of Japan 1990. *Underground Space* (in Japanese). Tokyo: Civil Engineer's Association of Japan.
2. Japan Rolling Stock Exporter's Association 1990. *Urban Transportation Systems in Japan.* Tokyo: Japan Rolling Stock Exporter's Association.
3. Keikakukyoku, T. and Johoka, S. 1988. *Planning of Tokyo.* Tokyo: Tokyo Metropolis.
4. Teito Rapid Transit Authority 1993. *1993 TRTA Handbook.* N.p.
5. Teito Rapid Transit Authority 1993. *TRTA Subway Brochure.* N.p.
6. Transport Economy Research Institute, n.d. *Transport and Environment* (in Japanese). Tokyo: Transport Economy Research Institute.

D Urban Transportation and Environment

Mitsuyuki Asano

INTRODUCTION

After experiencing about forty-five years of rapid growth since World War II, Japan now has a 16% share of the world's GNP (Gross National Product) at a time when the worldwide per capita GNP has also reached its highest level ever. Yet, many Japanese do not share a sense of being better off or even wealthy, as people may feel in Switzerland or other countries. This is presumably due to Japan's soaring land prices, poor housing, long commuting distances, and high consumer prices.

Conditions in Japan have spawned a dense urban society because of the limitation of land available for expansion in urban areas. Thus, in order to truly realize a wealthy existence in the twenty-first century, it is imperative that Japan find a way to create comfortable urban conditions and, in particular, provide mobility with high quality service to meet people's varied transportation needs. Japan already has a well-developed railway network. However, it is not easy to improve people's mobility in terms of safety and comfort in harmony with the urban environment, while competing with the increased affordability and the growing market of private vehicles.

Among the developed countries, Japan is foremost in actively promoting the expansion of transportation facilities in built-up urban areas. As Japan moves toward the twenty-first century, its cities will be transformed into a more mature, environmentally-oriented society. This chapter discusses the directions in development of transportation facilities and related services while attempting to maintain a healthy environment.

HISTORY OF THE URBAN TRANSPORTATION SYSTEM

In the half century after World War II, the concentration of population in urban areas has continuously been rising. During this period, the development of the urban transportation infrastructure has vigorously attempted to cope with the increasing traffic demand. A skeletal transportation network was formed in many cities that attempted to handle the increased transportation needs of city residents. It is this infrastructure, coupled with various urban development projects, that has been the foundation supporting Japan's continuous urban growth (Table III-D1).

Postwar Period and the 1950s

Urban road development, initiated under the Postwar Restoration Project (1946), was accelerated under the new regulations of the budgetary system established in 1954. This newest budget allocated a petroleum tax revenue specifically for road development. During this period, as the future direction of urban networks was discussed, road systems were increasingly regarded as a necessary part of city planning.

A continuous influx of people and industries to urban areas increased the volume of traffic. Consequently, traffic congestion became a serious problem because of the belated road and railway construction. Hence, major arterial roads, as well as the urban expressways of major metropolitan areas were quickly developed, the subway construction was promoted, and various approaches to increase the capacity of private railways were outlined. Operations between subways and private railways were also linked. Many streetcars which were once considered useful were abolished and their tracks were converted into road surface for motor vehicles.

In 1967, the first transportation survey was conducted of the commuters in the Hiroshima Metropolitan Area. Using such studies, a comprehensive method of transportation planning was established to replace former planning methods which were based on individual modes of transportation.

Later Trends

In the 1970s, the focus of transportation facility planning shifted from roads to the environment, as well as comfort and safety factors. This focus may be attributed to the marked increase in pollutant emissions and the first oil crisis of 1973. With these events, institutional improvements of transportation facilities took place at the district level. Plans for increasing the subway construction and capacity of private railways continued while bus patronage decreased remarkably.

In 1983 and 1987, the City Planning Council of the national government met to discuss the criteria necessary to determine the desirable levels of urban road planning and directions and measures for its development. As for public transportation, urban monorails and APMs (Automated People Movers) were planned in conjunction with other urban development projects and their operation was initiated. Subway service also started running in regional major cities, such as Sapporo, Fukuoka, and Sendai.

In the latter half of the 1980s, large-scale land-use conversion projects were pursued mainly in large metropolitan areas according to the changes which occurred in Japan's industrial structure. At the same time, the method of development of related transportation infrastructure became a serious issue. High density utilization of urban space and soaring land prices forced transportation facilities to be incorporated into multipurpose spaces, such as underground transportation networks, complex transportation terminals, reclaimed land combined with buildings, and over-road spaces.

Table III-D1 Brief history of urban transportation facilities development

Year	Urban roads development	Railways development	Remarks
Prewar			
Meiji (1st–45th): 1868–1912	1888 Tokyo Urban Area Improvement Code	1872 First railway (Shinbashi-Yokohama) opened 1889 Tokaido line (Tokyo–Osaka) completed 1895 First tramway in Kyoto 1897 First bus operation in hiroshima	1868 Meiji restoration 1894–1895 Japan–China war 1904–1905 Japan–Russia war
Taisho (1st–15th): 1912–1926	1919 City Planning Law (old) 1919 Road Law (old) 1925 Earthquake Restoration Started	1925 Yamate Line in Tokyo (Circular Line) Completed	1923 Great Kanto earthquake
Showa (1st–64th): 1926–1989		1927 First Subway (Ueno-Asakusa) Completed in Tokyo 1933 Subway Opened in Osaka	

Table III-D1 Continued

1939–1945 World War II

Postwar

1945 War restoration started		1947 New constitution enacted
1956 Japan Road Corporation established		
1959 Tokyo Metropolitan Expressway Corporation established		
1962 Hanshin Expressway Corporation established		1962 National comprehensive development plan
	1964 Tokaido Shinkansen opened	1964 Tokyo Olympic games
	1965 Tramway abolished in Osaka	
	1967 Tramway abolished in Tokyo	
1968 City planning law (new)		1969 New national comprehensive development plan
		1972 Sapporo Winter Olympic games
	1975 Sanyo Shinkansen opened	1977 3rd National comprehensive development plan

Present Development

The planning emphasis has been shifting according to the change in the socio-economic climate. However, the planning and development of urban transportation facilities have been continuously pursued to ensure the high mobility of people in conjunction with urban development projects. It is also true that the development of the transportation infrastructure needs to be accelerated to an even greater extent to catch up with the increase in demand of urban dynamics (Fig. III-D1). This gap between supply and demand has been filled so far by the development of high-quality service and technology, such as traffic control systems and door-to-door courier services, of which Japan can be proud. Such services and technology, however, have their limits. Therefore, the development of the urban transportation infrastructure has to be increased steadily in the future. Among developed countries, Japan is the only country where transportation facilities are actively developed in existing built-up areas. The direction of the facilities, however, are being currently studied and discussed in terms of the larger framework of city planning.

TRANSPORTATION FACILITY CHARACTERISTICS

The development of transportation facilities pursued in Japan can be characterized by the following facts:

- The road development in major cities is still insufficient since central city areas have historically used the design pattern of castle towns which were characterized by narrow and winding roads. For this reason, urban road implementation in downtown areas has been focusing on widening the existing roads and constructing new routes concurrently with the road development in the suburbs.

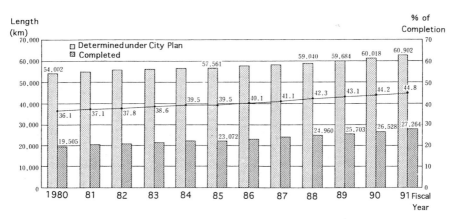

Figure III-D1 Development of city road planning in Japan (City Bureau, The Ministry of Construction, 1992, p. 16)

- Public transportation is the second major concern in large- and medium-sized cities. Although a large part of urban public transportation service has been provided by private operators, some local governments are now in charge of the construction and operation of public transportation facilities that are controlled by the national government.

Large cities with a population of around one million actually operate buses and subways under their own local supervision. As for urban rapid railways, a number of private railway lines were constructed at an early stage of urbanization and have been upgraded and operated since then in large metropolitan areas. Today, these private operators and the Japan Railway Companies (JR Group) play a dominant role in transportation.

- The basic principle in the construction and operation of urban public transportation in Japan has long been "self-finance." This economic doctrine has been applied particularly to urban railways, with the exception of national subsidies awarded for subway construction. As a result, the number of urban rail projects that have recently surfaced tend to be limited because only those projects with a high demand and with sufficient monetary support can proceed to the stage of construction.
- It is felt that medium-capacity urban public transportation modes are needed to fill the gap between the rail and buses. Thus, the construction and operation of urban monorails and automated guide way systems have been implemented using national subsidies from the urban road development budget.

RECENT TENDENCY IN URBAN TRANSPORTATION

Urban transportation characteristics differ by city size, geography, historical, and socio-economical background, as well as the level of development of the facilities themselves. In order to identify the future direction of urban transportation, it is important to recognize the following tendencies typically found in the transportation development.

Increase in Rate of Car Ownership

At the end of 1992, the number of vehicles in Japan reached 61.7 million. The ratio was approximately 499 vehicles per 1000 people, compared to 755 per 1000 persons in the U.S.A.; 621 in Canada; 463 in Great Britain; 505 in France; and 539 in Italy in the same year. Of this number in Japan, the ownership rate of commercial vehicles was the world's highest at 184 commercial vehicles/1000 persons, while the ratio of passenger cars to persons was lower than that of Western European countries by about 100 vehicles. The number of license holders in Japan in 1992 was about 64 million. Today, the trend seems to have moved from one vehicle per household to one vehicle per license holder.

Increase of Car Use and Decrease of Pedestrian Traffic

Recently, people's preferred mode of transportation has changed as the car ownership rate has increased. The present trend is:

- Car use is increasing all over Japan, particularly in local cities.
- Use of motorcycles and bicycles has increased as a means of individual transportation. Yet, its growth has stagnated recently, presumably showing a diversion to cars.
- Railway use is stagnant or decreasing except in large metropolitan areas and local cities where railways have recently been constructed.
- Bus use continues to decrease.
- Pedestrian traffic is declining in most cities, presumably due to the desire to have a comfortable walking space. This space is lacking in some areas.

In short, people's modes of transportation are shifting from the use of public transportation to more private and individual transportation, particularly private cars, which leads to a growth in private motorization. This transition from public to private transportation reflects an increasing aversion to walking (Fig. III-D2).

Increase in Travel Distance and Load on Transportation Facilities

The great reliance on private vehicles has given people more freedom to choose the sites of their residences, shops, offices, and factories and has resulted in the expansion of the urban scale. These scattered urban enterprises inevitably require mutual cooperation among transportation facilities. Thus, the travel distance has become lengthy and traffic congestion often serious.

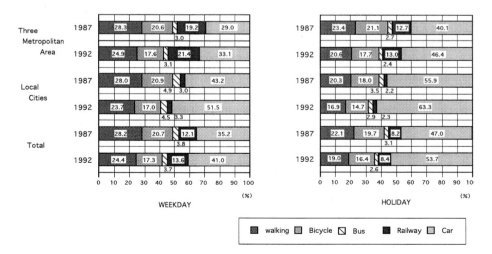

Figure III-D2 Modal composition and its changes in Japanese cities

Increase of Holiday Traffic

Another noticeable change is the increase of traffic on holidays. Although the volume of traffic is still less than on weekdays, the share of private cars on weekends and holidays is extremely high, and the travel distance is long.

ENVIRONMENTAL ISSUES OF URBAN TRANSPORTATION

Current Condition

The proliferation of cars, coupled with the adverse consequences of vehicular traffic on the environment, has emerged as a major issue in urban transportation. Among the major air pollutants, NO_2 has increased slightly, while others have declined slightly or have remained constant over the past several years. On the other hand, noise and vibration have increased in many areas, mainly along motor ways (Fig. III-D3).

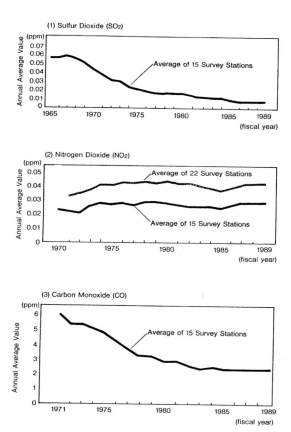

Figure III-D3 Trends of major air pollutants

Countermeasures

Countermeasures for the air pollution caused by vehicular traffic lie primarily in the improvement in the machinery of cars, so that exhaust will contain fewer air pollutants. In particular, progress is needed to improve the quality of exhaust emitted from diesel-powered vehicles. Other measures required are the regulation of goods distribution, the construction of bypass and circumferential arteries, and the dispersion of traffic by way of more effective traffic management.

The noise and vibration caused by vehicular traffic are attributable to the traffic volume, vehicle type, speed of travel, evenness of the road surface and pavement structure. It is rather difficult to reduce noise and vibration at their source. Countermeasures to alleviate noise and vibration, in addition to countermeasures for air pollution, include installing noise absorption dividers, strengthening road and pavement structures, and providing road side buffer zones and buildings.

Environmental Assessment

Environmental assessments are conducted on various large-scale projects to forecast and evaluate the potential effects on the environment, prior to the project's construction. The results of these assessments are officially announced and public opinion is invited to ensure that adequate measures will be undertaken during the implementation stage.

In August 1986, a decision was made by the Cabinet Council on the "Implementation of Environmental Impact Assessment." Subsequently, guidelines on environmental assessment were introduced whereby large-scale projects currently planned by the national agency were required to conduct impact assessments before starting construction. Similarly, environmental assessment is also required for large-scale projects managed by local governments. Projects requiring this assessment typically include national and urban expressways, large dams, railways, airports, and large-scale urban development projects. In 1991, thirty-four prefectural governments, including Tokyo and Kanagawa Prefecture, enacted ordinances on environmental assessment.

VIEWPOINTS ON URBAN DEVELOPMENT

With only a few years left until the twenty-first century, the keynote of urban development is moving towards creating an affluent and humane society. However, serious problems, such as the monopolar concentration of urban functions in Tokyo and belated urban infrastructure development, may hamper that goal. Also, ill-defined future perspectives may increase in relation to society and the economy, as greater unexpected changes may occur after the long-lasting high growth period has ended. However, urban development in the twenty-first century will lead steadily and gradually toward a stable expansion if the socioeconomic fluctuations are balanced. This aspect is briefly discussed from several viewpoints in the following.

Urban Population at its First Peak

After World War II, Japan's urban population continued to increase and in 1990, peaked at 78 million in the densely inhabited districts. Existing urban populations are located on the very limited amount of inhabitable land covering 80,000 km^2. Following this trend, in the beginning of the twenty-first century, the projected urban population will be 70% of the total population or 85 million people.

In 1992, however, the Population Activities Research Institute of the Ministry of Health and Welfare presented a projection that Japan's population would reach its peak at about 130 million in the year 2011 and that it would decline to about 126 million in 2025. According to provisional projections, the total population of Japan will further decrease to about 96 million in 2090. These projected population estimates have never been experienced in Japan before (Fig. III-D4).

Demographic Changes

In 1991, life expectancy was extended to a world high of 76.1 years for males and 82.1 years for females. This increase was due to improvements in the quality of life and advances in medical technology. Meanwhile, the birth rate is gradually declining. The specific birth rate has reached the world's lowest level of 1.53 children per family. This change is due to the tendency of women to marry late as they advance in the business world and pursue a higher education in greater numbers.

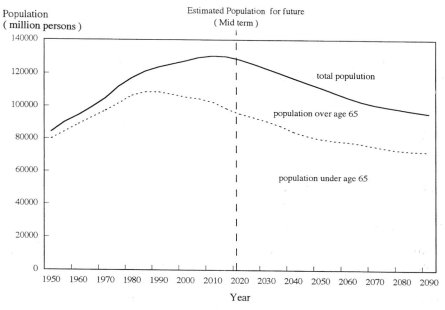

Figure III-D4 Estimated population in Japan between 1950 and 2090 (Institute of Population Issues, 1992)

Consequently, Japan's population will rapidly age and its effect will become noticeable at the beginning of the new century.

- The proportion of aged persons 65 years and older will increase to 25.8% of the population in 2025. Then, Japan will become the most "aged" country in the world.
- The share of the higher-aged (75-years-old or above) will be 15.5% in 2025. This is higher than the present percent of aged persons.
- Even in large metropolitan areas, where the percentage of aged people is relatively low at present, the aged population will sharply increase in the future.

Diversified Value and Lifestyle

With the increase of income and leisure time, people's values, lifestyles, and behavior are changing drastically. This change has been forcing the national focus to shift towards service and software functions. Also, with the internationalization and progress of our information-oriented society, around-the-clock business and commercial activity in large cities has become prevalent. In such an environment, a number of individuals with varied values and interests will seek out different lifestyles and hobbies which are not typically found in Japan and often would not adhere to existing Japanese social norms.

Cities and New Environmental Issues

Environmental issues raised in the 1970s were mostly related to air and water pollution as well as the identification of the source and area affected by this pollution. The polluter and victim were relatively easy to determine. Environmental issues of the twenty-first century, however, will be such that everyone will be both a polluter and victim at the same time, due to the CO_2 issue and the global warming problem. These phenomena will make it extremely difficult to recognize the problem and take countermeasures in a specific area. Expectations are high for science and technology to correct these problems. However, it is basically a problem inherent to or built into the social system. A typical example would be the case of vehicles which produce CO_2 from fossil fuels.

DIRECTIONS OF PLANNING AND DEVELOPMENT OF URBAN TRANSPORTATION SYSTEMS

Formulation of New Transportation Network Concept

As the city becomes larger, it will become more difficult to ensure the necessary mobility of people using all types of transportation on the existing road network alone. Only if the city structure is changed on a large scale, but with the effect of overshadowing or losing the city's historical background, can appropriate improvements be achieved. In this age of widespread private motorization, transportation planning should recognize the extent of the demand for cars. However, urban road development, only for the purpose of meeting the increased traffic volume, will lead to a vicious cycle whereby roads will continue to be built without ever alleviating the amount of road traffic. Hence, a proper combination of vehicle observation of environmental requirements, development of substitute sources of energy, and the use of software in vehicle design will be needed (Fig. III-D5).

Regulatory measures for a specific user group will be difficult to enforce from the viewpoint of social fairness. Consequently, the formulation of a future transportation network needs to be directed to maintain a certain level of density and quality necessary for city planning. The goal of future urban design should be to manage the volume of traffic or to create an equilibrium between service level and demand.

Creation of Open Transportation Facility Space

Cities in Japan do not have an overabundance of space for transportation facilities. Therefore, it is important to obtain available space for facility development despite the limitations faced in the early stages of construction. At the same time, as can be seen from recent trends, the space used for transportation provides a variety of other urban activities as well. Planning transportation facilities will be directed, therefore, towards creating a space that is friendlier and more accessible to the surrounding areas. The result will be a complex network of urban space with the transportation facilities at its center. These facilities must be open, whether underground or on the surface, to neighboring areas.

In order to realize this concept, the project supporters who act between the public and the private sectors will play an important role. The legal framework has to be strengthened to support such a development. An organization in charge of development, management, and operation should also be established since the spaces in question have different owners. In addition, a new institutional framework will be necessary to guide city planning in cases where urban renewal is planned in residential areas.

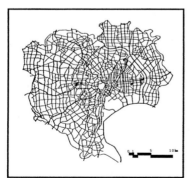

City Planning Roads Network in Tokyo

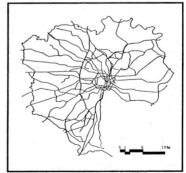

Railways Network in Tokyo

Figure III-D5 Transportation networks in Tokyo

Meeting Diverse Transportation Demands

In Japanese cities, it is taken for granted that water will flow when tapped, electricity will be supplied when switched on, and gas will heat when turned on. Yet, the common urban infrastructure necessary for the urban residents has changed because of transformations in the social, economic, and technical fields.

The role of the new urban infrastructure is large and expected to provide area air-conditioning systems, tube garbage collection systems, and cable television (CATV), which have already begun operation in many cities. Similarly, urban transportation services need to be upgraded to ensure comfort and convenience to meet socially diverse needs and the movement towards the "age of the aged." In particular, short-distance transportation systems need to be developed to assist pedestrians, with such devices as high speed moving walkways and automatic delivery/collection of goods using underground space. These will function as important urban conveniences in the twenty-first century.

In diversifying transportation services, advancements in technologies from various fields, including information processing and communications, will be applied in addition to energy and manpower saving technologies.

CONCLUSION

In the early twenty-first century, Japan's urban population will begin to decrease after reaching its highest peak ever. As a result, planning and improvement techniques of urban transportation systems will also change greatly. Space for transportation facilities developed by businessmen as a service level network will act to upgrade and enrich the quality of space. Urban transportation will offer comfortable and high-speed mobility after remedying the negative external conditions created by users. This will eventually be a first step towards building a stable and progressive city.

BIBLIOGRAPHY

1. Asano, M. 1994. How the cities in Japan accept a time of mature motorization (in Japanese). *Traffic Engineering* 29, no. 2.
2. Asano, M. 1993. *Planning and Development of Urban Transportation Facilities* (in Japanese). Tokyo: Shin-Toshi, 47, no. 8.
3. Asano, M. 1992. Transport planning in provincial cities—present and future issues. *The Wheel Extended* no. 82.
4. City Bureau, Ministry of Construction 1992. *Amenity Society and Urban Road Development* (in Japanese). Tokyo: Taisei Publishing.
5. City Bureau, Ministry of Construction 1993. *Urban Transport Facilities in Japan.* Tokyo: Transportation Planning Association.
6. Institute of Population Issues 1992. *Population Projections for Japan.* Tokyo: Ministry of Health and Welfare.

Part IV

Urban Planning and Design: The Present and Future in Japan

Introduction

A   National and Local Urban Development Plans of Japan
Yukio Sano, Fumio Tsubouchi, Tsutomu Uenomachi

B   Advanced Technology in Urban Development
Tatsuya Nagai

C   Urban Redevelopment Methods in Japan
Susumu Sakamoto

D   Japan's Urban Environment: The Potential of Technology
in Future City Concepts
Hideo Obitsu

E   Nodal System Planning for a Medium-size City
Yoshiro Watanabe

Part IV: Introduction

The grouped chapters of Part IV focus on the Japanese view of the current state and the future of urban design. Their common concern is the developmental policy, at the public and private as well as government levels, the methodology underlying the policy and the role of advanced technology in the construction process.

Since World War II, Japan has embraced Western urban planning methods and techniques along with modern construction technology. This progression influences the city's economy together with the social facet of Japanese life. The latter is entwined with the culture, which has changed little since World War II owing to the historically strong roots of the Japanese culture. To a large extent, the Japanese developmental policy of national, regional and local urban planning has followed the British example where all governmental levels play an active role as entrepreneurs in urban development and in the contribution of funds. Japan has also adopted U.S. technology and has gained the benefits of two worlds, the Eastern and Western. In fact, this synthesis is possibly the secret of the success of the Japanese economy and technology. However, nonmetropolitan areas have received much attention from the central government and private enterprise for the past few decades.

Following World War II, Japan has been facing the problems of overcrowded metropolitan centers. Mr. Yukio Sano and colleagues discuss the problems and solutions which urban planning has been offering. In the nonmetropolitan areas, Japan has faced serious problems of depopulated rural areas, a depressed industry, small cities with limited services as well as villages and towns with predominantly elderly residents. Different concepts have made it possible to revive small cities. Sano points out numerous countermeasures such as the construction of homes, the revival of industry, the creation of cultural centers, etc. to attract more Japanese to move back to small urban areas. This trend would then lead to an overall healthy balance between small cities and the metropolises. For the past few decades, developmental policy has focused on projects in metropolitan, regional, and rural areas. The Japanese vigor in the revival of the economy and services, strengthened the nonmetropolitan areas which in turn have contributed to the rise of Japan from developing to developed country. Still, the problems of the rural and regional development have yet to be resolved.

The advanced development of Japanese construction technology has deeply influenced the change in the nonmetropolitan as well as metropolitan landscape and the construction skills within and outside Japan. According to Mr. Tatsuya Nagai, the unique landscape and geological make-up of Japan supported the development of high-technology construction machinery. The soft sediments underneath Tokyo and its proximity to the waterfront pose a challenge to the urban planner and contractor. Modern machinery is involved during the construction process particularly in the Tokyo area (rotating shield machine, dynamic positioning system, automatic real-time control, etc.). Similar to the redevelopment industry, the overall construction industry in Japan nowadays suffers from the recession and the depopulation of rural areas.

Mr. Susumu Sakamoto explores the various systems of urban redevelopment in Japan and contrasts them with the U.S.A. To illustrate each system, the author describes a case to study the execution of an urban redevelopment plan which involves thorough planning and the involvement of citizens, the government, contractors and planners. In Japan, where landowners are given a voice in the planning process, redevelopment is a more complex process than in the U.S.A. Currently, redevelopment faces a bleak future due to stagnant land prices and the recession of the Japanese economy.

The impression usually perceived when Westerners interact with Japanese is that the latter operate in a very systematic, logical and justifiable method of their own. This performance also applies to their planning and development of the future city. To this effect, Mr. Hideo Obitsu introduces three concepts of future Japanese urban planning, particularly in Tokyo, to resolve the problem of chronic land shortage: super high-rise buildings to provide more space above ground; artificial platforms to create more land surface; and an (underground) geo-city as the location for infrastructure and automated factories. All these concepts, the author postulates, must be incorporated into a conscious urban planning effort with the ultimate goal of a more livable urban area.

To find a synthesis between overcrowded metropolitan areas and small towns, each with their own problems, Professor Yoshiro Watanabe suggests the careful planning of the medium-sized city. He presents a theory of settlement hierarchy by size and function in which business and residential areas of the medium-sized city could exist in an equilibrium. The medium-sized city would be an "open urban structure" with an openness towards the metropolis with which it would then enter a fruitful symbiosis of socio-cultural exchange. The chapter closes with concrete suggestions for the design of the medium-sized, nodal city (ladder pattern, ring pattern).

In conclusion, despite of what may appear rigid in the Japanese way of thinking, the Japanese have been open to rapid changes in technology and economics. Japan today is among the forerunners in international economy, a matter which has led Japan out of its isolation and into involvement with international politics. The Japanese culture is a culture where teamwork and community collaboration are understood as an obvious part of society, technology, planning systems and economics. Within the Japanese developmental system of government involvement in the role of entrepreneur, there is still space to encourage the private investor to become involved with construction projects. While in the U.K. the development of public transportation is almost solely controlled by the government, in Japan investments in public transportation projects are shared by private enterprise and the government.

G.S.G.

A National and Local Urban Development Plans of Japan

Yukio Sano, Fumio Tsubouchi and Tsutomu Uenomachi

INTRODUCTION

When talking about the cities of Japan, the Japanese generally refer to the metropolises only, like Osaka, Nagoya and of course, Tokyo. These metropolises, with their surrounding suburban regions, are the three largest and home to 45% of the Japanese population. Urbanization has offered a number of advantages to these cities, including the availability of work, densely spaced business activities, and advanced internalization.

However, about 50% of the Japanese people still live in the provinces and support the Japanese economy from the base. For this reason, it seems inappropriate that Japan gives all its attention to its metropolises when discussing the actual state of the cities of Japan. The issues of the provinces should be considered at the same time.

Mutual, yet contentious interdependence between urban and rural communities is not typical of modern Japan only, but has in fact been found in every country throughout the centuries since the dawn of history. Marx and Engels once wrote about an ideal future society where the confrontation between urban and rural communities would disappear. Now that metropolises are limited from developing further and provinces have begun to draw public attention, Japan has a chance to establish an ideal relationship between urban and rural communities, as well as between the metropolises and local cities.

In this chapter, the authors focus on the local cities in today's Japan and present the progress and current state of their development. The authors also introduce the measures taken by Japan's construction industry to cope with the problems between the rural/urban areas and metropolises/local cities. Kajima Corporation is already taking action by discussing possible directions for further urban development, which is where the construction industry now hopes to find answers.

LOCAL CITIES AND NATIONAL DEVELOPMENT PLANS

History of the Development of Local Cities

Definition of Local Cities

The administrative units or local public bodies of Japan can be classified into two levels: prefectures and municipalities. Japan is divided into forty-seven larger administrative units called prefectures which have an important intermediary position between the state and municipalities. The municipalities in Japan number 3246 and function as the administrative service agencies nearest to the people. Some municipalities with a population of 50,000 or more are generally called "cities." This definition is based on the Local Government Act.

In this chapter, the term "cities" is referred to as "local cities" except for the following:

- Tokyo, Osaka and Nagoya which are the three largest metropolises in their metropolitan regions.
- Sapporo, Sendai, Hiroshima, Fukuoka and Kita-kyushu, which are principal local cities with a population of approximately 1 million and form their own separate urban districts, respectively.

Outline of the National Development Plans

The Comprehensive National Development plans are government drafted guidelines concerning the regional development. Since the first Comprehensive National Development plan was drawn up in 1962, the plans have proposed methods reflecting the current needs of the times with the purpose of balancing development and correcting regional differences. Japan is now at its fourth plan, outlined in 1987. At the core of this most recent plan is a compound concept based on the growth of socio-economic conflicts and the continued gravitation of people toward metropolises.

Results of the Fourth Comprehensive National Development Plan

It is too early to make a final judgment on the results of the Fourth Plan. Some implications can be surmised from several movements which are now promoted by the plan. For instance, voluntary municipal projects have been introduced in the form of the "town activation movement" or the "movement for creating an original product for each town." These ideas evolved from the hometown concept of the Third Comprehensive National Development Plan.

There are also some local cities which have been successfully promoting their steady development using original ideas. Examples of prefectural and municipal development moving forward under the leadership of local government officials will multiply in the coming age of the provinces. One example of a movement based on an original product was put into practice by Hiramatsu, the governor of the Oita Prefecture. The art polis concept was realized by Hosokawa, the former governor of the Kumamoto Prefecture and the improvement to services for inhabitants and administrative reform was advanced by Iwakuni, the mayor of Izumo.

It is very significant that the "100 Million-Yen Project" for creating independent towns through independent thinking and acting was started in 1988. The subsidy was granted to this project by adding 100 million Yen to the local subsidy tax for discretionary use by each local community. This project is being employed everywhere for municipal development. The national subsidy had until then been granted only for the construction of specific institutions which satisfied specified standards, making this endeavor difficult to accomplish.

State of Local Cities and their Problems

State of Local Cities

The depopulation of rural towns continues despite attempts to hamper this trend. The 1165 cities, towns and villages, which account for 36% of all municipalities, are now categorized as depopulation zones according to government surveys. A "depopulation zone" is an area which meets one of the following conditions: (1) the population had a decreasing ratio from 1960 to 1985 of over 25%; (2) the population had a decreasing ratio of over 2% and the ratio of the population over 65 years old in 1985 exceeded 16%; and (3) the population had a decreasing ratio of over 2%, and the ratio of the population 15–29 years old in 1985 was under 16%. Although these municipalities cover 46.4% of the land area, they contain only 6.2% of the population. Without exception, the rate of the aged population is steadily increasing as young people move out. This emigration has also resulted in a continuously lowered productivity level of the local industries.

Efforts have naturally been made by the government and the residents to halt this exodus and to redevelop the local communities concerned. The Japanese government has granted subsidies and allowed the construction of agencies. The local governments have played a leading role in this endeavor. Various projects aimed primarily at the modernization of the local communities have led, however, to a flood of similar public agencies throughout the country.

On the other hand, private industries have invested in local communities to improve production and distribution facilities that translate into local employment opportunities, a rejuvenated infrastructure including roads, an increased tax base and an enhanced image of these local cities. These efforts, however, have been accompanied by various undesired effects, such as the destruction of natural environments and the appearance of monotonous shopping centers. Despite the criticism of these efforts, the rehabilitation of the infrastructure was direly needed. As regional redevelopment started from the base up due to the destruction from World War II, thorough preparations for reconstruction were required. However, neither the philosophy behind regional development nor the basic content of the institutions had been properly researched and, therefore, were not applied.

Problems Awaiting Solution

The promotion of private corporations and the local community development, with a rather strong dependence upon the central government, has led to larger differences between cities, or between local cities and metropolises. As the twenty-first century approaches, it is essential that Japan pursue the development of its local cities freed from the conventional dependence upon external influences.

To achieve this goal, people's perceptions of cities must be modified. The city has often been considered the site of political, administrative and economic activities, but it should now be viewed as a place for living, working and the relaxation of its citizens. In other words, officials and city planners must reconsider the city from the standpoint of its citizens and their needs.

It is quite inadequate to determine the direction of the local city development based on the conventional trends used in the past. To supplement a city with institutions typically found in other cities, but which do not fulfil the needs of the local people is not the answer. Rather, it is essential to outline the future vision of a local city without succumbing to trends and to find the means to implement the improvements after considering the role of the surrounding region.

MEASURES FOR ACTIVATING LOCAL CITIES

Measures on the State Level

Regional Development System

There are several laws and regulations relating to regional development. Some acts are applicable to individual blocks of national land (e.g. Capital Region Development Act, the Hokkaido Development Act, etc.) and others pertain to specific regions or districts (e.g. Tsukuba Academic New Town Construction Law, etc.). The Public Undertaking Relations Law is most often associated with the general municipalities. The construction of roads, harbor facilities and sewer systems is promoted within the framework of this law.

The laws and regulations concerning regional development are generally enforced in three stages. In the first stage, regions or districts are chosen for the application of such laws and regulations. Development plans are drawn up in the second stage and in the third stage necessary steps are taken for granting subsidies to execute such plans.

The laws and regulations are often applied by combining various measures according to their respective purpose. In many cases, specific rules for selecting such measures or the combination of the selection, planning and subsidization are not available. For example, some projects are advanced without a development plan, or the investors have poor security for subsidy. It can be said that the relating laws and regulations are very often applied on a case-by-case basis.

Financial incentives are provided for the local communities. The laws and regulations for regional development were established out of the necessity for exceptional financial treatment of financially weak communities. Through supplemental financial measures, projects can be promoted that reduce or eliminate regional differences. Exceptional financial measures for promoting such projects is strongly advised. The construction of roads and other infrastructure in the form of public work must actually be the basic objective of financial measures to anticipate the effects of such treatment.

Government Measures for Local Community Activation

The ministries of Japan plan and execute a wide variety of measures for district activation. Several examples of these measures are introduced below.

- The National Land Agency promotes a number of measures, including the development of comprehensive health resorts and the regional redevelopment around local cities. These measures direct action toward the goals of the Fourth Comprehensive National Development Plan. The agency also takes great interest in effective support of community activation through a "community activation support program."
- The Ministry of International Trade and Industry developed a program for the "promotion of dispersed offices" to spread satellite and resort offices into surrounding areas. This is an original Japanese concept to promote district development in harmony with the environment.
- The Ministry of Construction promotes the development and redevelopment of local cities as the economical and cultural center of each local society, by "urban development in coexistence with the environment." The aim is to sustain the growth of cities and create an urban environment with abundant amenities.
- The Ministry of Home Affairs takes administrative and financial measures for the support of local communities in the voluntary development of unique municipalities. Such projects include the "Hometown Project" and "Special Project for Town Development Measures." This ministry was started on the occasion of the "100 Million-Yen Project" mentioned in this chapter as the result of the Fourth Comprehensive National Development Plan.

Development Measures for Local Communities

Comprehensive Plans for Community Development

The comprehensive plans of municipalities have been compulsory since 1969 according to the Local Government Act. A comprehensive plan describes the future image of each local community and shows the basic direction of its developmental policies. Each community puts its various administrative measures forward on the basis of such an extensive plan. Further individual plans are drawn up in conformity with the town's vision to promote the buildup of the social infrastructure and the construction of buildings. Therefore, the comprehensive plans furnish information on the trend of the development measures of the local communities.

In many cases, the prefectures draw long-term comprehensive plans which are usually devised for one entire prefecture with plans to redevelop several blocks. The plans for such blocks are important since they guide the trend for the comprehensive plans of municipalities.

However, experience shows that the construction of institutions has progressed without examining which institutions are most needed for the district concerned. This could be due to the tendency of the municipalities to first try to ensure funds for construction, conscious as they are of the large subsidies of the state and prefectures.

New Trends of Local Community Development

The construction of facilities under the national subsidy system have almost come to an end. New attempts are made everywhere to create more affluent and comfortable living environments.

The investment in software or symposia for "town activation" is one such attempt. This trend has become stronger in recent years because of the intensified competition amongst local communities to invite manufacturing companies or establish an original industry in their community.

Other new attempts could be classified as follows:

- The training of leaders for local industrial development.
- Measures for raising living standards through health improvements and the support of cultural and educational activities.
- Enacting new measures for the town redevelopment, an urban landscape ordinance and esthetic building standards.
- Constructing unique cultural institutions, like the Mito Culture Museum and Bach Hall.

Community Development Facilities

Various local community development projects are now promoted in most local cities. There are many ways to approach community development measures, including their classification by their type of activities. The following are examples of this system.

- Cultural and art institutions:
  (1) cultural institutions with multipurpose halls, special halls, museums, archives, etc.
  (2) art institutions like galleries, special art museums, etc.
  (3) other organizations such as zoological and botanical gardens, etc.
- Sporting and recreational facilities:
  (1) sporting facilities in the form of multipurpose stadiums, gate ball courts, etc. Gate ball is a game that was originally born in Japan and is played by a large number of the elderly population. Two teams compete and each team consists of five persons. A player hits a ball with a T-shaped stick to direct it through "gates" before the ball hits a center pole beyond the gates on the far side.

(2) recreation facilities such as spring bath facilities, multipurpose plazas, etc.
- Tourist Facilities: these facilities serve mainly to entertain tourists and support local industries. They are often provided as the centerpiece of local development. Gardens, museums for craft work, local showrooms for tourists and information institutions are examples of such facilities.
- Lodging Facilities: these facilities serve the visitors of local cities with their leisure and recreation needs, in a natural environment. Visitors boost the local economy by spending time in local cities and by extending work opportunities in the service industries such as hotels, recreational centers like People's Vacation Village, villas and camp sites.

Execution Bodies

The community development procedures are put forward by the following bodies:

- Local Government: local communities plan and execute community development and activation measures, mostly involving the construction of cultural and artistic institutions, or sports and recreation facilities. Recently, local development policies which stress human services were also outlined. These measures are a system for preserving and restoring rows of traditional stores and houses on streets, for enacting the "urban landscape ordinance" or the "esthetic building standards," and to create and promote a beautiful urban landscape.
- Local Residents: local storekeepers and other volunteers participate actively in local development activities. Facilities that consume large costs are rarely involved. Usually, improvements to a shopping district and establishment of community identity are made under various financial and subsidy systems. Efforts have been made to train future leaders for the development of a local industry or to establish voluntary bodies for information dissemination.
- Private Corporations: today the private corporation is often seen as an asset to local community development. It extends its business to a district by opening its facilities to the local population or by constructing a gallery for exhibiting its own art collection, which enhances a town's cultural appeal. Private corporations are seeking not only a production base in a district, but also coexistence and mutual prosperity with the district.

The local government and private corporations cooperate to maximize their efforts in order to realize an ideal and efficient community development. Specifically, the local government organizes a network of leading persons while private corporations furnish the know-how for the development of original products.

CASE STUDIES

New Large-Space Architecture

Izumo City, Shimane Prefecture Projects

Izumo city, facing the Sea of Japan, has a population of approximately 83,000 and is the second largest city in the Shimane Prefecture, next to the prefectural seat of Matsue city in the high northwestern part of Honshu Island. The district of Izumo has been prosperous historically and is favored by abundant water and fertile land. A series of myths concerning the birth of the country have been passed down through generations and established Izumo's reputation as the "land of myths."

Having celebrated its fiftieth anniversary of becoming a city in 1991, Izumo city now promotes the image of a "strong and gentle Izumo" by acknowledging the development of its infrastructure and by providing additional human services. In short, the city has put forth various large-scale projects that meet all the functions of a city for work, life and leisure to build a humane city with a friendly atmosphere. This is accomplished on the assumption that the city's daytime population will number 200,000 and its residential population 100,000.

The key person behind these projects is Tetsundo Iwakuni, the present mayor. He grew up in the Shimane Prefecture, graduated from the University of Tokyo, and then studied further at Stanford University and Harvard University. He gathered experience as an international businessman at Morgan Stanley and held the position of senior vice president at Merrill Lynch's headquarters in the U.S.A. until 1988. After resigning from Merrill Lynch and returning to Japan, he was voted mayor of Izumo city in 1989.

Immediately after assuming this office, Iwakuni promoted the slogan, "Administration is the Biggest Service Industry," has advanced a conscientious reform of his staff and improved administrative support since that time. He further opened a holiday service corner, established a tree doctor system, a comprehensive welfare card system and introduced numerous other services.

The Izumo Health Park Project, one large project for the fiftieth anniversary of Izumo city, contained plans for a roof-covered, all-weather type stadium as a symbolic central institution of the Izumo cultural district. This project was to satisfy the desire of all generations for a site of sports and recreational activities, immune to irregular seasonal weather conditions, especially the strong winter winds.

In seeking a design which would be exceptional from an architectural view-point and would attract attention across the country, a dome-type stadium was selected which had no precedent at that time on a municipal level.

Mechanism of the Health Park Project

The Ministry of Home Affairs is a national system to support municipalities in promoting their individual projects actively on the basis of their original ideas and voluntary efforts. This system is applied only to public institutions, parks and green zones, open spaces, and cultural, sporting or recreation facilities as a symbol of each municipality's regional development plan.

However, the dome construction was recognized as a special project of town development by the Ministry of Home Affairs. When the objective of the project was recognized, 75–85% of its cost, excluding the cost of land acquisition, was appropriated from a regional comprehensive project bond first, while 30–55% of the amount of redemption, including interest, was compensated through a local subsidy tax. This project required 6.8 billion Yen (approximately 70 million dollars) in total. The city bond covered 5.31 billion Yen while the rest of the 1.49 billion Yen was appropriated from general financial resources.

The Izumo Dome

This all-weather type, multipurpose stadium (commonly called "Izumo Dome") was based on a design proposal which was submitted in a design competition by Izumo city. The city asked the competitors to propose a design solution for a multipurpose dome which would suit the tradition and culture of Izumo city and, at the same time, offer protection against intense wind and snow. The project aimed to promote town activity centering around the dome.

One of the seven leading general contractors nominated to participate in the competition, Kajima Corporation, proposed a multipurpose wooden dome design to harmonize with the traditional Japanese wooden construction expressed in the Grand Shrine of Izumo. This new shrine is one of the largest wooden buildings in the world. It has a membrane roof and its structure is suggestive of an umbrella with a bull's-eye design. The Kajima Corporation also proposed a concrete system of management and maintenance of the dome after its completion within the prescribed conditions. The proposal was accepted.

The old Grand Shrine of Izumo is 24 m high at present and is said to have been as high as 48 m in ancient times. The height of the Izumo Dome, about 49 m, was chosen to balance the height of the Grand Shrine. The Izumo Dome was built to the largest scale for a wooden dome with a membrane roof. Its framework is a hybrid structure consisting of wooden and steel members. Treated timbers of 2150 m^3 were imported from the U.S.A. for construction.

It also features an electric automatic stand which was then the first of its kind in the world. The automatic stand creates a multipurpose arena combined with a fixed stand for baseball, football and rugby. Other features are a lighting and acoustical system for multipurpose use, outside walls capable of natural lighting, large-sized revolving doors which integrate the dome with the park and form a protective bank against the wind and snow.

The landscape of the Izumo Dome was designed by Hellmuth, Obata and Kassabaum, Inc. and the structure by Professor Kimio Saitoh, a structural engineer. The project was completed in March 1992. This multipurpose stadium can accommodate 5000 people including fixed benches for 2500 people, or a total of 10,000 people if they are seated on the ground. The total area of the site is 68,810.26 m^2, the building area is 16,2177.42 m^2 and the total floor area is 15,742.14 m^2 which gives the dome a cubic capacity of 577,000 m^2. The arch-string structure is composed of glued, treated timber, steel, cable and a fabric membrane coated with Teflon. It is supported by concrete columns laid on a foundation of reinforced concrete. The average building height is 48.9 m with a maximum height of 53.9 m at its peak (Fig. IV-A1).

Figure IV-A1 External view of the Izumo Dome (Kajima Corporation) (Photo: Hishi Nihom Syabo)

The Izumo Dome, as the world's largest wooden dome, has numerous strong benefits. It can be used for exhibitions and fairs and attracts public attention as a regional base for sports and culture. Thus, it is actually used not only for athletic events by people, but also for various other purposes which contribute to the regional cultural development and activity. The dome is a current focus of interest and has become a part of the sight-seeing route along the way to Izumo which receives an average of about 1000 visitors a day.

Other New Large-space Architecture Projects

Kajima Corporation has taken part in the realization of many unique facilities by maximizing its comprehensive abilities. The construction of facilities for cultural activities, sports and other events in close relation with each local community has been promoted actively in recent years. Local communities are eager to have many large and high-quality facilities. Our corporation has followed this trend by offering proposals that satisfy the requirements of design, technology and management systems.

The first project of such nature is the Akita Sky Dome in Akita city, Akita Prefecture completed in 1990. This dome was in the spotlight as an institution for sports with an outdoor feeling throughout the year, even in a snowy area such as the Akita Prefecture. Kajima has further proposed new types of large-space architecture representing "the Age of the Province" such as the Global Dome for the Shinshu Exposition in 1993.

The speed-skate arena will be the main site of the Winter Olympics at Nagano, scheduled to be held in 1998. Its design is a product of the cooperation between six contractors, including the Kajima Corporation, which was awarded the best concept in the design competition (Fig. IV-A2).

Development of a Resort Area and Redevelopment of an Urban Area

Background of Resort Development

The 1980s were the age when Japanese workaholics were criticized during the growing friction of the international economy. Many people managed to acquire economic wealth but still longed for an enjoyable and high-quality life. At the same time, the Fourth Comprehensive National Development Plan was drawn to promote community development under "retention and exchange" (i.e. the retention of the hometown feeling while promoting exchange with other communities). The development of a resort area was also needed to create the sense of a place of exchange.

The Comprehensive Resort Development Act (commonly called the Resort Act) was established in 1987 to cope with this problem throughout the country. The act demands necessary measures for the promotion of comprehensive functions at resort areas to allow the people to relax and pursue recreational, educational or cultural activities, group meetings etc., during their leisure time.

Figure IV-A2 Outside view of the Akita Sky Dome (Kajima Corporation) (Photo: Kawasumi)

This would let private corporations realize a comfortable life for people and develop local communities. Each prefecture first draws up basic development plans. If a plan is recognized as the objective of the Resort Act by the government, the prefecture can have various restrictions eased for the development of the area concerned which includes the lowering of taxes on development funds. The system is thus favorable to both the local public bodies and private industry.

The Case of Tokamachi City, Niigate Prefecture

Tokamachi city, of the Niigate Prefecture, is located nearly one hour from the Echigo-Yuzawa station on the Joetsu Shinkansen Line, approximately 160 km north of Tokyo. This city, with a population of approximately 46,000, had once been a prosperous center of silk fabric production. Yet, owing to its geographical location in one of the highest snowfall areas and after suffering from a long depression in the domestic textile industry, Takamachi city, at present, exemplifies a local city with typical problems. It is characterized by a weakened local economic force, an outflow of young people and problems which seem almost impossible to solve. It was, therefore, a blessing for this small city as well as local developers to enter its name as a candidate for the Resort Act. The basic concept drawn up in cooperation with the neighboring municipalities was approved by the government in December 1988 to be released at full scale.

The promoter of the project was the Atema Kogen Resort Company, Ltd, which belongs to the so-called third sector (public private partnership). It is financed by several leading Japanese corporations, including the Kajima Corporation and the local public bodies of Niigate prefecture and Tokamachi city. The Resort Development Project has two purposes: first, to make the resort area a place for promoting personal exchange between metropolises and local cities and second, to make it a location of a new, established lifestyle for local cities. Unlike a conventional resort development project aimed at the construction and management of facilities for the support of recreational activities, this project is introduced as the solution for the two above-mentioned purposes.

The project contains a program to set up the "Atema Forum" which is modeled after the world-famous resort Aspen, Colorado. The concept of the Aspen Institute was studied in parallel with the resort master plan. "Atema Juku," its predecessor, was organized in February 1992 to serve as a place of exchange with local organizations. Staff meetings are often still held there to discuss the desirable form of the "Atema Forum."

The activities of the "Atema Forum" in the future will also range from consultation on resort development and community activation to software planning for the resorts management and execution of events. The central activity arena will be the forum center, provided in the central zone of the resort area. This center will accommodate institutions for mainly cultural activities, such as a library and workshops, and will provide a place for the secretariat of the "Atema Forum."

Furthermore, hotels, golf courses and various other sporting facilities are planned within the resort area of the Atema highland. Contrary to traditional resort areas in Japan where facilities compete with one another in luxuriousness, all of the Atema agencies will be designed to provide services suited to the local natural features and traditions. As such, it will become a facility offering even the average person a good time at a reasonable price. In other words, "Atema Kogen Resort" seeks to be an ideal resort and aims to establish a new standard for resorts in Japan. The site preparation work for this resort was started in 1993 and the first stage began in 1996 (Fig. IV-A3).

From Resort Development to Regional Development

In the case of the Atema Highland Resort Project, its coexistence with the local community has been planned from the beginning with the cooperation of Tokamachi city. This reflects the philosophy of the Atema Kogen Resort, that resorts and cities do not exist independently from each other but develop under mutual influences.

Kajima Corporation has, therefore, tried to continue dialogues with the local storekeepers' organization, The Rotary Club and average citizens from the initial stage of development. Its philosophy, as mentioned above, seems to have been acknowledged by them. A plan for turning one of the streets into a shopping district in the urban area was realized in cooperation with the storekeepers.

Traditional shopping streets of Tokamachi city would not expand like other shopping centers with large parking spaces developed conveniently along periph-eral roads as a result of extensive motorization. Since customers seem to prefer larger shopping areas, the purpose is to develop an about 300 m long part of the existing shopping street into a commercial street in the base city of the resort. Discussions went on for more than one year between the citizens, city hall, the

Figure IV-A3 Master plan of Atema Kogen Resort (Kajima Corporation)

local chamber of commerce and industry, and the staff of the Atema Kogen Resort. The concept of the shopping street is now taking final shape under the leadership of the citizens. The plan is to select the busiest street and change it into a pedestrian zone with a beautiful urban landscape design. Detailed investigations and negotiations of the plan with the authorities were conducted so that the shopping area can open concurrently with the resort area (Fig. IV-A4).

CONCLUSION: THE FUTURE OF LOCAL CITIES

The problems that local cities face can be summarized as a decreasing population accompanied with the increasing rate of the aged together with the depression of local industry. The introduction of new, different concepts, however, makes it possible to change this situation into one with a purpose and process without chance happenings.

Most of all, municipalities suffering from depopulation have designated the repopulation of their towns as their primary goal. The people of Nishikawa-machi, in the Yamagata Prefecture anticipate a certain reduction of the town's future population. The town will attempt to reverse this trend by active exchange with other municipalities and by inviting the people who come home for the holidays to stay.

Figure IV-A4 Perspective of a shopping street in Tokamachi City

On the other hand, Miharu-cho, in the Fukushima Prefecture, attempts straightforward town development. When a local community intends to develop or to redevelop itself, its success is commonly based on various domestic factors. Modifications to the old concept are going to open up a new future to Miharu-cho. For example, the agriculture of this town is very active because it lacks modernization. When Miharu-machi recognized its position in the world, it found that it is, in fact, blessed with an abundance of various crops. The "Miharu vegetables" produced here are tasty and in great demand in cities. This boost to the economy has been a result of the diversification of the values of people.

The first town planning act of Great Britain was enacted in 1909 and reached its peak in 1932 as the Town and Country Planning Act. This act prescribed that the utilitarian value of land should be fixed and an adequate portion of the profits from land development should be returned to the public. A mechanism allowing for the schematic and proper land utilization should also be required in Japan for community development.

In Bologna, Italy, urban redevelopment aims at the coexistence and preservation of the rows of old stores and houses on downtown streets. This project is a concrete example of redevelopment in accordance with the Landscape Preservation Act (1985) which is a landmark act for the control of land utilization by means of landscape planning. The act is based on the philosophy that the preservation of beautiful landscapes for future generations is necessary for the cultural growth of the nation.

The worst aspect found in community development in Japan is that there has been no monitoring of the outcome and that we have learned nothing from past experiences. It is important for Japan to remember the beautiful, natural environment and comfortable living arrangements that our country once had and to recognize their value again. Japan can also learn from the small attempts made elsewhere in foreign countries by studying their struggles to solve urban problems.

BIBLIOGRAPHY

1. Kajima Corporation n.d. *Kajima Corporation Brochure*. Tokyo: Kajima Corporation.

B Advanced Technology in Urban Development

Tatsuya Nagai

INTRODUCTION

After World War II, construction technology and the manufacturing industries progressed rapidly in Japan. The high level of postwar construction and restoration in the late 1940–1950s, to repair the damage inflicted during the war, led to great advancements in construction technology. Consequently, the economy and society witnessed high levels of development and prosperity in the 1960s, followed by a reform of the energy supply system due to the "oil crisis" in the 1970s and finally a restructuring of the industrial base in the 1980s. Urbanization also progressed in the Tokyo metropolitan area during those years, as did improvements in the management of core cities near Tokyo.

These changes in society have modified people's values and have also altered construction activities in the aspects of supply and demand. Mechanization, automation, industrialization, laborsaving and timesaving methods, and most recently, information-oriented processes have been the keywords of technological innovation in all sectors of the construction industry. The technical cooperation between various industrial branches, public sectors and countries worldwide has made the progress in research and development possible in the field of construction.

SOCIO-ECONOMIC AND NATURAL BACKGROUND

Construction Investment in Urban Areas

Public and private industries invest in the development and redevelopment of urban areas for different reasons. The public sector generally invests to facilitate and maintain the urban infrastructure, such as roads, harbors, airports, water and sewage systems, waste treatment centers, disaster prevention, as well as facilities for cultural, social welfare, medical and educational services. The private sector generally invests to redevelop old downtown sites, former manufacturing plant sites and old railroad freight-car yards. Both sectors invest to supply housing for city residents.

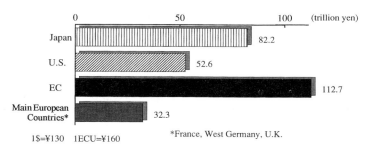

Figure IV-B1 Comparison of construction investment in Japan and other countries (1993) (Ministry of Construction, 1995, p. 2–8)

The amount of money spent on investments in construction in Japan is greater than that spent in the U.S.A. and 2.5 times more than that spent in major European countries (Fig. IV-B1). This total rate of construction investment is forecasted to maintain its present growth rate for the next twenty years (Fig. IV-B2). This high level of investment creates a big market for the construction industry. Major construction firms in cities receive more than 70% of their orders for the development of the urban infrastructure. Firms invested a total of 260 billion yen, approximately 0.5–0.7% of their sales turnover in 1992, to research and the development of advanced construction technology.

Construction Projects in the Community

A number of construction projects are carried out in densely populated urban areas. Construction can have an impact on the social and natural environment of neighboring communities in varying degrees. Existing buildings and infra-structures also affect their local environments.

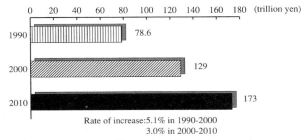

Figure IV-B2 Future growth of construction investment (public and private sectors) over the next twenty years (Ministry of Construction, 1995, p. 2–8)

The owners or developers of a proposed large-scale real estate project and high-rise building complex are under obligation to write up a preliminary report and assess the environmental impact of the project before starting its construction. They have to consent to accept remedial measures for negative environmental consequences, such as related pollution and reach a joint agreement through laborious public hearings and committee meeting sessions. Design and construction firms often cooperate to take preventative measures against any possible public nuisances the project may entail (Table IV-B1 and Fig. IV-B3).

Technology to curb or prevent negative environmental repercussions is developed with the mutual cooperation of academic research institutes and all sectors of the building industry, such as construction firms, building material manufacturers and construction machine manufacturers.

Table IV-B1 Nuisance factor impact for forecast and evaluation

	During construction				During operation		
	Machines, traffic	Building clearance	Building construction	Building existence	Related traffic	Exhaust from parking	Exhaust from DHC
Air pollution	✓	✓	✓		✓	✓	✓
Stench pollution							
Noise pollution	✓	✓	✓		✓		
Ground vibration	✓	✓	✓		✓		
Low-frequency air vibration							
Waste pollution							
Soil contamination							
Ground sinking			✓				
Configuration, soil			✓				
Plants and animals							
Sunlight prevention				✓			
Television wave prevention				✓			
Building wind				✓			
Landscape				✓			
Historical, cultural assets							

*District heat supply center.

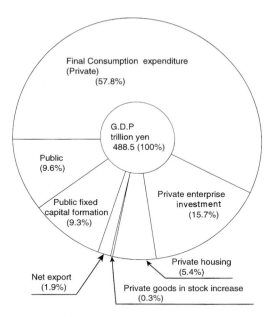

Figure IV-B3 Gross Domestic Product (GDP) in 1994 (Japan Civil Engineering Contractors Association, 1995, p. 4)

Labor and Safety

The number of workers in Japan's private construction industry is about 6 million, which comprises one-tenth of the total number of employees in all industries, including public services. However, the workforce is aging and the labor market is not as flexible as it once was. Currently, the skilled laborers in the construction industry are generally older workers. Unskilled laborers move away from home to find better-paying jobs in remote regions or overseas countries (Fig. IV-B4).

To eliminate dangerous working conditions, safety and health management are primary considerations in the planning and execution of construction work. Safety, in particular, is taken very seriously on the construction site. As the workforce ages, both safety and health measures become more costly, but the construction business is still a dangerous industry. Despite the great improvements in safety over the past fifteen years, the number of construction injuries and fatalities is still higher than that of all other industries. Thirty percent of all injuries and 40% of all deaths sustained in industrial accidents occurred in the construction business.

Yet, an increase in the productivity of the construction industry is crucial if Japan is to achieve a more attractive, comfortable and convenient urban living environment. Productivity in the construction industry is considerably lower

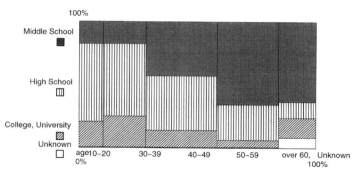

Figure IV-B4 Employees by age and education in the construction industry (1994) (Ministry of Construction, 1995, pp. 9–14)

than that in the manufacturing, transportation and communication industries (Fig. IV-B5). The trend in both productivity and annual labor hours has not changed but has remained constant for the past decade—a situation which hurts competition and prevents reducing costs.

The Natural Environment and Disasters

Most urban areas in Japan are located on the seacoast or on the alluvial fan. The Tokaido megalopolis belt-line includes Tokyo, Nagoya and Osaka and is formed on an alluvial plain composed of deep sedimentary silt, sand and gravel layers.

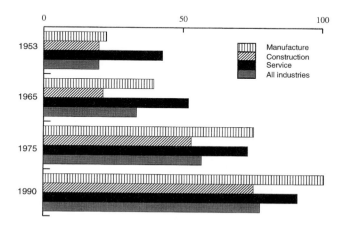

Note:Index 100 is average productivity form 1985 to1990 in U.S.

Figure IV-B5 Labor productivity in Japan and the U.S.A. (Japan Civil Engineering Contractors Association, 1995, p. 19)

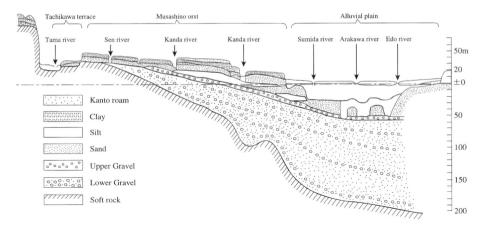

Figure IV-B6 Geological section of Tokyo ground (Hiroyuki Kawada, 1992; pp. 75–80)

The Tokyo metropolitan area and its population of 30 million people is located on the Kanto plain. Kanto is also the alluvial plain of the Tone, Arakawa, Tama and Sagami rivers and is covered with loam enriched with the volcanic ash from ancient Mount Fuji (Fig. IV-B6). Buildings and infrastructure are often constructed on this soft ground by using pile foundations or are protected with a waterproofed, underground slurry wall.

The Japanese Islands are located within the Asian monsoon region. Their average annual rainfall is 1800 mm, excluding the dry season. The northern part of the Sea of Japan coast is exposed to heavy snowfall in winter. The southern part along the coast of the Pacific Ocean experiences heavy rains and frequent typhoons in summer.

Active volcanoes and fault-lines pose the risk of earthquakes to the Japanese. Tsunami, high tides, floods, landslides, ground motion and ground liquefaction caused by earthquakes occur every year and severly harm the urban life and its economy. The turbulent natural conditions are repeated challenges for the Japanese people in general and building contractors in particular.

AUTOMATIC SHIELD TUNNELLING

Tunnels as Urban Infrastructure

The shield-tunnelling method has advanced tremendously technologically and is very popular because of its wide usage in urban areas with soft soils. It facilitates the construction of subway tunnels, road tunnels, waste-water tunnels, storm-water reservoir tunnels and common ducts in the soft soil underground. These tunnels often run underneath rivers and bays.

In Japan, the shield-tunnelling method has progressed rapidly in recent years for the following reasons:

- The "open cut and cover" method of an excavation in the open, which is then filled in through an underground tunnel after the concrete lining was built, is unsuitable to most projects due to severe road conditions and traffic congestion.
- The "shield" method, which requires a shield machine of steel to protect the excavation from soil and ground water pressures and is used for excavating underground tunnels in soft ground, is suitable for the complex layers of soil found in most Japanese urban areas.
- Mechanization and automation technology are rapidly introduced to the construction field, which gives way to apply new and improved construction methods immediately.

Automatic Positioning and Segment Erection

The automatic orientation, positioning, erection of segments, vertical and horizontal displacement, and advancement rate of the shield machine are monitored continuously by a gyrocompass and laser ray camera station, stroke meter, and inclinometer. The monitored data is processed and stored in knowledge-based expert systems on the computer. For example, the operating pattern of shield-pushing jacks is selected automatically by anticipating the direction and position of the shield machine. The erection of precast concrete segments for a large diameter shield involves issues such as weight of the segment, the risks of operation in a narrow space and the rate of productivity which can be solved by automatic conveying and erection devices (Fig. IV-B7). Conveying devices mounted on a carriage with a hoist crane and turntable can stock enough numbers of segments for the ring of lining.

Erection devices are operated automatically to check the gripping of the segment, precise erection position alignment and bolt fastening. Operations of these devices are controlled by computers which adopt the dialogue mode with a cathode-ray tube (CRT) monitor in real-time processing.

The Rotating Shield Machine

In conventional shield tunnelling procedures, a vertical shaft is made by employing caissons with enough sectional area to accommodate the shield machine for the horizontal tunnel excavation. The body of the rotating shield machine holds a revolving spherical head which launches the sub-shield machine inside the tunnel (Fig. IV-B8). The rotating shield machine excavates a vertical shaft to its designated depth; the spherical head then rotates to dig horizontally as a conventional shield would. The rotating shield machine can dig continuously, either horizontally or vertically after a turn of 90° (Fig. IV-B9). Since a caisson is not used, this method requires less land space for the shaft, shortens excavation time, and as a result, reduces the environmental damage to the surrounding area.

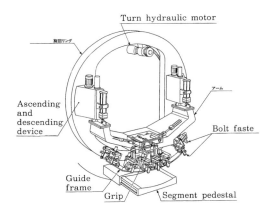

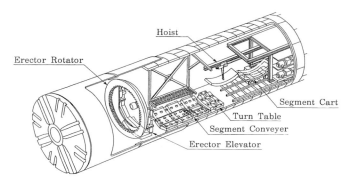

Figure IV-B7 Automatic segment erection device and system (Taisei Corporation)

Figure IV-B8 The rotating shield excavation process (models) (Taisei Corporation)

Figure IV-B9 Vertical and horizontal shield machine (Taisei Corporation)

This method was used to extend the Kannon River Rainwater Reservoir in Kawasaki City to 1.5 m in depth underground. The main reservoir tunnel is 260 m long and 4.5 m in diameter (Fig. IV-B10). Its branch tunnel, after a horizontal 90° turn, is 65 m long and 2.8 m in diameter. The main shield of the rotating shield machine measures 5.53 m and the sub-shield is 3.68 m in diameter. The sphere has a diameter of 4.95 m and is rotated by four oil-pressure jacks.

Figure IV-B10 Horizontal shield machine turned to 90° in the Kannon River Reservoir (Taisei Corporation)

Automatic Real-Time Control

The technology employed in the automation of shield tunnelling is already quite advanced. Automation has been introduced not only to the shield machine itself, but also to shield work as a whole. All shield operations are monitored and controlled automatically from a single monitoring station. Shield operations are divided into the following stages:

- Advanced surveying, position forecasting and shield orientation.
- Transportation, storage and erection of segments.
- Slurry shipping and handling as well as pressure control at the facing treatment.
- Backfill material transport and injection control.
- Safety control and disaster prevention.

High-speed communications in an optical-fiber cable network connects the subsystems of the mentioned functions using engineering workstations. The monitoring, measurement, and control of each subsystem is performed automatically.

GLOBAL POSITIONING SYSTEM FOR ARTIFICIAL ISLAND CONSTRUCTION

Dynamic Positioning System

A rapid and continuous measuring system is necessary to monitor the settlement of soil and the volume of removed or added soil when building urban structures on reclaimed, soft soil.

The Global Positioning System (GPS) is introduced to facilitate the survey of a large area, land reclamation work and the construction of artificial islands. A three-dimensional position is surveyed by processing the phase difference of radio waves transmitted from three different GPS satellites with two radio wave receivers. One receiver is placed on a known position and the other on an unknown position. A topographical survey can achieve consistently high accuracy rates using the receiver installed on a moving vehicle. This GPS survey system is called the "rapid dynamic surveying method."

Monitoring the Surface Level of Land Reclamation

Kansai International Airport opened in the fall of 1994 and was constructed into the sea of Osaka Bay. The rapid dynamic surveying method was introduced to survey the surface level of fill soil on this artificial airport island. A radio wave was received approximately every 0.5–2.0 s on an unknown point of fill soil surface by a receiver mounted on the roof of a moving vehicle. The number of surveyed points was 5200 on 21 ha of fill soil and 1300 on 9 ha of loading soil. It took about three hours to survey 6500 points on a total of 30 ha.

Monitoring of a Fill Soil Setting

Ground improvement work was undertaken on the Haneda International Airport offshore extension project built with 1000 ha of reclaimed land (Fig. IV-B11). The extension area was filled with dredged soil from Tokyo Bay to the 16 m maximum depth. The 2 m-thick soft surface layer was reinforced with cemented solidifier and covered with excavated soil from construction sites in urban areas to 3.5 m thickness. Then the reclaimed soil was hardened with sand-mat, paper drain and weighed down with covered soil. The project was undertaken while continuously monitoring the solidified surface layer setting induced by uneven loading of covered soil.

A measuring pole on the plate was placed at 157 survey points on the solidified layer of 360 m × 860 m. One pair of operators carried poles with a receiver antenna and a recorder. They could measure each survey point in a few seconds, so that it took a total of 2 hours to complete all the survey point measurements.

Land Dynamic Management System

A highly systematized management is necessary to properly handle information about complex geological composition and diverse soils. For example, a swift and simple measurement method can play a significant role in estimating the amount of cut and fill soil required. This survey procedure would entail heavy expenses for labor if the process measured data were mapped according to the conventional management of land reclamation work.

Figure IV-B11 Haneda International Airport reclamation (Taisei Corporation)

Important management items are:

- Complete amount of soil, by soil class.
- Measurement of each layers' boundary.
- Real-time measurement of filled soil.
- Excavation planning.
- Cut and fill soil transfer plan.

The three-dimensional high-speed topographic survey data obtained by the GPS dynamic measurement method is advantageous to the management of large land reclamation work. Cut or fill section-maps by soil class and various other useful data output are processed continuously (Fig. IV-B12).

LASER POSITIONING OF DEEP SLURRY WALL

Underground Structures on the Waterfront

Slurry walls, also called underground diaphragm walls, of various thickness are necessary to execute projects in an urban waterfront development area in Japan. This technology is efficient in the use of the underground space of an urban area and the construction of high-rise building complexes on the soft ground made of alluvial soil or the reclaimed land of dredged soil from the seabed.

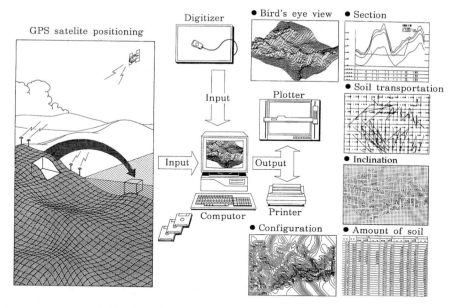

Figure IV-B12 Total land-work management system

A slurry wall or underground diaphragm wall is used for the following purposes:

• As a retaining wall to prevent water seepage during excavation.
• As an intercept wall to contain contamination by oil spills in subsoil water and soil.
• As a cell structure for preventing the sand liquefaction by earthquake.
• As an underground space structure (underground exterior wall).
• As an underground storage tank for water, oil and liquefied natural gas (Fig. IV-B13).

This technology was introduced from Italy in 1959. During the late 1960s and 1970s, new excavating machines and control systems were developed by Japanese companies.

After the 1970s, the use of this wall and site conditions became diversified:

• Moving from soft ground to hard ground, conglomerate and mixed layers.
• Close location to neighboring buildings or underground structures.
• To a deeper wall of varying widths.

These diversifications were needed to operate excavating machines automatically and highly accurately.

Figure IV-B13 Cylindrical slurry wall for LNG tank (Taisei Corporation)

Bridge Tower Foundation

Recently, long suspension bridges were constructed to connect the mouth of Tokyo Bay with the city. The Bay forms a convenient harbor but separates the city from both coastal areas and is perceived an obstacle to urban activities. To overcome a similar dilemma, the Hakucho Ohhashi bridge was constructed to connect the mouth of the Muroran Bay to Hokkaido. It forms a circular road into the city and connects directly with the highway. This 1.38 km-long suspension bridge has a clear span of 720 m.

The main towers used to support the suspension cables are 139.5 m in height from sea-level and were anchored 20 m deep into the seabed where the bearing rock layer inclines from the coast to the central part of the mouth of Muroran

Bay. The bearing rock layer is situated 73 m below the seabed at the foundation of the north tower. A circular slurry wall was constructed to connect the temporary cut-off wall with the retaining wall. The wall is 1.5 m and 106 m deep, with an inside diameter of 34 m. After excavating for the slurry wall, a perimetrical reinforced-concrete foundation wall was constructed from the top to the bottom of the wall and interior walls and floors were added. During this construction process it was crucial to accurately position the excavation machinery.

Artificial Islands

The Trans-Tokyo Bay Highway is a 15 km-toll highway that crosses the center of Tokyo Bay and connects Kawasaki and the Kisarazu Islands. Two 10 km-underwater tunnels and one 5 km-bridge highway are to form the Tokyo Bay Highway loop. The highway loop is to connect Tokyo, Yokohama, Kawasaki, Kisarazu and Chiba. The Trans-Tokyo Bay Gate highway is planned to form another loop.

Two artificial islands, started in 1989 and completed in 1996, will house ventilation facilities. The structures were constructed approximately 20–25 m deep on an alluvial seabed where the intensity of large-scale earthquakes and typhoons is very high and the soil under the seabed is soft to a depth of more than 30 m.

The Kawasaki artificial island is composed of a unique structure. In the early stages of the project, the soil was stabilized by sand compaction. A double cylindrical steel trestle structure which functions as a retaining wall and working platform was then constructed on the stabilized foundation. Soil fill was placed between two cylindrical trestle structures (Fig. IV-B14). During excavation, a thick and deep slurry wall was constructed within the fill to form a cylindrical

Figure IV-B14 Kawasaki artificial island under construction (Taisei Corporation)

retaining wall with a 100 m inside diameter. A reinforced concrete walled structure was built using the top down procedure after the fill was excavated. The islands served as a vertical access shaft during the shield tunnelling work and act as a ventilation tower now.

The Kisarazu artificial island was constructed to act as a transition structure from the tunnel to the bridge, as well as to house ventilation facilities. The underwater road tunnels were to be bored using slurry shield machines with up to 14 m in diameter.

High Accuracy Laser Positioning

A position control system is necessary to maintain accuracy before the construction of the deep slurry wall under severe site conditions. It is possible to control the maximum displacement of the wall within 50 mm at a depth of 200 m when excavating with a vertical multishaft and a reverse excavator.

This system uses a number of wires mounted on the excavator to detect its position. A laser displacement gauge on an accuracy control rack measures the displacement of the detecting wires during the excavation. The angle of inclination and the depth of the excavator body are measured by the inclinometer and depth gauge.

The position of the actual excavation at the center of the drum cutter is calculated with a three-dimensional data processing system. The excavated section is then displayed continuously on the monitor in real-time. Real-time processing and synchronization of measurement timing improve the reliability of the measure values. The position detecting process is fully automated, so the operation of the excavating machine can control positions without delay.

PARTS ASSEMBLY AND ON-SITE TRANSPORTATION

Parts Assembly in a High-rise Building

The layered construction method has become more popular in Japan, even for use in steel frame high-rise buildings. Each floor is built by assembling segmented parts of the building which are prefabricated at an off-site or on-site factory (Fig. IV-B15). The main parts consist of steel or composite framings, precast concrete exterior curtain walls, floor units, plumbing and sprinkler piping shaft units and air conditioning units. The floor units are framed by steel girders and beams as well as by steel mesh. They are installed complete with air ducts, conduit pipes, plumbing pipes and air conditioning ceiling units to reduce the number of items to be lifted.

These segmented parts are hoisted and assembled on each of the three floors with high-capacity twisting jib-tower cranes. Segmented parts are ordered in advance and prepared at on-site stock bays. Work teams take up their designated positions, then move to the next position as the task progresses.

Figure IV-B15 The assembly of segmented parts of a high-rise building

Climbing Jib Tower Crane Operation

The time required to erect segmented building parts has a great effect on the productivity of a high-rise building with a large floor area. It is necessary to adopt large capacity and high-speed transportation methods with various functions. The transportation time and work load at the higher floors can be reduced significantly when using climbing jib-tower cranes since segmented building parts are prefabricated in as large a dimension or weight as needed.

Climbing jib-tower cranes, croller cranes, raft cranes, high-speed cargo lifts, passenger and cargo elevators, and wide-span cargo elevators were adopted for the Tokyo metropolitan municipal office building which has forty-eight floors and is 248 m high. Jib-tower cranes have the lifting capacity of 900 t/m. The operating area covers 28 m in diameter and can lift parts up to a maximum of 32 t to each of the three floors in a 13-day cycle. The operating program of four jib-tower cranes is simulated by the computer and monitored by sensors to detect other crane's rotating or rolling movements. All these functions are in turn controlled by computers in the site office. When the crane boom enters a near-miss area, the alarm warns the operator and the crane boom is stopped automatically.

On-site Transportation

The higher the building to be constructed, the more important it is to solve the problems of efficient and timely transport of large amounts of various finishing

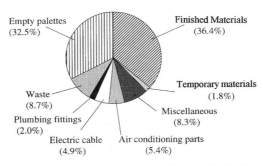

Figure IV-B16 Percentages of types of transported items (Taisei Corporation)

materials, mechanical and electrical units to the specified floors, temporary scaffoldings and the removal of waste from the finishing materials (Fig. IV-B16).

A new transportation system was adopted for the Yokohama Landmark Tower, the highest building in Japan. The tower, completed in 1994, has a height of 296 m with seventy floors, three basement levels, and a 39 ha floor area for office, hotel and public use. The transportation methods used during the construction of this building consisted of automatic carts, loaders, push-pull devices, high-speed lifts and forklifts. Transportation safety was maintained by electronic sensors which detect the workers' location, the cargo dimensions and obstacles which also adopt several interlock mechanisms.

Multi-crane Double Deck Transportation

The entirely mechanized construction system, called the T-UP method, is a unique pioneering approach to the construction of high-rise buildings. The construction process involves the transportation and assembly of modular building segmented parts. The system itself consists of several automated multiple crane operation systems and a temporary roof to reduce the construction time, to save manpower and enforce safety measures (Fig. IV-B17). An automated system provides integrated and consistently high-quality construction work.

There are four cranes, two traveling jib-cranes on the top of the service core above the hat and two overhead hoist cranes under the hat which climb with eight hydraulic jacks installed to the corner columns of the core frame. The building work starts with the construction of the service core structure of the high-rise building. The hat becomes a working deck and a roof-top after the building is completed and is housed near the service core.

Two twisting tower cranes are installed in case the conventional construction method is used for another similar high-rise building. The number of cranes on a site is restricted to avoid collision and to prepare more stock bays on the ground. Four cranes with six segmented-part stock bays on the ground can lift twice the number of parts per day as two twisting tower-cranes with two stock

Figure IV-B17 An entirely mechanized construction system

bays. All operation systems are monitored by televisions and three-dimensional laser scanning sensors, which are controlled by terminals located on-site and computer monitors at the site office.

CONCLUSION

The advanced construction technologies mentioned in this chapter are only a few examples of the initiatives that contribute to the urbanization and development of a city. Numerous large-scale construction and development projects do not form today's cities. Rather, a city is comprised of the numbers of individual and collective housing, office and commercial buildings and urban facilities in neighborhoods such as paths, parks and squares that are constructed and renovated again and again as the city changes. Increasing production capacity and effective technological innovation in all industries have stimulated the promotion of new construction technologies and the incentive to actively develop the city. A great degree of construction activity has affected socio-economic and natural environments in urban areas. In the meantime, various constraints to the supply of labor and materials have become more acute. The improvements to working environments and the conservation of natural resources are other important factors to be considered when upgrading the current construction technology.

Also, high levels of immigration to urban areas have left the remote regions throughout the country sparsely populated. Recently, it was deemed necessary to form an autonomous regional community network as a cultural and economic tool for easing the influx of people to the densely populated Tokyo megalopolis. The increase in social amenities and the structural change of Japan and its society act as incentives to reach further advancements in construction technology.

BIBLIOGRAPHY

1. Construction Economy Institute 1992. *Economy of Japan and Public Investment.* Tokyo: Construction Economy Institute.
2. Economic Planning Agency 1992. *Annual Report on National Economic Account.* Tokyo: Economic Planning Agency.
3. Japan Civil Engineering Contractors Association 1995. *Construction Industry Graph* March: no. 25.
4. Kawada, H. K. 1992. Subsurface development in metropolitan areas. *Soil and Foundation JSSMEE* 40, no. 8.
5. Ministry of Construction 1995. *Monthly Report on Construction Labors and Materials* April: 21.
6. Ministry of Labor 1991. *Annual Labor Force Survey.* Tokyo: Ministry of Labor.
7. Ministry of Labor 1992. *Monthly Labor Statistical Survey.* Tokyo: Ministry of Labor.

C Urban Redevelopment Methods in Japan

Susumu Sakamoto

INTRODUCTION

This chapter focuses on the Urban Redevelopment System, which is currently used in Japan and which is one of the most popular methods of urban renewal to emerge since the Urban Redevelopment Law of 1969. First, this report introduces Japan's major systems of urban redevelopment and then explains the Urban Redevelopment System itself, especially as there is confusion between the terminology of the Urban Redevelopment System and redevelopment in general. Secondly, a comparison is offered of Japan's general redevelopment system and the systems commonly used in the U.S.A. Finally, the newest elements of the Urban Redevelopment System are presented.

Urban renewal, in general, is classified into three categories: (1) redevelopment; (2) rehabilitation; and (3) conservation. Redevelopment is the partial or total clearance of a large-scale area which has been deteriorating physically and socially, for the purpose of redesigning it to improve the environment and its social quality of life. Rehabilitation is the renovation of some or all of a large area to maintain its overall structure. Its aim is to enhance the social environment, the standard of living and the landscape environment to meet modern norms and standards. Conservation is meant to retain the overall structure and its details in order to preserve the historical, esthetic and architectural values which have significant implications nationally, regionally or locally. The rehabilitation and conservation of structures is usually employed to preserve historical or cultural buildings that exist in the project area.

JAPAN'S URBAN REDEVELOPMENT SYSTEM

The rapid urbanization after World War II enabled many cities in Japan to recover from the war and attain their full capacities quickly. At the same time, however, urban master planning was inadequate as a guide to implement practical and efficient development techniques. Instead, the rapid growth caused urban sprawl, housing shortages, traffic congestion, the misuse of land space and many other urban problems, which severely hindered the cities' abilities to respond adequately to urban disasters like earthquakes or fires. Due to these circumstances, the Ministry of Construction established various guidelines and standards for the redevelopment of Japanese cities.

Urban redevelopment is accomplished through two aspects of the development process; the Planning Method, which is dictated by the laws enacted by the Japanese government, such as the City Planning Act and the Building Standards Act and the Project Method, which focuses on procedures to promote urban redevelopment projects.

Planning Method

The City Planning Act and the Building Standards Act are representative of typical Japanese planning control methods. The former regulates areas and land-use categories while the latter controls the use and structural safety of buildings. Since these control methods regulate the minimum standard of planning, it is difficult to create sound urban space using these Acts alone.

The government can modify the regulations of the Acts if a project contributes to the urban space in ways that affect both the public and private sectors, by declaring it a public–private partnership (PPP) redevelopment project. By the 1970s, various planning methods were established such as the Comprehensive Design System, the Specified Blocks System and the District Planning System (Fig. IV-C1).

Comprehensive Design System

This construction system seeks to increase open space and thus improve the urban environment. It encourages owners of real estate to pursue this goal by giving incentives according to the ratio of open space to built-up space at the site.

The Umeda Center Building, constructed in 1987 and located in the business and commercial zone of Osaka City, is an example of this design approach. Despite its convenient location for business, an old factory remained at

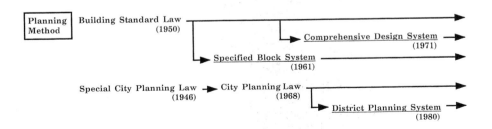

Underlined : mentioned in this report

Figure IV-C1 Flow of laws and systems of Planning Methods (Urban Renewal Association of Japan, 1991)

the site because of its irregularly-shaped block. The Takenaka Corporation proposed to construct a high-rise building applying the Comprehensive Design System. Despite the irregularly shaped block, a large open space which occupies 68% of the site accommodates many special features, including a sunken garden, promenades, lush greenery, a shopping mall and music hall (Fig. IV-C2).

Specified Block System

This system offers developers and owners incentives if they are willing to meet the desirable standards of bulk ratio, maximum height, and positioning of the building walls to contribute to a healthy urban environment. This application is limited to regularly-shaped blocks.

Figure IV-C2 Comprehensive Design System for an irregularly shaped block (Takenaka Corporation, 1992)

Figure IV-C3 Specified Blocks System for a regularly shaped block. Tokyo Opera City under construction (Site area 44,091 m²; proposed floor area 312,400 m²) (Japan Arts Council, 1993)

The Specified Block System is being applied to the proposed Tokyo Opera City with a projected completion date of 1998. Following the plan of the National Theater, the owners of an adjacent plot on the same block, together with the Takenaka Corporation and a group of consultants, are attempting to revitalize the area. In addition to the National Theater, the space will feature office and retail facilities as well as a small concert hall, with the development rights of the theater transferred to the office complex. The entire block development is known as "Tokyo Opera City" (Fig. IV-C3).

District Planning System

The District Planning System is a planning procedure at the district level. In the designated district, the local government establishes a district plan which will offer incentives in exchange for public facilities such as roads and parks.

The Hibiya Building, completed in 1987 in Tokyo, is an example of the District Planning System at work. For a long time, this area flourished as an entertainment strip. When the movie theaters relocated, the owner and Takenaka Corporation collaborated to redevelop the area. By applying the District Planning System, the development rights were transferred to an office and retail building (Fig. IV-C4).

Figure IV-C4 District Planning System. Photograph of Hibiya Building, Tokyo, 1987 (Site area 55, 23 m^2; floor area 59,581 m^2) (Takenaka Corporation, 1992, p. 8)

Project Method

To promote urban redevelopment projects, the Ministry of Construction has provided several redevelopment procedures which can be selected according to the physical and functional conditions of a given area. As opposed to the Planning Method, the Project Method is based on tax law, property title law and national subsidy systems other than planning law (Fig. IV-C5).

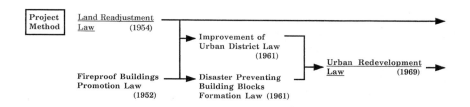

Underlined : mentioned in this report

Figure IV-C5 Flow of laws and systems of project method

Land Readjustment System

This system, based on the Land Readjustment Law, aims to improve public facilities such as roads and parks by replotting irregularly shaped parcels of land. Though a portion of each parcel of land becomes smaller in order to contribute to the infrastructure, its value remains the same due to the increase in its development potential.

The new Osaka Business Park, completed in 1987, was formerly the site of factories and warehouses. Surrounded by natural greenery and many historical buildings, the area was redeveloped as a business park according to the Land Readjustment System (Fig. IV-C6).

Urban Redevelopment System

In a densely populated area, this method, based on Urban Redevelopment Law, aims to improve both public facilities and buildings. The original property owner is entitled to retain sharing rights on the land and new buildings. This will be discussed in more detail later.

Figure IV-C6 Land Readjustment System. Photograph of the Osaka Business Park, Osaka, 1987 (Site area 18 ha; floor area 90 ha) (Osaka Business Park Development Joint Conference, 1990)

Comparison of the Systems

In the redevelopment systems of PPPs, the public sector provides many incentives for developers in the private sector depending on the potential contribution to the improvement of urban environment. Some of these incentives are presented in Table IV-C1 below, combined with the redevelopment method that would best accommodate a specific building incentive.

Due to the large-scale nature of the projects undertaken by Japan's developers, the three most commonly used redevelopment systems are: (1) the Comprehensive Design System; (2) the District Planning System; and (3) the Urban Redevelopment System.

Compared with the Comprehensive Design System and the District Planning System, an important component of the Urban Redevelopment Method is the subsidy incentive intended to directly improve the project's overall financial balance and to spread its benefits among the local cities where floor area demand is low and previous planning incentives have been ineffective.

THE URBAN REDEVELOPMENT SYSTEM, ITS LAWS AND PROJECTS

The profile of the Urban Redevelopment System is based on the Urban Redevelopment Law established in 1969. Since then, this Method has been adopted throughout Japan. By March 1994, 524 projects with a total area of 823.4 ha had been planned and 304 of these projects with a total area of 391.5 ha have been completed (Fig. IV-C7).

The building use varies somewhat from project to project, but most of the buildings consist of residences and retail stores. Other buildings house hotels, offices and cultural centers. Of these projects, 20,000 residential units have already been completed with an additional 26,000 units planned.

An Urban Redevelopment Project is carried out in cooperation with local governments, the private sector and local residents. Each group plays a distinct

Table IV-C1 Comparison of the planning and financial incentives of the five systems

Features of each system	Planning incentives			Project financial incentives		
	(A)	(B)	(C)	(D)	(E)	(F)
Comprehensive design system	✓	✓			✓	
Specified block system	✓	✓			✓	✓
District planning system	✓	✓	✓			
Land readjustment system				✓	✓	✓
Urban redevelopment system	✓			✓	✓	✓

(A) Ease of floor capacity regulation; (B) ease of building form regulation; (C) ease of building use regulation; (D) subsidy of nation and municipality; (E) special loan; (F) special tax treatment.

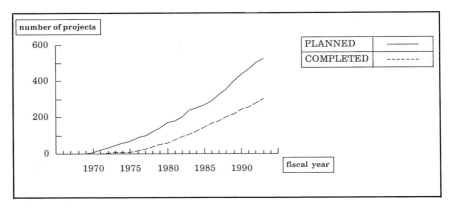

Figure IV-C7 Trend of total urban redevelopment projects (Urban Renewal Association of Japan, 1970–1994)

role in the accomplishment of the project. The funds required for a new construction are provided by individuals from the private sector who participate in the project to gain part of the land and floor rights for the new building. They may be developers or end users of the building. Local residents contribute their land to receive compensation in the form of a new plot of land and/or floor rights in the new building. The arrangement must involve compensation equal to the value of the previously owned land and buildings. Their titles remain intact and they do not need move to another area. Since the exchange of properties between many parties is involved, a subsidy is offered to stimulate the project, which is of critical importance at this point. The local government must closely supervise the project to protect the interest of all parties involved. Each redevelopment project requires the financial support from local and private sectors, supervision from the public sector and a contribution of land from local residents (Fig. IV-C8).

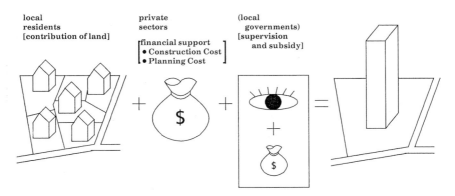

Figure IV-C8 Roles of parties involved

Project Procedures

Since urban redevelopment includes the liquidation of complex land and building rights, the submission of plans to the local governments is required to ensure fairness. The procedure demands a tremendous amount of time and negotiation and in many cases urban redevelopment consultants coordinate the projects entirely (Fig. IV-C9).

Examples

An urban redevelopment project is executed by either private individuals, urban redevelopment unions, local governments or other public sector groups like the

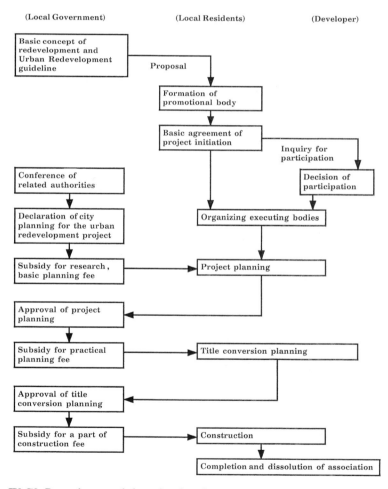

Figure IV-C9 Procedures and the role of each sector

Housing and Urban Development Corporation (HUDC). Among the completed projects, most were handled by either the redevelopment union, usually formed of local residents, or by the local government. Even in cases when the local government manages a project, local residents and the private sector play an important role that differs from the role played in purely public projects. The following examples represent projects conceived and completed by the two main bodies.

Mito Station North Area Project

The Mito Station North Area Project was supervised by the local government. Mito City is located approximately 100 km north of Tokyo and is the capital of the Ibaraki Prefecture. The north area of Mito Station is the main commercial zone, but some blocks have been decaying and suffer from chronic urban problems such as traffic congestion or underuse due to poor urban design. The Planning Department of the city outlined a basic redevelopment design for this area in 1983 and the execution of the project began in 1987 with the consent of the property owners (Fig. IV-C10).

The project had four main purposes:

- To enlarge the station plaza to secure pedestrians' safety.
- To construct underground bicycle parking to supplement the needs of cyclists.
- To enlarge the width of adjacent roads to reduce the number of traffic jams.
- To construct a new building to revitalize the area.

The local government of Mito City realized the project's many public purposes and decided to become its main sponsor. The implementation of the project has been estimated to take ten years.

The annual schedule was as follows:

1983 Mito city drafted a basic plan and proposed it to the local residents.
1984 The residents formed a promotional body.
1987 The residents agreed that the Mito City Government should oversee and execute the project.
1988 City planning for the Urban Redevelopment Project was authorized.
1989 The project planning was authorized and a developer joined the project.
1990 The title conversion planning was approved and the construction started.
1993 The Mito Station North Area Project was completed.

Site conditions and facility summary:

- Area of site   21,188 m^2
- Public facilities area   16,872 m^2
- Building area   4316 m^2
- Number of landowners and tenants   60
- Number of building stories   10 stories above ground, three stories underground
- Total floor area   37,681 m^2
- Total project cost   24.5 billion yen

Figure IV-C10 Photographs of comparisons of site area in 1987 (upper photo) and the Mito Station North Area Project at present (lower photo) (Urban Planning Department, 1993, pp. 2–4)

Nagasaki Chitose Project

This project was executed by the Redevelopment Union in Nagasaki. Nagasaki City is located in western Japan and has been flourishing as an industrial center, a fishing port and a tourist site for the past few decades. Although the area was the subcenter of a residential district in the city, there were many old wooden residential structures which hindered the area's ability to prosper. In response to the rising redevelopment needs of the local community, the city offered assistance and joined with the Redevelopment Union to initiate the project in 1978 (Fig. IV-C11).

Figure IV-C11 Photographs of the site area in 1987 (upper photo) and the Nagasaki Chitose Project at its completion in 1991 (lower photo) (Urban Development Department, 1991)

The project had three main purposes:

- To supply public housing
- To modernize retail areas
- To provide a public community center

The annual schedule was as follows:

1978 Residents appealed to the city to redevelop the area.
1981 The city held meetings with the residents.
1984 The city outlined a basic redevelopment plan. The residents, in turn, organized a redevelopment union.
1986 A developer participated in the planning of project details.
1987 City planning for the urban redevelopment project was approved.
1988 Project planning and title conversion planning were authorized and the construction began.
1991 The Nagasaki Chitose Project was completed.

Site conditions and facility summary:

- Area of site   15,907 m^2
- Public facilities area   4048 m^2 (formerly 3615 m^2)
- Building area   11,859 m^2 (formerly 12,292 m^2)
- Number of landowners and tenants   158
- Number of building stories   Fourteen stories above ground, three stories underground
- Total floor area   61,496 m^2
- Total project cost   11.1 billion yen

REDEVELOPMENT IN THE U.S.A. AND JAPAN: A COMPARISON

As mentioned above, the Japanese redevelopment system is unique in many ways. Although many Japanese methods are drawn from techniques used in the U.S.A., some significant differences can be found. To gain a better understanding of these differences, one must begin with an examination of the structure of the entire Japanese redevelopment system.

Japan's Urban Planning Mechanism and Urban Policy

In Japan, a majority of the population lives in densely developed urban areas due to the extensive network of mass transit and the scarcity of land suitable for settlements. The land available for large-scale development is extremely limited, especially in comparison to available land in the U.S.A. As a result, one of the the main issues in Japan has been the most effective way to redevelop the nation's already developed areas.

The municipal governments' primary concern is the improvement of densely built-up areas to protect them from natural disasters in Japan, like earthquakes, hurricanes and floods. Areas chosen for redevelopment have not necessarily been blighted. Many working class neighborhoods fall into this category. The typical motivating factor for redevelopment is the prevailing danger of structural weaknesses and the hazardous conditions found in old buildings. For this reason, scrap-and-build redevelopment has become the primary method of urban renewal. When a project adopts a scrap-and-build approach, it is quite different from the one employed in the U.S.A., where the main purpose for its adoption is to rid an area of blighted spaces and to promote economic development with the cooperation of developers who have incentives. However, from the property owners' point of view, scrap-and-build may appear similar to rehabilitation projects in the U.S.A. which actually tackle the renovation of both the entire interior and exterior of a given building.

For example, some redevelopment projects in Japan, especially those performed by unions, aim to revitalize their own commercial activities. The nature of cooperative development agreements allows owners of real estate to significant shares of the project's profits. However, the profit margin is frequently insufficient to benefit developers and some incentives are not available to them.

Residents' Concept of Land Ownership

Owning land in Japan is basic to the idea of having a home. The Japanese people's attachment to the land interferes with the notion of land as an investment. This tendency has made Japanese urban landscape unique, but in many cases it has prevented necessary redevelopment. The strong public sympathy for this concept impedes essential redevelopment planning without the consent of the residents. The notion of an eminent domain requires widespread public support and the clear understanding of the urgency of the project, although it is rarely used. The Japanese government has sought to establish a more flexible redevelopment system which would compel the residents to comply with a reasonable contract. For example, the Urban Redevelopment Law states that residents in an area must be allowed to remain after redevelopment—a proposition that stands in stark contrast with the ordinances in the U.S.A. (Fig. IV-C12).

In the U.S.A., houses which are older than one-hundred years are not uncommon. In Japan, however, building renewal takes place very rapidly. Low housing availability, coupled with the fact that many buildings constructed after World War II have been included in the redevelopment projects, suggests that residents' attachment to their buildings is relatively weak.

Role of National and Local Governments

In Japan, the national government plays an enormous role in the redevelopment process. All local and municipal governments must adhere to the system ordained by the national government. Local bodies have little power to change national regulations to suit their own conditions. Their adherence to national

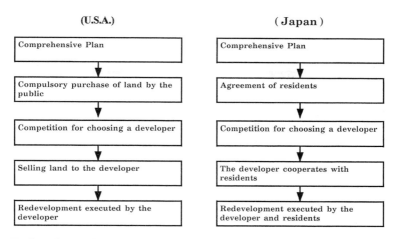

Figure IV-C12 General process of redevelopment promotion: a comparison between the U.S.A. and Japan

law is assured by the fact that they rarely possess the funds to promote a project without receiving considerable national subsidies.

In the U.S.A., the tax increment method and tax increment merging method seem to play an important role in the implementation of redevelopment projects. They allow local redevelopment agencies to dispose of money relatively flexibly without federal or local government intervention and, as a result, they can act independently. In Japan, on the other hand, there are no similar procedures to handle local redevelopment and primary public resources are national subsidies. It will be difficult for local Japanese governments to gain more power under the current financial system.

Redevelopment by Public–Private Partnerships (PPP)

When cooperation exists between the public and private sectors to promote a project, the Urban Redevelopment Method is known as a PPP. This, however, is different from the U.S. case for the following reasons:

- In Japan, employing a PPP Method facilitates planning, but the project's financial framework cannot be changed. In the U.S., PPP methods have more flexibility.
- In the U.S.A., a PPP is the relationship between the public and private sectors. In Japan, a PPP is the relationship among public sector groups, private sector groups and local residents.
- Area residents in Japan have a considerable voice in the project which is not unlike the situation in the U.S.A., but nonprofit organizations representing residents from the surrounding areas seldom exist in Japan. When they do, their influence is considerably weak as opposed to the influence of nonprofit organizations in the U.S.A.

General Contractor's Role

Urban renewal projects generally take a long time to promote and involve planning and coordinating many complex procedures. Leading general contractors in Japan participate as system organizers engaged in the redevelopment process. Below is a step-by-step guide of how the general contractors might get involved in the redevelopment projects. The project intitiation consists of a collection of related information and is based on the initial proposal from which a fundamental policy is formed. The ideas suggested by general contractors may be recommended and the location may be examined if necessary.

A feasibility study is based on an analysis of the marketability of the project. A land-use plan is devised which includes project executors, schemes and a summary schedule. A systematic plan is mapped out to coordinate the different needs of the participating government groups, tenants and developers, with the intention of making a basic agreement to satisfy all parties involved. The implementation of the plan requires more concrete coordination among the project parties to obtain complete unity, while detailed design, financial procurement and various legal procedures are investigated.

The construction supervision and control are based on the detailed execution plan. Progress on the construction is reported periodically to the client. The operation management process occurs after the facilities are completed. A periodic survey of the concerned parties is carried out so that the facilities and surroundings may meet to the complete satisfaction of the tenants. The general contractors in the United States mainly focus on the construction supervision and control, whereas in Japan the roles are more encompassing and are performed according to the needs of each project.

NEW ELEMENTS IN URBAN REDEVELOPMENT METHOD—A FUTURE PERSPECTIVE

More than twenty years have passed since the establishment of Japan's Urban Redevelopment Law. In the meantime, the law has been revised several times to keep pace with society's changing needs. Recently, through the cooperation of both the public and private sectors, research has been underway to develop more applicable redevelopment methods. It has received excellent results by providing many innovative methods for future urban redevelopment.

Large-scale Redevelopment System

In pursuit of better economies of scale and of a more harmonious urban design, developers have searched for a redevelopment method specifically devised for larger-scale redevelopments. In large-scale projects, policymakers should approach all sites with a general plan and then focus on each site individually. The phased execution of each site must be in accordance with that of a general plan. Redevelopment District Planning, established in 1989, enables stage-by-stage comprehensive redevelopment planning and has succeeded in attracting many developers to use it.

The Harumi Project

This project is an example of a proposed large-scale redevelopment project. It will be located in Tokyo and cover 10 ha. Due to its large scale, the area has to be divided into three parts with different redevelopment time schedules each. The first redevelopment project will provide the lead for the other two redevelopment projects functionally and financially. A description planned for the total project may be summarized as:

- Floor area   72.8 ha
- Construction began   1993
- Projected completion 2001

Mixed Land-Use and Function

In pursuit of the most efficient land-use, a public research group has been investigating Urban Complex Building (UCB). UCB includes public facilities such areas as atriums, skyways, public areas, pedestrian passages, monorails, greenery and other attractions inside and outside a building structure to blend and integrate public and private space.

Intersection Model Project

The main purpose of the UCB is to unify areas divided by roads or railways by an underground plaza. The proposed Intersection Model Project, with its massive underground plaza, will accomplish this goal (Fig. IV-C13).

Figure IV-C13 Scale model of the proposed Intersection Model Project (Building Technology Research Institute, 1991)

Project Financing

In Japan, the means of financing projects is still being determined. The Real Estate Compatible Mortgage is one pioneering method of project financing to increase real estate security. Project security involves the conversion of financial debt or equity into tradable investment securities. These methods, eagerly awaited by developers, can be more effective in promoting a redevelopment project.

The Shinjuku South Area Project

This project, with an estimated completion date of 1997, will be located in Tokyo on a former railway stockyard. The railway company wanted to sell the land, but the government denied the request because the sale would have raised land prices higher in the surrounding area. In 1992, the company adopted the Real Estate Compatible Mortgage Method and succeeded in selling seven shares of compatible mortgages for a total of 287 billion Yen (Fig. IV-C14).

Urban Design

The clients of a redevelopment project include all the residents and the developer. The two parties must reach an agreement on the property rights of the people involved in the redevelopment project. Any cooperative agreement takes time, especially when the handling of property rights is involved. As a result, there is generally little time left to discuss the overall urban design. Recently, residents have come to gradually recognize that thorough design itself is economically valuable and should be discussed in the earliest stages of the project planning.

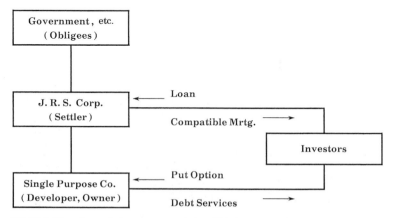

Figure IV-C14 The financial structure of the Shinjuku South Area Project (Kenchiku Chishiki Corporation, 1993, p. 301)

Yokohama Portside District

The Portside District, next to Yokohama station, has been undergoing fundamental changes which will make it part of a new international city dedicated to
art and design. The city government, HUDC, and main property owners formed
a town development community and concluded the Town Development Agreement in 1989. The agreement includes various urban design standards, such as
the skyline, color coordination and outdoor advertising (Fig. IV-C15). HUDC
was responsible for 4 ha of 25 ha of urban redevelopment in the Portside District.
Michael Graves, a U.S. architect, designed one of HUDC's residential buildings,
which was completed in 1993.

CONCLUSION

This paper presents various redevelopment systems and corresponding project
examples that represent the methods of urban renewal in Japan. The respect of
land ownership rights is a primary characteristic of these systems, a feature which
greatly varies from those in the U.S.A. More specifically, in most typical redevelopment projects, land belonging to the former owners is not "purchased" as a
rule and will continually exist as a new title in a modified form. The value of such

SKYLINE IMAGE OF THREE LAYER COMPOSITION

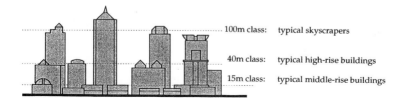

100m class: typical skyscrapers

40m class: typical high-rise buildings

15m class: typical middle-rise buildings

Figure IV-C15 Architectural drawing of the Yokohama Portside District (Urban Planning
Bureau, n.d.)

a title must not depreciate from the previous value and must be assessed fairly among the plurality of involved individuals. For this reason, developers and co-ordinators who promote redevelopment spend large amounts of time and energy mediating conflicting interests among the various parties involved. The delays which result from these discussions increase the redevelopment costs and post-pone the completion date of the project which causes changes in the areas socio-economic conditions and impedes the chances of business opportunities in connection with the project.

Furthermore, developers are usually motivated to participate in a particular project for mainly two reasons. One is the expectation of fulfilling the potential of a particular site, thus adding value to the entire environment. The other is the opportunity to engage in the profitable operation and management after the completion of the particular project. However, the current recession of the econ-omy in Japan has caused land prices to level off and the higher risks involved in the success of redevelopment projects have resulted in the waning desire and eagerness of the developers to invest.

An even greater problem is that the absolute value of the land price, which has stagnated recently, is still too high to buy land for the construction of buildings. This expense keeps these ventures from becoming profitable within a reasonable period of time. This trend makes redevelopment itself difficult. Parti-cularly in the central parts of large cities, land prices have skyrocketed to a level which makes it extremely difficult for ordinary citizens to buy or even rent houses. As a result, the nighttime population in these central areas has decreased, which creates problems such as urban sprawl and increases the commuter traffic con-gestion. Under these complex and rigorous conditions, future redevelopment methods will require drastic improvements. A solution must be found and implemented by combining the wisdom of people in various fields.

BIBLIOGRAPHY

1. Building Technology Research Institute 1991. *Urban Complex Building Proposal Broc-hure*. Tokyo: Building Technology Research Institute.
2. Hibata, Y. and Kimura, M. 1992. *Urban Redevelopment in the United States* (in Japanese). Kyoto: Gakugei Syuppansya.
3. Hibata, Y. 1992. *Micro Urban Planning and Land-use* (in Japanese). Kyoto: Gakugei Syuppansya.
4. Higasa, T. 1985. *An Overview of Methods for Urban Planning in Developed Nations* (in Japanese). Tokyo: Kyoritsu Syuppansya.
5. Housing and Urban Development Corporation 1990. *Harumi 1-Chome Area Redevel-opment Project Brochure*. Tokyo: Housing and Urban Development Corporation.
6. Japan Arts Council 1993. *New National Theater Brochure*. Tokyo: Japan Arts Council.
7. Kenchiku Chishiki Corporation 1993. *Reference Book for Urban Development and Architectural Planning*. Tokyo: Kenchiku Chishiki Corporation.
8. Ono, T. and Habe Evans, R. 1992. *Review of Urban Development*. Tokyo: Iwanami Shoten.

9. Osaka Business Park Development Joint Conference 1990. *Osaka Business Park Brochure.* Osaka: Osaka Business Park Development Joint Conference.
10. Sasaki, S. 1988. *Housing and Urban Policy in the United States* (in Japanese). Tokyo: Keizai Chosakai.
11. Takenaka Corporation 1992. *Major Works.* Osaka: Takenaka Corporation.
12. Takenaka Corporation 1987. *Umeda Center Building Brochure.* Osaka: Takenaka Corporation.
13. Urban Development Department 1991. *Chitose Area Urban Redevelopment Cooperative Brochure.* Nagasaki: Urban Planning Department.
14. Urban Planning Department 1993. *Mito Station Urban Redevelopment Project Brochure.* Mito: Urban Planning Department.
15 Urban Planning Bureau n.d. *Yokohama Portside Brochure.* Yokohama: Urban Planning Bureau.
16. Urban Renewal Association of Japan, Ministry of Construction 1990. *Urban Renewal Projects by Diagrams* (in Japanese). Tokyo: Urban Renewal Association of Japan.
17. Urban Renewal Association of Japan, Ministry of Construction 1993. *Urban Renewal '93* (in Japanese). Tokyo: Urban Renewal Association of Japan.
18. Urban Renewal Association of Japan 1985. *Urban Renewal Project Procedures* (in Japanese). Tokyo: Urban Renewal Association of Japan.
19. Urban Renewal Study, Ministry of Construction 1993. *Urban Renewal Law, Guide Notes* (in Japanese). Tokyo: Taisei Syuppansya.
20. Urban Renewal Association of Japan 1991. Urban redevelopment in Japan. *Urban Renewal Association of Japan* 3.
21. Urban Renewal Association of Japan 1970–1994. Urban redevelopment monthly journal. *Urban Renewal Association of Japan.*

D Japan's Urban Environment: The Potential of Technology in Future City Concepts

Hideo Obitsu and Ichirou Nagase

INTRODUCTION

The high-rise construction era began in the latter half of the nineteenth century with the development of new building techniques, such as steel-frame construction and with the invention of elevators. A century later, Japan is witnessing rapid changes in its social lifestyles as well as in its industrial structures. However, the vision of a desirable urban concept remains unclear and suggestions for new innovative urban designs are direly needed. Because of the technological process in a variety of fields, including information processing, the potential to develop new forms of buildings and more complex systems for entire cities lies behind this industrial progress.

Tokyo's problems today include the drudgery of daily commuting and deteriorating living conditions that are typical of any metropolis. Social and economic solutions need to be proposed that will also encompass new conceptual and structural forms. A resolution to urban problems requires the contributions of diverse fields.

This chapter discusses the possible physical forms that a city can assume and that are both technically feasible and nearly ideal. They are based on state-of-the-art science and technology that have seen dramatic progress during the twentieth century.

TECHNOLOGY FOR THE FUTURE CITY

The Obayashi Corporation, a comprehensive construction engineering company located in Japan, believes this research topic to be highly significant considering the hurdles facing our cities in the near future. To handle these obstacles demands the industry-wide focus and concentration on technological capability, including that of Obayashi's technology research institute. In this chapter, the company selected concepts and ideas that deal with the theme of the future city image from thirty-seven past issues of the publication *Quarterly Obayashi* and presented them here in abridged form.

The three concepts of urban design are based on three different levels: (1) an artificial platform city at a surface level; (2) a super high-rise building city at a high-rise level; and (3) an underground industrial city on the continental shelf at an underground level. The surface level extends over roughly five levels below the platform to another five stories above the platform totaling ten stories. The high-rise level involves super high-rise buildings and the underground level features the use of the great space below ground.

ARTIFICIAL PLATFORM—TOKYO LAPUTA PLAN

The image of Laputa in Jonathan Swift's *Gulliver's Travels* overlapped with our plan for an artificial platform built over an existing city, so we named the plan Laputa in honor of its first mention. The majority of the central Tokyo surface area is covered by a combination of small office buildings and residences with narrow roads built to resemble the mesh of a net. The urban infrastructure services, including water supply, sewage disposal and electric power, form an inefficient network above or under the road network.

To solve this problem of inefficiency, Obayashi Corporation has considered the possibility of creating a high-density but comfortable and convenient urban space. Such an urban setting would be designed to house the existing city area, including the streets, in single high-rise buildings, and everything else, including the urban infrastructure, would be relocated to achieve greater efficiency.[1]

Basic Concept of an Artificial Platform City

The basic module of the artificial platform city would consist of a rectangular-shaped foundation measuring 1 km^2 by 31 m in height from the ground surface level. By adding high-rise buildings for residences, the basic module would be capable of accommodating a working population of 53,000 and an additional 40,000 inhabitants. On and above the artificial platform level would be a residential zone and their related facilities, such as schools and parks. This arrangement could hold a working population about four times greater than that in the current central area of Tokyo. Building these basic modules at intervals of 1 km should supply the necessary functions equivalent to those currently available in Tokyo, as well as provide large green tracts. The modules could be connected via subways and main roads, and within a module, any destination would be within walking distance—a mere ten minutes by foot (Fig. IV-D1).

Existing urban areas including historical buildings, such as famous temples and shrines, gardens or other important sites, could be preserved within open spaces forming courtyards. Windows would then be placed overlooking the peripheral area of the artificial platform and the area which faces the courtyard to allow for the unobstructed view of such sights. The rooms positioned with a view of the green area would be used for offices or for rest and relaxation areas.

The space deep beneath the immense platform area where no natural light reaches would house factories, warehouses, recycling plants, sewage treatment

Figure IV-D1 Artificial platform—Tokyo Laputa Plan (*Quarterly Obayashi* 1989, 28, pp. 4–7)

plants and other facilities which would be automated and require a minimum of human intervention. Alternatively, it could also be used for halls, indoor athletic centers, movie theaters, parking lots and other facilities which require no natural lighting. The most negative consequence of this belowground construction would be the heat and quality of exhaust gas affecting the above surface land. However, advanced environmental technology could solve these problems in the near future.

Housing would be concentrated in the high-rise buildings which extend high above the new ground-level platform. These buildings would be designed to accommodate people who like urban-type condominiums. For those who prefer living in surface-level, independent houses, a housing zone would be provided within green spaces in the suburban or peripheral areas of the platform.

The new ground platform level, 31 m above the actual ground surface, would be supported by a base of 7 m × 7 m columns installed every 100 m. The platform would be made of thick slabs 2.5 m constructed by the unbonded flat slab method to form parks with ponds and trees. The landscape, featuring low houses, orchards, pastures and the like, would ensure a suburban appearance (Fig. IV-D2).

The artificial platform city would permit the introduction of extremely efficient equipment and systems similar to the familiar types currently featured in buildings. Sewage from the buildings would be purified in their own processing plants and recycled just as the precipitation on the new ground surface would be reused. Refuse would also be collected and dispatched to area-designated recycling plants via transport systems where it would then be incinerated and the energy from the waste heat would be sent to bioreactors. Thus, a highly self-sufficient city would be created.

Legal and Administrative Challenges

The plan for the artificial platform city is quite practical since it is based upon an extended line of today's state-of-the-art architectural and engineering technology. To execute the plan, however, it is necessary to adopt a new concept which transcends conventional systems of architecture and land-use. There are legal and administrative challenges to be met before the construction can begin. These challenges include adjustments in the administration of roads and public facilities in the case of disasters and ensuing evacuation, as well as in the ownership of land. The formation of the plan owes much to Professor Toshio Ojima of Waseda University, who has offered important advice on its preparation.

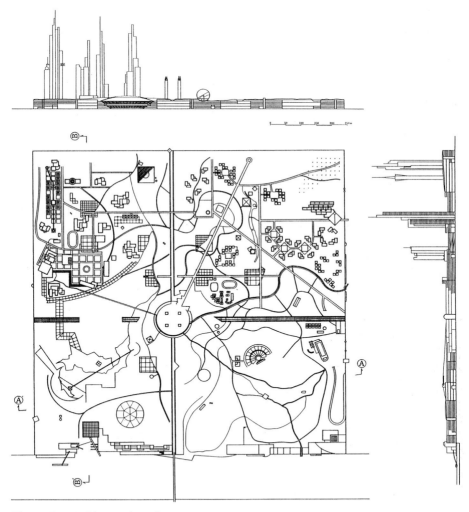

Figure IV-D2 Plan and sections of the artificial platform (*Quarterly Obayashi* 1989, 28, pp. 10–12)

SUPER HIGH-RISE BUILDING CITY—MILLENNIUM TOWER PLAN

Various problems need to be solved when constructing higher and larger buildings. Such difficulties include vertical transportation using elevators, the evacuation of residents, living environments, and the possible "shaking" and "swaying" of the structures caused by earthquakes and wind. Today, the 110-story Sears Tower in Chicago, Illinois, is the world's tallest building at 443 m. In Japan many high-rise buildings are also rising steadily; the Landmark Tower in Yokohama is 296 m high. The frequent earthquakes in Japan require that high-rise building technology fully investigate how to construct earthquake-proof structures that can ensure the residents' safety in case of extremely powerful quakes.[2]

Today, dramatic breakthroughs have been made in the height extension of buildings using technological innovations that include creative new damping approaches and structural analysis technologies. This innovative system would use new materials, such as ultra-high tensile-strength steel, a new disaster prevention system, and a fully automated construction method. The Millennium Tower plan suggests a future architectural image which overcomes conventional technological limitations on height. The Millennium Tower was named in the hope of achieving a first-rate structure with a longer life-span than the Century Tower in Tokyo.[3]

Throughout the world, there have been dreams of creating enormous, monumental buildings. Japan's super high-rise city plan, however, does not strive to set new records with the height of its buildings. It is designed to reinforce the diverse functions concentrated in existing cities and to provide efficient and comfortable high-density urban spaces.

With this view in mind, the megalopolis of Tokyo, which continues to grow despite the deepening problems relating to its high concentration of people and buildings, may be regarded as the site best suited for creating the super high-rise building city.

Basic Concept of the Millennium Tower

The Millennium Tower is designed to rise 150 stories to a height of 600 m above ground (a total of 800 m including the radio tower). Its effective total floor space of approximately 1 km^2 (1,000,000 m^2) would allow enough space to accommodate the entire central area of a large city. For this reason, a single building would be referred to as a city—a "building city" (Fig. IV-D3). The structure would include commercial, cultural and sports facilities, in addition to residences and offices. It would also contain public infrastructure facilities, such as an electric power substation and a sewage treatment plant, thus providing all the facilities necessary for a city.

A linear motor elevator, which would stop at a Sky Center every thirty stories, is designed to provide the main means of transportation for this architectural city. Each Sky Center, serving as a transfer connection point for local elevators,

Figure IV-D3 Millennium Tower

would also function as a public floor with a large open space in which commercial, cultural, and public service facilities would be concentrated. This story would connect to an evacuation shelter for emergency cases such as fire. About thirty upper stories, centering around this floor, would form a zone for daily activities as well as for disaster relief and evacuation (Fig. IV-D4).

Regarding resistance to earthquakes and wind, Obayashi Corporation has planned the building to outlast powerful earthquakes in a recurrence interval of 200 years and unusually powerful typhoons in a recurrence interval of 500 years. Therefore, much stricter criteria were used than conventional standards demand for the structural design of high-rise buildings in Japan.

Containment of the City

The Millennium Tower would form a compact city in itself and allow highly efficient urban infrastructures such as efficient recycling systems for waste-water and waste heat within the building, systems for waste collection and central air conditioning systems. Increasing the height of a building to 800 m will naturally lead to greater building costs and to a smaller floor area rental. The Millennium Tower, however, would offer the amenities of an urban infrastructure by providing mass transit and a public plaza, supported by the public investment in our conventional cities.

If the Sky Centers were viewed as public spaces and the linear motor elevators as a form of mass transportation, then the local tax levied on the inhabitants and businesses occupying the building could be assessed in advance to help finance the construction expenses, just as tax increment financing is performed in the U.S.A. If such public investment were to be used, the construction cost per floor area rental unit would become competitive with the current rent levels in central Tokyo.

The architectural design for the Millennium Tower was executed by Sir Norman Foster, a British architect hired by Obayashi Corporation. The study of the interior systems, the structural design, the equipment plan and the construction methods were prepared by the engineering team at Obayashi Corporation.

CONTINENTAL SHELF: UNDERGROUND INDUSTRIAL GEO-CITY CONSTRUCTION PLAN

The potential practical use of underground areas has recently entered a new era. More favorable approaches are currently designed to create an underground world. This endeavor represents a step beyond the mere underground space development to complement above ground level land-use. Its purpose is to achieve a future city that suits human needs. One active approach is to make use of the "great depth underground."[4]

The idea of this great depth underground was developed into the "Ungrado Plan" (Underground Golden City) by the late Mr. Shinzauo Koshimura.[5] The

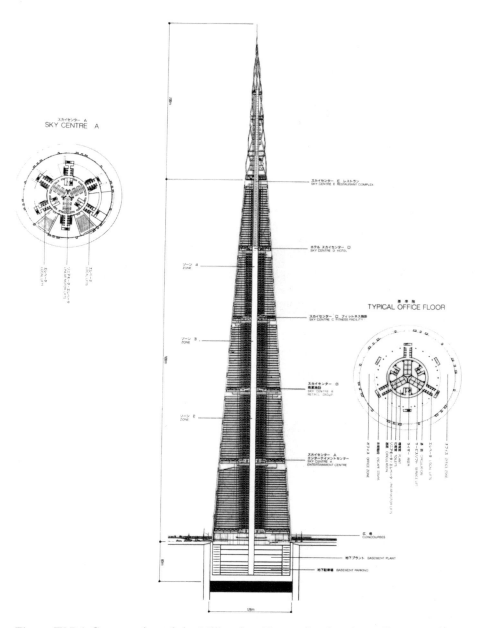

Figure IV-D4 Cross-section of the Millennium Tower showing the radio tower above 600 m and the five Sky Centers up to 600 m: (A) entertainment; (B) retail group; (C) fitness facility; (D) hotel; and (E) restaurant complex. The total height of the Millennium Tower City is 800 m.

name *Ungrado* is derived from combining the words *underground* with the name of the fabled city of gold, *El Dorado*, whose discovery was the quest of many great explorers.[6] The Ungrado plan proposes to accomplish the intensive use of underground space that would be many times greater than that of the above ground level. Such a development would be achieved by building a group of large-scale underground factories on the continental shelf. The plan is extremely attractive to Japan, particularly as it is surrounded by ocean.

Drawing on Mr. Koshimura's proposal for an underground industrial city, this chapter discusses the meaning of and possible methods for the construction of a large-scale group of factories underground on the continental shelf.

Basic Concept of the Industrial Geo-City

The basic concept of the industrial geo-city may be summarized as follows. The great depths directly beneath the central city area, which now attracts the attention of the industry, could very likely be used as a public space to locate infrastructure which will improve urban functions. In contrast, the underground area on the continental shelf would be designed to create a new dimension of an underground industrial zone. According to the plan, production facilities, such as the factories now scattered throughout the central area of the city, would be moved into tunnels built specifically for factories and situated in the underground area of the continental shelf. These would be unmanned factories operated by automated equipment, such as computers and robots.

The land in central Tokyo, vacated by production facilities, could be used for green spaces, residential areas, office sites and roads, thus improving the living environment aboveground. Such a reorganization can be summarized as the aboveground for humans, the urban underground for infrastructures, and the continental shelf for factories.

Outline of Factory Tunnels and Service Tunnels

Each of the factory tunnels placed at the center of the industrial geo-city would have an oval shape with a cross-section that is 30 m high and 20 m wide at the base (Fig. IV-D5). The scale of the cross-section was determined by considering the efficiency of the underground factory as a production space, as well as sufficient competence and safety in construction. The length of the factory tunnels would be 15 km, which is equal to the length of the site and the tunnels would be spaced at 50 m intervals. Thus, the number of factory tunnels per layer would be 101—a total of 505 in all of Ungrado—which would create a large group of underground factories. As described here, the inside of the factory tunnel would accommodate the production line and space for storing materials at the center; another sector in the upper area of the tunnel would house the network of distribution pipes, traffic, and a disaster refuge; and a third sector located in the lower and side areas of the tunnel would encompass the water supply and drainage, air supply and exhaust and electric power utility.

To support the functions of the factory tunnels, service tunnels would be provided at 1.2 km intervals and connect directly to the factory tunnels. The service tunnels would include vertical shafts to allow transfer of incoming and

Figure IV-D5 Cross-section of factory and service tunnels (*Quarterly Obayashi* 1990, 32, pp. 4–5)

outgoing materials, to supply energy, to feed and drain water for production or heat treatment, and to ventilate the air.

Construction Plan for the Industrial Geo-City

The site area for the tunnels would be 150 km^2 and separated into Zones A and B. The group of tunnels in Zone A, measuring 75 km^2, would consist of three layers and the group of tunnels remaining in Zone B of two layers (Fig. IV-D6).

The tunnels could be excavated using the most current technologies. Obayashi Corporation led an examination of the construction plan based on available technology and concluded that a thirty-year construction period would be required (Fig. IV-D7). This would include five years for the geological and environmental survey and the preliminary work for the construction as well as twenty-five years for the actual tunnel excavation. The construction period and building time could be shortened if robotization and further advances in high technology are acquired and implemented.

CONCLUSION

Three new city concepts, the artificial platform city, the super high-rise building city and the great depth underground city, could almost entirely be achieved using the currently available construction technology. Furthermore, the technological problems that remain unsolved today are expected to be completely solved by the beginning of the twenty-first century.

Figure IV-D6 Industrial geo-space city (*Quarterly Obayashi* 1990, 32, p. 8)

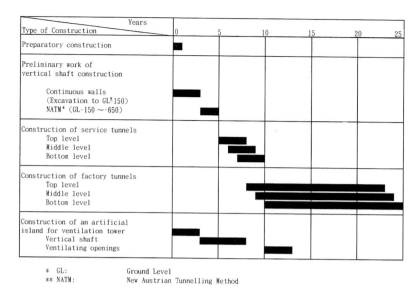

Figure IV-D7 Construction schedule for industrial geo-city (*Quarterly Obayashi* 1990, 32, p. 17)

The three models represent the ultimate application of high technology to establish unprecedented city forms. These highly planned and high-density land-use city forms would promote the efficient usage of space and are likely to benefit the global environment. Yet the potential impact on the existing society is unpredictable. Side-effects of the new concepts should be studied extremely carefully and the cost and advantages should be analyzed by various means. The planning process of these enormous urban projects is critical in order to obtain acceptable results for society.

The authors would be pleased if the high-performance compact city models, equipped with advanced equipment, would stimulate a debate across a broad range of disciplines which were to include discussions on the global environment, energy conservation, lifestyle and the economic efficiency. This summary of concepts has also been offered in the hope that these discussions will lead to the creation of a paradigm for new urban development.

NOTES

1. Earth 1989. *Quarterly Obayashi* 28; January 4–7.
2. Aeropolis 1989. *Quarterly Obayashi* 30; August 2–23.
3. *Telegraph Magazine* 1993. May 15, 21–25.
4. Continental Shelf 1990. *Quarterly Obayashi* 32; March 4–17.
5. Shinzabrou K. 1986. *Method to Make Japanese Land Ten Times Bigger* Tokyo: Shunju-sha Publishers, 43–72.

6. *Webster's Third New International Dictionary* 1986. Springfield, MA: Merriam-Webster. Defines *El Dorado* as a fabulously wealthy city or country that sixteenth-century explorers thought existed in South America.

BIBLIOGRAPHY

1. Earth 1989. *Quarterly Obayashi* 28; January.
2. Continental Shelf 1990. *Quarterly Obayashi* 32; March.

E Nodal System Planning for Medium-size Cities

Yoshiro Watanabe

INTRODUCTION

In this paper, the concept of a nodal system of city planning is used to deal with a medium-size city zone that would be located between a large and a small city. This medium-size city would serve as a transitional setting between the large and small city and would combine the assets of both types of areas.

In the study of a nodal system of city planning (or the medium-size city zone), three points should be considered: first, the social growth and change that is prevalent in contemporary Japan which affects urban development; second, the ideal urban structure that must be established with a long-range objective in mind; third, the choice of a suitable location which would meet the needs of the industrial, public and academic sectors as well as the population of residents.

With Japan's increasing prosperity, these themes have been the central focus of the country's efforts to increase the quality of life. Economic growth should positively influence social conditions and an improved living environment should, one day, reflect the fusion of international relations and technological innovations which are occurring in Japan. As part of the grand master plan of the nodal city as a system, the continuous planning development and ideal location for construction should actively be pursued. It would be desirable to create a parallel city system to achieve the ideal urban structure. The chosen operating methods are an attempt to keep an equilibrium between urban structures by selecting suitable developmental alternatives.

At this point in time, Japan must find other avenues to increase the quality of life which will outlast the changes. In this chapter key points which are relevant to nodal city system planning will be discussed, indicating which urban areas are suitable for a nodal system plan, providing several suggestions for methods that could be used to break away from the conventional concept of the nodal system and lastly, it will examine the common notion of nodal systems and suggest arguments to support the idea of improving the nodal system concept of city planning.

THE CASE FOR NODAL SYSTEMS

Features of the Nodal System

Many cities of different sizes are linked to the current information network, but not all cities have equal access to it. Some cities lack the necessary technology to take advantage of computer intelligence. The nodal system is dependent upon modern telecommunication networks, however, at present, there is an inequitable distribution of quality service which would impair the success of such a system. Large metropolitan areas have greater and better telecommunication services in comparison to small cities which have inferior ones. Additionally, discrepancies in the cost of living and average yearly incomes determine the location for developing a large city. With the advent of the nodal system, it is expected that industry and the social environment will improve, causing a more equal distribution of average yearly earnings and hence an increase in the likelihood of community access to quality telecommunication services.

The sphere, scale, location and character of nodal systems can be formed between a metropolitan city and a smaller, local city with a closed hinterland. The nodal system would serve the various needs of an urban population, yet be located close to a small city to retain the character of a town. The site of the intermediate city will depend on the integration of geographical, historical, natural and human conditions.

Furthermore, a means of transportation is an essential part of daily life and the nodal system concept has become a more pressing solution. Limited revenue in the small city makes it difficult to operate large public transportation systems, such as light railway transit (LRT). Accordingly, citizens of the small city must use their private cars for multiple purposes. The possibility of a public transportation system for small cities increases with the notions of the nodal system and city mergers since these efforts would increase revenue and traffic volume. It can be said, then, that the nodal system is becoming a necessity.

Problems with Large Cities

Tokyo has access to raw information through the immediate contact with the central government which serves as a useful resource of information. On the other hand, although Tokyo is also the strongest and most important urban area in Japan, it suffers from the various problems that accompany large cities with a diversity of functions.

The extent of information available to a cosmopolitan city influences business and commercial activities. One outcome is that land prices are stabilized by increasing the quantity of land area for businesses. Company employees working in the central business district (CBD) are obliged to commute long distances from their homes to their places of work. Under these circumstances, the notion of "my hometown" barely exists within such a city except during long weekends and holidays. Due to the commuting problem, workers have little free time to spare for leisure activities and invest many exhausting hours commuting to work. It often happens that, when employees retire at an early age, they experience a lonely life and feel unneeded by society as they age.

To correct these difficulties that exist in metropolitan areas, it has been proposed to develop an independent town as a "bedroom community" closer to the places of employment. This would provide people relief from the stress of commuting to a metropolis. The new town would serve as a parallel city that would be interconnected with the greater "mother city" in many ways.

To decrease commuting time, a large area should be designated as the site for a parallel city where the more affluent can build a second residence or weekend home, away from the core of the city. Hills and slopes should be investigated as possible sites for these weekend homes and recreation facilities which could be the future answer to the land shortage problems of Japanese society.

Endeavors and Tasks of Small Cities

The regional hub of the city, i.e. the downtown area or CBD, is its administrative core and the seat of the prefectural government. For an industrial city, factories and high technology are the source of growth and power, but small cities, which lack the CBD are stagnant. Despite their lack of business and government, these small municipalities endure because their residents live there out of nostalgia, the love for tradition and because they are less accepting of change. In small cities, there is an abundance of traditional culture. It is important to make the traditional culture a stable element for the younger generations who will inherit it and be responsible for passing it on to posterity. It may be necessary to leave the large city and return to the "bedroom" city to keep the traditional culture alive. In general, the automobile society has threatened the existence of the small city. Networks of express highways have allowed new shopping malls to be built on the outskirts of the cities which compete with the shopping areas of small cities. This development has caused small cities to lose a part of their economic base.

To relieve these ensuing financial problems, an examination of crop harvests, the location of high technology, and residential environmental considerations would be crucial in the effort to strengthen the durability of these towns. Residential space is an important indicator of affluence in modern society. The infrastructure and social amenities such as roads, parks and sewage facilities are more advanced than the ones found in larger cities while the industrial sector lags behind. To solve this problem, it is important to design a master plan for the small city that would also entice industries, increase employment and develop attractive cultural centers with shopping and other facilities.

Future of Cities in the Middle Zone

The business sector of a large city can be economically prosperous due to the influence of the global market, while at the same time, the residential sector can be poverty-stricken and feature crowded and unacceptable living conditions. Meanwhile, the small city faces the opposite circumstances of an abject business district and an affluent residential sector. It can be said that the cities in the middle zone between the large city and the small city are susceptible to all of the deficiencies and assets of both size cities.

The medium-size city would not serve as a satellite city to either the small or large city but would be an independent, complex city. With the recent development of a high-speed transportation service, this middle region could have greater and easier access to the hub or central business district of a large city and would be situated 70–100 km from the downtown area.

The key benefit would be that persons with knowledge about the industry could transfer information from the large city to the medium-size city and could carry the traditional culture of a small city to this area as well. Harmony could exist between the industrial workers, local people and new arrivals from the large cities. As its inhabitants gradually achieved harmony, the town would mature and grow into a central city. Therefore, it is desirable that the community core be made up of knowledgeable people to transfer their research, development functions and capabilities to the new setting. In a chain of community facilities, experts could contribute to this district as they develop a broader view of life and further their knowledge.

METHODS OF DEVELOPING CITIES IN THE MIDDLE ZONE

Popular Method

The objective for uniform growth of national land is to make a balance of service communication amenities provided throughout Japan. It is important to establish an urban system where communication services flow from the large to the small city and where cultural traditions flow in the opposite direction. A midway point, i.e. the medium-size city, could facilitate the exchange of these benefits. Therefore, it is recommended to establish an urban system at a central point, the medium-size city, whereby the merits of the large city could be passed to the small city and vice versa.

The concepts of "hometown" and leisure should be merged, not only for business to prosper, but also to restore humane conditions and to reestablish a "common consciousness" of the large city. As the first step, it is proposed that a community office be established and a telecommunication network be installed. Second, an international and comprehensive environment should become the key feature of this new area. The center management function and administrative function in the central business district would be transferred to the nodal cities. Thus, a nodal system would be created with an independent business function. In other words, both the initial stages and the core city planning, which would include an international airport, would evolve into a comprehensive environment, i.e. a residential environment balanced with the industrial environment.

Third, it is suggested that educated people with advanced training (educational, cultural and medical knowledge) become a part of the new environment. This proposal would create a higher quality of life with access to services. At the same time, such a comfortable and beautiful urban space system, with a core of high class urban functions, would provide a base for the next century and create a beautiful place to be nourished and maintained.

Metempsychosis Method

By using the middle position between the large and small city to promote growth, welfare and an attractive environment for cities, development should be pursued coupled with metempsychosis. Metempsychosis is a theory of systematic method with origins in Buddhism. The theory is that the cause produces the effect, then the effect produces a more fruitful effect by effort. It could be applied in the development and improvement of the nodal system. If the developers strive for developing an effective point and arrive at a suitable level, but are not satisfied with the outcome, they will strive for a higher target level. If this method is applied, the development is promising. This concept coupled with parallel management could be carried out effectively in five stages.

During the first stage, it would be expected that the accepted approach to profitable urban systems would improve the conditions to create a stronger industrial sites. The improvement of the accepted approach would necessitate serious project management and development. This in turn would require a large investment, land, and land readjustment in order to put district planning to practical use.

For the second stage, Japan could supplement the hub with amenities to bring it to a healthier and more attractive level for the individual. A healthier level means the satisfaction with urban life and the quality of services, even though the city may not be esthetically beautiful. However, the city's appeal would derive from the individuality of its region, the natural environment, its history and especially from its provision of an urban infrastructure with open space.

In the third stage, the cultural and informational exchanges between people are expected to influence the activities of the hub and its environment. Affluent people, who could afford two homes, could live in their own homes during the week and their second residence on weekends. This might encourage the less affluent to move to the medium-size city and to live there all week long. National or international culture and technology could be transferred to the core city and a new culture and technology would be created.

In the fourth stage, the newcomers would be expected to collaborate with the local inhabitants of the region who were willing to establish the urban community. The area would be full of useful resources with information for progress at the national and regional scale. The new state-of-the-art technology based on research and development would further the society.

The fifth and last stage, would be to create new jobs in neighborhoods near both residences and places of work. A more suitable job location will have the added value of providing commuting workers with more leisure time. Through the system of metempsychosis, a movement towards a higher level of the total area of the nodal city system would facilitate a wealthy and happy life. The citizens would enjoy a sophisticated urban environment as part of their new residential surrounding, with satisfying and useful information to reflect and reward their abilities.

CHANGING THE URBAN SYSTEM

From a Closed Urban Structure to an Open Urban Structure

By developing the midway region, expanding the large city to the local region and transferring the traditional culture of the local region to the large city, uniform service on the national level would be promoted. A symbiosis of the large city and the local, small city would correspond with the more open urban system structure.

The growth of an automated society, construction of express highway networks, spread of single family residential lots, along with an increase in the core function of cities beyond their current administrative boundary, would make up the background of the open urban structure. This transition should not be met with a rush into competing conditions between cities so that the weaker city becomes absorbed by the stronger city. Each city in the urban system should be planned to retain its own strengths but also to partially change some aspects of its structure to accomplish a dynamic and balanced relationship.

Changing from a Quiet to a Dynamic Balanced Relation

To achieve a satisfactory balance of proportional change by both the large and small cities, plans for this dynamic process must be selected to regulate and project consequences for the short-, medium-, and long-term transition. It is important to choose regulations that will protect and develop the projected comprehensive environment of the plan.

In the meantime, caution must be exercised when soliciting the consensus of the community by planning parallel and alternative systems which will further the objective of the master plan. Conventional ways of thinking should be abandoned, so this transition can be made from a practical standpoint. In addition, it is important that Japan put these plans into practice without feeling critical or self-conscious but remain confident as the leader of a new concept of urban construction. The coordination between the short-term and the long-term conditions could achieve a balanced relationship if a public policy is enforced by the Japanese people to reach these master plan goals. Such policies might include the establishment of environmental rules or the strengthening of social support networks, possibly through the work of interest groups.

From Planning to Construction

In urban construction, it is important that appropriate social needs for construction match the quality of comprehensive physical planning. People ask for the chance to make their fortune, to improve their quality of life and to enhance their surrounding environment. Therefore, it is natural to create a system which balances planning, construction and management, and which considers new technology, methods and budget sizes. It is crucial that the resulting infrastructure be enjoyed throughout the centuries to come.

At present, self-governing groups are examining the construction and maintenance of regional facilities, which are necessary features of shared living. The new system, deriving from the concept of individuality, would be a special system with decentralized authority. Thus, it may be worthwhile that the system of independent cities, yet with joint facilities to the large cities, be based on extensive physical planning and an environmentally sound policy.

Management and Harmony of the Various Units of Urban Areas

The number of urban structures are extensive. It is the conglomeration of individual urban units which produces the strength and power of a city. For example, the foundation of residential life depends on housing. Yet all urban functions are maintained through the complete and interdependent performance of cultural infrastructure as well as social and health services. It is then necessary to incorporate the services which will suit the needs of daily life. These services should be balanced taking into account all facets of life, i.e. natural, residential and industrial environments.

To organize the layout of a city design, the planners will have to determine the needs and constraints of the local area. To pinpoint which system to use, it may be recommended to employ the K.J. valuation method, a popular view of candidly evaluating the voices of the people. Then, between the total unit of the urban area, a transitory system would be transferred consciously from one spectrum of the society to another in order to make the transition occur smoothly. As a result, city planning and construction would be implemented without any prejudice or sacrifice.

Change from Horizontal to Vertical Pattern

Throughout history, when cities evolved into metropolitan areas with one core business center, negative phenomena resulted. As a consequence of the emergence of a concentration of various information networks, workers had to make long commuting trips, their leisure time diminished and rising land prices pushed residents to the outskirts of town.

It is now necessary to reorganize cities by moving more offices to the suburbs and locating residences and places of work nearby. It will take approximately fifty years to reach the stage of development where the core cities can be divided into shares of a big city. For the transitory period, people would have to accustom themselves to life without mass transit systems.

Accordingly, Japan should seek out a solution using both the vertical and horizontal patterns. To work out a countermeasure to the existing situation, the zoning of residential, business or industrial space is feasible vertically, with the new frontier of underground space and the reclamation of land and hills to be joined in a three-dimensional arrangement. This would be created by geotectural methods and flying replotting.

BASIC THINKING

For insight into the four kinds of changes for urban systems structure, it is important to satisfy the three levels described below.

First, space should be reserved for the expansion of the future urban area and the segregated use of land. It is important that the urban area double as a residential neighborhood and that sound city planning eliminate confusion and traffic congestion.

Second, a stable, balanced growth of the urban area and improvements in the quality of the urban environment should be promoted. Citizens would take pride in their town. This attitude would become widespread among people in the existing living environment.

Third, it is important to recognize that the urban system is a kind of socially-integrated society where partnerships create shared living. It is desirable that the urban system create future partnerships which would not compete with the other but recognize the characteristics of each individual. The services to citizens must not be monopolized or dominated for individual control.

Basic Pattern of Nodal Systems

Of the nodal systems, the ladder pattern is one possibility. The ladder pattern is a balance of working space with residential, recreational and educational spaces which would be accessible regionally and nationally. This ladder pattern would have express highways, a main railway, coastal ferries, an airport and alternative transportation networks to ensure the flow of people and goods (Fig. IV-E1A).

A second system, the ring pattern, consists of a large central space. Zones comprised of a lake, bay and mountains could offer people in crowded city sections a free and unrestricted area to enjoy nature and open space. For example, it could be most desirable to introduce a green area for every 500,000 citizens (Fig. IV-E1 B).

A third style, the twin-cluster pattern, could also be feasible. This pattern accommodates larger core cities and places smaller cities in a midway belt. This pattern is not the ordinary arrangement of the central business district in the "mother core city." It is expected that the "father" or "mother core city" would

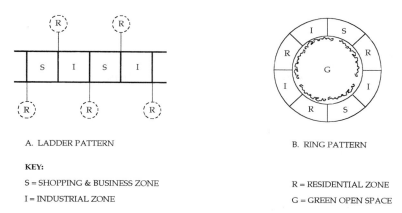

A. LADDER PATTERN   B. RING PATTERN

KEY:

S = SHOPPING & BUSINESS ZONE   R = RESIDENTIAL ZONE

I = INDUSTRIAL ZONE   G = GREEN OPEN SPACE

Figure IV-E1 Ladder pattern (A) and ring pattern (B)

be independent of the small town and would be influenced by high technological industry and have connecting commuting routes to these regions through a complex traffic system (i.e. road, LRT) (Fig. IV-E2). This traffic system would set up the living structure for potential expansion in the future.

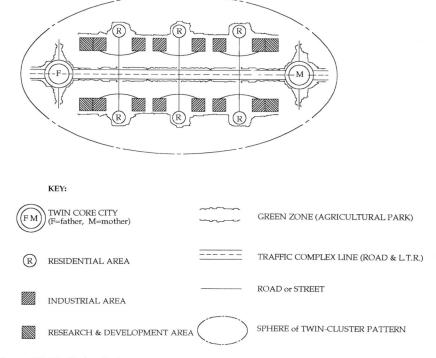

KEY:

(F M) TWIN CORE CITY
         (F=father, M=mother)   GREEN ZONE (AGRICULTURAL PARK)

(R)   RESIDENTIAL AREA   TRAFFIC COMPLEX LINE (ROAD & L.T.R.)

      INDUSTRIAL AREA   ROAD or STREET

      RESEARCH & DEVELOPMENT AREA   SPHERE of TWIN-CLUSTER PATTERN

Figure IV-E2 Twin-cluster pattern

CONCLUSION

With the aging of the population, the younger generation is shrinking in numbers. Furthermore, additional urban construction cannot be achieved without the redevelopment of built-up areas. In addition, low income wage earners from abroad are predicted to immigrate to Japan. All these factors will increase the problems of the urban environment.

Considering the changes expected in urban areas, the role of the medium-size city, the influence of experts, and the importance of joined urban patterns such as the ladder, ring and twin-cluster systems will be necessary methods of future progress and reform. This development will take place in Japan when the establishment of a nodal city system plan is controlled systematically on a large-scale as a new frontier.

BIBLIOGRAPHY

1. Institute of City Planning in Japan 1987. *Way to Amenity City*. Tokyo: GYOSEI.
2. Society for Core Cities 1989. *Community Office 2005*. Tokyo: PHP.
3. Watanabe, Y. 1991. *Story of New Frontiers*. Tokyo: Gihodo.
4. Watanabe, Y. 1990. Tunneling and underground space technology. *Deep Underground Space—the New Frontier. I.T.A*. New York: Pergamon Press.

Final Conclusion

The aim of the compilation of these chapters, written by diversified professionals and practitioners, was ultimately to produce an overall understanding of the nature and the distinction of the Japanese urban environment. In the belief that no single person can write such a book in its comprehensiveness, a team was formed to discuss this subject. We chose the challenging alternative of selecting, what we believe, are highly qualified Japanese intellectuals to research and write their findings about the distinction of the Japanese urban environment for the English-speaking reader.

Due to its interdisciplinary and comprehensive treatment, this book is unique. The key words of this compilation's theme are the urban environmental evolution, cityscape and socio-culturescape. It is the interaction process between these three elements and its outcome which constitute the book's theme. More specifically, the theme of this book describes how the evolution process of the Japanese urban environment takes place at two levels, the physical cityscape and the socio-culturescape. This development has been occurring during an era of rapid changes in technology when, throughout the evolution process, the shift from idealistic to materialistic values may pose a threat to the urban environment. The issue of confrontation between an indigenous socio-culturally preserved society with modern, materialistic norms not only creates a cultural shock but also has its impact on social values related to all levels of society. The Japanese have a traditional society which has been interwoven with definite and clear rules of behavior between the individual and the family, community, and other circles, which all hold society together. These ethics are certainly brought into the work place and set the tone for interactive relations there. In short, Japanese society contains spiritual as well as idealistic values. These spiritual values and their strong association with the Japanese ancestors were often expressed in the traditional Japanese architecture such as religious temples and shrines. Until now, this socio-cultural expression continues to be preserved within the Japanese urban environment and to a large extent, Japanese society still refuses to replace these socio-cultural norms by their Western counterpart. As for the Japanese socio-culturescape within the evolution of the urban environment, the Japanese have continuously preserved their culture within the invisible city.

At the cityscape level, the interaction between the traditional Japanese and the Western urban environment following World War II was easier than on the previously discussed level. At the outset, much of the architectural cityscape of today's Japanese cities visually resembles the physical Western urban environment. The Japanese proudly value their culture very highly and this feeling is mixed with a sense of superiority to Western culture. The pride of their native Japanese culture (behavioral norms and rules, standards, etc.) is so strong that abandoning it is almost unthinkable even among the young generation today. It is this socio-cultural distinction which preserves urban Japan's uniqueness. It seems to us, the Japanese justifiably perceive themselves superior to the West on the level of the socio-culturescape of their urban environment. Since their early interaction (during the Edo era, 1603–1868) with the West and until some decades of the post-World War II era, the Japanese felt technologically inferior to the West and consequently have welcomed Western technology on all levels including the visual, physical cityscape. The Western physical urbanscape features effective functions (escalators, elevators, building materials, etc.), which the Japanese deemed so practical that they adapted them to fit their own system. This process was the root of the sense of equality to the West and eliminated the previously prevalent feeling of technological inferiority. In short, modern Japanese architecture still imitates the Western cityscape to a large extent despite the fact that the development of Japanese technology has become self-confident and independent from Western tutelage. This explains why much of the Japanese cityscape is similar, yet not identical, to the Western city and why the Japanese architecture is not dominant within the urban environment excluding the religious temples and shrines. A similar process, with some variations, has been taking place in many developing countries since World War II.

This compilation focuses on diversified subjects which have formed the core of the book and its discussion. The subjects center around the complexity of the urban environment, which include human and socio-cultural aspects, the urban landscape, the impact of the West on the Japanese cityscape, values and environment, the influence of history on the present urban environment, and, last but not least, the future prospect of the Japanese urbanscape. We need to establish a discussion of the book's broader context and to outline the future development of those very issues.

Social and human dynamics in Japanese society differ from those in Western society. This difference should be taken into account when formulating our predictions for and expectation of Japan in comparison with the West; otherwise, we would misunderstand and misjudge Japanese society. First, we can generally state that the pace of social changes, as to be expected, is slower among Japanese society than our Western counterparts. Second, Japanese society, as a community, lives daily by strict rules and regulations. Thus, we can predict the humanscape for the foreseeable future relatively easily. Individual Japanese tend not to break rules and norms or work against them, but rather to conform with them. It is this ethic which significantly contributes to the urban environment of Japan. Third, Japan passed the age of the cross-cultural shock shortly after World War II. It is now at the state of maturity, or as we may call it, the post-cultural shock. In a sense, from this point of view, an equilibrium between the past and modern norms was created within the urban social environment. It is this author's prediction that this equilibrium will undergo some minor, but barely noticeable, changes in the foreseeable future. The fourth and most important issue, is the recent involvement of the Japanese economy with the international community which has led to the increasing interaction between the average Japanese person with the global community through extensive Japanese tourism throughout the world. In addition, there are a reasonable number of Japanese who have been migrating from Japanese cities to countries like Australia, Canada and the U.S.A. Finally, within the realm of social changes, the introduction of foreign laborers, who form enclaves within the urban environment of Japan, is another crucial event. The rise of new ethnic minorities of foreigners within Japan is a very recent phenomenon and it is our prediction that it will continue in the future. Although these minorities are physically settled within the Japanese cities and form a part of the humanscape of the city, they are far from being integrated into the Japanese society. There are and will continue to be, social problems between these two groups of city dwellers. As has happened in other countries in similar situations, a process of alienation has taken place among the two factions of the urban society, the minorities and the Japanese.

Economically, urban Japan has entered the pace of the dynamic and extensive changes since the Japanese adopted the Western economical system. Pragmatically, the Japanese have realized by now that these changes are an extremely positive development. Today, Japan is among the forerunners of the international economy and is becoming more and more involved with world politics. The Japanese entered the international finance market and trade exchange after a period of industrial development and modernization of the urban infrastructure to suit those changes. The city landscape underwent many changes in its physical dimensions, such as modern high-rise buildings and sky-rocketing urban land values, as well as the extensive use of belowground space with highly sophisticated, subterranean shopping centers. In addition, Western-style advertising dominates today's Japanese urban environment and this will most likely continue in the future. Most importantly, the development of express highways throughout the city will further accelerate urban growth. This will bring about a further increase in privately-owned cars on the road as well as the near disappearance of the waterfronts which used to dominate the Japanese urban environment. With the rise of the standard of living and increase in consumption, the Japanese cityscape will be more and more dominated by the Western style.

Socio-cultural Japanese norms contribute positively to the urban environment in Japan. Some of those norms usually impress the foreign observer and are related to the previous discussion in this book concerning the socio-cultural issues. For example, it is commonly understood that individuals have a set of rules and regulations of behaviors which they are expected to follow in their public lives and when interacting with others. The outsider views Japanese etiquette as the core of these rules while, in reality, it is merely their manifestation. These and other unwritten norms provide the individual and the community with clear expectations for the individuals behavior, particulary within the context of society as a whole. This pattern provides a sense of contentment in all parties involved since there is little space for unpleasant surprises. Japanese norms also set the tone for relations between individuals, the community of the work place and the employer. For example, it is the understanding of all the parties involved that when a given company offers a position to a candidate and the individual accepts it, both commonly enter a mutual life-long commitment. In addition, the company takes care of the social welfare of the individual, including recreation and family leisure. The individual is expected to be dedicated to the job beyond regular hours, to be an integrative member of a team and to spend some evenings and weekends with their colleagues. While Westerners are commonly used to individualistic/materialistic values, Japanese norms are based on the interest of the community. All these norms certainly provide a feeling of security for the individual and contentment to all parties involved. We believe that these behavioral norms are a by-product of the Japanese culture. As the Japanese urban society increases its interaction with the Western urban environment, these norms are subject to erosion and, therefore, to change. The recent trend is that a number of individuals move to a new work place and abandon the previous life-long job commitment.

The Japanese are becoming increasingly concerned about the physical part of their urban environment and less about its social aspect. The partly physical deterioration of the contemporary urban environment results from pollution, noise, overcrowding and traffic congestion. The physical environment introduces a threat to the health and safety of the Japanese city dweller. In the past, the Japanese were mostly concerned about two kinds of disasters; fires and earthquakes. Over time, the former has been diminished significantly since the Japanese shifted the building materials of their cities from wood to mostly noncombustible materials such as concrete and metals. Although significant research has been conducted by the Japanese on the characteristics of earthquakes and the means for protection, earthquakes still constitute a serious threat to the city. However, construction rules and regulations are enforced firmly.

Finally, the case of the Japanese urban environment in transition is a valuable model for developing as well as developed countries. Most developing countries in Asia and Africa, which have obtained their independence in the post-World War II era, have been going through a similar process of urban change and have been struggling with some similar, but not identical, urban problems. Their cities have become congested with rural-to-urban migrants and traffic which has resulted in a speedy urban expansion, an overloaded infrastructure, social changes and financial crises. Developed countries, under different circumstances but with similar problems, have also received a large number of rural-to-urban migrants and, in addition, an increased wave of immigrants from abroad; this situation creates a cross-cultural shock (e.g. as seen in Canada, U.S.A., U.K., France, Germany, and Australia). The modern changes have caused cultural confrontation, strong alienation (especially with imported laborers) as well as social welfare problems and associated issues in the metropolitan areas. In addition, developed countries, such as the U.S.A., have been facing socio-ethnic confrontation within the large urban centers which has led to considerable changes in the urban environment. It seems to us that Japan was able to handle these and other issues such as homelessness and poverty, adequately well with little or any social explosion and still retains an overall positive urban environment. Overall, the Japanese feel confident about the norms and standards of their social urban environment, since the safety and cleanliness of their cities is superior to most of the Western ones. The mission of this book is to introduce the Japanese example to policy makers, urban designers, economists and sociologists of the developed and developing countries.

G.S.G.

Japanese Urban Environment Bibliography (1990 and After)*

1. Allinson, G. D. 1997. *Japan's Postwar History.* New York: Cornell University Press.
2. Allinson, G. D. and Sone, Y. eds 1993. *Political Dynamics in Contemporary Japan.* New York: Cornell University Press.
3. Tadao, A. 1995. The city as public domain (in Japanese and English). *A + U: Architecture and Urbanism* no. 4. 295; April 2–5.
4. Applbaum, K. 1996. Endurance of neighborhood associations in a Japanese commuter city. *Urban Anthropology* 25; no. 1, 1–39.
5. Arakawa + Madeline Gins: reversible destiny city, Tokyo Bay 1995. *Architectural Design* 65, nos 1–2; November, December, 86–89.
6. Arnold, S. E. 1991. *The Information Factory: A Profile of Japan's Information and Database Infrastructure.* U.K.: Infonortics.
7. Ashkenazi, M. 1991. Traditional small group organization and cultural modeling in modern Japan. *Human Organization* 50; no. 4; 385–392.
8. Ben-Ari, E. 1995. Contested identities and models of action in Japanese discourses of place-making. *Anthropological Quarterly* 68; no. 4; 203–218.
9. Ben-Ari, E. 1992. Uniqueness, typicality, and appraisal: a village of the past in contemporary Japan. *Ethnos* 57; nos 3–4; 201–218.
10. Berque, A. 1996. Tokyo as an emblem of the city of tomorrow. *Architects' Journal* 203; no. 15; April 18, 31.
11. Berque, A. 1995. Da Chang'an a Kyoto e a Edo: capitali tra rappresentazione e realita (De Chang'an a Kyoto et á Edo: capitales entre representation et realite) (in Italian and French). *Spazio e societa* 18; no. 71; July–September, 106–113.
12. Bestor, T. C. 1989. *Neighborhood Tokyo.* Stanford, CA: Stanford University Press.
13. Brown, R. H. 1994. Economic, political, and cultural challenges of Japan's post-industrialization. *Culture, Politics, and Economic Growth: Experiences in East Asia.* 185–208.
14. Brown, T. 1993. The Kobe development campaign. *Urban Land* 52; no. 3; March, 42–43.
15. Buntrock, D. 1997. Tanpopo house. *Architectural Review* 201; no. 1199; January 64–67.
16. Bureau of Citizens and Cultural Affairs, Tokyo Metropolitan Government 1994. *A Hundred years of Tokyo City Planning.* Tokyo: Tokyo Metropolitan Government.
17. Castellano, A. 1996. La Millenium tower (Over 800 metres) (in Italian and English). *Arca* no. 100; January, 70–73.
18. Clark, G. 1991. *Japan: Landscape, Tradition, Season.* Rutland, VT: C. E. Tuttle.

*A few selected entries were published in the 1980s.

19. Coleman, S. 1991. *Family planning in Japanese society: Traditional Birth Control in a Modern Urban Culture*. Princeton, NJ: Princeton University Press.
20. Corporation Housing, Tokyo, Japan 1996. *World Architecture* no. 50; October, 122–125.
21. Cybriwsky, R. 1997. *Historical Dictionary of Tokyo. Historical Dictionaries of Cities of the World*, No. 1. Lanham, MD: Scarecrow Press.
22. Cybriwsky, R. 1991. *Tokyo, The Changing Profile of an Urban Giant.* Boston, MA: G. K. Hall.
23. Dearing, J. W. 1995. *Growing a Japanese Science City: Communication in Scientific Research.* New York: Routledge.
24. Development Assistance Committee 1996. *Development Co-operation Review Series*, No. 13. Paris: Organisation for Economic Co-operation and Development.
25. Doggart, C. 1994. *From Reconstruction to Development in Europe and Japan.* Washington, DC: World Bank.
26. Doubilet, S. 1989. The pied piper syndrome. *Progressive Architecture* 70; no. 10; October, 90–99.
27. David, M. D. 1993. *Exploring Osaka: Japan's Second City*. New York: Weatherhill.
28. Eccleston, B. 1989. *State and Society in Post-war Japan.* Cambridge: Polity Press.
29. Edgington, D. W. 1989. New strategies for technology development in Japanese cities and regions. *Town Planning Review* 60; no. 1; January 1–27.
30. Ehrentraut, A. W. 1995. Cultural nationalism, corporate interests and the production of architectural heritage in Japan. *Canadian Review of Sociology and Anthropology* 32; no. 2; 215–242.
31. Agency of Natural Resources and Energy 1990. *Energy in Japan: Facts and Figures.* Tokyo: Ministry of International Trade and Industry.
32. Government of Japan 1991. *Environment and Development: Japan's Experience and Achievement: Japan's National Report to UNCED 1992.* Tokyo: Government of Japan.
33. Friedman, D. 1988. *The Misunderstood Miracle: Industrial Development and Political Change in Japan.* New York: Cornell University Press.
34. Fu, C. W. and Heine, S. eds 1995. *Japan in Traditional and Postmodern Perspectives.* Albany, NY: State University of New York Press.
35. Fujimori, T., Yoshio, U. and Shusaku-sha 1995. Grass house (in English and Japanese). *Japan Architect* no. 24; 184–185.
36. Fujimoto, T. 1994. *Crime Problems in Japan.* Series of the Institute of Comparative Law in Japan, vol. 29. Tokyo: Institute of Comparative Law in Japan, Chuo University Press.
37. Fujita, K. and Hill, R. C. eds 1993. *Japanese Cities in the World Economy.* Philadelphia, PA: Temple University Press.
38. Fukami, H. 1992. *Japan's Energy Position. About Japan series*, Vol. 6. Tokyo: Foreign Press Center.
39. Fukuda, H. and Ojima, T. 1995. The residential environment left alone in "Ginza" Area (in Japanese with an English summary). *Nihon kenchiku Gakkai Keikakukei Ronbun Hokoku Shu* 476; no. 10; October 51–56.
40. Fukui, K. 1992. *Japanese National Railways Privatization Study: The Experience of Japan and Lessons for Developing Countries. World Bank Discussion Papers*, Vol. 172. Washington, DC: World Bank.
41. Funk, J. L. 1992. *The Teamwork Advantage: An Inside Look at Japanese Product and Technology Development*. Cambridge, MA: Productivity Press.
42. Gao, W. G. and Ojima, T. 1995. Study on planning an ecological city in Shitamachi,

Tokyo (in Japanese with an English summary). *Nihon Kenchiku Gakkai Keikakukei Ronbun Hokoku Shu* 472; no. 6; June 63–71.

43. Garon, S. 1994. Rethinking modernization and modernity in Japanese history: a focus on state–society relations. *Journal of Asian Studies* 53; no. 2; 346–366.

44. Geipel, K. 1994. Tradition der Kurzen Dauer: zur Frage der Identitat in der japanischen Stadtentwicklung (Tradition of short duration: concerning the question of identity in the Japanese urban development) (in German with English captions). *Arch Plus* no. 123; September 35–41.

45. Guth, C. 1996. *Art of Edo Japan: The Artist and the City 1615–1868.* New York: H. N. Abrams.

46. Hanayama, Y. 1986. *Land Markets and Land Policy in a Metropolitan Area: A Case Study of Tokyo.* Boston, MA: Oelgeschlager, Gunn & Hain in association with the Lincoln Institute of Land Policy.

47. Hasegawa, F. and the Shimizu Group FS eds. 1988. *Built by Japan: Competitive Strategies of the Japanese Construction Industry.* New York: Wiley.

48. Hasegawa, I. 1993. Architecture as another nature. *Columbia Documents of Architecture and Theory* 3; 139–147.

49. Hatsuda, T. and Suzuki, M. 1966. Historical study on architecture of the Tokyo Hoheikosho from the late Meiji era to the early Showa era (in Japanese with an English summary). *Nihon kenchiku Gakkai Keikakukei Ronbun Hokoku Shu* 489; no. 11; November 223–230.

50. Hebbert, M. and Nakai, N. 1988. *How Tokyo Grows: Land Development and Planning on the Metropolitan Fringe.* ST/ICERD occasional paper, no. 11. London: Suntory–Toyota International Centre for Economics and Related Disciplines: London School of Economics and Political Science.

51. Hein, L. E. 1994. In search of peace and democracy: Japanese economic debate in political context. *Journal of Asian Studies* 53; no. 3; 752–778.

52. The houses in "Ginza and Nihonbashi" area at the center of Tokyo (in Japanese with an English summary) 1994. *Nihon Kenchiku Gakkai Keikakukei Ronbun Hokoku Shu* no. 12; 466; December 95–102.

53. Howe, C. 1996. *The Origins of Japanese Trade Supremacy: Development and Technology in Asia from 1540 to the Pacific War.* Chicago, IL: University of Chicago Press.

54. Ichikawa, H. 1994. The evolutionary process of urban form in Edo/Tokyo to 1900. *Town Planning Review* 65; no. 2; April 179–196.

55. Imamura, A. E. 1987. *Urban Japanese Housewives: At Home and in the Community.* Honolulu, HA: University of Hawaii Press.

56. Inkster, I. 1991. *The Clever City: Japan, Australia, and the Multifunction Polis.* Melbourne: Sydney University Press.

57. The Development Center of Japan 1995. *International Development Center of Japan.* Tokyo: Development Center of Japan.

58. Ishido, K. and Myers, D. eds 1995. *Japanese Society Today: Perspectives on Tradition and Change.* Rockhampton: Central Queensland University Press.

59. Ishikawa, A. 1985. *Strategic Budgeting: A Comparison Between U.S. and Japanese Companies.* New York: Praeger.

60. Isomura, E. 1990. The capital city development in Japan. *Ekistics* 57; no. 340–341; January–April 44–47.

61. Iwao, S. 1994. *The Japanese Woman: Traditional Image and Changing Reality.* Cambridge, MA: Harvard University Press.

62. Iwaoka, T. 1996. Vivienda en Tokyo (Tokyo dwelling) (in Spanish and English). *ON Diseno* no. 174; 226–231.

63. Kalland, A. 1996. Geomancy and town planning in a Japanese community. *Ethnology* 35; no. 1; 17–32.

64. Kamstra, S., *et al*. 1995. *Tokyo Contemporary Art Guide*. Tokyo: Japan–Netherlands Institute.

65. Kato, K. 1983. Human resource management in times of recession and growth, a Japanese experience. Paper presented at the *Eleventh International Symposium on Public Personnel Administration*, Zürich, Switzerland, August.

66. Kawahara, I. ed. 1996 Tokyo—hope and recovery: urban civilization and environment (in English and Japanese). *Process: Architecture* no. 129; March, entire issue.

67. Kaplinsky, R. and Posthuma, A. 1994. *Easternisation: The Spread of Japanese Management Techniques to Developing Countries*. Portland, OR: F. Cass.

68. Kumagai, F. and Keyser, D. J. 1996. *Unmasking Japan Today: The Impact of Traditional Values on Modern Japanese Society*. Westport, CT: Praeger.

69. Kikutake, K. 1995. Profile. *World Architecture* no. 32; 26–47.

70. Kim, H.-K. 1996. The civil service system and economic development: the Japanese experience. Report on an international colloquium held in Tokyo, March 22–25, 1994. *EDI Learning Resources Series*. Washington, DC: World Bank, 1020–3842.

71. Kinko, S. 1984. *Why is There Less Crime in Japan? Orientation Seminars on Japan*, No. 15. Tokyo: Japan Foundation, Office for the Japanese Studies Center.

72. Kinzley, W. D. 1991. *Industrial Harmony in Modern Japan: The Invention of a Tradition*. New York: Routledge.

73. Knight, J. 1995. Tourist as stranger? Explaining tourism in rural Japan. *Social Anthropology* 3; no. 3; 219–234.

74. Kose, S. and Nakaohji, M. 1991. Housing the aged: past, present, and future; policy development by the ministry of construction of Japan. *Journal of Architectural and Planning Research* 8; no. 4; 296–306.

75. Koyano, W., *et al*. 1994. Social support system of the Japanese elderly. *Journal of Cross-cultural Gerontology* 9; no. 3; 323–332.

76. Kraft, S. 1994. Megalopolis Tokyo. *Arch Plus* no. 123; September 22–27.

77. Kuwahara, M. 1991. Transport in the Tokyo metropolitan region. *Built Environment* 17; no. 2; 172–183.

78. Mammen, D. 1992. Public works in Japan. *Livable City* 16; no. 2; 7.

79. Martin, J. H. and Martin, P. G. 1994. *Kyoto: A Cultural Guide to Japan's Ancient Imperial City*. Rutland, VT: C. E. Tuttle.

80. Lockwood, W. W. 1993. *The Economic Development of Japan: Growth and Structural Change, 1868–1938*. Ann Arbor, MI: Center for Japanese Studies, University of Michigan.

81. Macpherson, W. J. 1995. *The Economic Development of Japan, 1868–1941*. New York: Cambridge University Press.

82. Marshall, R. C. 1994. Urbanized hamlets, collective action, and municipal administration in Japan. *City and Society* 118–138.

83. Mikuni, M. and Nakamura, O. 1993. The characteristics of environmental conditions and the habitants' consciousness in the rural community groups (in Japanese with an English summary). *Nihon Kenchiku Gakkai Keikakukei Ronbun Hokoku Shu* no. 5; 447; May, 69–78.

84. Minami, R., *et al*. 1995. *Acquiring, Adapting, and Developing Technologies: Lessons from the Japanese Experience*. New York: St Martin's Press.

85. Minerbi, L., *et al*. 1986. *Land Readjustment, The Japanese System: A Reconnaissance and a Digest* (parallel title in Japanese characters). Boston, MA: Oelgeschlager, Gunn & Hain, in association with the Lincoln Institute of Land Policy.

86. Moody, P. R. Jr 1995. *Tradition and Modernization in China and Japan*. Belmont, CA: Wadsworth Publishing.

87. Motokura, M. 1996. Kenchiku design studio: FH Hoya-II [Tokyo] (in English and Japanese). *Japan Architect* no. 24; 152–155.

88. Murao, T. 1991. Reforming transportation in the megalopolis: focus on Japanese cities. *Wheel Extended* December 10–17.

89. Nafziger, E. W. 1995. *Learning from the Japanese: Japan's Pre-war Development and the Third World*. Armonk, NY: M. E. Sharpe.

90. Nagakubo, T., *et al*. 1994. A study on the value of urban waterfront area as one of the open space[s] with reference to the perception of residents (in Japanese with an English summary). *Nihon Kenchiku Gakkai Keikakukei Ronbun Hokoku Shu* no. 10; 464; October, 215–223.

91. Nardo, D. 1995. *Traditional Japan*. San Diego, CA: Lucent Books.

92. Nishimura, H. ed. 1994. *Farmland Use in Suburban Areas in the Developed Societies: Based on Studies in U.K., Germany, U.S.A., and Japan*. Tokyo: Fumin Press.

93. Odagiri, H. and Goto, A. 1996. *Technology and Industrial Development in Japan: Building Capabilities by Learning, Innovation and Public Policy*. New York: Oxford University Press.

94. Olds, K. 1995. Globalization and the production of new urban spaces: Pacific rim megaprojects in the late 20th century. *Environment and Planning A* 27; no. 11; November 1713–1743.

95. Patrick, H. T. and Park, Y. C. eds. 1994. *The Financial Development of Japan, Korea, and Taiwan: Growth, Repression, and Liberalization*. New York: Oxford University Press.

96. Pollock, N. 1991. Tokyo's tiny houses. *Metropolis* 11; no. 5; December 38–45.

97. Pollock, N. R. 1995. Law, order, and architecture. *Metropolis* 14; no. 7; March 64–67, 85, 93.

98. Asian Population and Development Association 1991. *Population and Development in Japan*. Tokyo: Asian Population and Development Association.

99. Price, D. C. 1995. Japan's 21st century utopias. *Asian Architect and Contractor* 25; no. 7; July 8–10, 12.

100. Rafael Vinoly Architects 1996. Tokyo international forum (in English and Japanese). *Japan Architect* no. 24; 48–51.

101. Rafferty, K. 1995. *Inside Japan's Power Houses: The Culture, Mystique and Future of Japan's Greatest Corporations*. London: Weidenfeld & Nicolson.

102. Ravina, M. 1995. State-building and political economy in early-modern Japan. *Journal of Asian Studies* 54; no. 4; 997–1022.

103. Region and environment [Urayasu-shi, Japan] 1988. *Kenchiku Bunka* 43; no. 505; 89–94.

104. Asian Population and Development Association 1992. *Regional Development and Population in Japan: Trends and Prospects in the 1990s. Population and Development Series*, No. 15. Tokyo: Asian Population and Development Association.

105. Reynolds, J. M. 1996. Japan's imperial diet building: debate over construction of a national. *Art Journal* 55; no. 3; 38–47.

106. Robertson, J. 1991. *Native and Newcomer: Making and Remaking a Japanese City.* Berkeley, CA: University of California Press.

107. Roehr, D. and Bosman, P. 1993. Tokyo's missing space. *Landscape Design* no. 225; November 34–37.

108. Okita, S. and Sewell, J. 1991. *The United States and Japan: Sharing Responsibility for Global Development.* U.S.–Japan Development Cooperation papers, No. 3. Washington, DC: Overseas Development Council.

109. Shelton, B. 1992. Rethinking our images of the Japanese city. *Australian Planner: Journal of the Royal Australian Planning Institute* 30; no. 3; September, 131–135.

110. Shinji, T. ed. 1993. *Japanese Capital Markets: New Developments in Regulations and Institutions.* Cambridge, MA: Blackwell.

111. Shiozaki, Y. 1995. Residential environment of housing estates on artificial islands (in Japanese with an English summary). *Nihon Kenchiku Gakkai Keikakukei Ronbun Hokoku Shu* 472; no. 6; June 101–110.

112. Slessor, C. 1994. Tokyo tectonics. *Architectural Review* 194; no. 1167; May 32–37.

113. Smith, J. 1991. *The High Tech Fix: Sustainable Ecology or Technocratic Megaprojects for the 21st Century?* Brookfield, VT: Avebury.

114. Stallings, B., *et al.* 1993. *Common Vision, Different Paths: The United States and Japan in the Developing World.* Washington, DC: Overseas Development Council.

115. Takamatsu, S. 1994. *Architectural Design* 64; nos 1–2; January–February 70–75.

116. Taniguchi, Y. and Taniguchi & Associates 1995. Kasai Rinkai water bus landing. *GA Japan: Environmental Design* no. 17; November–December 140–143.

117. Tanka, E. 1990. *Development of Land Relations in Japanese Agriculture Prior to the Second World War. Studies on Developing Countries*, No. 131. Budapest: Institute for World Economics of the Hungarian Academy of Sciences.

118. Tokyo Metropolitan Government 1995. *Tokyo and Earthquakes.* Tokyo: Liaison and Protocol Section, International Affairs Division, Bureau of Citizens and Cultural Affairs, Tokyo Metropolitan Government.

119. Tokyo Metropolitan Government 1992. *The Tokyo Metropolitan Housing Master Plan: Achieving The Goal of More Comfortable Housing.* Tokyo: Tokyo Metropolitan Government.

120. Tokyo Metropolitan Waterfront Subcenter–Tokyo Teleport Town (in English and Japanese). 1996. *Japan Architect*, no. 24; 106–109.

121. Tu, W.-M. ed. 1996. *Confucian Traditions in East Asian Modernity: Moral Education and Economic Culture in Japan and the Four Mini-dragons.* Cambridge, MA: Harvard University Press.

122. Uchida, E., Shunichi, A. and Murata, K. 1993. Socioeconomic factors affecting marriage, divorce and birth rates in a Japanese population. *Journal of Biosocial Science* 25; no. 4; 499–507.

123. Uchida, K. 1991. Current issues in Tokyo regional transport planning. *Wheel Extended* no. 77; September 2–9.

124. Ueono, C. 1996. Urbanism and the transformation of sexuality: Edo to Tokyo. *Columbia Documents of Architecture and Theory* 5; December 121–143.

125. Van Schaik, L. 1996. Ushida Findlay Partnership. *Transition* no. 52–53; 54–61.

126. Van Wolferen, K. 1989. *The Enigma of Japanese Power: People and Politics in a Stateless Nation.* New York: A. A. Knopf.

127. Vestal, J. E. 1993. *Planning for Change: Industrial Policy and Japanese Economic Development, 1945–1990.* New York: Oxford University Press.

128. Vittas, D. and Kawaura, A. 1995. *Policy-based Finance and Financial Sector Development in Japan/Policy-based Finance, Financial Regulation, and Financial Sector Development in Japan.* Washington, DC: World Bank, Financial Sector Development Department.
129. Vlastos, S. ed. 1998. *Mirror of Modernity: Invented Traditions of Modern Japan.* Berkeley, CA: University of California Press.
130. Wagatsuma, H. and De Vos, G. A. 1984. *Heritage of Endurance: Family Patterns and Delinquency Formation in Urban Japan.* Berkeley, CA: University of California Press.
131. Watanabe, A., *et al.* 1996. House in Seijo, 1996 [Tokyo] (in English and Japanese). *Japan Architect* no. 24; 186–191.
132. Westermann, T. D. and Burfeind, J. W. 1991.*Crime and Justice in Two Societies: Japan and the United States.* Pacific Grove, CA: Brooks/Cole.
133. Whitehill, A. M. 1992. *Japanese Management: Tradition and Transition.* New York: Routledge.
134. Worthington, J. 1991. Tokyo visions. *Town and Country Planning* 60; no. 5; May 146–147.
135. Yamamoto Hori Architects 1996. Housing and Urban Development Corporation, Tokyo branch (in English and Japanese). *Japan Architect* no. 24; 102–105.
136. Yamasaki, M. ed. 1994. Kyoto: its cityscape traditions and heritage (in English and Japanese). *Process: Architecture* no. 116; April, entire issue.
137. Yamazawa, I. 1990. *Economic Development and International Trade: The Japanese Model.* Honolulu, HA: Resource Systems Institute, East–West Center.
138. Kunio, Y. 1994. *Japanese Economic Development.* New York: Oxford University Press.
139. Yoshikawa, H. and Goossenaerts, J. eds 1993. Information infrastructure systems for manufacturing. *Proceedings of the JSPE/IFIP TC5/WG5.3 Workshop on the Design of Information Infrastructure Systems for Manufacturing, DIISM '93.* New York: North-Holland.
140. Yujobo, S. 1995. The development of landscape planning in Japan: toward a landscape design spirit suitable for Japan (in English and Japanese). *Process: Architecture* no. 127; October, 5–12.

Author Index

Subject Index